THE HOLOCAUST AND THE NONREPRESENTABLE

SUNY series in Contemporary Jewish Thought

Richard A. Cohen, editor

Books by David Patterson

Anti-Semitism and Its Metaphysical Origins
Genocide in Jewish Thought
A Genealogy of Evil
Sounding the Depths of the Soul
Jewish-Christian Dialogue (with Alan L. Berger)
Emil L. Fackenheim
Overcoming Alienation
Open Wounds
Wrestling with the Angel
Hebrew Language and Jewish Thought
Along the Edge of Annihilation
Sun Turned to Darkness
The Greatest Jewish Stories Ever Told
When Learned Men Murder
Pilgrimage of a Proselyte
Exile
The Shriek of Silence
In Dialogue and Dilemma with Elie Wiesel
Literature and Spirit
The Affirming Flame
Faith and Philosophy

Edited Volumes

Fire in the Ashes: God, Evil, and the Holocaust (with John K. Roth)
After-Words: Post-Holocaust Struggles with Forgiveness, Reconciliation, Justice (with John K. Roth)
Encyclopedia of Holocaust Literature (with Alan L. Berger and Sarita Cargas)

THE HOLOCAUST AND THE NONREPRESENTABLE

LITERARY AND PHOTOGRAPHIC TRANSCENDENCE

DAVID PATTERSON

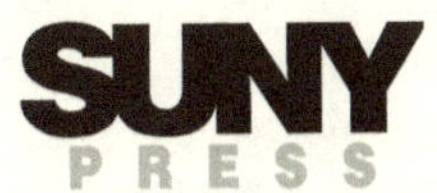

Published by State University of New York Press, Albany

For information, contact State University of New York Press, Albany, NY
www.sunypress.edu

Library of Congress Cataloging-in-Publication Data

Names: Patterson, David, author.
Title: The Holocaust and the nonrepresentable : literary and photographic transcendence / by David Patterson.
Description: Albany, NY : State University of New York Press, [2018] | Series: SUNY series in contemporary Jewish thought | Includes bibliographical references and index.
Identifiers: LCCN 2017032878 | ISBN 9781438470054 (hardcover) | ISBN 9781438470047 (pbk.) | ISBN 9781438470061 (ebook)
Subjects: LCSH: Holocaust, Jewish (1939–1945)—Historiography. | Holocaust, Jewish (1939–1945)—Moral and ethical aspects. | Aesthetics—Moral and ethical aspects. | Holocaust, Jewish (1939–1945), in literature. | Holocaust, Jewish (1939–1945), and art. | Photographs—Moral and ethical aspects. | Holocaust, Jewish (1939–1945)—Influence.
Classification: LCC D804.348 .P39 2018 | DDC 940.53/18072—dc23
LC record available at https://lccn.loc.gov/2017032878

10 9 8 7 6 5 4 3 2 1

Contents

List of Photographs

Acknowledgments

I would like first of all to express my deepest thanks to SUNY Press and to Rafael Chaiken for his support, encouragement, and insightful suggestions in the preparation of this book. My thanks also go to Richard A. Cohen of SUNY Press for his insightful reading of this book. I am also indebted to the reviewers of the manuscript for their astute and helpful criticisms and suggestions for revision, as well as to my PhD student Karl Sen Gupta, and I want to express my deep thanks to Eileen Nizer of the SUNY Press for her excellent work on this project. Finally, I owe a debt of gratitude to the Ackerman Center for Holocaust Studies of the University of Texas at Dallas and to its provost and interim president Dr. Hobson Wildenthal.

Preface

> For in each testimonial production, in each act of memory, language and image are absolutely bound to one another, never ceasing to exchange their reciprocal lacunae.
>
> —Georges Didi-Huberman, *Images in Spite of All*

Although a preface comes first, it is often written last, as has happened in this case. Still, the preface is about the premise, so I shall say a few words about the premise guiding this investigation. Because Part One provides a detailed introduction to the basis of this examination of Holocaust literature and photographs, here I shall be brief.

First, there is no problem of representation with regard to the Holocaust; where the Holocaust is concerned, the project of representation *is itself* the problem. When the Nazis set out to exterminate the Jews, the ultimate object of the annihilation program was nothing that could be named, nothing that could be seen. The war against the Jews was a metaphysical war that eludes thematization, generalization, and therefore representation. It concerns not only an event in the history of humanity but also a fundamental understanding of the transcendent meaning of history and humanity. And transcendent meaning is rooted in the ethical; it is what makes the direction of history and the destiny of humanity *matter*. Inasmuch as such a transcendent meaning is what sanctifies human life and human history, it belongs to the categories of the Good, which, in the words of Emmanuel Levinas, is a "non-present" that is "invisible, separated (or sacred) and thus a non-origin, an-archical. The Good cannot become present or enter into a representation."[1] Because the war against the Jews was characterized by an assault on the Good, this defining feature of the Holocaust cannot enter into a representation.

The interplay between word and image in the project of representation is largely about aesthetics rather than ethics. It is about transmitting a feeling or an experience of trauma, and not about a collision with an absolute commandment to pursue the Good. As soon as the ethical becomes central, however, we are turned over to an absolute demand, which belongs to the ineffable, the invisible, and therefore the nonrepresentable. Aesthetics stems from word and image; ethics stems from silence and the invisible. As the Greek root *aisthetikos* suggests, aesthetics is about perception and appreciation; ethics is about reckoning and implication. The literary and photographic transcendence of Holocaust representation rests upon the ethical; hence the urgency surrounding what we term Holocaust literature and Holocaust photography. For the current volume, then, the interest lies not in how the literary metaphor or the photographic image might "capture" something, but rather in what underlies the metaphor or image as a response to summons and outcry. Indeed, where the Holocaust is the focus, there is no subject matter to be "captured" but only a witness to be borne. Thus, the definitive inscription embossed in the entry to the U.S. Holocaust Memorial Museum, with all the biblical urgency and implication of the Absolute: "You are My witnesses" (Isaiah 43:10). Thus, we do not capture the Holocaust—it captures us.

The work at hand is also guided by two key philosophical positions. First, the thinking of Emmanuel Levinas figures prominently throughout the volume; his is the most prominent voice to resurrect ethics as first philosophy from the rubble of modernity. And since his thinking is steeped in the Jewish teaching and tradition that the Nazis slated for annihilation, this book is also steeped in the categories of that religious tradition, the categories of creation, revelation, and redemption that shape the written and oral Torah. With this in mind, Part One, as already suggested, lays the philosophical and methodological foundations for the book, with Part Two devoted to Holocaust literature and Part Three to Holocaust photography so-called. As Georges Didi-Huberman's epigraph above suggests, the two are interrelated: just as literary texts summon a word that springs from an image, so are photographic images charged with a word intended to be *read*. In each case, the axiological *word,* charged with the "exigency of the holy,"[2] is fundamental.

Let us proceed.

David Patterson
The University of Texas at Dallas

Part One

Reflections on Holocaust Representation and the Nonrepresentable

Theoretical Considerations

By Way of a Prologue

> The ultimate mystery of the Holocaust is that whatever happened took place in the soul.
>
> —Elie Wiesel, *Against Silence*

In the last twenty-five years more than forty books have been published on the problem of Holocaust representation. Most of them deal with the problem of representing evil, atrocity, and trauma. Few if any address the issue of why the Holocaust in particular poses such a representational problem. Why, for example, do we not find similar volumes on the problem of Armenian Genocide representation, Siege of Leningrad representation, or Rape of Nanking representation? What exactly are we representing in the effort to represent or re-*present* the Holocaust? And why should it be so problematic? Neither the suffering nor the degradation, neither the brutality nor the trauma of the Holocaust, was unique or unprecedented: sadly, evil and atrocity, terror and trauma, have long been part of the human experience. Why, then, does the *Holocaust* pose a problem of representation? Could it be that it calls for something otherwise than representation?

In *The Writing of the Disaster* Maurice Blanchot (1907–2003) offers his statement of the problem and what might be beyond "Holocaust," as well as a tentative response: *"The unknown name, alien to meaning: The holocaust, the* absolute *event of history . . . where the movement of Meaning was swallowed up, where the gist, which knows nothing of forgiving or of consent, shattered without* giving *place to anything that can be affirmed, that can be denied. . . . How can it be preserved, even by thought? How can thought be made the keeper of the holocaust where all was lost, including guardian thought? In the mortal intensity, the fleeing silence of the countless cry.*"[1] What is the *absolute* that Blanchot invokes? Perhaps a trace of it lies in the assault on the absolute, on the Good that exceeds the ontological coordinates of history, "outside history, but historically so,"[2] as Blanchot puts it, the Good that makes history matter and that stirs both in the soul and from beyond the soul, both in the event and from beyond the event—the Good, therefore, that exceeds representation. Perhaps that is how the movement of Meaning, of what is essential to the life of the soul, gets swallowed up in this singular assault on the soul. And yet, Blanchot creates an opening in *"the mortal intensity, the fleeing silence of the countless cry"* as a reply to the problem of Holocaust representation, for its countlessness is precisely what escapes the ontological categories. But what is this countless outcry? What is it fleeing from? It flees from a mode of thought that would think the Holocaust, from word to outcry, from representation to . . . what?

"The survivors," writes Dori Laub, "did not only need to survive so they could tell their story; they also needed to tell their story in order to survive. There is, in each survivor, an imperative need to *tell* and thus come to *know* one's story."[3] The imperative is a moral one: to know one's story is to know what must be done, beginning with telling the tale. Telling the tale is required in order to survive because the telling of tales was itself under assault. However, "the imperative to tell the story of the Holocaust is inhabited by the impossibility of telling and, therefore, silence about the truth commonly prevails"[4]—not because of some post-traumatic reticence on the part of the survivor but because of "the fleeing silence" that Blanchot invokes. Thus, says Laub, "what precisely made a *Holocaust* out of the event is the *unique* way in which, during its historical occurrence, *the event produced no witnesses.* Not only, in effect, did the Nazis try to exterminate the physical witnesses of their crime; but the inherently incomprehensible *and* deceptive psychological structure of the event precluded its own witnessing, even by its very victims."[5] Hence the *fleeing* silence.

Does the fleeing silence not give voice to the assault that eludes thought, since thought—at least as it is understood in the Western speculative tradition—belongs to the ontological categories that shape the very notion of representation? Do we not here come up against something otherwise than representation? Here is the problem: if representation is about *knowing* as *comprehension*—if it is more about epistemology than about responsibility—then it is not about the Holocaust. If it is about knowing, then it is about universalizing, so that the singularity of the extermination of Jews and Judaism is lost in the universal. Emil Fackenheim (1916–2003) states the problem this way: "How can thinking be both philosophical and Jewish? If it is rational, it makes values universal and only accidentally Jewish. If specifically Jewish, then it undermines the detachment and universality required of philosophy."[6] And yet, he writes, "It is precisely *because* of the uniqueness of Auschwitz, and *in* his particularity that a Jew must be at one with humanity."[7] Thus there is something to be affirmed, if not in the voice then through the voicelessness that attends to the "countless cry" of the assault on the body and soul of Israel.

The upshot? Any attempt to address the problem of Holocaust representation, including this one, is itself a representation of the Holocaust and therefore problematic. If that is the case, then such a reflection must come up against the nonrepresentable that eludes speculative thought. What follows, then, is a kind of reckoning, what in Hebrew is called a *cheshbon nefesh*. And so it must be: the Holocaust is nothing if not profoundly personal to anyone who collides with it: it singles me out, from beyond the ontological realm of speculation, to summon me to an absolute ethical responsibility, and not to an empathetic cry of pain. Here Eric Kligerman notes, "Although the process of identifying with the Other may start as an honest desire of the spectator to attain empathic identification with the victim, such a vicarious experience risks degenerating into an illusion of being the Other . . . where the act of facing the horror of the Holocaust would potentially lead to a cathartic encounter with its remnants."[8] In other words, if empathy or the knowledge of "what it was like" is the aim of representation, then representation ultimately undermines responsibility. Therefore, instead of the safe distance of either a speculative or a cathartic approach, this inquiry seeks to confront implication and complicity. At times, then, it may depart from the detached scientific method that since Aristotle has driven the project of knowledge and analysis, of comprehension and appropriation. But what other tools, it may be asked, do we have at our disposal? The short answer is this: we have at our disposal the mode of thought that the Nazis set out to obliterate. We have Jewish thought.

And so I shall attempt to break free from the ontological, totalizing categories of what Blanchot calls "guardian thought" and embrace the categories of Jewish thought that came under assault when the movement of Meaning gave way to a fleeing silence. My examination of the existing attempts to address the problem of Holocaust representation has led me to conclude that, generally speaking, they succumb to the thinking that produced an absolute assault on the absolutes of Jewish thought, an assault on categories such as creation and commandment, revelation and responsibility. In other words, generally (but only generally) speaking, the way in which the problem of Holocaust representation has been addressed so far—and I tremble at these words—plays into the hands of the thinking that resulted in the Holocaust itself. I may do no better. Such is the risk taken in any venture of this kind.

Naming *It*

> We are in the presence of a crime without a name.
>
> —Winston Churchill, speech given on 24 August 1941,cited in Martin Gilbert, *Churchill and the Jews*

"To approach the representation of the events," Andrea Liss observes, "is also to confront the difficult act of naming them."[9] What, then, are we attempting to name when we speak about the *Holocaust*? How shall we represent it? What image can capture it, if it can be captured at all? What shall we call it? The Nazis called it "the Jew War" or the "War against the Jews."[10] Hitler himself called it a "war of extermination."[11] If nothing else, the War against the Jews was a war against the absolute; from a Jewish standpoint, it was a war against two absolutes: the first and the sixth utterances at Mount Sinai: "I am God" (Exodus 20:2) and "You shall not murder" (Exodus 20:13). What, then, shall we name this crime of extermination that the Nazis deemed the Jew War and undertook as an assault on these two absolutes? Shall we refer to it, with Paul Celan, simply as "that which happened?"[12] Is it the Holocaust? The Shoah? The Churban? The Final Solution to the Jewish Question? The *Judenvernichtung*?

Since we are addressing the problem of Holocaust representation, let us start with the word *Holocaust*. Philippe Lacoue-Labarthe (1940–2007) demonstrates an understanding of its transcendent nature, saying, "To speak of a 'Holocaust' is a self-serving misinterpretation, as is any reference to an archaic scape-goating mechanism. There was not the least 'sacrificial' aspect in this *operation*, in which what was calculated coldly and with maximum efficiency and economy (and never for a moment hysterically or deliriously) was a pure and simple *elimination*."[13] How can the term *Holocaust* be construed as *self*-serving? Because to construe it as a sacrificial offering is to justify it and therefore absolve ourselves of the sin of indulging in issues of representation. Above all, it relieves us of issues of responsibility, which are precisely the issues of representation: confining our concern to such things as aesthetic convention, the limits of imagination, and working through trauma, we undertake various analyses of Holocaust representation in a flight from our responsibility for the Event.

Sidra DeKoven Ezrahi has also commented on the problematic nature of the term *Holocaust*:

> Even the rubric under which the horrors of those years are subsumed—the *Holocaust*—may be regarded as something of an evasion through verbal encapsulation. It is derived from the Greek word for whole-burnt and meant, presumably, to suggest the extent and even the "manner" of the death of the Jews of Europe. Yet the word *holokautoma,* which refers in the Septuagint to the "burnt offering" in the Temple of Solomon, raises problems through the sacrificial connotation that it attaches to the death of the Jews of Europe and which is, unfortunately, consistent with a prevailing Christian reading of Jewish history.[14]

The sacrificial connotation is problematic because it implies a kind of atonement and therefore something necessary, if unfortunate, about the Event. It is problematic also because it casts the deaths of the Jews in the mold of martyrdom, which, Fackenheim maintains, the Nazis denied the Jew by making the Jew into a Muselmann drained of the divine spark and therefore of any capacity to choose or reject martyrdom (more about the Muselmann later).[15] Although Fackenheim hesitates to call them martyrs, he accepts the Hebrew term *kedoshim* when applied to the Jews murdered by the Nazis. The word *kedoshim,* he correctly points out, does not mean "martyrs"; it means the "holy ones." It refers to "the many—the infants, the *Muselmänner,* and all the countless and nameless one who, without ever knowing what was happening, were murdered in the twinkling of an eye. . . . What then is the holiness of the *kedoshim*? *They suffered vicariously for their parents and their grandparents, but by no means, however, for their sins and their vices but, on the contrary, for their virtues and their saintliness, the fidelity with which they survived as Jews . . . the fidelity of all the past Jewish generations, way back to Sinai.*"[16] In a word, "the *kedoshim* suffered vicariously for God."[17]

This insight runs very deep indeed. It underscores the singularity of the problem of Holocaust representation as a representation of suffering for God, suggesting that the one in whom the divine image has been erased might nonetheless suffer for the divine—there lies *the fleeing silence of the countless cry.* Nevertheless, even if we view the murdered as the *kedoshim,* to situate the Holocaust within the parameters of sacrificial offering would amount to drawing it into the parameters of self-absolution and thus take it outside the parameters of representation. For the act of sacrifice or martyrdom is representable, as the history of Western art demonstrates, and, once representable, it is absolving. That is why Ezrahi calls our attention to an overarching difficulty in Holocaust representation as "something of an evasion." Is it possible that through the very use of the word *Holocaust* we represent it in order to avoid it, slipping into a kind of psychological denial of the Holocaust? Is there something beyond "Holocaust" that must be sought here?

The effort to represent the Holocaust often becomes an effort to relativize and thus trivialize it, incorporating it into the many agendas that go under the heading of tolerance, social justice, and anti-bullying. Says Alvin Rosenfeld, "As the mass murder of millions of innocent people is trivialized and vulgarized, a catastrophic history, bloody to its core, is lightened of its historical burden and gives up the sense of scandal that necessarily should attend it. . . . The more successfully it enters the public mainstream, the more commonplace it becomes. A less taxing version of a tragic history begins to emerge—still full of suffering, to be sure, but a suffering relieved of its weightiest moral and intellectual demands."[18] The *weightiest* of the Holocaust's moral demands extend back to the absolute, divine prohibition against murder, to the ancient demands of Judaism (later taken up by other traditions). As for the intellectual demands, although obvious, they are often ignored, for they include the demands of the study of history, religion, philosophy, languages, cultures, and many other areas. Relieved of its weightiest moral and intellectual demands, the Holocaust is relieved of its Jewish demands. Thus de-Judaizing the Holocaust, one may ward off perceptions of external reality that would be upsetting and withdraw attention from the stimulus, so that the arousal of negative affect is diminished.

There are, as already pointed out, other terms for the event. In Hebrew it is *Shoah,* a noun that suggests many things. In contrast to the sublime sacrificial connotations of *Holocaust, Shoah* means "abyss." It also means "pit," "destruction," and "ruin." Sharing the same root is another noun, *shav,* which translates as "lie" or "nothingness," suggesting that, as an assault on creation, the Shoah returned creation to the chaos and the void, the *tohu vevohu,* overcome in the act of creation (Genesis 1:2). Karla Grierson describes the outcome of this assault as "denatured nature."[19] Survivor Camille Touboul sees it in the absence of the natural world at Auschwitz: "Nature always has grass quivering in the wind, insects crawling among the pebbles, the cries of birds, a corner of the sky. Here there is nothing. An immense plain as far as the eye can see, receding into an unknown nothingness."[20] This nothingness, this *shav,* of the anti-creation extends beyond the time of the Holocaust and into the time of afterward, as Primo Levi (1919–1987) indicates: "The world around us," he says of his emergence from Auschwitz, "seemed to have returned to primeval Chaos, and was swarming with scalene, defective, abnormal human specimens."[21] These are the creatures who mirror the image not of the Creator but of the Chaos opposed by the Creation; these are the inhabitants of a brave new land, such as the one that the Germans made out of Eastern Europe. There, says Levi, "it was more than a sack: it was the genius of destruction, of anti-creation, here as at Auschwitz; it was the mystique of barrenness."[22] The anti-creation is the creation of nothing out of something, a return to the void of what strives to overcome the void.

Further, the verb *shah,* which shares a root with *Shoah,* means to "become desolate," to "be devastated"; the *hitpael* form, *hishtaah,* is to "wonder," to "be astonished," or to "gaze in wonder or awe." Thus, when Elie Wiesel (1928–2016) once asked a friend about his first impression of Auschwitz, his friend replied, "I found it a spectacle of terrifying beauty."[23] What can this aesthetic mean for our understanding of the *Shoah*? Exceeding the parameters of genocide, it is the systematic imposition of the abyss upon the world, turning the world over to the pit. It is the lie made truth, the unreal made real, the return of the world to the nothingness that creation now struggles to overcome. It is the astonishment not over what is unimaginable but over everything imaginable. Far more difficult than the representation of the unimaginable is the representation of everything imaginable.

Then we have the word *Churban.* In ancient times the most devastating events to plunge the Jews into the abyss were the destruction of the two Temples, first in 586 BCE and then in 70 CE. In Hebrew this "destruction" is known as the *Churban.* It is a cognate of *cherev,* the word for "sword"; both derive from the verb *charav,* which means to "destroy" or to "lay waste." A special term used to refer to the devastation wrought by the destruction of the Temple, *Churban* pertains to the darkening of the Divine Presence in the world, without which there is neither good nor evil, but only what is. It pertains to a radical assault on the Divine Presence through a radical assault on the Jews. Therefore, the Yiddish language uses this same word to refer to history's most devastating assault on God through the extermination of His Chosen: the Churban. It is a word that attempts to situate the destruction within the contexts of sacred history, which is already otherwise than representation, inasmuch as sacred history is the history of the incursion of more than all there is into the midst of all there is.

The Churban, moreover, has a date: it is the Ninth of Av, or Tisha B'Av. It is the day of the destruction of both Temples, as well as numerous other catastrophes in Jewish history.[24] On that date World War I began, a war that paved the way to the Third Reich; on 22 July 1942, the eve of Tisha B'Av, the first of the mass transports to Treblinka pulled out of Warsaw. In the time of the Churban in Europe, what Dan Cohn-Sherbok calls the Third Churban,[25] the Jews themselves took the place of the Temple. Like the Temple, they signify the presence of the Holy One in the world; like the Temple, they were consigned to the flames. In the words of Elie Wiesel, "with each hour, the most blessed and most stricken people of the world numbers twelve times twelve children less. And each one carries away still another fragment of the Temple in flames."[26] Yes, the children—they were the designated first targets in the Nazi war against God. Says Wiesel, "It was as though the Nazi killers knew precisely what children represent to us. According to our tradition, the entire world subsists thanks to them."[27] I have just one correction to his insight: it was not *as though*. In his diary from the Vilna Ghetto scholar and archivist Herman Kruk (1897–1944) often refers to the Gestapo's "Jew Specialists," such as the infamous Dr. Johannes Pohl, director of a department known as *Judenforschung ohne Juden*, that is, "Research on Jews without Jews."[28] It was their assignment to thoroughly familiarize themselves with the Jews and Judaism, with Jewish texts and teachings, and to use their information to destroy Judaism.

If, as it is written in the *Tikkunei HaZohar*, children are "the face of the Shekhinah,"[29] it is because, gazing into the eyes of a child, we catch a glimpse of the Divine Countenance and the Commanding Voice that the Nazis systematically set out to obliterate. Because children are the face of the Divine Presence, the Nazis rooted out that presence by creating realms that were void of Jewish children. "In the ghetto streets no children played," writes Yehiel De-Nur (1909–2001), the survivor and novelist known as Ka-tzetnik 135633. "In the ghetto there were no children. There were small Jews and there were big Jews—all looking alike."[30] In his memoir, George Lucius Salton (b. 1928) recalls the moment when, upon his liberation from Wöbbelin, he saw children for the first time in more than six years. They were German children: "The Jewish children had all been gassed."[31] According to Jewish tradition, moreover, only the prayers of our children reach the ears of God, "for the outcry of children," says Jacob ben Wolf Kranz (ca. 1740–1804), the Maggid of Dubno, "is formed by the breath of mouths unblemished by sin."[32] But one wonders whether this outcry ever reached the ears of the Holy One; with the extermination of the children it is as though God had been rendered deaf. And once rendered deaf, He is rendered irrelevant. Thus, in the assault on the children the Nazis attained their deicidal aim.

If the annihilation of the children is central to the Nazis' deicidal aim, so too is the obliteration of prayer. Indeed, just as the Shekhinah is associated with the community of Israel, so is she associated with prayers of Israel. The Baal Shem Tov (1698–1760), the founder of Chasidism, teaches that "when a man begins the Amidah [the prayer at the center of the liturgy] and says the opening verse: 'O Lord, open Thou my lips!' [Psalms 51:17] the Shekhinah immediately enters within his voice, and speaks with his voice."[33] Therefore, the annihilation of the Indwelling Presence—the Churban—required the annihilation of prayer. "Never before was there a government so evil that it would forbid an entire people to pray," Chaim Kaplan (1880–1942) records in the diary he kept in the Warsaw Ghetto.[34] Never before had a government undertaken such an assault on the Holy One *as a policy of state*. Central to that assault is the assault on the testimony to the Holy One manifest in prayer. "Only when you are My witnesses," it is written, "am I God, but when you are not My witnesses, I—if one dare speak thus—am not God" (*Pesikta de-Rab Kahana* 12:6; see also *Sifre* on Deuteronomy 33:5).[35] The Nazis understood that both the Source and its seekers, both God and His witnesses, had to be destroyed.

We understand, then, why the Nazis transformed places of prayer into latrines, stables, scrap depots, and other such facilities. Often they were not content merely to desecrate the places of prayer; they put them to the torch, with praying Jews inside, and thus consigned God Himself to the flames. The assault on the place of prayer is an assault not on a building or a space but on the encounter between God and the soul that characterizes prayer: in order to assail God, the Nazis launched an attack on the prayer that is itself divinity. Chaim Kaplan bears witness to this assault. On the eve of Tisha B'Av 5700 (1940), he writes, "Public prayer in these dangerous times is a forbidden act. Anyone caught in this crime is doomed to severe punishment. If you will, it is even sabotage, and anyone engaging in sabotage is subject to execution."[36] Note well: the Nazis deemed prayer *an act of sabotage*. Why? Because prayer affirms the divine, transcendent authority behind the commandments of Torah, beginning with the prohibition against murder. Only where there is a place for this absolute, divine prohibition does the Divine Presence find a dwelling place in the world, and only where there is a dwelling place for the Divine Presence is there a place for prayer.

So the term *Churban* provides its own inkling of what must be represented and why it is not representable: it is the radical assault on the Holy One, on holiness, on the Shekhinah as she is driven into exile, on the absolute prohibition against murder. What must above all be represented and is above all nonrepresentable is this *absolute*. Indeed, this absolute is tied to what is final about the *Endlösung* or Final Solution, another term for this event that some would represent. Final Solution to what? To the *Judenfrage*, the Jewish Question: *die Endlösung der Judenfrage*. But what exactly is the Jewish Question? Why does it require a Final Solution? And what does it tell us about the problem and even the wrongheadedness of Holocaust representation?

The term *Jewish Question* was first used in Great Britain around 1750; it appeared during the debates surrounding the Jew Bill of 1753, which enabled Jews to become naturalized citizens of England through application to Parliament.[37] The phrase became a familiar one in the German-speaking world with the publication of *Die Judenfrage* in 1843 by philosopher and historian Bruno Bauer (1809–1882); some of Karl Marx's (1818–1883) most notorious anti-Semitic statements came in his reply to Bauer, where he wrote, "What is the profane basis of Judaism? *Practical* need, *self-interest*. What is the worldly cult of the Jew? *Huckstering*. What is his worldly god? *Money*."[38] For Marx and other anti-Semites, the Jews did not suffer any oppression at the hands of the nations, but rather the nations were oppressed by the conniving Jews. Early on, then, the Jewish Question was not the question of how to assimilate the Jews under a program of civil rights for all; no, it was the question of how to get rid of the Jews and Judaism altogether. Although *die Endlösung der Judenfrage* is a distinctively Nazi phrase, the desire for a Final Solution to the Jewish Question did not originate with them.

The total, absolute solution to the Jewish Question could come only with the total, absolute elimination of the Jewish Question. In other words, the question had to be not only resolved but also eliminated. For the Nazis, as long as a single Jew was alive, the question was alive: every Jew and all memory of the Jews had to be annihilated in the *Final* Solution to the Jewish Question. Thus, in 1942 the Nazis trekked to Tromsø, Norway, 217 miles north of the Arctic Circle, to send the seventeen Jews residing there to Auschwitz; one does not venture into the Arctic out of economic envy, xenophobia, racial animosity, ethnic prejudice, or the longing to find a scapegoat. No. Because the God of Abraham is omnipresent, the assault on the God of Abraham had to be omnipresent. Jewish teaching and testimony was the designated target of the extermination project, for Jewish tradition is itself a manifestation of the God of Abraham, Isaac, and Jacob. The total elimination of the Jewish Question is, indeed, an elimination of the Jewish God. The Hebrew word for "question," Wiesel reminds us, "is *she'elah,* and the *alef lamed* of God's name are part of the fabric of that word. Therefore God is in the question."[39] To eliminate the question—to finally resolve the Jewish Question—is to eliminate God.

So what is the Jewish Question for which the Nazis systematically sought a Final Solution? It is not a question of what to do with the Jews, precisely; rather it is a question of what to do with the infinite ethical demand that they represent by their very presence in the world. Because the demand is infinite, it cannot be settled or assimilated, dominated or domesticated. " 'The jews,' " Jean-François Lyotard (1924–1998) reflects, are "the irremissible in the West's movement of remission and pardon. They are what cannot be domesticated in the obsession to dominate."[40] And if they cannot be domesticated, they must be annihilated. Thus, Lyotard outlines the history of anti-Semitism: "One converts the Jews in the Middle Ages, they resist by mental restriction. One expels them during the classical age, they return. One integrates them in the modern era, they persist in their difference. One exterminates them in the twentieth century"[41]—which is the final solution to the Jewish Question. What is said of the Jews, moreover, can be said of God: He cannot be domesticated. One makes God into a Christian or a Muslim, He resists by mental restriction. He is expelled and replaced by the "I think" in the classical age, He returns. He is integrated into a cultural phenomenon in the modern era, He persists in His otherness. One exterminates Him in the postmodern age by exterminating His people. And so we have the Final Solution to the Jewish Question. The representation of the Final Solution must, if possible, represent the irremissible, indomitable, inassimilable, ethical absolute signified by the very presence of the Jews.

Thus, the annihilation of the Jewish people termed the *Judenvernichtung* is the annihilation not only of a people but also of a millennial teaching and tradition. It is the annihilation of the questions that constitute the true Jewish Question, the question put to Adam—"Where are you?" (Genesis

3:9)—and the questions put to Cain—"Where is your brother?" (Genesis 4:9) and "What have you done?" (Genesis 4:10). That is what makes the Final Solution a *Judenvernichtung*. The representation of the *Judenvernichtung* is a representation of what was targeted for annihilation in the annihilation of the Jews, which is what eludes representation. It eludes representation because it belongs to a metaphysical realm that is otherwise than being, whereas representation belongs to the ontological landscape of all there is. The term *Judenvernichtung* refers to more than mass murder; least of all does it signify "man's inhumanity to man," a trite and meaningless combination of words. The *Judenvernichtung* is neither one instance of inhumanity among others nor one horror among others. It designates an assault on the very metaphysical category, the ethical category of human sanctity, that makes other horrors horrific.

Taken together, the various terms for the Holocaust—Shoah, Churban, *Judenvernichtung,* and so on—are one, much as God, Israel, and Torah are one. They harbor not only a memory but also the summons to remember, the summons to which we are tasked to answer, "*Hineni!*—Here I am!" Indeed, we are summoned to do more than remember—we are summoned to act. The task for the artistic word and image is to represent the non-representable "Commanding Voice of Auschwitz," as Fackenheim calls it. "Jewish opposition to Auschwitz," he argues, "cannot be grasped in terms of humanly created ideals but only as an *imposed commandment*. And the Jewish secularist, no less than the believer, is *absolutely singled out* by a Voice as truly *other* than man-made ideals—an imperative as truly *given*—as was the Voice of Sinai."[42] There lies the difficulty posed for any representation of the Holocaust: to make heard the Commanding Voice silenced in Auschwitz, a Voice that yet commands precisely in its reverberating silence. Once again, we come up against the question of what to call it.

Naming Auschwitz

> And praised. *Auschwitz.* Be. *Maidanek.* The Lord. *Treblinka.* And praised. *Buchenwald.* Be. *Mauthausen.* The Lord. *Belzec.* And praised. *Sobibor.* Be. *Chelmno.* The Lord. *Ponary.* And praised. *Theresienstadt.* Be. *Warsaw.* The Lord. *Vilna.* And praised. *Skarzysko.* Be. *Bergen-Belsen.* The Lord. *Janow.* And praised. *Dora.* Be. *Neuengamme.* The Lord. *Pustkow.* And praised . . .
>
> —André Schwarz-Bart, *The Last of the Just*

"In order to understand ourselves and to illuminate our trackless way into the future," writes Leo Strauss, "we must understand Jerusalem and Athens."[43] Among the matters Strauss understood best was the tension between Athens and Jerusalem. Whereas the former, he explains, signifies "free inquiry," the latter signifies "obedient love."[44] If the difference between Athens and Jerusalem lies in free inquiry over against obedient love, it lies in autonomous self-legislation over against divine commandment. And if that is the case, then one may trace a path leading from Athens to Auschwitz, where no one was ever more autonomous, more self-legislating, than the Nazis and no truth ever under a more radical assault than the truth of a divinely revealed commandment. What began with modernity's thinking God out of the picture ended with shoving the Jews into the gas chambers. Philosophy turns its ear to Auschwitz and hears only a sound and a fury signifying nothing, hears only the screams of the children and the silence of the Muselmann. And it is paralyzed.

In contrast to this paralysis we have the Israelites' response when Moses presented them with the Torah: "All that the Lord has said, we shall do and we shall hear" (Exodus 24:7). This is precisely the response to the Commanding Voice of Auschwitz that must now be made. The path to truth, then and now, lies in *acting*, out of love, in response to the revealed word, for only by thus bringing the Commanding Voice to life through our deeds can we ever hope to hear and understand it. Insisting that the path to truth lies in the "free inquiry" of reasoned reflection, philosophy would first deduce the right path and then take a first step. In the words of Strauss, "by saying that we wish to hear first and then to act, we have already decided in favor of Athens against Jerusalem."[45] In the twentieth century, Athens was superseded by Auschwitz. The implication for our reflection on Holocaust representation is that, if we are to oppose Auschwitz, we are summoned to think in the categories of Jerusalem, not of Athens. It is not for nothing that the word *Auschwitz* heads the litany of names echoing from the anti-world in the defiant prayer with which André Schwarz-Bart (1928–2006) closes his novel *The Last of the Just*. It is because, as Brett Kaplan has understood, "the word 'Auschwitz' takes on a more than synecdochal force when it comes to represent not only all other camps, but all other horror."[46] It is a name that appears in numerous titles of books that deal with the Holocaust and its representation. What, then, are we naming with this name?

The town of Auschwitz has existed since the thirteenth century, when it was originally known as Ośpenchin. Since the fifteenth century it has been called Auschwitz in German and Oświęcim in Polish. In the late Middle Ages and Early Modern periods the town prospered as a center of trade until it was destroyed in 1655 with the Swedish invasion of Poland. By the end of the nineteenth century Oświęcim prospered once again as an important rail junction, which would serve the Nazis well in the twentieth century.

One more item of interest: Elie Wiesel relates a tale of two Chasidic masters, Rebbe Elimelekh of Lizensk (1717–1787) and Reb Zusia of Onipol (1718–1800), who were known for their travels throughout Eastern Europe to spread the teachings of the Baal Shem Tov: "One day they arrived in a little town as dusk was falling. Noticing an inn, they went inside, hoping to spend the night there. Exhausted, they lay down behind the stove, which was the customary place for wandering beggars. Soon the place fell silent. And dark. All of a sudden, they woke in a panic, overcome by an inexplicable fear. So violent was their fear that they left the inn and the village in the middle of the night. The name of the place: Oushpitsin—better known to our generation as Oświęcim, or: Auschwitz."[47] Thus, the two Chasidic masters fled the place from which their descendants would be unable to flee.

Consider, too, the following from French philosopher Fabrice Midal, who flees not only from the site but from the very word: "Auschwitz. It is difficult for me to write the word itself. It seems to me impossible to know the order of the letters. I must look at it several times. In the end I do not want to know. Is it because this word designates a site where order has disappeared forever?"[48] No synecdoche here. No metonymy. No aesthetic tools of representation. Ironically, grimly, the name *Oświęcim* brings to mind the Polish verb *oświecić,* which means to "enlighten" or "illuminate." Throughout how many nights was Oświęcim illuminated by the flames of the crematoria? How might the word *Auschwitz* illuminate our ignorance?

I am reminded of a remark that Yehiel De-Nur made to me in the summer of 1991, as he related the story of how the Israeli prosecuting attorney Gideon Hausner (1915–1990) pleaded with him to testify at the trial of Adolf Eichmann (1906–1962): "I told him, yes, I was there. I saw the beatings, the exhaustion, the starvation, the smoke rising from the chimneys, and the ashes raining down. I saw men humiliated and mutilated, reduced to non-men. But that is not Auschwitz. What Auschwitz is, I tried to explain to him, I cannot say." Can it, indeed, be said?

In the end, Hausner got De-Nur to agree to testify. When the time came for him to take the stand on 7 June 1961 in Session 68 of the trial, he attempted to say what Auschwitz is:

Witness Dinur: I do not regard myself as a writer and a composer of literary material. This is a chronicle of the planet of Auschwitz. I was there for about two years. Time there was not like it is here on earth. Every fraction of a minute there passed on a different scale of time. And the inhabitants of this planet had no names, they had no parents nor did they have children. There they did not dress in the way we dress here; they were not born there and they did not give birth; they breathed according to different laws of nature; they did not live—nor did they die—according to the laws of this world. . . . They were clad there, how would you call it . . .

Q. Yes. Is this what you wore there? [Shows the witness the prison garb of Auschwitz.]

A. This is the garb of the planet called Auschwitz. And I believe with perfect faith that I have to continue to bear this name [Ka-tzetnik] so long as the world has not been aroused after this crucifixion of a nation, to wipe out this evil, in the same way as humanity was aroused after the crucifixion of one man. I believe with perfect faith that, just as in astrology the stars influence our destiny, so does this planet of the ashes, Auschwitz, stand in opposition to our planet earth, and influences it. If I am able to stand before you today and relate the events within that planet, if I, a fall-out of that planet, am able to be here at this time, then I believe with perfect faith that this is due to the oath I swore to them there. They gave me this strength. This oath was the armour with which I acquired the supernatural power, so that I should be able, after time—the time of Auschwitz—the two years when I was a Muselmann, to overcome it. For they left me, they always left me, they were parted from me, and this oath always appeared in the look of their eyes. For close on two years they kept on taking leave of me and they always left me behind. I see them, they are staring at me, I see them, I saw them standing in the queue . . .

Q. Perhaps you will allow me, Mr. Dinur, to put a number of questions to you, if you will agree?

A. [Tries to continue] I remember . . .

Presiding Judge: Mr. Dinur, kindly listen to what the Attorney General has to say.

[Witness Dinur rises from his place, descends from the witness stand, and collapses on the platform. The witness fainted.][49]

If Midal could not name Auschwitz because the very word signifies the collapse of order, De-Nur himself collapsed in his attempt to name it. Can this witness's attempt to say what Auschwitz is be construed as an instance of Holocaust representation? Saul Friedländer has said that "the limitations which weigh on the literary and artistic representation of the *Shoah* reappear in the domain of historical interpretation."[50] Do those limitations also weigh on the courtroom testimony of a witness who would undertake his own representation of the Holocaust? Does this literary figure not venture into the domain of historical interpretation? I think he does. But he does far more than offer evidence at a trial.

Indeed, this testimony encapsulates the issues of Holocaust representation. Something unspeakable weighed on the witness, something he could not speak, the weight of the entire "concentrationary universe."[51] In Auschwitz, writes Jean Améry (1912–1978), "It was not the case that the intellectual . . . had now become unintellectual or incapable of thinking. On the contrary, only rarely did thinking grant itself a respite. But it nullified itself when at almost every step it ran into its uncrossable borders. The axes of its traditional frames of reference then shattered."[52] As De-Nur tried to speak it, even as he tried to think it in "a shuddering of the human quite different from cognition," to borrow a phrase from Emmanuel Levinas (1906–1995),[53] that universe swept over him from beyond uncrossable borders and sent him into a swoon in his attempt to narrate a time outside of time, a time that cannot be thought. Time is a key. "Time there," De-Nur testified, "was not like it is here on earth. Every fraction of a minute there passed on a different scale of time." Elsewhere he says that time "on planet Auschwitz revolved around the cogwheels of a different time-sphere."[54] That different scale of time, that different sphere, belongs to none of the circles of heaven or hell, where a principle of justice rules; as Primo Levi has said, "for us the Lager is not a punishment."[55] In Auschwitz, the Jews served no sentence: they were not "doing time." Outside of time, Auschwitz can be located within the landscape neither of being nor of nothingness: in that anti-space-time more was real than was possible. The cogwheels turned and twisted, but not according to the measure of time that belongs to creation.

"Time in Auschwitz", says survivor and psychiatrist Eugene Heimler (1922–1990), "was not divided into minutes, hours, and days."[56] There is no sun "like the one that shines upon Majdanek," as the Majdanek Anthem goes,[57] because the Majdanek sun does not trace the time of the orbit of the sun placed in the heavens to rule the day. Human time, life time, is measured according to human relation; hence, the Jews measure time not from the first day of creation but from the sixth day, the day of the creation of Adam, which is Rosh Hashanah, the Day of Judgment. In Auschwitz, however, there is no judgment, no punishment, nothing but the chaos and the void of the arbitrary in a time radically out of joint. In Auschwitz, the time of one's life, the time of human relation, came under a radical assault. Recall one of the most chilling lines in all of Holocaust literature, when an inmate informs the young Eliezer in Wiesel's *Night* that in the camp "there is no such thing as father, brother, friend. Each of us lives and dies alone."[58] Thus, the witness testifies before humanity to an anti-time in an anti-world void of humanity. Here we have a clue to the problem of Holocaust representation as a problem of relating the destruction of all relation.

Because human relation is made of language, this rupture of time, which is a rupture of the real, is a rupture or breakdown of language. For De-Nur, who tried to put Auschwitz into words, there was a literal breakdown of language, a breakdown that was part of his testimony. Lea Wernick Fridman has a sense of this "rupture of language" running through the witness's "representations of the Holocaust."[59] Fridman, however, misses the *Holocaust* in her discussion of its representation through language. For the rupture of language that distinguishes the Holocaust belongs to the rupture of the divine image in which the human being is created as a "speaking being" (a *medaber* in Hebrew, *not* to be confused with the Greek *zoon phonate* or "speech organism").[60] It is a rupture not only of a speech process but also of a divine commandment, not only of an aesthetic endeavor but also of an ethical absolute. Hence, the survivor's sense of an absolute ethical obligation to the dead ruptures his life, his ego, his entire sense of identity.

In the late spring of 1945 Yehiel De-Nur, now an escapee from Planet Auschwitz, lay dying in a British army hospital in Italy. But before succumbing to death, he resolved to fulfill a promise made to the dead whose ashes had been cast to the winds. He asked for pen and paper. Some two weeks later, the patient produced the manuscript of the first Holocaust novel, the first attempt to name Auschwitz, *Salamandra* (*Sunrise over Hell* in the English edition). He also made a miraculous recovery, as though his testimony to and for the dead had released him from the grip of the Angel of Death. He entrusted the book to Eliyahu Goldenberg, a member of the Jewish Brigade. Noticing that the manuscript had no name on it, Goldenberg asked, "Who shall I say wrote this?" To which came the reply: "Who wrote it? *They* wrote it! Put *their* name on it: Ka-tzetnik!"[61] As his character Harry Preleshnik, the persona of the author, says in *Phoenix over the Galilee*, "My name was burned with all the rest in the crematorium at Auschwitz."[62] How, then, are we to name this site of the burning of names?

And yet, as the site of the burning of names, Auschwitz and its dead summon the survivor by name from the depths of a human relation that extends beyond the time of the living. "I owe the dead my memory," says Elie Wiesel. "I am duty-bound to serve as their emissary."[63] This point is crucial in the matter of Holocaust representation as a representation of Jewish history. Jewish history entails handing down a metahistorical "message" or *meser* in Hebrew, a message concerning ethical responsibility as an expression of a higher relation. This view of history transforms the one to whom the testimony is handed down into a witness and a messenger. It means that the living remain in a relationship with the dead; only if we are in such a relationship with the dead can the transmission of their memory be ethically charged, and not just a matter of academic curiosity or aesthetic engagement. Wherever Auschwitz is named or represented—if, indeed, it can be represented—we have the representation of an absolute ethical demand that devolves upon the ego and deposes it.

Notice in this connection that in his attempt at the Eichmann trial to say what Auschwitz is, De-Nur turned to relating something of his story—the story of his responsibility, the story of the abrogation of his ego—confirming an observation from Michael Bernard-Donals in his book on Holocaust representation: "To witness is to forget yourself; it's being in the position of forgetting who 'I' am, because to say 'here I am' is to cast yourself out of phase with yourself, to make the speaking self noncoincident with its own language—with testimony—and with the position from which it speaks—the event, the 'here.' "[64] This forgetfulness of the "I," this abrogation of the ego, signifies the realization of the ethical demand that somehow penetrates the heights eclipsed by the ashes of Israel. It is what Levinas calls a "breakup of identity, this changing of being into signification, that is, into substitution, is the subject's subjectivity, or its subjection to everything, its susceptibility, its vulnerability."[65] For De-Nur, the heavens went mute, so that the cry of those marked for death "split the heavens," as it is written in *Sunrise over Hell*, "but Heaven remained lofty and silent as though God had deserted its temples."[66] And yet the injunction broke through the heavens and devolved upon him through the eyes of the Jews on their way to the gas chambers. Even the silence of God harbors a divine imperative, one that finds its way into Holocaust representation as the nonrepresentable.

De-Nur's repeated refrain of "I believe with perfect faith" is also worth noting: it is the Hebrew phrase *ani maamin b'emunah shlemah*, from the Thirteen Principles of Faith found in Maimonides's (1135–1204) commentary on the Mishnah (*Sanhedrin* 10).[67] The Thirteen Principles are recited in the prayer known as the *Yigdal*, which has become part of the Jewish liturgy of prayer. Invoking this liturgical utterance, De-Nur chooses Jerusalem over Auschwitz. In this connection, Ezrahi poses a salient question: "In what conceivable language can a Jew speak *to* God after Auschwitz, and in what conceivable language can he speak *about* Auschwitz?"[68] But, for a Jew, to speak *about* God is to speak *to* God; it is a form of prayer in reply to a summons. One form that it takes, as we have found, comes at the end of Schwarz-Bart's *The Last of the Just*. If one is to say what Auschwitz is, perhaps it can only be said in a prayer, in reply to a summons. As Blanchot states, "The question concerning the disaster is part of the disaster; it is not an interrogation, but a prayer, an entreaty, a call for help."[69] What Blanchot says of the question concerning the disaster may also be said of the question concerning the representation of the disaster. Or is it to be said in a swoon, realizing that the call for help comes both from the human and from the beyond? Is that when De-Nur finally "said" what Auschwitz is? Is that how Planet Auschwitz is to be represented? Is that how it is to be spoken? And what becomes of language and all that we thought we knew about language in the attempt to speak it?

Terror has undone time, and with it that being that is the life of the human being, the being of the word. The attempt to speak the Holocaust, to put it into words its extremity, opens up a situation in which language works against itself. "This contradictory quality of the extreme," explains Michael Rothberg, "the fact that it always exceeds language but always inhabits it, also constitutes its implication in the everyday. This implication represents in turn the traumatic potential of extremity."[70] The issue, however, is not so much about extremity as it is about what is beyond extremity, beyond the beyond, a presence within language from beyond language, a presence that constitutes the meaning of language. The problem of Holocaust representation, then, opens up new possibilities for an understanding of language. If it is a "new" understanding, however, it has ancient roots in the Jewish tradition.

Post-Auschwitz Implications for an Understanding of Language

> Come, let us go down and confuse their language . . .
>
> —Genesis 11:7

Holocaust scholar Dorota Glowacka has astutely observed that "what Holocaust testimonials bear witness to first and foremost is this abyssal, *Babelian* condition of post-Holocaust speech."[71] The survivors who would bear witness to and thus offer some "representation" of the Holocaust attest to Glowacka's assessment. In the case of Primo Levi, Daniel Schwarz points out, "language is the protagonist of [his] books, the means by which he seizes light from darkness. For him, it is the means of creation and understanding, the one antidote to chaos,"[72] and chaos always lies in a confusion of tongues. If language is a protagonist, it is a protagonist in much the same sense as the dead are the protagonists of Holocaust testimonies: language itself lies among the dead. Here the survivor does indeed confront a "Babelian condition" of speech. It is a condition that is both rooted in the event and that follows the event into its aftermath.

There are ancient Jewish teachings on the "Babelian condition" that may help us to fathom this distinctively contemporary, post-Holocaust dilemma of representing the Holocaust through language. The Holocaust transpired in a place and a time of a bloody tearing of meaning from words. The Nazis never spoke of killing people but only of "resettlement," "special treatment," and "processing units." In that anti-world something primeval seeped through the ontological fabric of a discourse that belied reality, a "confusion" or *bilbul,* that characterized the collapse of the word at the Tower of Babel, which was literally the Tower of "Confusion." Just so, according to Levi, the carbide tower in Buna was deemed the *Babelturm,* or Tower of Babel. "Its bricks," he writes, "were called *Ziegel, briques, cegli, kamenny, mattoni, téglak,* and they were cemented by hate."[73] Hate is a defining feature of the tearing of word from meaning; it cannot happen without hate. Hate *is* the tearing of word from meaning and therefore of human from human.

The confusion of tongues is manifest in the collapse of human relation and of the understanding of what makes the other human being *matter*. It has nothing to do with any shift in some system of signifiers. This confusion that characterizes the time of the event carries over to the time after the event, to the time of Holocaust representation. And it stems from ancient times.

Contrary to the popular misconception, the biblical tale of the Tower is not intended to explain how the multitude of languages came to be. In his thirteenth-century commentary, the Baal HaTurim says that the confusion lay in the fact that they "had one language with unique words" (Genesis 11:1), where any word could mean anything, so that words were "empty and void" (Baal HaTurim on Genesis 11:1; cf. *Zohar* I, 75a). According to the fourteenth-century sage Ovadiah Sforno, the confusion lay in the supposition that the people could "make a name" for themselves and therefore generate identity and meaning from their own autonomous selfhood (Genesis 11:4): they had no knowledge of the Name of the Holy One, from whom all names and all meaning issue, as it is written in the Zohar (*Zohar* II, 124a). It also lay in the fact that through building a tower to the heavens they thought they could define their own dimension of height (Sforno's commentary on Genesis 11:4). Making one's own name and forging one's own height go hand in hand: the height is in the name and the name signifies a height, but, as in the case of anyone who makes his own name, the dimension of height is here a counterfeit.

The Midrash reveals the consequence of this confusion: when a man fell to his death during the construction of the Tower, no one even noticed; but when a brick was dropped and broken, a great lamentation went up, and the people cried out, "When will another come in its stead?" (*Pirke de Rabbi Eliezer* 24). Hence, we have the reading of Genesis 11:7 from the eighteenth-century sage Rabbi Yaakov Culi, who notes that in the phrase *navlah sham sfatam*, "let us confuse their tongues," the word *navlah* (a cognate of *bilbul*) may also be read as *nevelah*, which means "corpse."[74] Read in this way, says Rabbi Culi, the verse means "let us make their speech produce corpses."[75] And so it has come to pass: the confusion of tongues was a confusion of life and death. With the tearing of the ultimate from the word there comes a corresponding tearing of sanctity from the human being. And so during the Holocaust a confusion of speech produced corpses: the Holocaust is not only the culmination of a modernity enamored of abstractions but also of a postmodernity that would eliminate absolutes.

Consider, for example, how meaning was torn from the word *bread* in that realm. Bread, says Levi, was the "grey slab" of "bread-brot-Broid-chleb-pain-lechem-keynér" that in this realm is their "only money."[76] Bread is not bread when bread is currency; meaning was torn from the word *bread,* and with the tearing of meaning from this word, human was torn from human. For the word *bread* takes on its meaning in its offering to another human being. Levinas offers an insight in this connection: "It is because subjectivity is . . . signification [through the word] . . . that a subject is of flesh and blood, a man that is hungry and eats, entrails in a skin, and thus capable of giving the bread out of his mouth, or giving his skin."[77] This giving skin is the concrete signifyingness of human subjectivity as a signifier, as the one-for-the-other. The divine commandment to be there for the sake of the other human being is a commandment to snatch the bread from one's own mouth and offer it to another, a commandment to give skin. Else the word loses all connection to meaning.

In the last chapter of *Survival in Auschwitz,* "The Story of Ten Days," Levi shows that when the meaning of the word *bread* is restored, human relation is restored, which is to say: the *meaning* of "human being" is recovered. For the moment came during those ten days when one person offered bread to another, so that bread was no longer currency—bread was bread. And when bread is once again bread, human beings are once again human beings. "It really meant that the Lager was dead," writes Levi. "I believe that that moment can be dated as the beginning of the change by which we who had not died slowly changed from Häftlinge to men again."[78] This tearing of bread from one's own mouth to offer it to another constitutes not only the restoration of bread—it is the restoration of the link between word and meaning, beginning with the restoration of the name. Which name? The name of the human being and the name of the Holy One, both of which are tied to the name of the Holocaust, which was an assault on both the name and the Name.

Other scholars have addressed the issue of language surrounding Holocaust representation, beginning with the word *Auschwitz.* James Young, for example, writes, "Whether or not one wants meaning in Auschwitz, it is automatically created the instant its smoke and ashes are represented—that is, figured—for us in *language.*"[79] Language and metaphor, he maintains, "tell us as much about how events have been grasped and organized as they do about events themselves."[80] In her study of Holocaust testimony and representation Zoë Vania Waxman makes a similar claim.[81] But what do the events tell us about language itself, particularly when at the core of the events is a systematic assault on language?

If that assault is characterized by a tearing of meaning from word and thereby a tearing of human from human, then we are led to understand language as something other than a system of signs and signifiers. Indeed, the assault on the Good that lies at the core of the Holocaust's singularity is not reducible to an assault on a semiotic web of signs, since, as an ethical absolute, the Good cannot be determined by such webs. Left only with systems of signifiers, not only do we lose the flesh-and-blood human being, but we also lose the absolute, *caring* Voice of any ethical imperative that may arise from the event, as David Hirsch realized: "Did not Hitler prove, Derrida and deconstruction to the contrary, that there is more to language than just an infinitely regressive series of signifiers?"[82] Hitler proved that words inflict wounds, that they create and destroy worlds. Words—words torn from meaning, torn, therefore, from every ethical absolute—created the anti-world of Auschwitz. Can representations of the Holocaust transmit this tearing of the word that went into the creation of the Holocaust?

There is a certain safety within systems of signifiers. They impart a sense of security, universality, and predictability, the illusion of a firm ground under our feet that leaves us free to indulge in language games, free of the prelinguistic, preoriginary, immemorial call to responsibility. From this counterfeit freedom issues what Hirsch calls "deconstructionist nihilism," noting that a consequence of "deconstructionist nihilism is the imposition of the dogma that all human acts must remain morally undifferentiated, since *différance* exists only in the language systems, only as differences in sounds and concepts, in signifiers and signifieds, so that the only difference between a collaborator and a resister is a difference in sound images."[83] This superficial difference between a collaborator and a resister carries over into the issue of language and Holocaust representation. The question that must be decided is this: Shall we indulge in the diversion of language games that belong to systems of signifiers, or shall we embrace a view of language that exceeds the system and leave off with the seductions of game playing?

Those of us who are enthralled by the Sirens' song of semiotic systems fall prey to the game society embodied in Levinas's image of the café:

> The café . . . is a place of casual social intercourse, without mutual responsibility. One goes in without needing to. One sits down without being tired. One drinks without being thirsty. . . . The café is not a place. It is a non-place for a non-society, for a society without solidarity, without tomorrow, without commitment,

> without common interests, a game society. The café, house of games, is the point through which game penetrates life and dissolves it. Society without yesterday or tomorrow, without responsibility, without seriousness—distraction, dissolution. . . . In the café there are no themes. Here you are, each at your own little table with your cup or your glass. You relax completely to the point of not being obligated to anyone or anything; and it is because it is possible to go and relax in a café that one tolerates the horrors and injustices of a world without a soul. The world as game from which everyone can pull out and exist only for himself, a place of forgetfulness—of the forgetfulness of the other—that is the café.[84]

Need it be said that here Levinas is speaking of something more than the café? He is speaking of a condition made possible by what Hirsch calls "the scandal of twentieth-century European philosophy": "That so many thinkers could have remained detached from reality while their countrymen were turning Europe into a continent of death camps, that 'philosophers' could sit in the eye of the whirlwind, thinking sublime thoughts, oblivious to the disintegration of human values occurring before their eyes—these realities are the scandal of twentieth-century European philosophy."[85] Suddenly I understand why De-Nur once remarked to me with a scowl: "*Philosophy*: it is a *shabby* word."

A scene in Wiesel's *Night* articulates a "theory" of language that may be helpful in the matter of Holocaust representation. It an understanding of language from the standpoint of the Jewish tradition that was targeted for annihilation. After Eliezer and others had completed their initiation into the camp and were gathered in the block for the night, the young Pole in charge urged them to "have faith in life, a thousand times faith. By driving our despair, you will move away from death. . . . And now, here is a prayer, or rather a piece of advice: let there be camaraderie among you. We are all brothers and share the same fate. The same smoke hovers over all our heads. Help each other." And then we come to the comment: "Those were the first human words."[86] These are human words not because they belong to a system of signs but because they attest to the sanctity of human relation. They are words that retain their bond with meaning, for a word's tie to meaning lies in its capacity to draw one human being into a relationship with another. Indeed, if language were nothing more than a system of signs, representation would not be an issue. Without the nonrepresentable, there is no representation; where there is representation, the Good abides in the immemorial background. "Antecedent to the verbal signs it conjugates," Levinas makes this point, "to the linguistic systems and the semantic glimmerings, a foreword preceding languages, it is the proximity of one to the other, the commitment of an approach, the one for the other, the very signifyingness of signification."[87] If language is to represent the radical assault on the human word and human relation as embodied in Jewish teaching and tradition, then it must restore the tie between word and meaning as a bond between human and human.

What is called for, then, is an understanding of language that views the bond between word and meaning as a bond between human and human, and not just a link to other signifiers within a semiotic system. Such a view of language opens up a vision of the vertical dimension in the young Pole's statement: he refers to his advice as a "prayer." Taking on the aspect of prayer, his words take on the aspect of a commandment, a *mitzvah,* from on high. Understood as *mitzvah,* a commandment is not a rule to follow or an order to obey; stemming from the root *tzavta,* it is a "connection" or a relation that we enter into. Where language has meaning it harbors a commandment and a connection, not between signs but between human beings. That connection is made of an ethical absolute that penetrates into this realm from above, from elsewhere, from what Levinas calls the "otherwise than being." And surely the language of Holocaust representation should have meaning—not the meaning we give to words but the meaning words give to us. As Sara Nomberg-Przytyk (1915–1990) recalls in her Holocaust memoir, "the new set of meanings" that the Nazis imposed on the word "provided the best evidence of the devastation that Auschwitz created."[88] Therefore, one method for approaching the language of Holocaust representation—one way of naming Auschwitz—is to proceed from the Jewish understanding of language that came under assault in Auschwitz and thus to resist the new set of meanings that the Nazis imposed upon the word. Holocaust representation must assume the form of such a resistance.

At the core of a Jewish understanding of language is the notion of a holy tongue, which stems from the Torah itself (Exodus 35–38). There it is related how Betzalel was chosen to oversee the building of the Holy Tabernacle as a dwelling place for the Shekhinah. According to the Talmud, he was chosen for this most sacred of tasks because he knew the secret meanings and combinations of the Hebrew words and letters that God uses at every instant to do the work of creation (*Berakhot* 55a). Which means: Betzalel had the wisdom, understanding, and knowledge to sound the depths of the holy word contained within the Ark of the Covenant. For out of that word heaven and earth—the sum and significance of life—came into existence. If "Hebrew words describe not only an object but its very essence," as the Maharal of Prague, Rabbi Yehuda Loeve (1513–1609), taught,[89] then the object is in some sense made of its Hebrew word. It is written, for example, that "whatever the human being [Adam] called a living soul was its name"; the Hebrew phrase is *vekol asher yikra-lo ha-adam nefesh chayah shmo* (Genesis 2:19), where *yikra-lo* literally means he "read" its name: the soul of the creature was already inscribed in the name, and Adam had the wisdom to read the name that constituted the creature. Betzalel's wisdom lay in understanding the bond between word and reality.

From a Jewish standpoint, such a connection profoundly comes to bear in matters of Holocaust representation, as illustrated by an example from the Talmud. It is related that whenever the Holy of Holies required mending, a craftsman would be lowered into the sacred enclosure in a *tevah* or a "box" (*Midot* 37a). There were openings in the box just large enough for the craftsman to see what had to be repaired and to do his work, so that he would not be tempted to feast his eyes upon the glory of the Shekhinah. Now the word *tevah* signifies not only a vessel; it also means "word." Entering the vessel of the word—entering the *tevah*—in the wake of the Nazi assault on the word, we may descend into the world to undertake the task of restoring the world as a holy place, a place where the holiness of the human being is affirmed in the bond between word and meaning.

If, as Levinas says, "language is the fact that always one sole word is proffered: God,"[90] the assault on the word is also an assault on the Holy One. A text from the abyss of the Churban sheds additional light on this matter. It is the *Esh Kodesh* or *Sacred Fire*, the journal of Torah commentary written from 14 September 1939 to 18 July 1942 by Rabbi Kalonymos Kalmish Shapira (1889–1943), Rebbe of the Warsaw Ghetto, who was murdered in the concentration camp Trawniki on 3 November 1943. In the *Esh Kodesh* the Rebbe compares the holiness of Hebrew to the holiness of the Sabbath. Just as the Sabbath imparts meaning and sanctity to the other days of the week, he maintains, so does the Hebrew language impart meaning and sanctity to the other languages of humanity.[91] Rabbi Shapira's insight stems from the teaching of the talmudic sage Rabbi Yochanan, who maintains that when God created the heavens and the earth, His first utterance broke into seventy sparks. From those seventy sparks emerged the seventy languages of the world (*Shabbat* 88b). Hebrew is not among the seventy languages of the seventy nations; rather, as the vehicle of the divine voice, it precedes those languages. It is the language of the immemorial, of the ethical injunction couched in human words: help one another. Surely, in the contexts of Holocaust representation we must consider this ethical aspect of language itself.

If Hebrew letters and words are "the energy building-blocks of all reality," as the sages have taught,[92] then language is the substance of human relation, the substance of the human soul. How does one undertake an assault on the soul? By undertaking an assault on the word that binds human to human. Indeed, Abraham Isaac Kook (1865–1935) writes, "The soul is full of [Hebrew] letters that abound with the light of life, intellect and will."[93] As far as I can determine, no other language that uses an alphabet contains such teachings and traditions surrounding the very letters of its alphabet. "To Hebrew," says the sage Judah Halevi (ca. 1075–1141), "belongs the first place, both as regards the *nature of the language,* and as to *fullness of meanings*" (*Kitav al khazari* 2:66; emphasis added). This understanding of Hebrew is not so much an article of faith concerning a language as it is a distinctively Jewish way of thinking about language itself, a way of thinking about language that the Nazis set out to obliterate in their extermination of the Jews. It is a means of getting at the truth of language and the language of truth; it is the avenue through which being is sanctified and thus made meaningful from beyond being. That is why the Nazis undertook a radical assault on language, beginning with the Hebrew word, consigning the folios of Hebrew texts to the flames. Georges Didi-Huberman understood this point when he wrote that Auschwitz "was a hell made by humans for the *obliteration of the language* of their victims."[94] The only difference is that there is a language of justice associated with hell: Auschwitz was not hell.

Here, too, the Hebrew language informs this inquiry into language, meaning, and representation. The Hebrew word for "meaning," "sense," or "significance" is *mashmaut,* from the root *shema,* which means to "hear." Like language, meaning is first of all *heard,* and it is heard as an ethical imperative; like language, meaning *addresses* us, from beyond systems of signs and signifiers. To have a sense of meaning in life is to hear something or *someone* calling out to us, as the dead call out to De-Nur and Wiesel. And if their summons bears an ethical imperative, it comes from beyond the dead themselves. It is a calling to a particular path: to have meaning is to have "direction," *kivun* in Hebrew, which is a cognate of *kavanah,* another word for "meaning." It also means "purpose" and "devotion," words that imply a *love* for someone. A cognate of *kavanah, mekhuveh,* drives home this point; it means "named," "called," and "designated." Here lies a key to the analysis at hand: our response to representations of the Holocaust becomes a loving response to the one who calls our name (more about this below), a saying of "*Hineni!*—Here I am." The issue of meaning in representations of the Holocaust, then, becomes an issue of identity, both for those who testify and for those who receive the testimony. It is an issue of answering to the witness, who singles us out by name.

Consider this: the most overwhelming of the memorials at Yad Vashem, the Holocaust memorial and archive center in Jerusalem, is the Children's Memorial. Entering the memorial is like entering a tomb. But there are no bodies laid to rest in the tomb. On the contrary, there is an abysmal sense of unrest. That is the reason for the handrails: it is not the darkness—it is the swoon of feeling the ground crumble from beneath your feet. No, there are no bodies in this tomb: instead of bodies there is a darkness seared by a million and a half points of light generated by using mirrors to reflect the light of five candles. Instead of bodies there are names, hundreds of thousands of names. Every few seconds you hear the name, the age, and the birthplace of a murdered child. Every few seconds your soul is wracked not by the million and a half little ones but by *this one*. The researchers at Yad Vashem have identified less than one-third of the names of the murdered children. It takes three years to get through the list of names. In that utterance of each name you hear the utterance of the Name. You hear your own name. You hear a Commanding Voice put to you a question: "What is your name?"

To name Auschwitz is to name the site of the assault on the Name and on the name. It is a fundamental indicator of the assault on language and the task of the restoration of language for Holocaust representation: no one can undertake such a task innocently. To attempt a representation of the Holocaust—to attempt an analysis of Holocaust representation—is from the outset *confessional*. The flight from such a confession often takes the form of turning to numbers instead of names, a move that plays into the hands of the murderers, for whom the very numbers were a camouflage. In *Essays in the First Person*, Holocaust survivor and novelist Aharon Appelfeld (b. 1932) writes, "We have been taught to speak about the Holocaust in the language of big numbers, and no language distances you from contact more than such a language."[95] Nothing reduces the person to an object more than a number does, which the Nazis did with totalitarian efficiency: the number is the first weapon drawn in the assault on language and the soul.

Thus, seeking the recovery of their humanity, the authors of numerous memoirs set out to recover a name by remembering a number. For example:

Elie Wiesel: "I became A-7713. From then on, I had no other name."[96]

Miklós Nyiszli (1901–1956): "Henceforth I would be, merely, KZ prisoner Number A 8450."[97]

Sara Zyskind (1927–1995): "Mine was 55091—my new name from now on."[98]

Alexander Donat (1905–1983): "I looked at my number: 7,115. From that moment I ceased to be a man."[99]

Rudolf Vrba (1924–2006): "That, indeed, was the last time I used my name . . . for now I was prisoner number 44070."[100]

Nathan Shapell (1922–2007): "A filthy needle . . . erased Natan Schapelski from the human race and brought into being Häftling 134138."[101]

Olga Lengyel (1908–2001): "I was number '25,403.' I still have it on my right arm and shall carry it with me to the grave."[102]

Moshe Sandberg (1900–1966): "We ceased to be human beings with family names. . . . In my metamorphosis I was No. 124753."[103]

"Ceased to be a man," "erased from the human race," "ceased to be human beings": memory clutches at such phrases in an attempt to speak Auschwitz, to articulate the death that the survivors survive but never live through, for it follows them from the massive grave that was Planet Auschwitz to their own grave. "You must watch over your name and your soul," says Rabbi Nachman of Breslov (1772–1810).[104] Sensing this, the Nazis assailed the Jewish soul by forcing these men and women to watch over a number rather than a name.

"This is an indelible mark," the tattoo declares, "you will never leave."[105] "You will never leave" means that the confinement to Auschwitz exceeds space and time; it exceeds language. The problem of representation through the word is not a problem of imagination—it is a problem of bearing a name and an identity, a problem of *who,* and not a problem of *what.* Through the needle Auschwitz invades the flesh and stains the image of the human being; through the flesh it enters into his soul and substance, into his *language.* Through the pen it leaks into the language that would represent it. Primo Levi dwells at length on the significance of the number in the anti-world, describing the details of the tattooing process, as well as the aftermath of the process. Prisoners would not be fed, he explains, without first showing their numbers and repeating them in German.[106] Not only is the number alien to the man, but the German language in which the number is spoken adds to the Jew's alienation from himself. The eclipse of the name is tied to the breakdown of the body: showing the number in exchange for food, the prisoner declares his namelessness and his nothingness, as he wastes away on the meager ration. "For many days," says Levi, "while the habits of freedom still led me to look for time on my wristwatch, my new name ironically appeared instead, a number tattooed in bluish characters under the skin."[107] Thus, the man who seeks the time only to find the number—not *on* the skin but *under* it—continually collides with the collapse of time, with his exile from time, and with the end of his life time.

The task of representing the Holocaust in language is a task of restoring a "memorial and a name," of answering to our name as we receive that testimony. With the number inscribed in their flesh, the witnesses do not merely experience the Holocaust; rather, the Holocaust "experiences" them to become part of their essence ever after. They leave Auschwitz, but they do not leave it behind: the prisoner is not in Auschwitz—Auschwitz is in the prisoner, and the unspeakable haunts every effort to speak it, beginning with the effort to name the assault on the name. Paradoxically, if anything names Auschwitz, it is the number inked into the flesh that becomes not only part of the body but also part of the soul. But a number is not a metaphor. Or is it?

To answer this decisive question in the context of Holocaust representation, we must raise another question: Who first utters the name that situates the human being within the language of meaning, the language of divine creation, the language that itself came under a radical assault? In a word, it is the mother. Here lies a profound key to understanding both the Holocaust and the problem of Holocaust representation. Indeed, for Ka-tzetnik, it is a key to understanding what Auschwitz is.

The Nonrepresentable and the Murder of the Mother

The silent face of my mother—
With her last glance turned to the sky;
And her last thoughts, most likely of her children;
Mother was set ablaze. A mother burns!

—Ka-Tzetnik 135633, *Kaddish*

The assault on language that finds its expression in the assault on the name bring us to what, for many survivors, is a metaphor for the Holocaust itself: it is image of the murdered mother, as when Isabella Leitner (1924–2009) writes, "The air was filled with the stench of death. Unnatural death. The smoke was thick. The sun couldn't crack through. The scent was the smell of burning flesh. The burning flesh was your mother."[108] Ka-tzetnik, too, invokes the burning flesh of the mother in the silent face about to be burned and reduced to ash. The face that is the origin of the word, of language—and here the theory of language espoused above applies—is the face of the mother, who is the origin of the name. That face is silent, set ablaze, making it impossible for the sun or the word or any representation to "crack through." And so the metaphor of the mother speaks more than can be said, more than can be represented, not only because of the suffering or the trauma endured in her death but because of the metaphysical horror that seeps into the ontological assault.

Mikhail Bakhtin (1895–1975) provides a clue as to how we might understand this "seeping." He points out that "the child receives all initial determinations of himself and of his body from his mother's lips. . . . It is from [her] lips, in the emotional-volitional tones of love, that the child hears and begins to acknowledge his own *proper name*. . . . For the first time, he finds himself and becomes aware of himself as a *something*."[109] The mother is the closest tie that we have to the Creator, the Supernal Mother, as the Zohar describes Her, who gives birth to creation through the womb of the *beit,* the first letter of the Torah, which is shaped like a womb (*Zohar* I, 22b). She is the absolutely Other, who is revealed in the absolute non-indifference, in the preoriginary language, of love. Love is the key, conceived not as one feeling among many but as a living presence between two. "Feelings one 'has,'" explains Martin Buber (1878–1965). "Love occurs. Feelings dwell in man, but man dwells in his love."[110] The between space of human relation is made of this love. If the Holocaust entails a fundamental assault on human relation, it entails a fundamental assault on the mother, so that the problem of Holocaust representation is a problem of representing the assault on the love of the mother.

Confronted with the representation of this assault, we are confronted with the nonrepresentable assault on the bond between word and meaning, which *is* the bond between mother and child. In this relationship, to borrow from Levinas, "the 'movement' that meets the *Thou* does not resemble thematization,"[111] and therefore cannot be accommodated by representation. It is otherwise than representation. As the one ultimately targeted for extermination in the Kingdom of Night, the mother emerges as a metaphor for saying what Auschwitz is. If, through the mother, the human being first becomes aware of himself or herself as *something,* then when the mother is lost, the human being is reduced to *nothing,* which is the Nazis' definition of the Jew.

Thus, with terrifying beauty, Charlotte Delbo (1913–1985) invokes the metaphor—and the reality—of the mother in her effort to "represent" the nonrepresentable horror that is the Holocaust:

> My mother
> she was hands
> she was a face
> They set our mothers before us naked
> Here mothers are no longer mothers to their children.[112]

With the removal of the hands that offered the embrace of love—with the erasure of the face that spoke the first words of love—the little girl is orphaned before she is orphaned. The Holocaust turns humanity over to this *being alone.* Such is the ontological starting point for Holocaust representation—and the metaphysical endgame that transpires in the collision with the nonrepresentable: "mothers are no longer mothers to their children." A people and a world are ontologically and metaphysically orphaned, their essence redefined as the essence of the orphan, an essence that representations of the Holocaust must convey and, because nonrepresentable, must *fail* to convey: Holocaust representation is about this failure, a failure here inscribed in my own effort to articulate it. It is about what is otherwise than representation.

The mother is the one who comforts her child, saying, "It's all right, I am with you." With the obliteration of the Jewish mother from their midst, the Jews were left with no one to be *with them* as a mother; they were turned over to the anti-world where, in the words of Primo Levi, "everyone is desperately and ferociously alone." Yes: *ferociously* alone. Sara Zyskind begins her memoir with the memory of her mother's last Mother's Day.[113] Very soon she loses her mother to the anti-death of ghetto death and is left only with the agonizing cry: "I don't want to be an orphan, Mother!"[114] The cry of "I don't want to be an orphan" is the cry that issues from the war against memory, which here is the war against the mother. The orphan's memory is the memory of the loss of the one who forever remembers her child, when no one else remembers the child. The bottomless void, the infinite emptiness, experienced by the orphan is the void and the emptiness of being forgotten. Losing those hands and that face, the child loses her own hands and face, her own deeds and words, to become "the shadow of another shadow," as Ana Vinocur (b. 1926) expresses it. "I felt an infinite emptiness in my mind and heart," she recalls. "They've taken my mother away. I'm nothing but the shadow of another shadow."[115] When the mother is turned to ash, creation is returned to the *tohu vevohu,* to the chaos and the void, antecedent to every origin.

Indeed, the first word in Vinocur's *Book without a Title* is the word *mother.*[116] From this word arise all other words in the memoir. "Mama!" Isabella Leitner screams the word in an attempt to reattach the word to its meaning. "If you don't turn around I'll run after you. But they won't let me. I must stay on the 'life' side. Mama!"[117] No good-bye. We know why "life" is placed in quotation marks in these lines from Leitner's memoir: there is no "life" side in this non-place. If the memory of Auschwitz echoes in the metaphor of the mother, it is because the mother is the source of everything meaningful in the Jewish tradition; only through her, says the Talmud, does blessing come to a home (*Bava Metzia* 59a). The origin is precisely what is *meta-* in the metaphor, beyond signs and semiotics. As a metaphor of the Auschwitz, the murder of the mother is a metasign and signifies a metalanguage, opening up a meaning and a relation that transcends semiotics and systems of signs.

One night in 1988 in Tel-Aviv, De-Nur entrusted to me the manuscript of the English edition of his memoir *Shivitti* that his wife Eliyah had just translated. The key to Auschwitz, he told me, came not in his novels but in this book of visions, his first work of nonfiction. Perhaps that is why it took him ten years from the time he had completed his therapy with Dr. Bastiaans until he could pen the book's opening line. Perhaps that is why he wrote the book in a trance-like state, as he told me, and had no memory of having written it, a memory that brought him to the edge of memory:

> My mother. I see her naked and marching in line, one among Them, her face turned towards the gas chambers. "Mama! Mama! Mama!" A voice comes rolling down to me out of the Auschwitz sky. The echo of each separate word is a hammer crashing on my eardrums. It's my mother, naked. She's going to be gassed. I run after her. I cry out, "Mama! Mama!" I, outside that line, run after her: "Mama! Listen to me! Mama!" My mother naked. Going

> to be gassed. I behold my mother's skull and in my mother's skull I see me. And I chase after me inside my mother's skull. And my mother is naked. Going to be gassed. I'm choking![118]

This is the key. This is the metaphor. How are we to draw on the ontological categories to represent this assault on the metaphysical ground of the ontological? If, as Levinas has said, "the soul is the other in me,"[119] here the other in me is the mother in me. This assault on the mother and on all that she signifies was systematic and calculated: it is the essence of the singularity we call the Holocaust, and De-Nur has conveyed it in all its metaphysical depth. His vision is truly visionary in a way that borders on the prophetic; it is not a memory from his own life dredged up by the LSD. *For in his own life, his mother passed away before the war broke out.* Perhaps what is required for Holocaust representation is more akin to prophetic vision than to artistic inspiration.

That the metaphor of the mother is related to the Nazi assault on the Holy One can be seen from various teachings in the Jewish tradition on the feminine. The Talmud affirms that the Shekhinah is not only a feminine presence but is also a maternal presence (*Kiddushin* 31b). When she accompanies Israel into exile, she does so as a mother looking after her children. When the Jews were gathered at Mount Sinai, it is written, the Torah had to be accepted first by the women before it could be received by the men. For the House of Jacob mentioned in Exodus 19:3 precedes the reference to the Children of Israel, and the House of Jacob refers to the mothers of Israel (Rashi's commentary on Exodus 19:3). If the Torah is the foundation of creation, the mother, through her tie to the *beit,* the first letter of the Torah, is the foundation of the Torah itself. As we have seen, the *beit* is the womb from which creation is born.

The mystery of value and meaning in human life—the very thing that the Nazis annihilate in the annihilation of the mother—unfolds wherever we make room for another human being. A mother opens up space where there is no space: she is precisely the one who does not usurp the place of another. Instead, miraculously, she creates room for another life within herself, in the very depths of her physical being. Both physically and metaphysically, a mother embodies the radical opposite of the ontological interest in occupying space, which was the Nazis' interest in *Lebensraum* or "living space." Associated with the "womb," or *rechem,* the mother personifies the "compassion," the *rachamim,* that lies at the core of our humanity. Levinas sheds light on these connections when he notes, "*Rachamim* (Mercy) . . . goes back to the word *Rechem,* which means uterus. *Rachamim* is the revelation of the uterus to the other. . . . *Rachamim* is maternity itself. God as merciful is God defined by maternity."[120] Hence, the Nazis' assault on the mother was central to their assault on God. From the depths of the mother's compassion—from the *rechem* within the *rachamim*—human life and the meaning of human life, to which the presence of the Jews bears witness, begin to stir. That is why the mother is a metaphor for the Holocaust: if the crime of the Jew was existing, then the most heinous of criminals was the one who brought the Jew into existence: the mother.

Just a couple of examples from the diaries written in the heart of the maelstrom illustrate this point. "These Jewish mothers with babes in their wombs!" the words cry out from the pages of Yitzhak Katznelson's (1886–1944) *Vittel Diary.* "That was their chief joy! To destroy women with child!"[121] Yes: *their chief joy.* It was their chief joy because it was an expression of their primary aim. The horror that overcomes Katznelson oozes from the words of Avraham Tory (1910–2002) when on 24 July 1942 he makes this entry in his diary from the Kovno Ghetto: "From September on, giving birth is strictly forbidden. Pregnant women will be put to death."[122] When a pregnant woman is put to death, more than a pregnant woman is murdered, physically and metaphysically. Exceeding the horror of slaughtering pregnant mothers, the Nazis often waited until these mothers held their babies in their arms before murdering them and their infants with them: the very relationship was the designated target of this physical and metaphysical murder, this nonrepresentable murder that exceeds murder. We do not know how to represent it; indeed, here the very word *representation* smacks of obscenity. All "representation" is here transformed into a crescendo of horror. For the word that would determine that the human being is a *something* is murdered with the murder of these mothers.

The danger of representation lies in its drowning out the screams—and the silences—of the Nazis' victims. Terrence Des Pres (1939–1987) once asserted that the Holocaust "produced an endless scream which, given time, has transmuted itself into the voices of many witnesses."[123] Here too we circle back to the mother, and nowhere more so than in Sara Nomberg-Przytyk's memory of a transport of Jewish children—yes! a *transport of children*—burned alive—*yes!* burned *alive!*: "Suddenly, the stillness was broken by the screaming of children . . . a scream repeated a thousand times in a single word, 'Mama,' a scream that increased in intensity every second, enveloping the whole camp. Our lips parted without our being conscious of what we were doing, and a scream of despair tore out of our throats. . . . At the end everything was enveloped in death and silence."[124] The Nazis set out to tear meaning from the word in a tearing of human from human, and the word from which meaning was most radically torn is *Mama*. No one ever uttered a prayer that came more profoundly from the depths than these children's scream of "Mama!"—a scream that, in the end, is enveloped in silence, as is every attempt to represent the Holocaust.

The Silent Scream

> Anyone who was in the ghetto, in the camp, or hiding in the forests knows silence *in his body*.
>
> —Aharon Appelfeld, *The Story of a Life*

"Surely we feel," writes Blanchot, that the silence "is linked to the cry, the voiceless cry, which breaks with all utterances, which is addressed to no one and which no one receives, the cry that lapses and decries."[125] And yet, addressed to no one amounts to being addressed to everyone. These words should be kept in mind when venturing onto the campus of Yad Vashem, near the Children's Memorial, where we collide with Leah Michelson's sculpture titled *The Silent Scream* (Figure 1.1).[126] It is a faceless figure: the word that issues from the face has been obliterated in the obliteration of the face. Draped in a long stone robe, this stone image is wearing intractable stone *tefillin,* the phylacteries that Jews don for their morning prayers. His hands are over his ears, as if to keep out a deafening silence, a deafening silent scream, a silent scream that issues from the figure itself, who screams like a Chasid—silently.[127]

Or does the scream issue from on high? Is it the scream of the Holy One, the scream that Rabbi Shapira invoked when he wrote, "Possibly because God is infinite—and hence unknowable in the world—His pain at the suffering of the Jewish people is also infinite. . . . And so, the world continues to exist steadfast, it is not obliterated by God's pain and His voice at the suffering of His people and the destruction of His house, because God's pain never enters into the world"?[128] It does not enter, Rabbi Shapira concludes, because God retreats to a place of concealment to weep and cry out in pain. The Talmud, in fact, names the place of God's retreat: it is "called *Mistarim* [meaning 'concealment'], in the inner chambers" (*Chagigah* 5b). For God's pain—His fear of His own scream—cannot enter the world

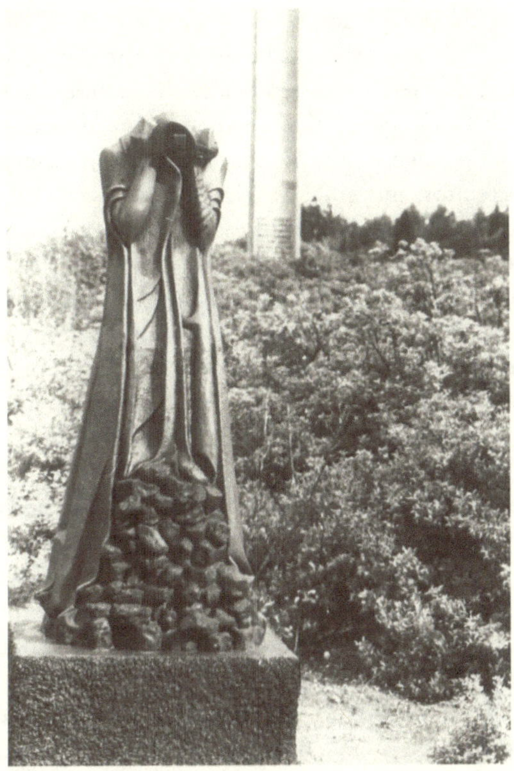

FIGURE 1.1. Jerusalem, Israel Leah Michelson's statue "The Silent Scream," Yad Vashem Photo Archive, Jerusalem, ID 7084, Archival Signature 5432/15, with permission of Yad Vashem.

without destroying it. Thus, the angel Metatron, who rules over this world (*Sanhedrin* 94a; *Yevamot* 16b; *Shemot Rabbah* 17:4), weeps in God's place (*Tanchuma Vaetchanan* 6). God is driven into hiding, where He weeps in secret and roars in silence, so that just enough of the Divine Presence abides to sustain Creation. Or does it?

In the Shema, the "Hear, O Israel," prayer that Jews recite each day, are the lines from Deuteronomy 11:21 affirming that the promise of the Covenant will endure "as long as the heavens are above the earth." But there came a time when the heavens were no longer above the earth, when the dead were buried in a sky transformed into a cemetery. If the silent scream comes from the silent heavens, then it may well be the scream of the dead. Their silent scream, like their silent ashes, rains down from the heavens to cover the earth and shake us from our sleep. *Shachrit,* the rite of morning prayer, is symbolic of the arousal from sleep, when Jews don their prayer shawl and tefillin to step before the countenance and recite the Shema, like Michelson's statue. The cognate *shachar* means both "dawn" and "darkness": it is the edge of darkness about to be transformed into light, the horizon where life's "meaning" or "significance"—two other meanings of *shachar*—struggles to come to light through the prayers. The verb *shachar,* moreover, means to "seek out" or "diligently search for," reminding us that meaning lies much more in the seeking than in the finding. Seek out what? The human relation and the higher relation that came under the Nazis' assault. For the prayers are preceded not by the recitation of a creed but by the declaration, "I take upon myself the commandment: 'You shall love your neighbor as yourself.' "

At what hour in the morning, the rabbis ask, shall a Jew put on his tefillin, when the darkness succumbs to the light? The answer: when it is light enough for him to recognize the face of his neighbor (*Kitzur Shulchan Arukh* 10:2). To be sure, according to the Midrash, God's hiding place is the realm of darkness, from which God drew the plague of darkness, the darkness in which "a man could not see his brother" (Exodus 10:23); that is the darkness, that is the silence, that makes God weep and cry out in pain (*Midrash Tehillim* 1:18:16). If you cannot behold the face of your neighbor in an answering of "*Hineni!*—Here I am for you," you cannot enter into a relation with the Holy One. Hence, the declaration of what is commanded in Leviticus 19:18: "You shall love your neighbor as yourself." To don tefillin is to affirm that there is no Torah without the face of the other human being, no face without the Torah. Putting on tefillin, then, is no mere ritual; far more than that, it is, in the words of Levinas, the confirmation of "the conception of God in which He is welcomed in the face-to-face with the other, in the obligation towards the other."[129] The faceless figure of *The Silent Scream* represents the systematic assault on the face of the neighbor and the silencing of the scream that erupts from a face upon the obliteration of the word. The silent stone sculpture represents the Holocaust, if, indeed, it can be represented.

At the feet of the praying image is a sculptured pile of stones. Those who visit the site will also find stones placed upon the sculpture, like stones placed on a *matzevah,* on a grave's memorial stone, symbolizing the persistence of memory. Jews add stones to the memorial stone to combat the elements that over time may wear away the memorial stone, the way time eats away at memory. It is a means of waging a war for memory in the aftermath of the war against memory. The implication is that the sculpture itself is a kind of matzevah. The embodiment of the scream of the Holocaust in the silence of stone is expressive of the prayer turned to stone, a prayer in the mode of a scream, perhaps to a God who has turned to stone, who has taken on the indifference of a stone. In this image of stone are gathered the screams that spread through the camps and the convoys, through the ghettos and the hiding places, to rain down on a humanity turned to stone by the Medusa of the Holocaust.

A prescient literary giant comes to mind: Dante (1265–13121), the one beloved by Primo Levi. Memories of *The Divine Comedy*, said Levi, "made it possible for me to reestablish a link with the past, saving it from oblivion . . . in short, a way to find myself."[130] Indeed, in *Survival in Auschwitz* he devotes a chapter to "The Canto of Ulysses," as he translates passages from Dante for his friend Pikolo with a profound sense of urgency, trying desperately to convey to him "something gigantic that I myself have only just seen, in a flash of intuition, perhaps the reason for our fate, for our being here today."[131] Here, however, as we seek to fathom Michelson's sculpture, we recall a different canto, Canto IX, the "Canto of the Heretics":

> "Turn your back and keep your eyes shut tight;
> for should the Gorgon come and you look at her,
> never again would you return to the light."
>
> This was my Guide's command. And he turned me about
> himself, and would not trust my hands alone,
> but, with his placed on mine, held my eyes shut.
>
> Men of sound intellect and probity,
> weigh with good understanding what lies hidden
> behind the veil of my strange allegory! (Canto IX, 52–60)[132]

If the Gorgon of myth turns one to stone, the Gorgon of the Holocaust turns us over to the stony silence of a world turned to stone by the Kingdom of Night, never again to return to the light. So it happened to Susan Sontag (1933–2004) when she first gazed upon photographs of Bergen-Belsen and Dachau and her life was divided "into two parts," before and after: "Some limit had been reached, *and not only that of horror*; I felt irrevocably grieved, wounded, but part of my feelings started to tighten; something went dead; something is still crying."[133] Interestingly, throughout her analysis in her book *On Photography* she never again mentions those photographs. She was literally struck *dumb*. Men of sound intellect and probity will behold in the *Inferno*'s Gorgon an allegory of the nonrepresentable in Holocaust representation.

"I don't think you can focus on the horror of the Holocaust," says W. G. Sebald (1944–2001). "It's like the head of the Medusa: you carry it with you in a sack, but if you looked at it you'd be petrified."[134] Has Michelson's figure gazed upon something that turned him to stone? Or is his head bowed so that he might avert his gaze? Perhaps those who would represent the Holocaust, as well as those who would analyze its representation, are like Perseus, laying claim to the Gorgon while averting her gaze. Or are they, rather, like Lot's wife, who upon turning her gaze to the horrific destruction of Sodom and Gomorrah was turned to a pillar of salt (Genesis 19:26), with the difference that we look back not upon the destruction of depravity but upon the destruction of the Good? Perhaps that is why Martin Walser asserts, "We are all subject to the temptation of defending ourselves against Auschwitz. We look toward it, and then immediately we look away. It's not possible to live with these images."[135] Didi-Huberman reminds us that Perseus was protected from the gaze of the Gorgon by holding up the shield of Athena—the goddess of wisdom, civilization, knowledge, and reason—so that he could slay the creature by looking at its reflection in the shield. "It is not surprising," he notes, "that [German art historian] Aby Warburg [1866–1929] should have cast Perseus fighting the Medusa as an exemplary personification of the 'sum of European intellectual history,' as a ceaseless struggle of *ethos* against the powers he called the *monstra,* the monsters of savagery."[136] If we glance at what we would represent, we see the *monstra* that is the Gorgon, but if we gaze long into her countenance, we collide with a greater horror, a petrifying horror: hers is the image not of savagery but of the monstrosity that would pass for wisdom, civilization, knowledge, and reason—the image of Athena herself!

Ka-tzetnik understood this point immediately: to represent the Holocaust is to represent modernity. In *Sunrise over Hell,* Auschwitz inmate Harry Preleshnik discovers the corpse of his friend Marcel Safran, who one day simply collapsed and thus succumbed to the fate of the archetypal inhabitant of Auschwitz, the Muselmann. "Prone before his eyes," writes Ka-tzetnik, "he saw the value of all humanity's teachings, ethics and beliefs, from the dawn of mankind to this day. . . . He bent, stretched out his hand and caressed the head of the Twentieth Century."[137] Yes, the head of the *Twentieth Century,* the culmination of twenty-five centuries of the moral and philosophical sophistication that stems from Athens. The value of humanity's teachings and of the human image itself meet this fate at the hands not of ignorant brutes but of highly educated people—the heirs to Kant and Goethe, to Wagner and Nietzsche—who acted in a meticulous, calculated, and systematic manner. It is well known, for example, that at one time or another all four commanders of the *Einsatzgruppen* killing units had doctorate degrees,[138] as did eight of the thirteen men whom Reinhard Heydrich (1904–1942) summoned to the Wannsee Conference on 20 January 1942.[139] The purpose of this meeting of great German minds was to discuss the logistics of murdering the Jews of Europe. There, indeed, we see what had become of "higher learning" in Germany. Perhaps that is why those who would name the silence risk being petrified, reduced to the stony silence of the silent scream.

In the end, philosophical peregrinations through language and metaphor in Holocaust representation lead us to the Site of Silence, for there is no word "to express this offense," as Primo Levi says, no word for "the demolition of a man."[140] The demolition of a man, and *not* the mundane crime of murder, was the essence of the Third Germany, both through torture and through murder. If, as Emil Fackenheim has argued, "the murder camp was not an accidental by-product of the Nazi empire" but "was its pure essence,"[141] then torture, too, is a defining feature of who the Nazis are, as Jean Améry realized: "I am convinced, beyond all personal experiences, that torture was not an accidental quality of this Third Reich, but its *essence*."[142] In torture, explains Elaine Scarry, "World, self, and voice are lost . . . through the intense pain of torture and not through the confession."[143] The human being is no longer a speaking being—he is a screaming being. That is what the torturer demands: the scream. Neither information nor confession, neither expiation nor recompense. Just the scream engulfed by the infinite silence: no one hears, no one answers. For the scream announces the demise of the soul of the mortal victim, as it is possessed absolutely by the divine torturer. The demolition of a man—the demolition of the *medaber* or the "speaking being," as Jewish tradition defines the human being—*is* the demolition of the word, for which there is no word; it is the reduction of the man to a screaming silence.

The demolition of the word is the demolition of what imparts meaning and value to a human being, and in the Holocaust it begins with the demolition of the Jew. It is the demolition not only of the expressible but also of the ineffable, the immemorial, the *hidden*. In Auschwitz everything was stark and nothing was hidden; with Auschwitz, in the words of Blanchot, "the invisible has made itself forever visible."[144] Auschwitz is "beyond understanding," as Nicholas Chare points out. "Events were not known or knowable, they were instead *shown* to the inmate. They had an immediacy that is absent in the everyday."[145] There was, in other words, no link between word and meaning because there was no link between the expressible and the ineffable, and therefore no relation between human and human, which is a relation between hidden and hidden in a calling of deep unto deep.

In Auschwitz there was no *depth,* no *height,* as in the time of the *Mabul,* the Great Flood, when above and below collapsed into a sameness, but with a difference: in the time of the Holocaust, the earth below and the heavens above were buried by the silent ashes of the Jews. Defined by the *stark,* Auschwitz is the archetype of *clarity,* which, in a sense, renders it representable. And there lies the horror. Listen to Levinas: "Clarity is the disappearance of what could shock. Intelligibility, the very occurrence of representation, is the possibility for the other to be determined by the same without determining the same, without introducing alterity into it; it is a free exercise of the same. It is the disappearance, within the same, of the I opposed to the non-I."[146] And: "To be sure, representation is the seat of truth: the movement proper to truth consists in the thinker being determined by the object presented to him. *But it determines him without touching him, without weighing on him.*"[147] And if the representation of the Holocaust does not weigh upon us, it is not a representation of the Holocaust. Where there is representation, then, there is the danger of an abrogation of the responsibility announced in the silent scream.

"The assembling of being in the present," writes Levinas, "is representation. . . . Representation does not integrate the responsibility for the other inscribed in human fraternity; human fraternity does not arise out of any commitment, any principle, that is, any recallable present."[148] Human fraternity is prior to any project of representation; that is why representation runs the risk of evading encounter. Representation is a flight from response in the face of a preoriginary responsibility, a flight into the silence of indifference, a silence broken only by the nonrepresentable responsibility to and for another. Indeed, inasmuch as it tends toward the monological, representation *silences.* It *means* nothing because what can be represented means nothing; in its very utterance, representation turns the event over to the universally determined, to the said, to what Bakhtin calls "the dead flesh of meaning."[149] Auschwitz, then, is the ultimate ontological nightmare: it is what it is, nothing more, nothing less. It is the apex of the cry of "The horror! The horror!" that erupts in Kurtz's dying words in Joseph Conrad's (1857–1924) *Heart of Darkness*,[150] echoed in the last line of the diary of Hélène Berr (1921–1945), the French girl who was murdered in the Holocaust: on 15 February 1944 she wrote, "*Horror! Horror! Horror!*"[151] The horror is not that the evil is so great or the atrocity so extreme that it cannot be represented; no, the horror is that there is no evil to represent, no good, no meaning. There is simply what *is*, neutral, valueless, indifferent—and *silent*. There lies the problem of Holocaust representation. Hence, the *silent* scream.

The Nonrepresentable Site of Silence

> No screams here, no speech. The Site of Silence. Soundlessness was all around, engulfing the outflow of humanity from the cattle trucks. The different laws governing here were instantly tangible; the air was different; the platform lights here shed a different glow. Night here had an essence all its own. Night here was at the beck and call of an omnipotent sovereign, a sovereign supreme over the Planet. Night muffled, stealing inaudibly on tip toes to envelop you, inaudibly, so as to keep from trespassing upon the terrifying silence reigning supreme.
>
> —Ka-tzetnik 135633, *Shivitti*

"Darkness in my mouth," Ka-tzetnik records the first of his visions in *Shivitti*. "I can taste it."[152] The darkness in the mouth is the darkness of silence: the Kingdom of Night is the Kingdom of Silence. No screams. No speech. Ka-tzetnik expresses the cosmic nature of this silence in *Star of Ashes*, where he writes, "Silent are the heavens, silent the yellowed fields; silent the readied rifles, silent the ghetto hovels."[153] Silent the heavens that reign supreme over the soul: since the soul or essence of the human being lies in a capacity for speech, as Maimonides has said,[154] the Site of Silence is the site of the assault on the soul, which is an assault on the heavens. In the Aramaic Targum of Onkelos, where the Hebrew text relates that God breathed His breath into the human being to create a "living soul" (Genesis 2:7), Onkelos renders it, God breathed the word into the human being to create a "speaking spirit" (*l'ruach memalla*).[155] At the Site of Silence the word was sucked forth—and with it all utterance, spirit, and soul—into the chaos and void, the *tohu vevohu,* of the anti-creation that was Auschwitz.

The breath of God breathed into the human being is the image of God, and the image of God is associated with the Divine Presence or the Shekhinah. Because the word vibrates on the breath, the mystical tradition associates the Shekhinah with the faculty of speech.[156] Noting further that the Shekhinah is a maternal presence, Ka-tzetnik realizes a link between the metaphor of the mother and the site of silence. In the ghetto, he writes, the little ones "push again their mother's belly, as if seeking to get inside once more. Their scream, embryonic, unuttered, howls out of the mother's eyes."[157] Hence, the Shekhinah is no more; the mother is no more. Which means: speech is no more.

"Auschwitz," writes André Neher (1914–1988), "is, above all, silence."[158] In Auschwitz, he says, "Silence—the 'inert' silence, great and solemn—comes forward not as a temporary suspension of the Word but as a spokesman for the invincible Nothingness. Thus Silence replaces the Word because Nothingness takes the place of Being."[159] In *Badenheim 1939*, a novel set in the time of the onset of the Holocaust, Aharon Appelfeld writes, "The silence was dense, and from day to day it grew denser."[160] When Eugene Heimler was finally freed from the concentrationary universe of silence, the silence followed him into an open field. "I became aware that the silence was within me, too," he writes, "a silence such as there must have been before the days of creation."[161] Why the silence before the days of creation? Because this is a silence imposed by an absolute, ontological destruction; it is "the emptiness and silence of an imposed Absence," as Alvin Rosenfeld calls it,[162] the silence of the word torn from its meaning and of the man torn from a life that inheres in language. "There is the silence which preceded creation," Wiesel has said, "and the one which accompanied the revelation on Mount Sinai. The first contains chaos and solitude, the second suggests presence, fervor, plenitude."[163] But in Auschwitz there was fervor without plenitude, except the plenitude of the void. Referring to Wiesel's remark, Neher insists that "a man's true self can be discovered only in one or another of these silences, and the revelation of this ontological potential of silence is undoubtedly the major achievement of the phenomenology of silence in Elie Wiesel."[164] But there is a third silence, a nonrepresentable silence, in which a man loses himself and his soul. This emergence of the third silence announces the problem of Holocaust representation.

Wiesel was aware of this third silence, as one can see from his main character in *The Testament*, the Russian Jewish poet Paltiel Kossover, who collides with a paralyzing silence. Listen to Paltiel, as he speaks from the solitary confinement of a Soviet prison cell:

> As an adolescent in Liyanov, I yearned for silence. . . . I begged God to find me a mute master who would impart his truth—and his words—to me wordlessly. I spent hours with a disciple of the Hasidic school of Worke, whose rebbe had turned silence into a method. . . . At midnight, our eyes closed, our faces turned toward Jerusalem and its fiery sanctuary, we listened to the song of its silence—a celestial silence and yet terrible silence in which both voices and moments attain immortality. No master had ever warned me that silence could be nefarious, evil. . . . No master had ever told me that silence could become a prison.[165]

Here we recall the insights from Levinas, in his discussions of the "there is." With the appearance of the "there is," he writes, "the absence of everything returns to us as a presence, as the place where the bottom has dropped out of everything, an atmospheric density, a plenitude of the void, or the murmur of silence."[166] That "murmur" of silence is a death sentence—or worse, as Paltiel discovered: it is a sentence to languish under the gaze of Dumah, the angel whose very name means "Silence," who silently presides over the dead, for whom death is not the last but is continually the last. Like the horror of the "there is," this silence means: there is no getting it over with. And, very often, the aim of representation is precisely to get it over with.

Can this silence be the key to what Auschwitz is, the key to the representation of the anti-world, of the nonrepresentable? Is silence the best way of naming Auschwitz? In 1952, composer John Cage (1912–1992) wrote a three-movement composition for any and all instruments; the score instructs the musicians to sit in silence for the duration of the piece, the title of which is the time of its silence: *Four Minutes, Thirty-three Seconds*. While there is a post-Holocaust context for this experimental composition, it can have no bearing on the problem of Holocaust representation. Framing the silence within the work of art undermines the silence, so that as soon as silence is used as a means of representing anything, it subverts what it would represent. Just as there is no sun like the sun that shone over Majdanek, there is no silence like the silence that reigned supreme over Auschwitz. Not even the silence of *Four Minutes, Thirty-three Seconds*.

The silence of Auschwitz, where the word came under a radical assault, is the obverse of the silence of the Divine Presence that abides within the word, the silence of all tongues, signified by the silent letter *alef*, which, according to the Baal Shem Tov, abides in every word, every letter (*Keter Shem Tov* 45). Made of a *yud* above, a *vav* between, and a *yud* below, the letter *alef* has a numerical value of twenty-six, the same value as the *yud-hey-vav-hey* of the Divine Name, so that with the *alef* a divine spark abides in every word, as the Talmud suggests (*Shabbat* 88b). Recall the statement from Levinas cited above: "Language is the fact that always one sole word is proffered: God." For the word *God* is proffered in every word. Abiding within the word, the Voice within the silence—the Voice in the mode of silence—speaks from the depths of the word, which is the depths of the cosmos, as Neher has said: "The silence of the cosmos is simply the most eloquent form of the Divine revelation,"[167] like the silence that accompanied the revelation at Mount Sinai. Hence, the talmudic teaching of the sage Rabbi Sheshet: "God's appearance is announced by a deep silence" (*Berakhot* 58a). Meaning, then, is not in the word—it is in the silence curled up in the word, the silence that summons another word and another silence, the silence that transcends utterance and representation. More than the word can contain, meaning arises from a realm of "speech before speech," Franz Rosenzweig (1886–1929) states it, "the speech of the unspoken, the unspeakable."[168] Meaning belongs to silence: the word is uttered and defined, while the silence that belongs to the word opens up an inexhaustible dimension of meaning. The task for representation is not to fill the silence but to transmit it, so that we "somehow charge words with silence," as Wiesel describes his own endeavor.[169] "If I use words," he says, "it is not to change silence but to complete it."[170] If Auschwitz is the Site of Silence, it is the site of the nonrepresentable assault on the divine silence. The task of Holocaust representation is to represent that assault as an assault on the divine revelation revealed most profoundly in the silence of all tongues.

The silence of the concentrationary universe, however, is a silence that follows upon draining the word of its silence, of its meaning, of all that is hidden within it. The deep silence invoked by Rabbi Sheshet is what the Nazis would transform into a blank silence by tearing meaning from the word and the name from the human being. And they did it with a sound and a fury signifying nothingness, with the roar of barking and bellowing, of flames and furnaces. They did it with the *raash* that is not only "noise," "outrage," and "tumult," but is also an "earthquake," one in which the ground of meaning crumbles with the crumbling of the human being. It is not for nothing that Holocaust survivor Serge Dancy saw *Night and Fog* not as "historical iconography" but as "seismography."[171] The Hebrew word *raash* announces the truth that when all we hear is an indifferent rumbling, the earth shifts beneath our feet, and we plunge into the despair of wordlessness. "Suppose," writes Lyotard, "that an earthquake destroys not only lives, buildings, and objects but also the instruments used to measure earthquakes directly and indirectly. The impossibility of quantitatively measuring it does not prohibit, but rather inspires in the minds of the survivors the idea of a very great seismic force."[172] Hence, Alexander Donat's remark in his memoir *The Holocaust Kingdom*: "We could feel the ground slipping out from under our feet."[173] The earth that heaves is not an earth that we can walk. In the anti-world, however, at the site of silence, even earthquakes do not make a sound.

Is there any image more unnerving than the scene from Charlotte Delbo's memoir, where she writes, "Fifteen thousand women stamp their feet and it makes no noise. The silence is solidified into cold. . . . We are in a setting in which time is abolished. We do not know if we exist"?[174] There is another silence with which she collides, the silent earthquake within the soul that swallowed up with the site of silence: "The women pass near us. They cry out. They cry out and we hear nothing. This cold and dry air would be conductive if we were in an ordinary earthly environment. They cry out to us but no sound reaches us. Their mouths cry out, their outstretched arms cry out, and every bit of them cries out. . . . So many torches that flame in cries of terror, so many cries that have assumed the bodies of women. Each woman is a materialized cry, a scream that is not heard."[175] To understand the task of Holocaust representation is to understand the shriek of silence that reverberates throughout these passages and into many passages of Holocaust literature, such as the one with which Ka-tzetnik ends his novel *Atrocity*. As the child, the *pipel*, collapsed and died, "the earth gathered him like a mother cradling her little one to sleep. Hush. . . ."[176] The original text is punctuated by the ellipses. "Ellipses, it seems," Christopher Bigsby notes, "are a mark of Holocaust literature."[177] Why? Because, as Dorota Glowacka astutely observes, "ellipses and parataxis in Holocaust testimonials are the simplest rhetorical figures of silence."[178] This "hush," moreover—the novel's last word, which in Hebrew is not a word but the *shshshsh* of the repeated letter *shin*[179]—is more terrifying than comforting. Written with the ellipses, it is the sound of the shriek of silence.

Josef Bor's *Terezín Requiem*, a novel about the camp at Theresienstadt, is a good example of this shriek of silence. In his novel, silence itself may be counted among the characters, a persona at play in the tale:

> The silence had penetrated here, Schächter realized, from outside, from above, from everywhere, and now it spread throughout

> the room, strident and imperative; it overwhelmed everything, froze the walls into dumbness, maimed the people; not even a quiver of air moved here now. The murmur is silenced, the hum of everyday life, which at other times flows everywhere, in the streets, in the house, even in yourself, though you are solitary. The walls receive it and return an echo, the air is tremulous and warm with it, there is so much of it everywhere, and yet you never notice it. As you never feel the air you breathe. And suddenly the hum has ceased. At first you don't even realize that something has happened. There is only a chill somewhere in the marrow of your bones, as though the coldness of the dark night had touched you. As though the breath of death itself had wafted over you. . . . Then suddenly you are aware of the silence.[180]

The place is not silent; rather, silence is the place, or the non-place, of the anti-world and all that transpires within it: the Site of Silence. The silence is not around you—it is inside you, in your body and in your bones, in your *etzem* in Hebrew, which is your "essence." Like darkness and death, silence is a veil that hides the light, the life, and the Word of the Ineffable. It is the nonrepresentable that cries out for anything but "representation," for something otherwise than representation. It is as though there were something complicit about the very project of representation. In order to make manifest the holiness of the Holy One, those who undertake a "representation" of the Holocaust must transform silence into word—not by "filling" the silence with words, words, words, but by making the silence itself speak. But how? That is the question for Holocaust representation. To be sure, it is only through the word that silence *can* speak. But what sort of silence are we dealing with? For many, it is the silence of God. If, however, representing God is problematic, how much more so the problem of representing the silence of God? If it were only the silence of an indifferent cosmos, "the eternal silence of these infinite spaces" that filled Pascal (1623–1662) "with dread,"[181] then John Cage would do. But no, he will not do.

To the extent that Holocaust representation deals with silence, it deals with a most fearsome aspect of God. As Paltiel Kossover says in *The Testament*, "I didn't know it was possible to die of silence. . . . And I understand why God created heaven and earth, why He fashioned man in His image by conferring on him the right and the ability of speak his joy, to express his anguish. God too, God Himself was afraid of silence."[182] Perhaps He was most afraid of His own silence; after all, His silence is the world's silence as when *di velt hot geshvign,* "the world remained silent," the original Yiddish title of Wiesel's memoir *Night.* The rabbis raised this question long before any of today's erudite scholars thought to ask. In a Midrash on Exodus 15:11, where it is written, "*Mi k'mokhah b'elim*?, Who is Like You among the mighty?" we have "*Mi k'mokhah b'ilemim*?, Who is like You among the mute?" That is, how long will you stand by silently while Your children suffer? (*Mekilta Shirata* 8). How would a literary text or a photographic image representing the Holocaust represent *this* silence, the silence of a God gone mute? This appears to be the impossible task posed for Holocaust representation: we may refuse God or affirm God, but we cannot ignore God, even though we cannot represent God. Indeed, perhaps we can undertake a recovery of the Name after this assault on the Name only by refusing *and* affirming. Is that how we are to name Auschwitz? And is the recovery of the Name the whole purpose of Holocaust representation? If so, then the problem of Holocaust representation is the problem of returning to a higher relation, a problem of a *teshuvah* or "return" that is essential to a *tikkun* or "mending" of the world, which is a tikkun of the Name and of the Holy One Himself.[183] That is where the nonrepresentable comes into play. Here we come to yet another aspect of the problem of Holocaust representation.

Naming the Name, the Nameless, and the Assault on the Name

Jacob said, "Please tell me your name."

—Genesis 32:39

"Ma'am," Sara Nomberg-Przytyk calls out to a fellow prisoner who gave her a blanket that saved her life, "please give me your name . . . your name . . . your name!"[184] She asks repeatedly but receives no reply. Why was she so desperate to know the name of the woman who provided her with a blanket in the dead of a January night on an open-air railroad transport out of Auschwitz? As Jacob received a blessing and a name, Sara received a blessing and a blanket that saved her life on a transport of prisoners evacuating Auschwitz. Here another voice comes to mind, another prescient voice from another time and place, the voice of Spanish novelist and philosopher Miguel de Unamuno (1864–1936), who wrote: " 'Tell me thy name!' is essentially the same as 'Save my Soul!' We ask Him His name so that He may save our soul, so that He may save the human soul, so that He may save a human finality for the Universe. And if we are told that God is called He, or that He is the *ens realissimum* or Supreme Being, or given any other metaphysical name, we are not satisfied, for we know that any metaphysical name is an X, and we go on asking for His name."[185] The metaphysical X is the nonrepresentable. If His Name lies anywhere, it reverberates in the persistent asking after His Name, in the asking after the name of the one who has saved a life: *the Name is itself the asking of the Name*. Thus, Sara asks for the name of the one who had saved her soul, not with the blanket but with the act of loving kindness, so that she might have some trace of some contact with the One who commands the loving kindness, the One whom the Holocaust obviated.

Pursuing a metaphor to represent Holocaust representation, I have drawn on suggestions that to gaze upon the Holocaust is to gaze upon the face of the Medusa. Invoking another metaphor of this metaphorical gaze upon the "disaster," Maurice Blanchot turns to the figure of Narcissus, saying, "The water in which Narcissus sees what he shouldn't is not a mirror, capable of producing a distinct and definite image. What he sees is the invisible in the visible—in the picture the undepicted, the unstable unknown of a representation without presence, which reflects no model: he sees the nameless one whom only the name he does not have could hold at a distance. It is madness he sees, and death. . . . These are the words of Ovid on Narcissus that should be retained: *'He perishes by his eyes'* (by seeing himself as a god—which recalls: Whoever sees God dies)."[186] More to the point, whoever sees himself as a god not only dies—he murders, for there can be no usurpation of the divine with the abrogation of the divine prohibition against murder, as taught in the Midrash. There it is written that we are to read the first utterance at Mount Sinai with the sixth utterance, not from top to bottom but from right to left (in Hebrew): "I am God" (Exodus 20:2) means "Thou shalt not murder" (Exodus 20:13) (*Mekilta Bachodesh* 8; *Pesikta Rabbati* 21:19; see also *Zohar* I, 90a). Gazing, like Narcissus, upon the images that emerge from the event, or reading the lines that surface from the literature of testimony, we behold not only the face of Abel but also the face of Cain, who killed Cain in a mad attempt to kill God. And we perish, paralyzed by what penetrates the soul after the assault on the soul: it is *my own* image that peers into my eyes from the shield of Athena, from the pool of Narcissus, and from the glass of the glass booth where Eichmann sits. It is the image of I who am created in the image and likeness of the Holy One and who would undertake an assault on the Holy One.

Ka-tzetnik glimpsed just such an image in *Shivitti*, in a vision of the day when we was loaded into a truck to be sent to the gas chamber in Birkenau; he sees it in the sleepy yawn of the SS man sending him to his death:

> Does he hate me? He doesn't even know me. . . . Do I hate him? I don't even know his name. . . . All I know about this German is that on a cold morning he'd certainly prefer snuggling under the covers of his warm bed without having to get up this early because of some load that has to leave for the crematorium. All at once an additional horror seizes me, one I've not yet known: if this is so, then he could have been standing here in my place, a naked skeleton in the truck, while I, I could have been standing there instead of him. . . . Oh Lord, merciful and compassionate Lord, am I the one, the one who's created Auschwitz? It's much worse than that he . . . could have been in my place. It's that I—and this is the paralyzing horror—I could have been there in his place! Oh Lord of Auschwitz heavens, illumine my ignorance of your handiwork, so that I might know who is the being within me now delivered to the crematorium—and why? And who is the being within him delivering me to the crematorium—and why? For you know that at this moment the two of us, dispatcher and dispatched, are equal sons of man, both created by you, in your image.[187]

Later he has another realization: "God created us in His image and gave us the imagination to create Him in turn. God did not make Auschwitz. Neither did a devil. It was man. And in making Auschwitz, man made a new image of God."[188] Are we able to represent our own handiwork? In the image of what shall we represent it? Of ourselves? What, exactly, does Auschwitz *itself* represent? If it is the human being's infinite capacity for evil, then how do we represent that infinity? After all, as Elie Wiesel has said, "infinity cannot be challenged with impunity,"[189] and to represent it is to challenge it, which is to risk madness. For if it is a matter of naming infinity, it is a matter of naming the Infinite One, the One known as the *Ein Sof*, who is "without limits." Thankfully, representation is inherently limited.

"What man did at Auschwitz," Wiesel takes a slightly different view, "could not have been done outside of God; in some way He too was at work—was He questioning man? Was He showing His face? What a face! In a sense, at Auschwitz God was afraid—afraid of Himself."[190] If God was afraid of Himself, shall we not be afraid of . . . Him, Her, It? In the context of Holocaust representation the question of whether or not we believe in God is irrelevant. The question is: How shall we represent that assault on God, even if we do not believe? To be sure, the question rests not on belief but on the ineluctable reality of what human hands have wrought. What, then, shall we say? "I believe, O Lord, help my unbelief"? Facing the God for whom *all* things are possible, from Eden to Auschwitz—facing the God who was afraid of His own face—what shall we say about Holocaust representation? None of the studies I know of raises this question. And yet, it is, in my view, the most fundamental of questions concerning Holocaust representation: How do you represent the assault on the Name as the silent assault on silence?

Thus, naming the assault on the Name returns us to the Site of Silence, to the *Makom,* the "Place," as God Himself is referred to in Hebrew. Many memoir writers recall the savage screams and shouts and curses that greeted them when they rolled into Birkenau. They also recall the silence that pervaded the anti-world, both in the ghettos and in the camps, as we have seen. Levi writes that when he arrived in Auschwitz "everything was as silent as an aquarium."[191] There was movement, but it was the muffled movement of another world, where one had to be careful not to drown in the sea of a silent horror. Yes, the shouting and screaming, brutal and inhuman, were there. But pervading all of it was the silence. The Hebrew word *ilem* applies: it means both "silent" and "mute." In his Warsaw Ghetto account of the Nazi assault on the Name inscribed in the soul of Israel, Rabbi Shapira reads *ilem* as a silence that overcomes a person "so broken and crushed that he has nothing to say; who does not appreciate or understand what is happening to him; who does not possess the faculties with which to assess or assimilate his experiences; who no longer has the mind or the heart with which to incorporate the experience. For him, silence is not a choice; his is the muteness of one incapable of speech."[192] Because this muteness is the muteness of a human being, however, within it lies hidden an outcry. Indeed, the muteness itself "stands erect," as Rabbi Shapira says, like Joseph's "sheaf," which, in a play on *ilem,* is *alumah.*[193] The muteness of *ilem* is more than deafening—it is haunting. Like the Muselmann, it haunts anyone who would say what Auschwitz is.

Here our reflection on the assault on the Holy Name brings us to the assault on the one created in the image and likeness of the Holy One. Simply stated, this evil lies in the radical undermining of both the human-to-divine and the human-to-human relations, which are of a piece. The product of this assault is the Muselmann, who should be dead but is not, who is neither alive nor dead, the one whom Fackenheim deemed the Nazis' "most characteristic, most original product."[194] Says Leon Poliakov (1910–1997), "When they could still walk they moved like automatons; once stopped, they were capable of no further movement. They fell prostrate on the ground; nothing mattered any more to them. Their bodies blocked the passageway. You could step right on them and they would not draw back their arms or legs an inch. No protest, no cry of pain came from their half-open mouth. And yet they were still alive. . . ."[195] Still alive. . . . But what can this "still alive" mean? Trapped in their namelessness, in their mute paralysis, can they still be alive? Rudolf Vrba describes the Muselmänner as entities "whose eyes were empty, whose flesh had fled, whose blood was near to water."[196] Here, the murder of the soul encompasses the murder of the body. The assault on the soul, which is an assault on the Name, is an assault on something very concrete: once the soul has been slaughtered, the blood turns to water. For the soul is in the blood, as it is written (Genesis 9:4), as is the life of the flesh (Leviticus 17:11). With the fleeing of the flesh there is a fleeing of Torah and a draining of life from the blood itself. Empty of the light of life, the eyes are drained of the light of Torah, the light of the face that forbids us to murder, as Levinas has said.[197] How to represent the emptiness of those eyes in which the divine spark has been extinguished?

As it goes with the Holy One, so it goes with the human one: the assault on the Name renders the human being nameless. Thus, in his own effort to convey what Auschwitz is, Levi, too, conjures up the image of the Muselmänner, describing them as "the backbone of the camp, an *anonymous* mass, continually renewed and always identical, of non-men who march and labour in silence, the *divine spark* dead within them, already too empty to really suffer. One hesitates to call them living: one hesitates to call their death death."[198] Recall the words that De-Nur spoke at the Eichmann trial: they did not live, they did not die, *they had no name.* Once again, we discover that silence is the key, the silence that ensues upon the extinguishing of the divine spark, a silence that eludes representation through word or image, not because the Muselmänner cannot speak but because they were once speaking beings, because they were once human beings: only a man or a woman can become a Muselmann. Levi attests to the fact that the assault on the divine spark within the human entails an assault on death itself, but not in in the sense of the Martin Heidegger's (1989–1976) *Sein-zum-Tod*, or "being-towards-death."[199] This is where Giorgio Agamben's (b. 1942) analysis of the Muselmann is not only mistaken but buys into the Heideggerian categories of thought that went into the making of the Muselmann. The reason why the Muselmann's death is not death, he says, is "a reason that calls into question the very possibility of authentic decision [as defined by Heidegger]. . . . Just as in Being-towards-death, the human being authentically appropriates the inauthentic, so in the camp, the prisoners exist *everyday anonymously* [and inauthentically] toward death."[200] An "authentic" stance toward death, as Heidegger and Agamben understand it, has to do with the inner resolve of the isolated ego (which collapses in the Muselmann), rather than a relation to another that would entail dying for the sake of another (which also collapses in the Muselmann).

Elsewhere in his memoir, Levi declares that Auschwitz is made of hunger.[201] If the Muselmann is the backbone of the camp, hunger is its essence; an incarnation of silence, the Muselmann is the incarnation of hunger. Like the silence, the hunger is ubiquitous and definitive. If, as Levinas insists, "to recognize the Other is to recognize a hunger,"[202] the silence of the Lager is the silence of the radical nonrecognition of the other human being, a nonrecognition of his or her name in the midst of an assault on the Name. "To be torn from oneself despite oneself," says Levinas, "has meaning only as a being torn from the complacency in oneself characteristic of enjoyment, snatching the bread from one's mouth. Only a subject that eats can be for-the-other, or can signify."[203] Therefore, to recognize the other human being *as* a human being is to recognize him or her as *hungry* and to offer him or her bread or a blanket. Which returns us to the question: How do we represent the nonrepresentable void of that nonrecognition? If the Muselmann embodies "all the evil of our time in one image," as Levi says,[204] it is because he or she embodies the hunger that in turn exemplifies the destruction of the divine image within the human being, a destruction that is the outcome of a deadly assault on the Name.

And yet, "God is one," as Wiesel says. "He is everywhere. And if He is everywhere, then He is in evil and injustice too, and also in the supreme evil: death. It is man's task to free God of this evil."[205] Evil, it must be noted, lies not in the *violation* of a commandment, but rather in its *elimination* through the elimination of the One who commands. Levinas argues that "evil claims to be the contemporary, the equal, the twin, of the Good. This is an irrefutable lie, a Luciferian lie. It is the very egoism of the ego that posits itself as its own origin, an uncreated sovereign principle, a prince."[206] And, he adds, evil refuses "any synthesis in which the wholly otherness of God would become visible. . . . The excess of evil by which it is a surplus in the world is also our impossibility of accepting it. The experience of evil would then be also our waiting on the good—the love of God."[207] Can God be present in the representation of this assault on God? Perhaps there can be an assault on the Name only where the Name abides, just as the representation of that assault is an expression of a refusal to accept it. To be sure, only in the name of a false god can one undertake an assault on the Name. If God is to be freed of this evil, might the liberation of God be the true task of Holocaust representation, by naming the assault on the Name?

Elaborating on the face of God that we encounter in Auschwitz, Fackenheim has noted that "while Nietzsche and Sartre may have found exhilaration in the idea that God is absent, there is only terror at a God who is still present but has become an enemy"[208]—or who has become afraid of Himself, afraid of His own creation. Fackenheim relates a tale about a group of Jews gathered in a synagogue to pray in a city in Nazi Europe. Suddenly a pious Jew, stealing his way through the city's streets, bursts through the door, and, in a loud whisper says, "Shhhh, Jews! Do not pray so loud! God will hear you! Then He will know that there are still some Jews left alive in Europe!"[209] Is there a similar terror in representing a God turned enemy? Can there be any Holocaust representation that is not steeped in this fear and trembling, in this "Shhhh"? Here, God becomes the absolutely Other—the Name Other to Himself, afraid of Himself—implicating not only His creation in an undoing of the pronouncement that it is "very good," but indicting also the human being created in his image.

Reflecting on this condition, André Neher has said that God "vanishes to the rear," but "there is no purpose in seeking Him in that rear, for God is already out there in front, on the horizon-edge of a Promise which only restores what it has taken, without ever being fulfilled."[210] Any literary text or visual image that would represent the Holocaust must represent this vanishing of what is revealed not in its manifestation but in the human longing for what was lost, the longing for the benevolence of the God who was lost. In that longing abides God's memory of and longing for Himself, an infinite longing for His own deliverance from the valley of the shadow of mass murder. "Let Him remember," Wiesel writes, "for He alone can make us remember."[211] And yet in nearly every discussion of Holocaust representation He is the first one forgotten, despite the fact that in nearly every effort to represent the Holocaust He is there, either affirmed or denied, either silently or explicitly. If, as Levinas says, God reveals Himself through the disturbance of the witness,[212] He reveals Himself perhaps most profoundly in the rebellion of the witness. That too becomes an issue for Holocaust representation. "God's final victory," Gregor's father tells him in Wiesel's *The Gates of the Forest*, "lies in man's inability to reject Him. You think . . . you're crying out your hatred and rebellion, but all you're doing is telling Him how much you need His support."[213] In the project of Holocaust representation we discover how much *He* needs *our* support, how much He needs our outcry and outrage over His absence. There can be no representation of the assault on the Name that is not steeped in that outcry and outrage.

"Did God take leave of his senses?" asks Isabella Leitner.[214] Pushing the question farther, Eugene Heimler asks more boldly of God Himself: "Almighty God, why have you done this to us? . . . You are wicked, O Lord, as wicked as man."[215] Jewish tradition holds that God is the shadow of man: when men do nothing, God folds His arms, so that God is both as kind and as wicked as man. Therefore, as Heimler suggests, there is a parallel between the movements of God and the actions of human beings. The slumber of the one is the sleeping sickness of the other. Hence, Ana Vinocur cries out to awaken both humanity and the Guardian who neither sleeps nor slumbers (Psalms 121:4). Both must be stirred if the Name that exceeds representation is to be recovered. "It may be too late by the time you wake up," she shouts to the world. "And God . . . ? I sometimes thought that the crying of the children was too weak to reach Him. But He had to hear them, because there was more and more crying. O God! Wake up and see what they have done to the people who have always kept faith with you!"[216] The Guardian of Israel is the soul of Israel, so that if the Sleepless One should sleep, then Israel would no longer be Israel—a point certainly not lost on the Nazi killers. How is God to be awakened? How shall we get the Nameless One to answer to His Name? Perhaps by addressing Him through the remembrance and representation of the nonrepresentable that summons humanity. Is that not the aim of Holocaust representation—to stir an indifferent humanity to non-indifference? For the silence of the one is the silence of the other. It is the silence that rumbles as the background noise, the white noise, of a post-Holocaust world awash in noise, noise, and more noise, the silence that Holocaust representation must oppose, even if it is with another silence.

The Nonrepresentable Assault on the Nonrepresentable Good

The Good cannot become present or enter into a representation.

—Emmanuel Levinas, *Otherwise Than Being*

The Muselmann is created in the image and likeness of the void that remains when the Good is obliterated. The void, however, is not empty—it is full to overflowing, full of a silence that surpasses terror, a silence that swallows the word before it can escape the lips, a silence that washes over humanity like a tsunami. There, too, lies the problem of representation. Neither something nor nothing, this void is akin to what Levinas describes as the indifferent, neutral, horrific "there is." "We do not grasp it through a thought," says Levinas. "It is immediately there. There is no discourse. Nothing responds to us, but this silence."[217] The "there is," he explains, appears as an "anonymous and senseless rumbling of being,"[218] as the *raash,* manifest not as thought but as an absolute indifference, a sovereign It. The Muselmann's wasted body embodies the "there is." Yet he is not the one who encounters the murmur of silence or the rumbling of being that characterize the "there is." Indeed, he *encounters* nothing; only one in whom the word still abides can encounter something outside himself. The "there is" is what *we* encounter and collide with in the project of Holocaust representation. Therefore, the emptiness to be overcome in the effort to represent the Holocaust is as much ours as it is the Lager's, as the Lager casts its shadow far beyond the gates embossed with the words *Arbeit Macht Frei.*

Gazing upon the gates, it is not just that we come to the uncrossable, where we cannot enter; more than that—more terrifying—there is something from the other side of the gates that reaches into us, from within the depths of the denizen of the gates, from the Muselmann. From the Muselmann it creeps into the survivor; from the survivor it creeps into us. This is the ontological heritage and the ontological horror that is Auschwitz. It is the horror confronted by representations of the Holocaust, the horror that creeps into Holocaust representation itself—not only the horror of what is represented, but also the horror that surrounds the very project of representation.

The antidote to the "there is" does not lie in more clever modes of representation: aesthetics is of no help here. Aesthetics belongs to a world in which the Good abides, waiting to be given artistic form. In the aftermath of Auschwitz only a "responsibility for the other, being-for-the-other," Levinas writes, can "stop the anonymous and senseless rumbling of being,"[219] in such a way that the rumbling is eclipsed by the Commanding Voice of Someone. It is an infinite responsibility that arises in the wake of the assault on the Infinite, that stems from more than all there is, from a revelation and a summons, from a transcendent imperative that inserts itself into being from beyond being, from what Levinas calls the "otherwise than being." Where words and images come to bear after the demolition of the word, the task of representation is not merely to describe what took place or to convey "what it was like," but also to attest to why it matters, in a response to what was announced to Primo Levi: *Hier ist kein Warum*: here there is no Why.[220] Where there is no why, there is no Who, no Commanding Voice through whom the Good is revealed.[221]

Ann Richardson raises a question in this connection: "If no form of representation is adequate to convey the extreme pain and suffering experienced by the Holocaust survivor, is it morally and/or ethically correct to attempt representation at all? As a corollary to this question, who precisely should make that decision? . . . Is it then a possibility that the very question of the representation of the Holocaust could in some cases cause offence?"[222] Her question concerning the possibility of ethical offense is legitimate. Says Levinas, "The Good cannot become present or enter into a representation. The present is a beginning in my freedom, whereas the Good is not presented to freedom; it has chosen me before I have chosen it. No one is good voluntarily."[223] And no one confronts the Holocaust voluntarily; we engage it because, on some level, we are aware of an imperative, of an absolute ethical demand. As Levinas has said, "The attributes of God are given not in the indicative, but in the imperative. The knowledge of God comes to us like a commandment, like a *Mitzvah*. To know God is to know what must be done."[224] To know God is to know the Good, and to know the Good is to be commanded, absolutely: it is a knowledge that lays claim to the knower. Not the other way around. Such knowledge cannot be deduced—it comes only with being commanded, only by being summoned to answer, "*Hineni*—Here I am for you," to and for another. Without this answering, Holocaust representation is worse than vanity—it is exploitation, appropriation, and accession. The task of Holocaust representation is taken up by those who know what must be done. It cannot be otherwise, if it is to be the representation of the nonrepresentable assault on the Good, on what Levinas calls "the exceptional."

Survivor Germaine Tillion sat through the testimony presented at the Ravensbrück war crimes trials. "All the while," she relates, "the representation—re-presentation—of their crimes unfolded, and I became all too aware of the widening gap between what really happened and that imprecise representation known as 'history.' "[225] If it were just a matter of precision, however, the problem of Holocaust representation would be no different that the problem of representing any historical event. To be sure, in the case of the Holocaust, we are dealing not with precise representation but with the nonrepresentable. Whereas representation necessarily operates within the ontological categories of historical precision, "the exceptional, extra-ordinary, transcendent character of goodness," writes Levinas, "is due to just this break with being and history. To reduce the good to being, to its calculations and its history, is to nullify goodness. The ever possible sliding between subjectivity and being, of which subjectivity would be but a mode, the equivalence of the two languages, stops here. Goodness gives to subjectivity its irreducible signification."[226] If this is the case, then representations of the Nazi assault on the Good may not only fail—they may be complicit in the nullification of goodness. In the case at hand, the irreducible signification of subjectivity, moreover, lies in the absolute implication of subjectivity in the assault on the Good.

Thus, nowhere is ethics first philosophy more than in the project of Holocaust representation. Without this ethical *otherwise than being*—without this ethics as first philosophy, this metaphysics—Holocaust representation is amoral, nonethical, or absolutely unethical. One who would represent the Holocaust as an assault on the Good, whether through literary art or photographic image, therefore, steps before the Countenance and comes under a judgment in the aftermath of a radical assault on the face. And yet the impossible task posed for Holocaust representation is to represent the face that comes under a radical assault without losing the face to the framework of representation itself. "The face with which the other turns to me is not reabsorbed in a representation of the face," Levinas explains. "To hear his destitution which cries out for justice is not to represent an image to oneself, but is to posit oneself as responsible."[227] To posit the nonrepresentable that shadows representation is to posit this responsibility; without the transcendent nonrepresentable, there is no responsibility. In the Holocaust, the Jew is the one who is destitute. The Holocaust is the systematic creation of widows, orphans, and strangers who lose their status and meaning as widows, orphans, and strangers. In an effort to avoid the face, we often turn to group images of the dead, as Barbie Zelizer points out: "Group images tended to be less graphic than those of individuals, partly because the rarely visible eyes and faces worked against the possibility of identifying the victims being depicted."[228] The group belongs to the said, the individual to the saying.

Listen to Levinas:

> To say is to approach a neighbor, "dealing him signifyingness." This is not exhausted in "ascriptions of meaning," which are inscribed, as tales, in the said. Saying taken strictly is a "signifyingness dealt the other," prior to all objectification; it does not consist in giving signs. The "giving out of signs" would amount to a prior representation of these signs, as though speaking consisted in translating thoughts into words and consequently in having been first *for-oneself* and *at home with oneself,* like a substantial consistency. The relationship with the other would then extend forth as an inten-tionality, out of a subject posited in itself and for itself, disposed to play, sheltered from all ills and measuring by thought the being disclosed as the field of this play. Saying is communication, to be sure, but as a condition for all communication, as exposure.[229]

Representation as saying is representation as communication, as the communication of a testimony, bearing a witness that is unbearable in the cry of "*Hineni!*—Here I am!"

Recall, by contrast, Levinas's remarks about the "game society," a pseudo-society that avoids "dealing signifyingness" at all costs, for to "deal signifyingness" is to deal responsibility, indeed, a radical responsibility in the face of a radical evil's assault on the Good. There lies the exposure and the implication attendant to the project of representation. There is no ascription of meaning to the horror of the assault on the Good, because the assault on the Good is an assault on meaning: the Good is what announces meaning, as a summons and ascription, as assignation and excession. The assault on the Good undermines all being *at home with oneself.* In fact, living in a camp, in a ghetto, or in hiding, *every Jew in Nazi Europe was rendered homeless* before he or she was rendered ash. Thus, we realize that the Good abides only where dwelling abides. Finally, understood as saying—or as the representation of a saying that surpasses representation—Holocaust representation must be understood as exposure, not only to what is nonrepresentable but also to what is all too representable.

Meaning derives not from the said of representation, but rather representation takes on meaning in the light of a preoriginary saying, which is the preoriginary condition of having *already* been chosen by the Good. This is the meaning of chosenness, a chosenness by the Good prior to all choosing, to which the Jews bear witness and which the Nazis would obliterate. "The attachment to the Good precedes the choosing of this Good," says Levinas. "The Good is good precisely because it chooses you and grips you before you have had the time to raise your eyes to it."[230] That is what makes the representation of the Holocaust *matter*: we are already responsible for the Good because we are already chosen by the Good. Levinas elaborates: "Already the Infinite speaks through the witness I bear of it, in my sincerity, in my saying without said, preoriginary saying which is said in the mouth of the very one that receives the witness. . . . It thus retains in its statement the trace of the excession of transcendence, of the beyond."[231] The trace of the excession of transcendence lies in the absolute ethical responsibility that singles us out as witnesses. If the Holocaust can be represented as an assault on the Good, it is represented in the nonrepresentable saying that underlies the representations of the said. Which is to say: the problem of Holocaust representation lies as much with the project of representation itself as it does with the Holocaust.

A fundamental expression of the Nazis' assault on the Good lies in their effort to exterminate Judaism in their extermination of the Jews, as the Nazi ideologue Alfred Rosenberg (1893–1946) insisted: "Our race has been poisoned by Judaism," and not simply by Jewish blood, because the -ism is in the blood.[232] Rosenberg's statement is reaffirmed in Martin Bormann's (1900–1945) assertion that "everything is linked within National Socialism and everything aims at the fight against Judaism,"[233] which is the fight against the nonrepresentable Good. Thus, "the negation of Judaism," Uriel Tal has observed, "had to be transformed into the annihilation of the Jews, this time not spiritually, but rather physically, not symbolically but in substance."[234] And so we realize that, contrary to popular misconception, the Nazi view of the superiority of the Aryan people is not reducible to mere racism. As the Nazi economist Peter Heinz Seraphim (1902–1979) declared, National Socialist anti-Semitism is not reducible to racism or ethnic differences; it has nothing to do with xenophobia, economic envy, or scapegoating.[235] More than an anthropological category, "race" in this instance is a *metaphysical* category.

In Nazi ideology, the notion of race is rooted not just in color or physiognomy or even in the genes, but *in a concept of human essence*: it is an ideological category in which body and soul, biology and being, are fused into one. The category has a name: it is *Rassenseele*. Explaining the Nazi concept of *Rassenseele* or "race-soul," Rosenberg writes, "Soul means race viewed from within. And, vice-versa, race is the externalization of soul."[236]

If race may be viewed from within, then it is not reducible to any outward manifestation such as skin tones or hair texture; rather it is *conceptual* and therefore an abstraction. "This heroic attitude [of National Socialism]," said Rosenberg, "departs from the *single* but *completely* decisive avowal, *namely from the avowal that blood and character, race and soul are merely different designations for the same entity*."[237] Hence, the threat of Judaism to humanity "would not be altered," Rosenberg explains, "if the Jew denied the Talmud, because the national character, which remains the same, would continue to represent an equally inflexible, dogmatic viewpoint in other areas."[238] In a word, the Jew is an *essential* threat to the Aryan *essence*. Therefore, not just the body of Israel, but the very soul of Israel, must be obliterated: the ideology demands it. The degradation, humiliation, and torturous brutalization—all of it was *ideologically demanded*. How shall that ideological demand for the obliteration of the soul, which is an obliteration of the Good, be represented?

The Nazis were not anti-Semites because they were racists. No, they were racists because they were anti-Semites: the anti-Semitic principle has to be determined in order to arrive at a racist position. The assault on the Good that would be subject to representation is an assault on the teaching and testimony of Judaism that the Jews signify by their very presence in the world. Steven Katz elaborates: "The conflict of Aryan and Jew is an inner-historical actualization of normative, metahistorical antitheses. As such, the struggle between Aryan and Jew is not only necessary and inevitable but also a clash of world-historical (*because more than historical*) significance. Though actualized through blood in time, the depth of the historical encounter is rooted in eternity. In conformity with the recognition of this ontological truth, killing Jews, or, more precisely, eliminating 'the Jews' becomes a sacred obligation."[239] The "metahistorical" or "more than historical" aspect of this history is what makes its representation problematic: the metahistorical is the Good that exceeds representation. More learned and more meticulous than their predecessors, the Nazis understood that the presence of the Jews in the world *is* the presence of the Holy One in the world. The Nazis "aimed to make the world *rein* of *Juden*, but also of *Judentum*," says Fackenheim,[240] adding that the term *Judentum* is not exactly the equivalent of the English word *Judaism*; rather, it means "what Jews do collectively"[241]—in other words, what Jews do as *Knesset Yisrael*, as the "Community of Israel," which the Zohar equates with the Shekhinah (*Zohar* II, 93a). And Fackenheim was quite familiar with this teaching from the Zohar.[242] Again, the Shekhinah that is the Divine Presence is not the concept of the Good but the persona of the Good, who goes into exile with her children, driven into hiding and into the ghettos, and who ascends into the heavens in columns of smoke and pillars of fire with the burning of the bodies of her children.

The assault on the nonrepresentable Good always entails an assault on the human soul, who is beyond essence and therefore otherwise than representation. Which means: the assault on the Good is an assault not only on the flesh and blood of mothers, fathers, and children but on the very meaning of mothers, fathers, and children. In Judaism that meaning is grounded in the view that the human being is an insertion of something otherwise than all there is into the midst of all there is. Therefore, a human being is not reducible to the accidents of race, gender, culture, or ethnicity, all of which belong to the ontological categories of representation. Created in the image and likeness of the Holy One, the human soul harbors the presence of what sanctifies all of being from beyond being. In a word, the human being is a breach of being, defined by the commandment from beyond being, summoned to an uncompromising love for the *other* human being. According to Judaism, *every* human being is my fellow human being, indeed, is part of my family, descended as we are from a single human being. Rabbi Shimon ben Azzai maintained that the origin of all humanity from one human being is the most fundamental of all Jewish teachings (*Talmud Yerushalmi, Nedarim* 9:4). Why did God begin humanity with just one human being, and not two? The sages say it was so that no one may declare to another, "My side of the family is better than your side of the family" (*Tosefta Sanhedrin* 8:4). There is only one side of the family, which means that all of humanity is interrelated, physically through Adam, metaphysically through the Creator. This interrelation is knotted in an infinite responsibility. There is no teaching more inimical to National Socialism's claim—namely that there is no connection between the Aryan and the non-Aryan—than this teaching that defines Judaism.

The problem of Holocaust representation is rooted in this absolute, infinite responsibility to and for the other: Holocaust representation, if there can be such a thing, is the representation of that infinite responsibility. "The responsibility for another," writes Levinas, "is precisely a saying prior to anything said. The surprising saying, which is a responsibility for another is against 'the winds and tides' of being, is an interruption of essence."[243] It is therefore an interruption of representation: the project of representing the assault on the Good is necessarily self-undermining. The preoriginary saying is the saying and the summons of the immemorial that summons and sanctifies all that can be remembered. That is why the transmission of *this* history through representation transforms the one who receives the memory and the testimony of the witness into a witness and a messenger, and anyone who maintains an engagement with the Holocaust has undergone that transformation and the attendant trauma. Only if understood and represented as an assault on the Good can the Holocaust be understood as a responsibility that draws the living into a relationship with the dead, and only if we are in such a relationship with the dead can the transmission of their memory be ethically charged by the immemorial, and not just a matter of academic curiosity.

If, as both Elie Wiesel and Primo Levi have said, the Holocaust was a war against memory,[244] it was a war against the ethical relationship commanded by the Good, a war against the immemorial. Yet, as an instance of the said, Holocaust representation undermines the relationship to the point of a certain denial, not of the event but of the nonrepresentable responsibility for the Good that accompanies the assault on the Good, which, in a sense, amounts to Holocaust denial. Holocaust representation represents, in other words, a betrayal of what it would represent. Says Levinas, "The beyond being, showing itself in the said, always shows itself there enigmatically, is already betrayed."[245] The project of representation constitutes just such a betrayal of the immemorial, of the otherwise than representation. And analyses such as this one run the risk of being complicit in that betrayal.

The assault on the Good requires a usurpation of the Angel of Death himself, as suggested earlier. If the "death camps" are so designated, it is because in those camps there was an enactment of a radical assault on death itself, just as in the labor camps, transit camps, and internment camps there was an assault on the meaning of labor, transit, and internment. Which tells us that in a very important sense, God is not dead—He is death, and if He is to be obliterated, so must death itself be obliterated. Stated otherwise: if God is "announced by a deep silence" (*Berakhot* 58a)," as the Talmud says and if "death is silence," as says André Neher,[246] then the Holocaust that we seek to represent is an obliteration of death and the silence of death, the silence of God Himself. Recall, too, Neher's assertion that "Auschwitz is, above all, silence."[247] If Auschwitz signifies the death of the Angel of Death, Neher is quite right when he says, "Auschwitz is, above all, silence." It is the "silence" that in Hebrew is *shtikah,* a cognate of the word *shituk,* which means "paralysis." As one character from A. Anatoli's (1929–1979) novel *Babi Yar* expresses it, "The utter silence made my head swim. It was like being tied up in a black sack or buried alive deep under the ground, where you couldn't budge and it was no use wriggling about because there was no way out."[248] This is the silence of the muted Angel, of the muted man transformed into a Muselmann. But what sort of silence follows in the wake of this assault on the death that is silence, robbing the Jews even of their deaths? And how is it to be represented? In short, how does one "represent" or "make present again" the obliteration of death as an assault on the Good?

The Assault on Time, the Death of Death, and Holocaust Representation

> The new enemy, no mere Haman, not only succeeded where Haman failed, for he murdered the Jewish people. He murdered also Ezekiel's image of Jewish death.
>
> —Emil L. Fackenheim, *The Jewish Bible after the Holocaust*

The eleventh-century sage Bachya ibn Paquda teaches, "Life and Death are brethren, dwelling together, clinging closely to one another, inseparable, holding fast to the two ends of a tottering bridge over which all the world's creatures pass."[249] Situating life and death together as brethren, the family sanctifies life upon every burial and every memory of the dead; our family brings us into the world and lays us into the earth. Thus, the Kaddish, the Prayer for the Dead, sanctifies the Name and affirms the dearness of life. Recall here a statement made by Dr. Josef Goebbels (1897–1945) on 19 June 1942 in the National Socialist weekly *Das Reich*, as reported by Hannah Arendt (1906–1975): "Not one Kaddish will be said."[250] In their ontological overturning of Jewish being the Nazis decreed and carried out the murder of Jewish death and with it the measure of Jewish time.

In *One Generation After*, Elie Wiesel relates his return to Sighet to dig up the watch that he had buried just before his deportation. "I was laboring to exhume not an object," he writes, "but time itself, the soul and memory of that time,"[251] which had come under a radical assault on time. Where ethics comes to bear, time comes to bear: time—the life time of the human being—is made of the ethical. As an assault on the Good affirmed by the millennial Jewish testimony, the Holocaust is an assault on time, both on the time of human relation and on the time of sacred history. If, as Wiesel maintains, "the opposite of the past is not the future but the absence of future," and "the opposite of the future is not the past but the absence of past,"[252] it is the ethical aspect of human relation that makes it so. Further, if Holocaust representation is to assume an ethical aspect, then it must become what Levinas calls "a way of being against death,"[253] that is, against the death of the *other* human being; this being against death is a being for the future, since "the other is the future," as Levinas has said.[254] Being against the death of the other, being for the future, means living and dying for the sake of the other human being. During the Holocaust, this *dying for the sake of* came under a radical assault, so that the task of representation lies not in the representation of a horrific death but in the representation of the death of death pursuant to an assault on time. Far from robbing life of its meaning, death defines the parameters of the yet-to-be, from which life derives its direction and therefore its meaning. If the Muselmann is emblematic of the Holocaust, he also embodies the assault on time that defines the Holocaust. He is the one who has no way of being against death and who, therefore, cannot die for the sake of another. He is the one exiled from time in the Nazi assault on time and death.

"All the musselmans who finished in the gas chambers," writes Primo Levi, "have the same story, or more exactly, have no story,"[255] that is, they have no *storia,* to use the word from Levi's Italian text,[264] a word that also means "history." In this word that means both "story" and "history," suggesting both "tale" and "tradition," we come to a deeper insight into the divine spark dead within the Muselmann and what it is made of. It is made of the human being's tale and tradition; it is made of his or her story. And his or her story is made of time. Where the divine spark is gone, the story and the time of life are gone. The more intimately we enter into a relation with others, the more familiar we become with their stories. Indeed, where one human being lives in relation to the other, each is part of the other's story, just as God and humanity are part of each other's story. When God breathes the divine spark, the soul or *neshamah,* into the human being, He breathes His story, which is His Torah. In a word, He breathes time into the human being. Thus, the human being inherits the tale and tradition that make every human being's story meaningful. Each time the tale is related, the spark is transmitted. With each transmission of the tale, there is an increase of light in the world. And with the extinguishing of each story, there is a diminishing of the light.

As the vehicle of ethical demand, says Levinas, the duration of human time assumes "the form of a worrying about the other, a spending without counting, a generosity, goodness, love."[257] Here, the ethical, to borrow a phrase from Franz Rosenzweig, lies in "a future which, without ceasing to be a future, is nonetheless present,"[258] in the embrace we have *yet* to offer, in the act of kindness we have *yet* to perform. That eternal *yet to be,* which is the substance of *the present,* lies at the core of who I am, since I *am* the one who has *yet* to perform *this* act of goodness; I am the one eternally implicated with "one responsibility *more* than all the others," as Levinas declares.[259] Thus, we have a basic link between identity and eternity. That link is undermined with the assault on time: in the Lager, where the blood of the Muselmann turns to water, there is no *yet to be.* In his commentary on Isaiah 63:3 Abraham ibn Ezra (1089–1167) writes, "The blood is called *netsach,* literally 'time,' because through the blood man lives his time."[260] Time is the soul that is in the blood, and the soul, the divine spark, is precisely what came under the Nazis' assault. Indeed, the assault on time is an assault on the divine, since, as Abraham Joshua Heschel (1907–1972) states it, "time is the presence of God in the world of space."[261] Inasmuch as Holocaust representation is a representation of time as history, it is the representation of a certain sacred history: the sacredness of sacred history lies in the *time* of sacred history. "The existence of God," Levinas makes this point, "is sacred history itself, the sacredness of man's relation to man through which God may pass."[262] God and history, time and humanity, being against the death of the other human being—all of it comes under assault in the Holocaust. All of it belongs to the nonrepresentable that haunts attempted representations of the Holocaust, especially when they would avoid any notion of sacred history.

As a history of time itself, sacred history is the history of death—of the death that the Nazis set out to obliterate. Lyotard offers an important insight here:

> The authority of the SS comes out of a we from which the deportee [the Jew] is excepted once and for all. . . . The deportee, according to this accounting, cannot be the addressee of an order to die, because one would have to be capable of giving one's life in order to carry out the order. But one cannot give a life that one doesn't have the right to have. Sacrifice is not available to the deportee, nor for that reason accession to an immortal, collective name. . . . The individual name must be killed (whence the use of serial numbers), and the collective name (Jew) must also be killed in such a way that no we bearing this name might

> remain. . . . This death must therefore be killed, and that is what is worse than death. For if death can be exterminated, it is because there is nothing to kill. Not even the name Jew.[263]

The "we" in this passage is the "we" of history. Excluding the Jew from history, the Nazi does not want the Jew dead. The Nazi does not want the Jew alive. The Nazi wants to erase every predicate from the Jew, every dry bone. Here we glimpse the horror of the Nazi war against memory: it is a war against the memory of one's own name and therefore a war against death.

"Even death is too good for a Jew?" asks Isabella Leitner.[264] To this question the Nazi answers, "Yes." To be a subject who lives and dies—to be a human being with a name—is to take up the project of making sense of a world. Bereft of both world and sense, the human being is not alive—he or she is simply there, a solitary pocket of emptiness in the midst of a crowded void. The world has no inherent meaning or value—it too is simply there, a deafening silence in the midst of an incessant noise. But the phenomenon of the anti-world rests upon a world that harbors an inherent meaning and value. In the anti-world, which is void of any valuation of life or death and therefore of any distinction between life and death, there is no human *being*. Bodies are not consigned for burial; like trash, they are collected for disposal. Mourners neither pray nor sit *shivah* (the week-long ritual of mourning for the dead)—there are no mourners. In the concentrationary universe, death is not a rite of passage; neither rite nor passage, it simply is. Which amounts to saying: it is simply *nothing*. Hence, death dies. The heart continues to beat when it should have come to a stop. The soul continues to live, and yet it *has* no life, for it has been stripped of the sign, of the category, that would seal the tomb of the past and open up the way to the future: it has been stripped of the cemetery. That is what makes the concentrationary universe an anti-world: it is empty of all cemeteries.

Miklós Nyiszli describes Planet Auschwitz as a "cemetery of millions, a cemetery without a single grave."[265] As Wiesel has said, "My generation has been robbed of everything, even of our cemeteries."[266] Millions were murdered. But no one was buried. Hence, their deaths were murdered with them. In the world of humanity we bury the dead, mark their graves, and leave the cemetery; burying the dead and marking their graves enables us to leave the cemetery. But there is no leaving the cemetery without a grave. The Nazis are literally grave robbers: they rob the Jews of their graves. Thus, the one who departs from the anti-world—from the "world" without a grave, the "world" inhabited by denizens whose death was not death—becomes a grave himself. Even in the ghettos the Nazis regarded the Jewish dead not only as objects of contempt but as sources of amusement. Michael Zylberberg reports from the Warsaw Ghetto that the Germans "gleefully photographed the dead . . . and even went as far as taking snapshots of the corpses as they were laid out in the mortuary. . . . This, rather than the cinema, was a place of amusement for them."[267] When a mortuary becomes a place of amusement, it is no longer a mortuary, and the dead are no longer the dead. "The dead have lost their traditional importance and sanctity," writes Chaim Kaplan on 9 October 1941. "The sanctity of the cemetery is also being profaned."[268] A month later, he notes, "Henceforward people accompanying their dead for burial will be denied permission to enter the cemetery grounds."[269] No stones are to be laid on the gravestones, no measures to be taken against the loss of memory and the loss of a name.

"They have forbidden burials at the Praga cemetery," writes Jewish Council head Adam Czerniaków (1880–1942),[270] so that soon the bodies of the dead became nothing more than fixtures on the ghetto streets. "The police district chiefs," Emmanuel Ringelblum (1900–1944) pens the entry in his diary for 26 August 1941, "simply throw the bodies from one streetcar to the next."[271] And so we have the image of the murdered riding around the ghetto alongside the yet to be murdered: the tram is turned into a hearse bound for every stop except the cemetery. Before long, the cemetery itself would become the object of annihilation, as Vladka Meed (1921–2012) attests in her memoir. "Wherever I turned," she recalls, "there was nothing but overturned tombstones, desecrated graves and scattered skulls. . . . Yes, the Jews were persecuted even in their graves."[272] And on 12 May 1942, Ringelblum writes, "The Praga cemetery, which is more than 150 years old, is being leveled. The devils won't even let the dead rest."[273] In his Lvov Ghetto diary Rabbi David Kahane (1903–1998) records a similar action: "A special labor battalion of Jewish workers from the camp was ordered to uproot and smash all the tombstones on the cemetery."[274] Not only do the Nazis undertake the task of desecrating the dead and removing death from Jewish life, they force Jewish hands to engage this task of destroying the graves where they once said the Kaddish over their mothers and fathers. And so the assault on death is taken to the dead themselves in a campaign to destroy Jewish death. When the graves and the prayers over them are obliterated, the world and the life that constitutes it are also obliterated. Thus anti-death and anti-world are interwoven.

How is this absence, this "anti-," to be represented? Perhaps the makeshift forms of representation themselves take the place of memorial stones to serve as matzevahs for the dead robbed of their deaths, as markers for what is unmarkable. "For me," Wiesel asserts, "writing is a *matzevah,* an invisible tombstone, erected to the dead unburied."[275] Those who receive his testimony are put in a similar position. If the signifiers that go into representations of the Holocaust would lay to rest the dead unburied, they also mark a life ended for one who has lived through his own death. Recall the words of Moishe the Beadle in Wiesel's *Night*, when, like the paradigmatic survivor, he crawled out of a mass grave "to describe to you my death."[276] Recall, too, the words of Charlotte Delbo:

> I came back from the dead
> and believed
> this gave me the right
> to speak to others
> but when I found myself face to face with them
> I had nothing to say
> because I learned
> over there
> that you cannot speak to others.[277]

Thus, the nonrepresentable. Representation in this instance is an effort to die on the part of someone who cannot die away from the horror because he or she cannot speak the horror. For this death has been murdered in the obliteration of the gravesites of Jewish mothers, fathers, and children.

To be sure, the word *death* is drained of meaning. Even—or especially—in phrases such as "death camp" and "death factory," we have nothing more than a euphemism that veils the truth of the Nazis' assault on time and death. "Natural death no longer exists," declares Emil Dorian (1891–1956).[278] That is why the Nazis targeted the old and the ailing for murder: refusing to simply wait for them to expire, they were determined to see to it that no Jew would die, that the new Nazi god would eliminate Jewish death itself from the world. And so they drained the word *murder* of its meaning as well: the Holocaust was not an instance of mass murder, not a case of genocide. No, it was . . . what? What word or image is sufficient for its representation? What analysis of the project of representation itself can get at this unreality? The Angel of Death himself—the Angel with a Thousand Eyes, who looks over our shoulders each time we would represent the Holocaust—dies upon the death of Jewish death. How, then, are we to represent death in the throes of death? Does this not belong to what is otherwise than representation?

Where the assault on time and the death of death are concerned, the issue of representation is not about working through trauma; it is about the recovery of time and death. For the survivor, this problem manifests itself in the guilt over having survived: survival itself is traumatizing. Here, we see how deep the Nazi horror runs: survivors whose crime was being alive now feel guilty of some crime precisely because they are alive. When Leon Wells (1925–2009), for instance, returned from the concentrationary universe, the only thing people wanted to know was why he was alive.[279] For Alexander Donat, the question that turns him over to a constant atonement for nothing he *did* comes not from the other but from within himself: "Why was *I* permitted to live?"[280] Zivia Lubetkin (1914–1976) also wonders how she could possibly answer the recurring question: "How will I be able to explain how I survived?"[281] By now we can see that there is much more than mere guilt underlying the question. Deeper than guilt, what is at work here is the problem of liberation confronting a person robbed of his death and now faced with being a marker for those who have no gravestones. Thus, the survivor eternally seeks her liberation by seeking the death denied her, the death that would enable her to detach herself from the past. For death denied is a living death. And the recovery from a living death is ever open-ended.

In *The Jews of Silence* Elie Wiesel tells the story of a woman who was shot but only wounded at the mass grave site known as Babi Yar. After crawling out of the mass grave, she managed to find shelter with a Ukrainian, only to be handed over to the Germans. Again she was taken to the mass grave; again she was shot and merely wounded. This time, too, she managed to escape. But, says Wiesel, "her mind had snapped. Now she rants aloud, remembering forgotten things, and people say, 'Poor woman, she lives in another world.' "[282] This woman's condition exemplifies the condition of the survivor. While it may be true that not every survivor has had his or her mind snap, every survivor has had his soul wounded. And the wound refuses closure; refusing closure, it refuses liberation, trapped in a persistently recurring dehiscence. "The injury," Primo Levi insists, "cannot be healed."[283] And if the injury cannot be healed, it cannot be represented. We have examined the facets of this torment: the movement from one silence only to collide with another, the assault on time, the murder of Jewish death and of the death by which the Jew may die away from the event. The upshot? The survivor leaves the death camp, but the death camp does not leave the survivor. "It's not me who's doing the thinking," Fania Fénelon (1922–1983) insists, " 'it' thinks *for* me. . . . I spend every night there—every night!"[284] And, writes Isabella Leitner, "Bye, Auschwitz. I will never see you again. I will always see you."[285] For she will always be seen, always summoned, by the dead who have no graves, whose cemetery is the sky that looks down upon us all. "I belong here," Kitty Hart (b. 1923) remembers her return to Auschwitz. "I have never been away."[286] She returns to the site of the anti-world seeking a liberation from it, just as memory returns in a search for recovery. But it does not come; the movement remains open-ended, unconsummated, and otherwise than representation.

The Midrash offers an important teaching in this connection. On each of the first five days of the Creation (except the second day), God pronounced His labor to be good; but on the sixth day He declared it to be *tov meod*, that is, "very good" (Genesis 1:31). The word *meod* means "more." What could possibly be more than good? The Good that belongs to Creation becomes "more" with the creation of the human being; the human being is *more* than being. What is the sign of his being *more*? It is his death, which, conceived as a task, becomes his infinite offering for the sake of the infinitely dear, in a being-against-the-death of the other human being. Therefore, Rabbi Meir maintains that the *meod* in *tov meod* signifies death, a category belonging to human life alone (*Bereshit Rabbah* 9:5; see also *Zohar* II, 103a).[287] To choose life is to choose this *tov meod* that distinguishes the animate from the inanimate, the human from the animal, and a living Good from a conceptual good. Choosing the *tov meod* means understanding that the basis of our relation to another human being—underlying the commandment to love our neighbor—is our fear for his or her death. In their metaphysical overturning of Jewish life and death, the Nazis decreed and carried out the annihilation of this *tov meod* that is death. Those who would undertake the task of representing the Holocaust must articulate that fear—that is what is traumatizing in the representation of trauma: it is not only the trauma that others have suffered but also the trauma of the realization that I am the one responsible for their trauma. If Holocaust representation is about remembrance, it is a remembrance of the responsibility attendant to memory.

A Memory and a Name

> And to them will I give my house and within my wall a memory and a name that will not be cut off.
>
> —Isaiah 56:5

George Steiner has noted that there is a definitive link between "the possibilities of human discourse in regard to God and to the Shoah."[288] The Third Commandment provocatively, if not prophetically, hints at a connection: *Lo tisa et shem Adonai Eloheikha lashav,* that is, "Do not take the Name of the Lord your God in vain" (Exodus 20:6). Tisa also means "carry," "bear," or "deliver": do not transmit the Name, *HaShem*—do not name the Name—*lashav,* where *shav,* as we have seen, is the root of Shoah. Do not make the Name that came under assault in the Shoah into the Shoah, into a lie, into nothingness, lest you play into the hands of the evil that would obliterate the Name. Here, a profound caution sweeps over all who would delve into the issue of Holocaust representation, and Omer Bartov understood as much. He observes that "the multiplicity of names for the mass murder of the Jews is to some extent the obverse side of God's multiplicity of names."[289] Just so, the Holocaust is invisible in its definitive, metaphysical aspect, and therefore nonrepresentable. At best, it can be glimpsed only as a trace, as when God declared to Moses, "You cannot see My face," and passed by so that Moses could catch sight only of a trace of God's "back" (Exodus 33:20–23). You cannot see the "face" of the Holocaust.

Representing the Holocaust, then, is like trying to represent God, inasmuch as it was an assault on God and on every trace of God that might show itself. Where is He represented? In the Torah, which, when read as a single word, from the first letter to the last, is the Holy Name, as it is taught in the Zohar: "The whole Torah is an enfolding of the Divine Name, the most exalted Name, the Name that comprehends all other names" (*Zohar* II, 124a). This teaching is based on the Talmud's commentary on God's first utterance at Mount Sinai, the saying of *anokhi* or "I," which is to be read as an acronym for *Ana nafshi ketavit yehavit,* or "I shall give My soul to you in writing" (*Shabbat* 105a). While all other names are subject to representation, however, the Name that comprehends them—the Name from which they emanate—belongs to the nonrepresentable. He is the One whom the enemy sets out to destroy in the destruction not only of the Jews but of every trace of Jewish teaching, testimony, and tradition. Hence, the difficulty in naming the Holocaust, which is fundamental to the difficulties surrounding Holocaust representation.

"At last you must admit, Rabbi," we read in the first of Ka-tzetnik's visions in *Shivitti,* "that God of the Diaspora himself is climbing into this truck—a musselman."[290] The ontological assault on the human becomes a metaphysical assault on the divine. Recognizing this assault on the Holy One

Himself that characterizes the Holocaust, Fackenheim insists that with the Holocaust there can be no philosophical "overcoming,"[291] and representation itself is a kind of "overcoming"; it is a subsuming of the event under the categories of comprehension, where comprehension is a seizing or grasping of the event, an appropriation of the event. "Why," Fackenheim asks, "did they do it?" And he answers: "Perhaps this was the purpose: to kill God."[292] If one should object that the Nazis targeted both religious and nonreligious Jews for annihilation, we need only recall Rosenberg's assertion that *all* Jews are prone to think "talmudically . . . whether they are atheistic Bourse-speculators, religious fanatics, or Talmudic Jews of the cloth."[293] Whether religious or not, every Jew carries the "contagion" of Torah. This evil that deems Torah the quintessential evil is itself in a metaphysical category.

As early as 1934, Levinas recognized that National Socialism "stems from the essential possibility of *elemental Evil* into which we can be led by logic and against which Western philosophy had not sufficiently insured itself."[294] And Holocaust representation is a project that stems from Western philosophy, a tradition steeped in the ontological, totalizing, epistemological project of appropriation that ends in mass murder. Examining the philosophical ground of the Holocaust, Levinas would go on to realize a deeper insight: "A philosophy of power, ontology [culminating in Heidegger] is, as first philosophy which does not call into question the same, a philosophy of injustice. . . . Heideggerian ontology, which subordinates the relationship with the Other to the relation with Being in general, remains under obedience to the anonymous, and leads inevitably to another power, to imperialist domination, to tyranny."[295] Elsewhere, he puts it this way: "Heideggerian philosophy precisely marks the apogee of a thought in which the finite does not refer to the infinite (prolonging certain tendencies of Kantian philosophy . . .), in which every deficiency is but weakness and every fault committed against oneself. . . . Heideggerian ontology subordinates the relation with the other to the relation with the neuter, Being, and it thus continues to exalt the will to power, whose legitimacy the other alone can unsettle, troubling good conscience."[296] If an analysis of Holocaust representation is to assume any ethical aspect, those who take up such a project must ask themselves where they stand in relation to this ontological tradition.

That tradition demands what Immanuel Kant (1724–1804) demanded, namely "the euthanasia of Judaism,"[297] which in the Nazi period translated into the murder of God, Torah, and Israel. Said Pinchas of Koretz (1728–1790), a disciple of the Baal Shem Tov, "God and Torah are one. God, Israel, and Torah are one."[298] God and Judaism are one: to assault one is to assault the other through an assault on Torah. Testimony from the event itself confirms this view. In his diary from the Vilna Ghetto, Zelig Kalmanovitch (1885–1944) writes, "A war is being waged against the Jew. But this war is not merely directed against one link in the triad [of Israel, God, and Torah] but against the entire triad: against the Torah and God, against the moral law and Creator of the universe."[299] In her Holocaust memoir, to take another example, Judith Dribben (1923–1977), relates the following: "One morning some Germans saw me on the stairs. Richard, a blond and fresh young man who spoke Ukrainian, stopped me. 'Last night we set your synagogue afire! Didn't it burn wonderfully? The Jewish God is burnt to ashes.' "[300] This brief scene is emblematic of the mission of the millennial German Reich.

Here, an insight from Levinas comes to bear in the context of Holocaust representation and why it is problematic: " 'Here I am' as a witness of the Infinite, but a witness that does not thematize what it bears witness of, and whose truth *is not the truth of representation,* is not *evidence.* There is witness, a unique structure, an exception to the rule of being, *irreducible to representation,* only of the Infinite. The Infinite does not appear to him that bears witness to it. On the contrary, the witness belongs to the glory of the Infinite. It is by the voice of the witness that the glory of the Infinite is glorified."[301] Rather than providing evidence, the testimony that characterizes Holocaust representation is an opening of a portal through which a Commanding Voice may be heard, the Voice that puts the first question to the first human being: "*Ayeka!?*—Where are you? Or better: How could you!?" (Genesis 3:9). What we call the Holocaust, then—how we "represent" it—determines not only what we remember but also our ability to hear the call of the Jewish men, women, and children consumed in the Holocaust, when the Jewish God was burned to ashes. It is a summons in which our own name resounds. If Holocaust representation is tied to memory, it is tied to a memory of the Name and a memory of the immemorial that transcends memory. "The immemorial is not an effect of a weakness of memory," Levinas explains, "an incapacity to cross large intervals of time, to resuscitate pasts too deep. It is the impossibility of the dispersion of time to assemble itself in the present."[302] It is otherwise than representation; it belongs to the ineffable that makes the effable meaningful. It makes our name meaningful in an answering of "Here I am!" to our name.

I once saw an interview with a Holocaust survivor filmed in 1945, just after the war. He began the interview by saying, without exaggeration or flair, "My name, when I can remember it, is. . . ." And so we recall the words of Primo Levi: "They will even take away our name, and if we want to keep it, we will have to find ourselves the strength to do so, to manage somehow so that behind the name something of us, of us as we were, still remains."[303] From 1938, when the Nazis added the name *Israel* to every Jewish male and the name *Sarah* to every Jewish female, the erasure of the name of the Jew was central to the assault on the soul. Indeed, Jewish tradition teaches that the name and the soul are of a piece.[304] For the Jews, the struggle to keep their names was a struggle to keep their souls, since the soul is made of the divine utterance of its name, a name in which is inscribed the destiny and the meaning of a life. The Hebrew word for "destiny," *yiud,* is a cognate of the word for "testimony," *edah,* suggesting that a link between a testimony and a name, in which we recover not only the names of the nameless dead but also our own names.

According to the tale, on the night before Jacob was to reconcile with his brother Esau and return to the land of his birth, the Angel of Death fell upon him, and the two of them wrestled until dawn. Jacob overcame the Angel and would not release him until he obtained a blessing from the unearthly being. The blessing began with a question, the question that the angel puts to each of us: "What is your name?" And the man answered, "Jacob." To which the Angel of Death replied, "No longer will you be called Jacob. Henceforth you will be called Israel, for you have struggled against God and men, and you have prevailed" (see Genesis 32:25–31).

What can it mean for Jacob to have "struggled against God [*Elokim*] and men?" Menachem Mendel Schneerson offers the following insight: " 'Elokim' in this context means 'angels' [cf. *Chullin* 92a], and generally connotes the 'seventy heavenly princes' through whom flow the Divine emanations which sustain physical existence, and who thereby act to conceal Godliness. 'Men' signifies a still greater concealment, for men are capable of denigrating the Jew for performing God's will, and this is a harder concealment to bear."[305] At no time in history was the denigration of the Jew by men more pronounced than in the time of the *Judenvernichtung*. And at no time was the concealment of God greater: the two are interrelated. How does a Jew in the post-Holocaust era break down the concealment of God, of the One whom we call "the Name?" By assuming his own name, the name of Israel. That is why the Jew—then as now—is faced with wrestling from the Angel of Death the name of Israel. Holocaust representation represents just such an encounter, just such a wrestling. In the time of the Shoah the Jewish people wrestled incessantly with the Angel of Death.

The Nazi affliction of the Jewish soul entailed an assault on the memory and the name, an assault on understanding and origin, on meaning and redemption. Ka-tzetnik's Rabbi of Shilev understood this point even as he and his fellow Jews awaited their turn for the gas chambers of Birkenau. "Can't you see," he addressed a man named Ferber, "God's spirit hovering here now above this Destruction and Creation? Can't you feel that Jacob—in our bones—now wrestles with the Angel? We are the sinew of his thigh vein in this struggle!" And Ferber asked him, "Rabbi of Shilev, for whose sake does Jacob wrestle with the Angel, if his children did not cross the river, but stayed here in the blackness of the night?" And the Rabbi answered, "From the very blackness of this night Jacob will bring forth the name 'Israel!' "[306]—from the blackness of the night and from the blackness of those ashes. For the Zohar tells us that the dust raised when Jacob wrestled the name "Israel" from the Angel "was not ordinary dust, but ashes, the residue of fire" (*Zohar* I, 170a). If, as the Midrash says, the Torah is made of black fire written on white fire (*Tanchuma Bereshit* 1; *Devarim Rabbah* 3:12), the word that would represent the nonrepresentable Holocaust is made of the black ash of the body of Israel written on the terrible flames of the crematoria. Indeed, "fire was the dominant image of the Event," as Wiesel has said,[307] and it is a dominant image in the representation of the Holocaust as nonrepresentable. Hence the prophetic words of Madam Schechter, the woman in the sealed train in Wiesel's *Night*: "Fire! I see a fire!"[308]

The images of fire and ash that so frequently arise in representations of the Holocaust underscore not only the event that has passed but also our engagement with representations of the Holocaust. We may be outside the Event, but the Event is not outside of us. "We flounder," says Terrence Des Pres, "in a torment having nothing to do with us yet felt in some strange way to be very much a part of our deepest, most secret being. The terror of the camps is *with* us."[309] More than that, it is all *around* us, as well as *within* us. The dead and the ashes of the dead were dumped into the rivers that flow into the sea and encompass the earth, as when the Danube ran red,[310] and yet the sea is never full. The sea from which life itself emerges teems with the body of Israel. As for the *within* us, in an effort to grasp the graphic meaning of this point, remember the disaster that occurred in Chernobyl on 26 April 1986, when a cloud of radioactive material was released into the air from one of the chimneys at a nuclear power plant. Two weeks later, radiation levels in Montana were elevated. In fact, earth scientists claim that one can determine air pollution levels over the years by taking a plug of snow and ice from Antarctica. *Antarctica!*

"O the chimneys!" cried Nelly Sachs (1891–1970). "And Israel's body as smoke through the air!"[311] In the time of the Holocaust the remains of the Jewish people flowed into the sea and bellowed into the air in columns of fire and smoke and ash, not for one day but for a thousand days, not from one chimney but from dozens. Then there are the tens of thousands of Jews exhumed from their mass graves and burned in an effort to hide the evidence of the crime without a name. And so it happened, in the words of Schwarz-Bart, that the Jews of Europe "turned from *Luftmenschen* into *Luft*. I shall not translate. So this story will not finish with some tomb to be visited in memoriam. For the smoke that rises from crematoriums obeys physical laws like any other: the particles come together and disperse according to the wind that propels them."[312] If, as the talmudic sage Rabbi Ammi once taught, he who eats from the earth of Babylon is as though he ate the flesh of his ancestors (*Zevachim* 113b), what shall we say of this bread that we now harvest from the ashen earth? The winds have spread the ashes of untold millions of Jews over the face of the earth, east to west, pole to pole. They inhabit the soil from which we harvest our bread. They abide in the bread we put into our mouths, in a dark eucharistic union that binds us to the body of Israel. As we are made of that bread, so are we made of those ashes: we are the grave to those denied a grave.

Thus, we understand the lines from Czech survivor and novelist Arnošt Lustig (1926–2011):

> These ashes would be indestructible and immutable, they would not burn up into nothingness because they themselves were remnants of fire. . . . No one living would ever be able to escape them. . . . These ashes will be contained in the breath and expression of every one of us and the next time anybody asks what the air he breathes is made of, he will have to think about these ashes; they will be contained in books which haven't been written and will be found in the remotest regions of the earth where no human foot has ever trod; no one will be able to get rid of them, for they will be the fond, nagging ashes of the dead who died in innocence.[313]

And in their nagging abides a nagging question, the question put to us by the Angel of Death: What is your name? That too is the Jewish Question for which the National Socialists sought a Final Solution, the question they snatched from the mouth of the Angel of Death. The task for representation is to sustain the question. There lies the problem: how to represent the restoration of the question put to the human being from beyond being, the question that eludes all mastery.

Representation is mastery, which is the aim for the ontological project; setting out to seize or ensnare, representation tends to seek a security found in settling matters. To the extent that it would settle matters by re-presenting and thus overcoming the Holocaust, it is universalizing and, in the end, trivializing and relativizing. "Men shun the scandal of the particularity of Auschwitz," writes Fackenheim. "Germans link it with Dresden; American liberals, with Hiroshima. Christians deplore antisemitism-in-general, while Communists erect monuments to the victims-of-Fascism-in-general, depriving the dead of Auschwitz of their Jewish identity even in death. Rather than face Auschwitz, men everywhere seek refuge in generalities, comfortable precisely because they are generalities."[314] There's the rub: the Nazis undertook an assault on the God of Abraham, Isaac, and Jacob, and the project of Holocaust representation—wittingly or otherwise—runs the risk of slipping into the same mode, the same assault through universalizing and thereby trivializing the event. Representation is universalizing, whereas the Holocaust is a singularity, even though it may have universal implications.

The matter of Holocaust representation rests on the responsibility that, as Barbie Zelizer outlines, has undergone a process, a history, of abrogation: "An initial need to take responsibility for what was witnessed, experienced directly after the Holocaust, soon gave way to a period of amnesia—the forgetting to remember that stretched from the 1950s through the 1970s. It was replaced by an obsession with Holocaust memory—a period of remembering to remember that has lasted till the present day. But as memory proliferates in the public imagination, the act of bearing witness is growing thin, and our often empty claims to memory work render us capable of little more than remembering so that we may forget in its shadow."[315] So where are we now? How shall we answer the One who puts to us the question: Where are *you*?

Part Two

The Literary Transcendence of Holocaust Representation

Speaking the Ineffable

Opening Thoughts: Epiphany and the Ultimate

> And subscribe the deeds, and seal them. And call witnesses.
>
> —Jeremiah 32:44

> There is no such thing as Holocaust literature—this cannot be. Auschwitz negates all literature.
>
> —Elie Wiesel, *A Jew Today*

One cannot examine the literary response to the Holocaust without citing the famous words of Theodor Adorno (1903–1969): "Cultural criticism finds itself faced with the final stage of the dialectic of culture and barbarism. To write poetry after Auschwitz is barbaric. And this corrodes even the knowledge of why it has become impossible to write poetry today."[1] The post-Holocaust corrosion of culture—the descent into the relativization and trivialization of all good and therefore of all evil—has indeed corroded the knowledge of why the aesthetic might become barbaric so as to make it impossible to write poetry. Where criticism is couched in the cultural, it cannot be otherwise; the Holocaust has once and for all demonstrated the bankruptcy of culture as a ground for the Good. What makes the aesthetic endeavor barbaric is a radical disconnect between the aesthetics that culture would espouse and the ethics it cannot sustain. Hence Adorno's problem: once good and evil have been relativized and trivialized by culture, there is no ethical action to be found in poetry, but only an aesthetic indulgence.

Gertrude Kolmar (1894–1942) makes a distinction between being a poet and being a writer. In a letter she wrote from Berlin on 23 July 1941to her sister Hilde Wenzel, she says, "I'm a poet; yes, I know that; but a writer I would never want to be."[2] For Kolmar, writing poetry was much more a matter of ethical demand than of cultural expression. If poets such as Kolmar had the courage to write poetry then, are we to denounce it now? Are we not ethically obligated to heed the words of Romanian poet Emil Dorian, who on 12 July 1938 wrote, "All is not lost while the hope of writing a poem is still alive"?[3] By 15 September 1942, however, his pursuit of poetry had become problematic: "When you hear around you in what absurd and arbitrary ways an existence still full of inner life is destroyed in a few minutes, fear and rage overwhelm you and undermine the layer of resigned calm, plunging you into helpless despair. No doubt now is the moment when I ought to turn to poetry for its nourishing strength. . . . But today poetry comes very hard to me."[4] In his concern with the word, the diarist here opposes the meaningful to the absurd in an act of testimony. The same might be said of the post-Holocaust literary response to the event (I do not say literary representation of the event), even while acknowledging the bankruptcy of meaning and value. To be sure, that very bankruptcy summons the literary response that transcends literature.

"I do not regard myself as a composer of literary material," we recall the words of Yehiel De-Nur in his testimony at the Jerusalem trial of Adolf Eichmann.[5] Likewise, Holocaust survivor Suzanne Birnbaum declares that in writing her memoir she "does not pretend to be writing a work of literature."[6] In his account of his experience in Dachau Charles Joyon similarly insists, "This is not a work of literature."[7] And on 10 October 1943, Hélène Berr confessed in her diary, "To write all the reality and the tragic things we are living through, giving them all their naked gravity without letting words distort them is a very difficult task and requires constant effort. Then there is the considerable repugnance I feel at thinking of myself as 'someone who writes.' "[8] Yet Imre Kertész (b. 1929) asserts, "The concentration camp is imaginable only and exclusively as literature, never as reality,"[9] a statement that introduces a tension between truth and reality, between truth and literature. If Auschwitz was a realm in which more was real than was possible, then more was possible than representable. In this realization we have an indication of literature's "capacity to turn against itself," as R. Clifton Spargo phrases it,[10] something that exceeds the capacity of "historical" narrative. But what is this turning against itself, this contravention of representation?

Understood on different levels, Kertész and De-Nur and Wiesel, Birnbaum and Joyon, are right: Karin Bauer has shown that ever since Richard Wagner (1813–1883) and Friedrich Nietzsche (1844–1900), if not before, literature has degenerated into an aesthetic diversion, robbed of its ethical aspect.[11] Attesting to this understanding of post-Holocaust literature, Piotr Rawicz (1918–1982) writes in his novel *Blood from the Sky*: "Our only real betrayal is the one we commit against silence."[12] How does one betray silence? According to Rawicz, it is by indulging in the discourse of literary representation: "Literature: anti-dignity exalted to a system, to a single code of behavior. The art, occasionally remunerative, of rummaging in vomit. And yet, it would appear, *navigare necesse est*: one *has* to write."[13] One *has* to bear witness to what Terrence Des Pres calls "excremental assault,"[14] and thus rummage about in excrement. One *has* to become a messenger, despite the impossibility of delivering the message. But why does one *have* to? The "one *has* to" can be determined only from an absolute, transcendent ethical demand from on high, and not from some cultural norm, no matter how "sophisticated." Like it or not, despite ourselves, the Shoah has torn a hole in the fabric of all the cultural niceties and aspirations and has transformed us into messengers of this tearing.

And it changes us to our core, as in the case of Thérèse Goldschmidt, the survivor Doriel's psychoanalyst in Elie Wiesel's novel *A Mad Desire to Dance*. After several sessions with him, her husband declares to her, "You've changed since you've been treating him."[15] Anyone who undertakes what we undertake here is changed; there is no coming out of this unscathed. Goldschmidt has changed because she has been transformed into a witness. This transformation is effected through a collision with a transcendence encountered in the face of the other human being, in a moment of epiphany. One task facing the writer of Holocaust literature is to effect an encounter with the face and with the Nazi assault on the face. "It is here," Emmanuel Levinas explains, "that the transcendent, infinitely other, solicits us and appeals to us. . . . His very epiphany consists in soliciting us by his destitution in the face of the Stranger, the widow, and the orphan."[16] Indeed, more than solicitation, to be transformed into a messenger is to be laid claim to and accused by the Ultimate.

To confront the testimony of Holocaust literature is to collide with the destitution of strangers, widows, and orphans, in all their biblical gravity. What begins as an "aesthetic experience" becomes an ethical collision in a moment of epiphany: "Thou shalt not murder." This gravity, says Levinas, "is stronger than murder, already resists us in his face, is his face, is the primordial *expression,* is the first word: 'you shall not commit murder. . . .' The epiphany of the face brings forth the possibility of gauging the infinity of the temptation to murder."[17] If Holocaust literature is about anything, it is about the primordial commandment, "Thou shalt not murder," and the Nazis' assault on the commanding Voice. What thus "appeals to me" *from on high* seizes me and transforms me into a witness: I cannot slip away, any more than Adam could hide.

No wonder André Schwarz-Bart interrupts his narrative as his characters approach the gas chambers, saying, "I am so weary that my pen can no longer write. 'Man, strip off thy garments, cover thy head with ashes, run into the streets and dance in thy madness. . . .' "[18] What is the literary response to the Holocaust but a dance of "midrashic madness," as Emil Fackenheim calls it? It is what Elie Wiesel invokes when he titles his novel *A Mad Desire to Dance.* It is an aggadic madness that brings to mind a teaching from the *Sifre* on Deuteronomy 11:22: "You wish to recognize the One who spoke and brought the world into being? Learn Aggadah for in Aggadah you will find God." The engagement with the aggadic response to the Holocaust, however, is an engagement with a radical assault on God: you wish to recognize that assault on the Holy One, who did not speak as the world was turned over to nothingness? Read the unprecedented "Psalm" of Paul Celan (1920–1970), where he writes,

> No one moulds us again out of earth and clay,
> No one conjures our dust.
> No one.
> Praised be your name, no one.[19]

Noting that this last "no one" is *Niemand,* with a capital *N,*[20] we understand something that eludes representation; representation is the representation of some*thing* or some*one*. Shall we dare to name this *Niemand*? Learn the post-Holocaust Aggadah, these new tales from a new Bible, as Primo Levi has described them.[21] And so we have the ethical demand of a mad Aggadah, the demand for a literary response to the event that transformed literature itself.

Fackenheim elaborates: "Midrashic madness points to *an existence in which the madness is transfigured.* Midrashic madness is the Word spoken in the anti-world which ought not to be but is. The existence it points to acts to restore a world which ought to be but is not, and this is *its* madness.

After Planet Auschwitz, there can be no health without *this* madness, no joy, no life. Without this madness a Jew cannot do—with God or without Him—what a Voice from Sinai bids him do: choose life."[22] There lies the ethical demand couched in the literary response to the Holocaust: choose life *as a Jew,* even though such a choice, for a Jew, is madness, since to choose life as a Jew could get you killed.

The one who undertakes a literary response to the Holocaust—and therefore attempts to choose life in the very act of testimony—takes the word spoken in the anti-world and transmits it to our own world by restoring its bond with meaning and therefore with life. He or she does so by answering, "Here I am for you," to an imperative that comes not only from Mount Sinai but from the undoing of Mount Sinai, from what Fackenheim calls "the Commanding Voice of Auschwitz."[23] To answer that commandment with an affirmation of "Here I am" in the act of literary testimony is to touch upon an Ultimate that exceeds what Saul Friedlander calls the "event at the limits."[24] At the limits, in the words of Maurice Blanchot, the disaster "is the unknown name for that in thought itself which dissuades us from thinking of it, leaving us, by its proximity, alone. Alone, and thus exposed to the thought of the disaster which disrupts solitude and overflows every variety of thought, as the intense, silent and disastrous affirmation of the outside."[25] This "disastrous affirmation" lies in an imperative *from on high,* from *the outside,* and it lies in the possibility of an epiphany in the literary testimony to *this* event, which unfolds not in history but in a transcendent metahistory, in the very soul, as Wiesel has said.[26] Hence, the epiphany and the Ultimate.

One encounters this sense of the Ultimate in the earliest investigations of Holocaust literature, dating back to 1970 with the publication of Irving Halperin's *Messengers from the Dead*, where he views the authors of Holocaust literature "essentially as moral teachers."[27] This is a striking statement, one that constitutes a first step toward defining Holocaust literature as a genre unto itself, in some ways as an antigenre or a countergenre, a genre of the Ultimate. If, as Sem Dresden says, "literature and writing in general meet a limit they cannot transgress without dissolving themselves,"[28] it is not the aesthetic limit of imagination but this ethical limit, the limit where the Infinite flashes in a moment of epiphany; the epiphany is the realization of an infinite responsibility summoned by the Infinite. In what other literary genre is revealed moral teaching an *essential* feature of the "genre," one that stems not from reason or art but from above? In what other literary "genre" are the voices that go into the text viewed as messengers from the dead? In what other literary genre might we come across Wiesel's assertion that "when I write I feel my invisible teachers looking over my shoulders, reading my words and judging their veracity,"[29] where his "teachers" are not only the sages of Jewish tradition, but also the dead whose voices are entrusted to him?

"Holocaust literature," Alvin Rosenfeld affirms, "is at its heart of hearts revelatory in some new way."[30] Yes! The "revelatory" lies in the infinite ethical obligation to the dead outlined in Part One; only where the otherwise than being transcends being, only where we touch upon an Ultimate, can there be the ethical obligation to the dead that defines Holocaust literature. Surely this is the meaning of Saul's attempt not to save a life but to save a death, to find a way to say kaddish for his dead son, in Lázló Nemes's film *Son of Saul* (2015). In the past, the literary representation of life has belonged to the categories that define the ontological landscape. No more, at least not in the case of Holocaust literature, where in an epiphanic instant, as Michael Bernard-Donals and Richard Glejzer state it, the witness catches sight of "what escapes understanding," something that "exceeds the limit of knowledge."[31] Thus, writes Wiesel in his novel *Twilight*, "It is sometimes necessary to seek in order not to understand,"[32] in order to realize what surpasses understanding, namely that something—or someone—has *already* laid claim to us. The Holocaust that transformed the premise of our understanding of reality has dissolved the parameters of literary genre, so that the transcendence of the genre, of the representable, has come with the testimony to the Good in the aftermath of the assault on the Good, the testimony that defines Holocaust literature (if, indeed, that term still obtains).

Halperin demonstrates that from the beginning scholars have recognized the testimonial nature of the literary response to the Holocaust as a response to the transcendent summons of the Good, which, as we have seen, belongs to the nonrepresentable. Contrary to the claims of Ruth Franklin, for example, the confrontation with Holocaust literature is not about empathy.[33] Much closer to the mark and much more profound is Dorota Glowacka's notion of the "poethics of disappearing traces": "Disrupting mimetic paradigms of representation, the 'poethics of disappearing traces' roots literature and art in ethical responsibility. At the same time, it foregrounds the necessity of producing words and images, since it is only in such representations that the other can leave a trace of his or her existence."[34] That trace lies in the silent outcry of the face: to undertake a literary representation of the Holocaust is to step before the commanding presence that emanates from the face, a presence that transcends representation. It is an attempt to restore the face that came under a radical assault, as the Nazis sought to destroy not only the body of Israel but also the soul of the Jew, not only the memory and the name of the Jew but also the memory and the Name, the *yad vashem*. In order to destroy the name of which the soul is made, they had to destroy the Good; and in order to destroy the Good, they had to destroy the response to the summons of the Name. In the midst of this response the voice of HaShem is heard and the covenantal relation is realized.

The underlying transcendent in the literary transcendence of the Final Solution to the *Jewish* Question is the Jewish *covenant,* a covenant of fire that the Nazis consigned to the flames. Given the images of fire that dominate the Event, the study of the literary response to the Holocaust takes on unprecedented meaning when we recall the teaching from the Zohar that says *bereshit,* "in the beginning," should be read as *brit esh,* "covenant of fire" (*Zohar* I, 89a). We grasp on a deeper level images of the covenant of fire that find their way into the literature of the Holocaust, from Madame Schechter's cry of "Fire!' in Wiesel's *Night*,[35] to Arnošt Lustig's insistence in *A Prayer for Katerina Horovitzova* that "these ashes would be indestructible and immutable, they would not burn up into nothingness because they themselves were remnants of fire."[36] There lies the nagging cry of the dead, the nagging ethical imperative that issues from the dead who ascended into the heavens on pillars of fire.

The engagement with Holocaust literature becomes an attempt to recover a trace of the covenant that was assailed in the assault on the Word, which paved the way to Auschwitz and now shapes the literary response to it. It was an assault whose seeds were planted long before the Nazis. As Jonathan Sacks has understood, "The assault on the Word [that characterized the advent of modernity in the nineteenth century] could not but be an assault on the Jewish God. Nor can we escape reflection on the fact that within a century, the culture which had reduced the book of the Covenant to fragments had reduced a third of the people of the Covenant to ashes."[37] As Alon Confino has realized, on Kristallnacht "burning the synagogues and the Bible was not directed at Jews as liberals, Bolsheviks, or potential emigrants from the Reich, nor as racial enemies. Instead, Kristallnacht created a new imagination: it was not about Jews as individuals but about Judaism."[38] Viewed in the context of covenant, the Jewish testimony to the mass murder therefore has a metaphysical aspect; written as an ethical response to the assault on the very meaning of the ethical, which is the very meaning of the human being, the literary response to the Holocaust harbors an outcry to God and an affirmation of the Covenant. "The dialogue—or duel, if you like—between man and his God," writes Wiesel, "doesn't end in nothingness. Man may not have the last word, but he has the last cry. That moment marks the birth of art."[39] Just so, Holocaust literature is a summons to, from, and for the other human being, a cry of deep unto deep. The issue of "believing" in God is irrelevant; decisive is the sense of urgency, of having had something infinitely precious placed in one's care, the sense of an infinite responsibility that devolves upon the witness, in spite of what he or she might believe. *Navigare necesse est.*

Recall Fackenheim's evocation of Pelagia Lewinska (1907–2004), who in her memoir says that once she "grasped the motivating principle" of Auschwitz, she "felt under orders to live."[40] And Fackenheim asks, "Whose orders? Why did she wish to obey? And—this above all—where did she get the strength? We answer the last question by discovering that it is unanswerable. Once again 'willpower' and 'natural desire' are both inadequate. Once again we have touched an Ultimate."[41] Under orders to choose life, Lewinska and others were under orders to speak, to write, and to testify outside the parameters of willpower and natural desire. The ethical obligation underlying the witness's sense of duty, therefore, takes us beyond the usual aesthetic engagement with a literary text. Transcending aesthetics, the literary response to the Holocaust arises from a condition of being commanded to write, in all of its pathos, in all of its ethos.

Other seminal studies of Holocaust literature confirm the literary transcendence of Holocaust representation. In 1975, Lawrence Langer published *The Holocaust and the Literary Imagination*, in which he explores the conflict between "historical fact and imaginative truth."[42] Again, however, Glowacka takes an earlier insight to a deeper level: "Ethical imagination carries the other toward the image, where the witness discovers the truth that is 'not the truth of representation.' In that sense, a Levinasian art of disappearing traces radically calls into question traditional aesthetics; representation is undone by the trace [of the absolute ethical commandment]."[43] Why? Because the trace is an epiphany of the Ultimate articulated through the efficacy of the image. In the image, "the part counts for the whole, is the image of the whole," says Levinas. "The image has to symbolize the whole. Truth consists in a being whose images are . . . also its symbol, being identified through new images. . . . But this immediacy is, in the knowing of the truth, always repressed,"[44] because it is a knowing that undoes the categories of knowledge, a "knowing" that is a not-knowing, an epiphany. "What we have come to understand as knowledge," write Bernard-Donals and Glejzer, "occludes access to it. . . . The objects through which we do have access to the event . . . are representations of a traumatic, sublime object that are themselves resistant to knowledge,"[45] because the ethical absolute cannot be appropriated by knowledge. It is therefore resistant to representation.

This conjunction of the traumatic and the sublime is crucial: if knowledge of the truth is suppressed, it is because of the diachrony of time and identity. Time is this diachrony experienced upon the entry of the otherwise than being into the midst of being. Indeed, the presence of God—the presence under assault—defines this diachrony, which is precisely *time*. If "for the Nazis, the Jews symbolized time,"[46] as Confino has said, it is because for the Nazis, the Jews symbolized God. Hence, the presence of God—the presence that the Nazis would obliterate—is the presence that Holocaust literature would restore in a transcendent restoration of the voice of the dead and, thus, a restoration of time.

Says Golda in Schwarz-Bart's novel, "When death knocks at the door, God is always there."[47] Likewise: when the dead knock at our door, the Good is always there, putting to us the question put to the first human being, the question from which we would hide, as the first human being hid: "Where are you?" That is the question that the would-be author of "Holocaust literature," as well as those of us who collide with it, must answer. In Schwarz-Bart's tale, after hearing Ernie Levy telling the children on a transport to Auschwitz that it is only a trip to the Land of Israel, a woman asks him how he could deceive them so. " 'Madame,' " he says, rocking the corpse of a child in his arms, " 'there is no room for truth here. . . .' 'Then what is there room for . . . ?' And . . . she murmured softly, 'Then you don't believe what you're saying at all? Not at all?' She was weeping with bitter sorrow and laughed a short, terrified, demented laugh."[48] That laughter is the sound of the implosion of dream and reality, of truth and delusion; it is the sound of the epiphanic appearance of the Ultimate that haunts the literary response to the Holocaust.

The literary transcendence of Holocaust representation lies in its evocation not only of a truth that came under assault but of a truth always promised, always future, always hoped for in the hope for wisdom. Delving into the limits of representation, we approach the immemorial, which is the nonrepresentable, and thus touch upon an Ultimate. There lies the literary transcendence of Holocaust representation. And so, in 1980, in her groundbreaking study *By Words Alone*, Sidra DeKoven Ezrahi addressed the collapse of aesthetic convention in the literary representation of the Holocaust and the problem of situating the Holocaust "in literature."[49] The collapse of aesthetic convention, however, comes on the heels of the collapse of the ontological "convention"; it comes, in other words, with the collapse of the *idea* of the human, without which there is no aesthetic convention. The collapse of aesthetic convention in the literary representation of the Holocaust, in other words, comes with the Nazis' obliteration of the ethical demand that forms the foundation of the human being. Hence, Wiesel has said that at Auschwitz not only was man murdered, but the very idea of the human being was annihilated.[50]

In the same year that Ezrahi published her study, Rosenfeld's *A Double Dying* came out, where, taking the investigation to an even deeper level, he astutely examines the "contradiction between the impossibility but also the necessity of writing about the death of the idea of man in order to sustain that idea."[51] Recall Levi's assertion that there is no word "to express this offense, the demolition of a man,"[52] no speech to convey the silencing of the speaking being. The author of Holocaust literature is faced with the task of drawing upon the word to represent the demolition of the word, which is the demolition of the human being, which, in turn, is the demolition of the Good, as we see in Levi's memory of Lorenzo. There, he relates that through Lorenzo's "natural and plain manner of being good" his friend unearthed from within Levi himself a trace of humanity, so that he realized the truth that "Lorenzo was a man" because Lorenzo was good: to be a man is to be *good*.[53] To sustain the idea of man is to sustain not just the idea but the concrete reality, the *Who*, of the Good, "something and *someone* still pure and whole, not corrupt, not savage, extraneous to hatred and terror."[54] It is as concrete as the help that Lorenzo provided to Levi, which was the transmission of a word from the outside into the anti-world, a letter from home, from the *Who* of a relation, outside of which the soul suffocates.[55] There lies the impossibility of Holocaust representation, which in this case is the representation of the transcendent Good, the representation of a nonrepresentable Ultimate that lays claim to all of us: it is the transmission of a word from the anti-world into the world, a letter from the *Who* of a relation under assault.

A Word about Method: Substitution and the Transcendent

> Who wrote it, you ask? *They* wrote it!
>
> —Ka-Tzetnik 135633, *Shivitt: A Vision*

Recall once again a moment from Levi's memoir. It happens when he is trying to convey to his friend Pikolo the flash of an insight that came to him while reciting for Pikolo the lines from Dante's Canto of Ulysses:

> "And three times round she went in roaring smother / With all the waters; at the fourth the poop / Rose, and the prow went down, as pleased Another." I keep Pikolo back, it is vitally necessary and urgent that he listen, that he understand this 'as pleased Another' before it is too late; tomorrow he or I might be dead, or we might never see each other again, I must tell him, I must explain to him about the Middle Ages, about the so human and so necessary and yet unexpected anachronism, but still more, something gigantic that I myself have only just seen, in a flash of intuition, perhaps the reason for our fate, for our being here today."[56]

The method here undertaken is similar: it lies in the pursuit of an epiphanic flash of something gigantic that erupts like an earthquake in the literary transcendence of Holocaust representation.

In the analysis of the literary transcendence of Holocaust representation that follows I take an altogether new methodological approach to (1) the Holocaust, (2) Holocaust literature, and (3) the parameters of representation. This approach is grounded in the Jewish teachings and traditions that the Nazis sought to obliterate. Such an approach touches upon an Ultimate, inasmuch the Jewish people's very presence in the world is a testimony to the penetration of the Ultimate into this realm; it is a witnessing to what belongs to no ontological category, as in the *ein k'mokha,* "there is none like You," of the Eighty-Sixth Psalm (Psalms 86:8). The realization of meaning in history, Fackenheim has argued, "requires the incursion of God,"[57] an incursion that always brings with it an ethical demand. What Fackenheim says of history may be said of the prophetic literary response to *this* history, where the prophetic is more about proclamation than prescience. "To the modern historian," Heschel makes this point, "history is not the understanding of events, but rather the understanding of man's experience of events. What concerns the prophet is the human event as a divine experience."[58] The methodological premise adopted here rests upon a similar, prophetic understanding of the literary transcendence of Holocaust representation, where the literature *proclaims* a matter of great urgency.

Therefore, I undertake more than an examination of works and authors, of characters and motifs, of settings and themes—the usual categories of aesthetic engagement and literary analysis. Beyond those categories, what concerns me is the epiphanic moment of transcendence found in these literary moments of the nonrepresentable, for in the epiphanic moment lies a moment of hearing the Commanding Voice that the Nazis set out to silence. It is a hearing tied to meaning, as suggested in the Hebrew word *mashmaut,* the word for "meaning," which has the same root as the word *shema,* which is to "hear." To have a sense of meaning is to have heard something, an ethical outcry of the Good that the Nazis would eliminate. The aim of a literary response to the Nazis' radical assault on the Good is to *hear* something, in a return to a relationship between above and below, between human and human.

Glowacka observes that, with regard to Wiesel, "to write about the Holocaust is to say 'Here I am' to the unrelenting specter of Moishe, to be his hostage."[59] As we recall, the madman Moishe in Wiesel's *Night* crawled out of a mass grave to relate the story of his own death.[60] Like Moishe, the survivor returns from the depths of the mass grave that was Europe to tell his tale, but he is a messenger who cannot deliver his message. "He no longer mentioned either God or Kabbalah," Wiesel relates. "He spoke only of what he had seen. But people not only refused to believe his tales, they refused to listen. Some even insinuated . . . that he was imagining things. Others flatly said that he had gone mad."[61] Wiesel adds, "Finally he understood and fell silent. Only his burning eyes revealed the impotent rage inside him. His muteness bordered on madness."[62] Words and images eluded him. Like Moishe, other survivors, authors of what we call "Holocaust literature," were locked into their silence by the silence they encountered in the gaze of the condemned plodding inexorably to their inexorable deaths.

Undertaking a literary response to the Shoah, the witness answers *Hineni!*—"Here I am"—not only to the One on high, but also to the dead, who are now the ones on high, abiding in a sky transformed into a cemetery. Recall the words of the psalmist, words whose meaning is transformed by the Shoah: "His might is in the skies" (Psalm 68:34). Recall, too, the patient Zelig in Wiesel's novel *Twilight,* whose gaze is constantly turned toward the sky: " 'Look, over there," he tells the novel's main character Raphael. " 'An old man holding his grandson's hand. . . . A woman with her little girl. . . . They too are holding hands. . . . And there, to the left, a man is searching for his lost children. . . . A rabbi is summoning his disciples. . . . And coming toward us a procession of adolescents, their eyes riveted to a flaming mountain. . . .' "[63] Here too we have a link between HaShem and Shoah, an expression of the overturning of the heavens and the earth, as discussed in Part One. In this transformation, in this overturning, lies the transcendence of Holocaust representation: if it is anything, the representation of the Holocaust is the representation of an overturning, of a flash as blinding as the flames of the crematoria, as we turn our eyes toward a sky awash in blood and smoke and ash. *Blood from the Sky* is not only the name of a work of Holocaust literature—it is a designation of the literature itself, a literature made of blood from the sky and ashes from the earth.

If the witness and the one transformed into a witness are held hostage by an ethical demand, they are held hostage by the heights. To be thus taken hostage and drawn into a condition of substitution entails the overturning of the ego into nothing in the face of an Ultimate, as when Abraham, beginning to understand the higher, covenantal relation, utters the words, "I who am but dust and ashes would nevertheless venture to speak" (Genesis 18:27). The literary response to the Holocaust is fraught with this biblical venture, as the witness would speak of *these* ashes and thus become as nothing. We find in A. Anatoli's novel *Babi Yar* an explicit expression of this becoming: "I know, of course, that this has been carefully analyzed by experts in all the '-isms'. . . . Everything has been examined, proved and all is clear. All the same, *I do not understand.*"[64] This "not understanding" is a leaving off with the project of comprehending and grasping, of possession and appropriation, which belongs to the epistemological aspiration of the Western ontological tradition. It is a leaving off with the project of knowing, which is a project of power and control. This "not understanding" is the only way to ask the pardon of the dead, a pardon that can never come. Hence, the Levinasian condition of hostage, who does not grasp but rather is grasped, seized, and laid claim to.

"To substitute oneself," Levinas explains, "does not amount to putting oneself in the place of the other man in order to feel what he feels. . . . Rather, substitution entails bringing comfort by associating ourselves with the essential weakness and finitude of the other; it is to bear his weight while sacrificing one's interestedness and complacency-in-being, which then turn into responsibility for the other."[65] Substitution has nothing to do with either sympathy or empathy; it is not a matter of knowing how it feels or what it is like to be the other. No, it is a matter of taking on the wounds of the other in an affirmation of a profound physical and metaphysical connection to him or her, a connection made of an ethical demand. What Levinas calls "being outside-of-oneself" is a certain forgetfulness of oneself, an abrogation of the ego, in a renewal of the life of the soul through sanctification by substitution. There lies the meaning of *Kiddush HaShem* or "the Sanctification of the Name": sanctification entails substitution.

Those of us who engage this literature are summoned to undergo a movement of substitution in answer to a summons to sanctification. Far more than a matter of empathy or knowing "what it was like," it is a matter of taking upon oneself the burden of testimony, of being transformed into the messenger of an absolute by an absolute. In her introduction to her translation of Tadeusz Borowski's (1922–1951) *This Way for the Gas, Ladies and Gentlemen*, Barbara Vedder articulates this point, noting that Borowski's "writing carries a burden of meaning [for the reader] that far transcends the merely actual."[66] Assuming the "burden of meaning" is a matter of assuming the trauma of meaning undone in the light of having been chosen by the absolute Good that has come under a radical assault. "The implication of the one in the-one-for-the-other in responsibility," says Levinas, "goes beyond the representable unity of the identical, not by a surplus or lack of presence, but by . . . my uniqueness as a respondent, a hostage, for whom no one else could be substituted without transforming responsibility into a theatrical role."[67] Nothing is more tempting, more comfortable than this "theatrical role" steeped in the presumption of knowing "what it was like." That is why we find among the attempts to "analyze" Holocaust "literature" and Holocaust "representation" so many cases of flight from the ethical into the aesthetic in an avoidance of the Commanding Voice of Mount Sinai, which echoes in the Commanding Voice of Auschwitz. Already assigned and forever summoned, we move from collision to collision as we pore over these texts, wondering, as one of my students once wondered, "How do I get to the next line?"

In *Otherwise Than Being*, a book dedicated to the Six Million, Levinas articulates the condition confronting anyone who would confront the literary transcendence of Holocaust representation: "Vulnerability, exposure to outrage, to wounding, passivity more passive than all patience, passivity of the accusative form, trauma of accusation suffered by a hostage to the point of persecution, implicating the identity of the hostage who substitutes himself for the others: all this is the self, a defecting or defeat of the ego's identity. . . . It is a substitution for another, one in the place of another, expiation."[68] Yes, expiation. Expiation for what? For the human evil encountered and for the presumption of undertaking the study itself. Who is the hostage, the substitute here? It is one who has been transformed into a witness, not by receiving more information, but by glimpsing a flash of the Ultimate, something gigantic that comes in a revelation, in an epiphany, driving home something about what the literature would re-present, something of the Holocaust that resembles the biblical tales Primo Levi refers to.[69] Yes: *biblical* tales—a designation that takes Holocaust literature out of the realm of representation and into the realm of revelation. This biblical aspect of Holocaust literature makes it into "an appeal, an outcry to God on behalf of His desperate people and also on His behalf, an offering to night, to heaven, an offering made by wise old men and quiet children to mark the end of language—a burning secret buried in silence."[70] Who is the hostage? Who is buried in the silence of the end of language? It is you, reader, and it is I: we are summoned to a substitution, for the sake of an absolute dearness, infinitely fragile, that bears an absolute ethical demand.

"In substitution," writes Levinas, "my being that belongs to me and not to another is undone, and it is through this substitution that I am not 'another,' but me. The self in a being is exactly the not-being-able-to-slip-away-from an assignation that does not aim at a generality."[71] Here we see that substitution is just the opposite of representation: in substitution there is a transcendence of representation. Indeed, it can happen that representation amounts to a flight from the ethical demand of substitution. Where representation is about the self, substitution is about the soul, the "other in me," whose hostage I am by virtue of his or her being entrusted to my commanded care. The methodological premise guiding this investigation of the literary transcendence of Holocaust representation is that any engagement with Holocaust literature brings with it an ethical demand to address the singled-out condition that arises in the encounter with singled-out texts. In the engagement with Holocaust literature, the reader is unable to slip away from an assignation that disturbs the comfort of the usual literary analysis. This—and not the contravention of convention, the bankruptcy of imagination, or the failure of description—is why a novel about Treblinka is either not a novel or not about Treblinka. Like any attempt at a literary representation of the Holocaust, this analysis falls into a different category, into something akin to prayer.

"The substance of language," writes Wiesel, "and the language of silence—that is what prayer is."[72] In an attempt to restore to language the silence of the ineffable in the aftermath of an assault on language, Holocaust literature assumes an aspect of prayer, both in its utterance and in its listening, in the aftermath of the Nazi assault on Jewish literature itself, including the prayer books. "The scornful laughter of the SS myrmidons," writes Filip Müller (1922–2013), "was always heard when prisoners from the *Sonderkommando* had to burn prayer-books and religious works."[73] And Livia Jackson (b. 1931) remembers the "volumes of the Bible, leather-bound Psalms, phylacteries turn and twist and burst into myriad fragments of agony.

Pictures and documents. . . . Our soul."[74] This literature and this prayer are intertwined. Says Wiesel, "Both prayer and literature impart to and confer upon everyday words another sense."[75] This "other sense" surpasses sense; it is otherwise than sense. The subject of Holocaust literature is not only the Holocaust; its subject is the life of the soul targeted for annihilation. It is about intoxication and madness, despite me and for another, as Levinas says: "All my inwardness is invested in the form of a despite-me, for-another. Despite-me, for-another, is signification par excellence. . . . It is the very fact of finding oneself while losing oneself,"[76] in storm and fire and dizziness.

In *this* literature we encounter a transcendence of sense, of the categories of representation, in a turbulent attempt to restore a sense that perhaps can never be restored. "What I lack is words," says Gauthier Bachmann, the main character in Holocaust survivor Jakov Lind's (1907–2007) novel *Landscape in Concrete*. "I'm afraid of the words I lack."[77] As so often happens, the author's character bespeaks the author's dilemma: there is no word for this offense, the demolition of a man. Enter Mordi, one of the main characters in Haim Gouri's (b. 1923–2018) novel *The Chocolate Deal*: "I thought that periodically I'd shriek one day-long shriek which would earn me the title of Champion Shrieker."[78] And so the Holocaust novelist shrieks a shriek of silence, fearing the words that he or she lacks, seeking to reconnect the word with a meaning torn asunder in a tearing of the soul from the human being. It is a shriek transformed into a prayer.

"Each word," Wiesel has said of his writing "corresponds to a face, a prayer, the one needing the other so as not to sink into oblivion."[79] He divides his novel *The Town beyond the Wall* not into chapters but into prayers. In this tale the main character, Michael, endures the torture of standing at a wall in order to save the life of his friend Pedro, just as Jews stand at the Western Wall to pray. The aim of prayer—if it is prayer—is always to save a life. The root of the Hebrew word for "prayer," *tefillah*, is *pilel*, which may imply supplication, but it is also associated with decision, analysis, and judgment; its cognate *naftolin* means "struggle" or "wrestling," so that prayer is not a request but a confrontation—at times adversarial—between God and the soul, as when Jacob wrestled with the angel at Peniel. There are times when wrestling is a form of the closest attachment to God, of what in the mystical tradition is known as *devekut* or "clinging" to God; those who have wrestled know that in wrestling one gets *very* close to his opponent. Because prayer is an *inter*action, it requires both speaking and listening. Therefore, the talmudic sage Abba Shaul urged that when you pray, "prepare your heart and let your ears hear" (*Berakhot* 31a). In prayer, we do not merely speak to God—God speaks to us, cries out to us: viewed as prayer, the aggadic outcry to God is his outcry to and *through* the one who cries out. The guiding method here is undertaken with an ear to aggadic outcry, which exceeds the categories of thought.

Once again we recall an insight from Levinas: "Language would exceed the limits of what is thought, by suggesting, letting be understood without ever making understandable, an implication of meaning distinct from that which comes to signs from the simultaneity of systems or the logical definition of concepts. This possibility is laid bare in the poetic said, and the interpretation it calls for ad infinitum. It is shown in the prophetic said."[80] Therefore, Levinas declares, the creation of the poem is "not in order to see ideas, *but in order to prohibit evasion*; the first meaning of that insomnia that is conscience—rectitude of responsibility before any appearance of forms, images, or things."[81] That's it: what we seek to address here is the epiphany that opens up not just the moment but the moment *before* the appearance of the utterance and the image. It is the epiphany of the face that prohibits evasion, laden with ethical implication. There lies the link between a substitution that cannot be evaded and a transcendence that demands response and responsibility.

The prophetic moment of epiphany comes in the revelation of a *kol demamah dakah,* of the "thin voice of silence," revealed to the prophet Elijah (1 Kings 19:12), but with a difference. Fear and darkness are the very stuff of the silence with which the memory of the Holocaust does battle; fear and darkness are the signifiers of the transcendence of representation that belongs to the restoration of the bond between word and meaning. It is the fear of a voicelessness that drains the human being of his soul, since the divine spark that ignites the soul, the "candle of God" (Proverbs 20:17), draws its breath from the word; it is the darkness of an anti-creation pitted against the light created upon the first utterance of Creation. "The silent voice," says the Zohar, "is the supernal voice from which all other voices proceed" (*Zohar* I, 210a), as when the Holy One breathed the Word into the dust to forge a human being. But when the "supernal voice" falls silent in the silence and the hunger that is Auschwitz, the "divine spark," in Levi's words,[82] is extinguished.

And so the human voice of memory must seek its recovery in a testimony to the extinguishing of the divine spark, a recovery that happens—if at all—not in representation but in revelation. This is one implication of André Neher's insight when he writes, "The first step after Auschwitz . . . is the moment of Silence, of that Silence which once, at the beginning of the world, held back the Word while also being its womb."[83] In the literary response to the Holocaust, testimonial memory and memorial testimony become just such a transcendent womb from which the Word struggles to emerge. This moment of transcendence rests upon a movement of substitution, such as the one Wiesel describes when he writes, "Novelists should not speak. Their mission consists in listening to other voices."[84] But, in the approach adopted here, what is required is far more than listening; it is more akin to the *Shema,* to the "hear and heed," of Jewish tradition, the word at the root of *mashmaut,* of "meaning," as we have seen. Such is the mission of the one who would engage these novelists, poets, and playwrights. Trying to understand this literature without the *Shema* of attending to "other voices," both of the dead and of the sacred tradition they represent, is like trying to understand Dante or Milton without the Bible. Images and motifs from the Bible, Midrash, Talmud, Kabbalah, and Aggadah—every text that the Nazis would consign to the flames—hover between the lines and float in the margins of Holocaust literature. The Chasidic master Levi Yitzchak of Berditchev (1740–1809) taught that when God gave Moses the Torah, He gave not only the words but also the silence between and around the margins.[85] And so it is with this new Torah, these new biblical tales: we must attend not only to the words but to the silence between the words and in the margins.

In what follows, therefore, the collision with the literary voice that transcends representation in an act of substitution has little to do with what we might consider the "indescribable." Karla Grierson writes, "To say that an event, experienced or not, is 'indescribable' is to affirm in an indirect voice that its horror has been understood . . . [the word] *indescribable* is already a description, and, as in the case of a discourse on the impotence of a 'literary' language, this discourse on the inability of language is simply the trap of the reflexivity of language, which permits no commentary other than itself."[86] Both "describable" and "indescribable" are not only offensive but ethically errant, inasmuch as both belong to the categories of representation, appropriation, comprehension, and control—all of which evade and avoid the commanded substitution and the transcendent summons of Holocaust literature that guide the method here adopted.

Of the myriad epiphanic moments that pervade the literary response to the Holocaust, we can examine only a few, but enough to make the point. It is an effort not to articulate but to glimpse the impossible that confronted Yehiel De-Nur at the Jerusalem trial of Adolf Eichmann, as one might glimpse a trace the flashes between the words and in the margins of the text: it is an effort to say what Auschwitz is. To say what the Holocaust is. To say how this event not only in history but in an irruption of history confronts the generations and the individuals who follow, not just with an aesthetic anomaly but with an ethical absolute.

The Extermination of the Eternal

> Whoever kills, becomes God. Whoever kills, kills God.
> Each murder is a suicide, with the Eternal eternally the victim.
>
> —Elie Wiesel, *A Beggar in Jerusalem*

In Part One we saw that the Holocaust is fundamentally an assault on God, which is an assault on the Eternal. If, as Levinas says, anti-Semitism is "hatred for the other man,"[87] then the Eternal is indeed eternally the victim, for the hatred that defines anti-Semitism is hatred of the Eternal as manifest in the holiness of the other human being. In the time of the Churban—what made the Holocaust a *Churban*—the Eternal was not only eternally the victim, but it was repeatedly, savagely, and systematically the victim, without precedent. What does it mean to say the Eternal is eternally the victim? First of all, it indicates an ontological assault on the metaphysical, an assault of the *What* on the *Who,* of the representable on the nonrepresentable. The Eternal is not a long, long time. It is time viewed as the presence of God in the realm of space. It is the otherwise than being that sanctifies time; it is the constituent of time as a fundamental relationship with God and with the other human being. "The very movement that leads to another," Levinas argues, "leads to God,"[88] that is, to the Eternal, to the Holy One. And because the holy is revealed in a *relation,* its breach of being is manifest not in the "I" but in the "you," as Levinas maintains.[89] If the Eternal is eternally the victim, the You is eternally the victim.

This is where time enters into a consideration of what it means to say that the Eternal is eternally the victim, a point that bears implications both for the witness and for those of us turned into witnesses, as we encounter these moments of epiphany in Holocaust literary testimony. In time and the Eternal we come up against what it means to say, as Levinas does, that I have one responsibility *more* than the other.[90] Time is made of this "more," of this *od* in Hebrew, because the responsibility to be met for the sake of the other is one responsibility *more,* to be met *once more,* forever yet to be accomplished. Therefore, in our reading of "Holocaust literature" we encounter a trace of "eternity," of what transcends the parameters of representation—a point that becomes clear when we observe that *od* also means "yet" or "still" and that its cognates *ad* and *idan* mean "eternity" and "time" respectively. All of these meanings come together in the literary Holocaust "testimony" or *ed* offered to another for the sake of another. When we declare to another, "Here I am for you," we attest to the dearness of the human that derives from the divine, and thus to the urgency that eternity imparts to time.

The literary response to the Holocaust is about the future as well as the past, and "the other is the future," Levinas states. "It seems to me impossible to speak of time in a subject alone, or to speak of a purely personal duration."[91] Which means: when we step before the face of one who takes up *this* literary response to the Holocaust, we come before the face of Another, the One who spoke at Mount Sinai and remained silent at Auschwitz. And yet the divine *silence* is also a divine revelation that resounds in the epiphanic moment transmitted in the literary testimony. Like the Sabbath that is an insertion of the holy into time, the face—and the coming before the face—is a manifestation of the holy in space. And there is no stepping before this literature without stepping before the human face. "It is in the human face," writes Levinas, "that—beyond the expression of human singularity and perhaps because of that ultimate singularity—*the trace of God is manifested, and the light of revelation inundates the universe.*"[92] It also inundates Holocaust literature in epiphanic moments.

The relation of reader to the epiphanic textual voice, therefore, is always face to face; to betray the relation is to turn our back on the voice that cries out from the words and the silences of these texts, as well as from above. Indeed, here as everywhere, the face speaks, and in its speaking resounds the revealed, absolute prohibition against murder. (I am reminded of something Harry James Cargas once shared with me: in an interview with Arnošt Lustig, the Czech survivor said to him, "I believe I can be a writer only because I have never killed.") Thus, the face summons, and we respond precisely by showing our face. Neither the Voice of Sinai nor the silence of Auschwitz is behind us—both are before us, contemporary with us, resounding from the face of this human being who finds the courage to pen this literature. Only in the response to this summons from the face and by moving toward the face do I take on a face. Time, says Levinas, is precisely this responsibility,[93] which is manifest as a commandment, as a mitzvah.[94] This defining dimension of the Holocaust can be neither described nor demonstrated, neither represented nor replicated—it can only be revealed in a blinding flash that radiates from between the lines, from between the words, and in the margins of a literary response to that assault.

So what is being exterminated in the extermination of the Eternal? In Hebrew, the Divine Name, the Name of the one whom the Nazis set out to murder, articulates the Eternal that encompasses time, inasmuch as the Name of Y-H-V-H contains all the tenses of time: *hoveh, hayah, ehyeh,* "is," "was," and "will be." Assuming this proper Name, the Eternal becomes the Who, which in turn is couched in the Why, and the Why belongs to the hidden. When Levi is told, *Hier ist kein Warum,* he is told "Here there is no Who,"[95] nothing hidden, no time, no tale, no Eternal: just the timelessness of the Lager, which is the opposite of the Eternal. Likewise, where there is no Who, there is no height, no Eternal as the *Gavuhot Shel Olam,* the "Height of the Universe." Where there is no Why, no Who, there is no vertical dimension. The literary response to the Holocaust—by its very existence—struggles to restore that transcendent dimension.

This is where the issue of naming discussed in Part One assumes even greater depth. As the Holy One, God has a name because God is beyond essence and therefore otherwise than representation. His is the Name of the Nameless One because He is more than He is: He is eternally *more* and therefore eternally *more meaningful.* Known as the *Chey HaOlamim* (for example, Daniel 12:7), He is the "Life of the Worlds" or the "Life of the Eternal." The life we hold in our hands and encounter each day is holy because it harbors a trace of the *Chey HaOlamim.* Likewise, another expression denoting God as eternal is *Elokei Kedem,* which means the "Ancient God" or the "Eternal God," eternal because ancient, where ancient refers not merely to a time long ago but to what is eternally *already*, to the immemorial. Thus, Fackenheim invokes the "need for a radical turning—a turning to the ancient God in the very midst of modernity."[96] Because God is eternal, it *already* matters how we speak, act, and treat one another, before any of us enters into a particular situation. And it *already* matters how we respond to the literary response to the Holocaust.

The situation does not determine the good; rather, the good judges the situation from a position that is always *prior* to the situation, always older than any context, eternally *kodem* or "before." This "before" vibrates in the "after" of Holocaust literature wherever a moment of epiphany transcends the representable through a radical diachrony, with the appearance of the immemorial in the midst of memory. With that appearance—or with the trace of that appearance—comes the ethical injunction, not of "Never again" but of "Where is your brother?" and "What have you done?" Thus, after the time of the assault on the eternal in time, we are cast into the diachrony of a time out of joint, where a trace of the Infinite passes by in a moment of epiphany. "The idea of Infinity *is revealed,*" Levinas avers, "in the strong sense of the term."[97] But what is revealed is much more than idea: it is a *Voice*.

"Diachrony," explains Levinas, "is the refusal of conjunction, the non-totalizable, and in this sense, infinite. But in the responsibility for the Other, for another freedom, the negativity of this anarchy, this refusal of the present, of appearing, of the immemorial, adjures me and ordains me to the other, to the first one on the scene, and makes me approach him, makes me his neighbor. It thus diverges from nothingness as well as from being. It provokes this responsibility against my will, that is, by substituting me for the other as a hostage."[98] Once again, we realize that to engage this literature is to be taken hostage by the other in whose voice of remembrance reverberates the Commanding Voice of the immemorial, the Voice that the Nazis set out to silence and that *this* literature sets out to resurrect.

> Admit now, Rabbi of Shilev, God of the Diaspora Himself flounders here in this snarl of bones—a Mussulman!
>
> —Ka-tzetnik 135633, *Star of Ashes*

When the number takes the place of the name, the unit takes the place of the human being. Recall, for example, the moment in Levi's memoir when a Nazi officer wanted to know how many were on the transport to Auschwitz. He did not ask, "How many people?" or even "How many Jews?" but "*Wieviel Stück*—How many pieces or units?"[99] When God is dead, the human being is a unit or a piece, but a piece of what? No more than a piece of bone amid a snarl of bones, so much raw material about to be made into fertilizer or scattered as pavement over a road leading to a camp.[100]

Ka-tzetnik's *Star of Ashes* (*Kokhev Ha-Efer*, 1966) contains very few character names; Auschwitz itself is the main character. What stands out much more than names in this series of vignettes from the anti-world is the silence of which we spoke in Part One. It is this silence that ultimately leads an inmate named Ferber to cry out to a rabbi, "Admit now, Rabbi of Shilev, God of the Diaspora Himself flounders here in this snarl of bones—a

Mussulman!"[101] The silence of God so pronounced in Holocaust literature is not a blank or an absence of noise; no, it is the silence of the snarl of bones called "Muselmann." Neither a blank nor an absence of noise, it has a sound, as we see when the novel's narrator finally emerges from the anti-world: "Back of him lay Auschwitz—mute, petrified. He screamed. Heard a voice. Startled, he looked around. It was his own voice bounding back at him."[102] Simultaneously addressing himself and the reader, he declares, "You are outside. On top of the earth. You weren't buried in the pit,"[103] thus transforming the reader into a voice, as he and we flounder before this snarl of bones in which the Eternal eternally flounders. This is the new Incarnation, the Incarnation that exceeds representation. In the face of the new Incarnation the author/survivor of *Star of Ashes* vows to be a voice "unto the Ka-Tzet now voiceless and consumed."[104] Nothing representable makes the survivor or the reader into such a voice. Once the event is represented, matters are settled: once the event is represented, we have the last word. The nonrepresentable, by contrast, is radically unsettling and inexorably demanding. The nonrepresentable has the last word, but it is a word that can never come, for it surpasses utterance.

And so we understand how to read the question that Ka-tzetnik raises in his novel *Atrocity*, a tale based on what befell his younger brother Moni in the anti-world: "Will this cry reach an ear after we have all passed from the world? A voice cannot be burned. Roots. Mute tree roots on Auschwitz soil. When the time comes will *they* be able to recount one whit of it?"[105] Those roots are nourished by ashes and a snarl of bones. Because a voice cannot be burned, the God who flounders in the snarl of bones now flounders in those ashes that nourish the trees from which we harvest our fruit, a strange fruit indeed, a forbidden fruit from the trees of the collapse of good and evil into a sameness, with the collapse of the Eternal into a snarl of bones. There lies the true evil, the transcendent, nonrepresentable evil that is the Holocaust.

> I grabbed a handful of rocks and began to throw them at the sky. And at a certain moment the sky *shattered*. You understand? . . . Then I said to myself, "Yankel, if God is in little pieces, what can it mean to be a Jew?" . . . But then, as closely as I could look I couldn't see anything but blood, and more blood, and blood again. But meaning?—none.
>
> —André Schwarz-Bart, *The Last of the Just*

The God who flounders in a snarl of bones is a God shattered into little pieces—this time shattered by a sole survivor named Yankel, who relates his account to Benjamin Levy. Benjamin is the father of Ernie Levy, the title character in André Schwarz-Bart's *The Last of the Just*; it is the story of the last in a line of Just Men who met his end when he joined a transport of children to Auschwitz. Although Yankel is the survivor of a pogrom in Poland, and not a ghetto *Aktion,* his tale is to be read through the lens of the Holocaust, appearing as it does in a Holocaust novel. It is a way of viewing the Shoah through a kind of filter, such as one might use when gazing at the sun. The sky shattered when it was transformed into a cemetery, when it was no longer above the earth. This catastrophic shattering of the Eternal is not to be viewed as a "normal" reaction to a traumatizing event. More than "How could God let His people be annihilated?" the question is "How could God allow Himself to be obliterated?" Here, God is the one who is traumatized.

Is there any way to "picture" the shattering of the sky? Is there any way of understanding it? Or is this where we must lower our eyes and refuse to understand? What are the pieces of a shattered sky made of? Perhaps they are made of a snarl of shattered bones. Yet even when the Eternal flounders within a snarl of bones, there abides an *above* in this *within.* Still more profoundly, this *above* of a shattered sky defines the *between* of the shattered space and time between author and reader. Explaining how this *within* and *above,* this *above* and *between,* are interrelated, Levinas writes, "Height is heaven. The kingdom of heaven is ethical. This hyperbole, this excellence, is but the for-the-other in its disinterestedness. . . . Here the human is brought out by transcendence, or the hyperbole, that is, the disinterestedness of essence, a hyperbole in which it breaks up *and falls upward,* into the human,"[106] just like the title character in Wiesel's play *Zalman, or The Madness of God,* the Russian Jew who, in a swoon before his congregation, fell upward.[107] Like the fall upward, the shattering of the sky is the shattering of the dimension of height; it is a shattering of the ethical, which is a matter of the human-to-God and the human-to-human relation, *ben adam l'Makom* and *ben adam l'chevero,* as expressed in Hebrew.

If God is in little pieces, if He flounders in the midst of a snarl of bones, then what can it mean now to be a Jew? It is a question that studies of Holocaust representation seldom, if ever, address. And it is the most decisive question for anyone engaging the question of Holocaust representation. The Holocaust is, after all, the Juden*vernichtung,* the annihilation of the *Jews.*

If the God of Abraham, the God of the Diaspora, flounders to the point of being shattered, what can it mean to be a Jew? Does not this Jewish Question resound in the question that rises up from the burning anguish of Yehiel De-Nur when he cries out, "God, who created Auschwitz?"[108] The outcry ascends not only from within one of his novels but also from within his first "memoir," if that term applies to *Shivitti*, from the memory of a journey into the collisions and visions of the anti-world as he both knew it and was terrified to know it.

What can it mean to be a Jew, when the definitive Nazi project was the extermination of the Jews and all that Judaism has taught? Indeed, what can it mean to be a human being? The obliteration of God is interwoven with the obliteration of humanity, on physical and metaphysical levels. Where there is only blood and more blood and more blood again, only *dam*, there is no *adam*, no human being and therefore no witness to the holiness of the human being: no Eternal One. As a beggar expresses it to Doriel in Wiesel's *A Mad Desire to Dance*, "God isn't God, for man is no longer human."[109] Note well: *the divinity of God lies in the humanity of man*. Hence, says Simon Wiesenthal (1908–2005), "It is impossible to believe anything in a world that has ceased to regard man as man. One really begins to think that God is on leave. Otherwise the present state of things wouldn't be possible. God must be away. And He has no deputy."[110] He has no deputy because He has no Jew. He has no *Stellvertreter* in the original,[111] which means no "representative," no one to *represent* this absence, this collapse, this shattering, this curse, this cessation of any regard for the human being as a human being, this end of the Jews that the *Stellvertreter* now struggles to recover in the literary transcendence of the representation of the nonrepresentable loss that is the Holocaust.

One of the dangers of Holocaust representation lies in the resolution or in the omission of what it means to be a Jew. If it means nothing to be a Jew, then the absent God has no deputy and therefore remains absent. If the voice that emerges from the depths of the Holocaust speaks for those who cannot speak, it speaks as much for the absent God as it does for the absent human beings who have been robbed of their very graves. There lies the task of representing the nonrepresentable. Inasmuch as the Judaism that defines a Jew rests upon the nonrepresentable—upon the Name that surpasses utterance and exceeds all ontological categories—the project of representation when applied to the Holocaust runs the risk of de-Judaizing it. If there is no God, there is no Jew. And if there is no Jew, there is no human being.

> God of Auschwitz, know that I must remember Auschwitz. And that I must remind You of it. God of Treblinka, let the sound of that name make me, and You, tremble now and always. God of Belzec, let me, and You, weep. . . . Remember that only memory leads man back to the source of his longing for You. Remember, God of history, that You created man to remember. . . . Even if you forget me, O Lord, I refuse to forget You.
>
> —Elie Wiesel, *The Forgotten*

This is Holocaust survivor Elhanan Rosenbaum's prayer to a forgetful God, from the opening pages of Elie Wiesel's novel *The Forgotten*. Dr. Rosenbaum is a distinguished psychiatrist who has become a victim of Alzheimer's Disease: he is losing the only thing left to him as a human being, his memory, the very thing that the Nazis set out to obliterate, the very thing that Holocaust literature sets out to restore. So how do you represent the loss of memory in an act of remembrance? What does it mean to represent the loss of memory that ensues upon the war against memory, which is a war against the soul of the human being? Like the novelist transmitting the memory to his reader, Elhanan transmits his fading memory to his son Malkiel. Subsequently, Malkiel returns to the Carpathian Mountains, where the horrors that haunt his father took place. There he encounters a gravedigger, a kind of Melkhitzedek or Elijah figure, who tells him a tale of slaughter. Telling the tale, he binds one generation to another, as well as each generation to God, within a novel immersed in all the trappings of prayer.

"The shout becomes a prayer in spite of me," says Michael in *The Town beyond the Wall*.[112] Like *The Town beyond the Wall*, which is divided into prayers, this novel begins with a prayer; like all of Holocaust literature, it assumes the aspect of a prayer. And prayer is epiphany. Far from being a mere act of supplication, prayer in the Jewish tradition is transcendence. It is as much about listening as it is about speaking. "Men believe they pray before God," a tzaddik once said, "but this is not so, for the prayer itself is divinity."[113] Said the Koretzer Rebbe, a disciple of the Baal Shem, "God and Prayer are One."[114] The prayer takes hold of the one who prays and sets a task before him: to pray is to be commanded to act. In this case, the one in prayer is commanded to refuse to forget not only what took place but also the Eternal You subjected to systematic extermination: I refuse to forget You, which means: I refuse to forget *the You* subject to a radical assault. For "in every You," as Martin Buber has said, "we address the eternal

You."[115] The trace of the divine in the other human being is the You in the other human being. In the case of the remembrance that defines Holocaust literature—which above all defines *The Forgotten*—the other human being is one among millions subjected to a death that transcends even murder and that therefore transcends representation.

For the Jew who would address the question of what it means to be a Jew, there is no remembrance of the Shoah without a remembrance of the *mitzvah.* For according to Jewish thought, the response to prayer is not God's reply to a request but our engagement in action. For the author, as for the reader, the *mitzvah* lies in bearing witness. This is what Heschel means when he describes a *mitzvah* as "a prayer in the form of a deed."[116] Wherever we find a literary transcendence of representation as in *The Forgotten,* we find a *mitzvah,* a prayer in the form of a deed. Wherein lies the transcendence? It lies in the *tzavta* of the *mitzvah,* in the "connection" that binds the *above* to the *between,* even—or especially—when the prayer is voiced in an act of defiance. This is what it means to open a novel with a prayer, which belongs to the nonrepresentable.

And so, as in his novels, Wiesel prays the epiphany in *Ani Maamin: A Song Lost and Found Again*, beginning with the outcry:

> Ani maamin, ani maamin.
> For you, O Lord.
> With you.
> In you.
> Against you.[117]

And ending with the outcry:

> Whether God is silent
> Or weeps,
> Ani maamin.
> Ani maamin for him,
> In spite of him.
> I believe in you,
> Even against your will.[118]

In these words we hear Elhanan's refusal. This is the song lost to the ashes but found again in the defiant memory of God. It is a memory steeped in a defiant clinging to the Jewish tradition that came under assault. It is a tradition that teaches that God likes to be overcome by His children (*Talmud Bavli, Bava Metzia* 59b), particularly in the light of what befalls His children—even in their refusal to believe.

The Annihilation of the Father

> No prayers were said over his tomb. No candle lit in his memory. His last word had been my name. He had called out to me, and I did not answer.
>
> —Elie Wiesel, *Night*

> Father, save me!
>
> —Isaac Bashevis Singer, *Shosha*

In *Legends of Our Time*, Elie Wiesel writes, "In dying, my father looked at me, and in his eyes where night was gathering, there was nothing but animal terror, the demented terror of one who, because he wished to understand too much, no longer understands anything. His gaze fixed on me, empty of meaning."[119] And so the look of the father fixes upon the reader of Holocaust literature, empty of meaning. In that look there is epiphany: the meaning of this literature is meaninglessness. For the father is the ground of meaning. The father assures a future, a memory and a name, no longer assured. There is no representing this moment. Gazing long into those eyes where night was gathering, we gaze into an abyss that gazes back at us.

In the father we have the truth that provides a ground for life, the wisdom that underlies all thinking about life, and the order that constitutes the reality and substance of life. When the father's existence is rendered illegitimate, truth, thought, and reality come under attack. In Jewish terms, these are the truths of tradition as an avenue of revelation. All of this is lost in the loss of the father, so that the memory of the murder of the father entails far more than a mournful reminiscence surrounding the head of a household. The father confers a name upon the child, as the author confers a name upon the character. Yet the creative process reverses itself, so that the one whom the father names seeks salvation in the name of the father. "It was my father who saved me," says a patient in Wiesel's *Twilight*. "His face appeared before me. . . . I was sure that *he* had not forgotten his name. His name, his name: if only I could remember it, I would be saved."[120]

Holocaust literature is about remembering the name of the father. As "the whole Torah is an enfolding of the Divine Name, the most exalted Name, the Name that comprehends all other names" (*Zohar* II, 124a), so is all of Holocaust literature about remembering the name of the father, which is the name of the Torah. For the assault on the father is an assault on the Name.

Each night before going to bed, Gamaliel, the surviving character in Wiesel's novel *The Time of the Uprooted*, would repeat his name, his father's name, and his mother's name.[121] Noting that, like Gamaliel, almost all of the survivors of the Shoah were *orphans*, we catch a glimpse of the horror not only of the systematic murder of the Jewish father but of the imposed *abandonment* of the Jewish father. Livia Jackson, for example, cries out, "Oh, Daddy! . . . How could you leave me?"[122] Eugene Heimler pleads, "Father, my father . . . do not forsake me."[123] In both instances it is as if the father himself had chosen to abandon the child. This *as if* is carefully engineered. No *father* would ever abandon his children. Yet the Nazis' undoing of the ontological image of the father is calculated to impose a sense of this abandonment in the imposition of a radical Absence.

Absence of what? Absence not only of the source of truth, thought, and word, but also absence of memory. The attack on the father is, in fact, an attack on memory itself, and the memory at work in Holocaust literature arises as a remnant of the father and all he signifies. Memory belongs to the father, who is responsible for handing down the tradition. Thus, Filip Müller begins his *Auschwitz Inferno* with the murder of a father. The memoir opens by relating an account of how the block clerk Vacek was the first to be singled out for death one Sunday in May 1942. He "was a father of four," notes Müller. "Before he became an inmate of Auschwitz he had scraped a living by reciting the Kaddish, the prayer for the dead, in the synagogue of his native town."[124] The saying of the Kaddish is itself an act of remembrance and the recovery of a nonrepresentable trace, an affirmation of the sanctity of life and of the Creator of life. The memory of the murder of the father is a refusal of that murder and an affirmation of the nonrepresentable, of all that is murdered in the slaying of the father—not a denial, be it noted, but a refusal. Just so, Fania Fénelon recovers the name of her late father upon her deportation to Auschwitz: "If I was going to die, I preferred to die under my father's name, Goldstein."[125] To retain the name of the father is to retain the truth, the wisdom, and the word signified by that name.

The memory of the loss of the father often begins with a memory of the crumbling of his image. Recall, for example, Gerda Klein's (b. 1924) description of her father's reaction when her brother Arthur was forced to leave their home: "Now he was as helpless as I. . . . I embraced Papa. The touch of my arms made him shiver, and a suppressed and terrible sobbing cry rose from his throat, a cry which I will never forget, which had no resemblance to the human voice; it sounded rather like the cry of an animal when it has been stabbed and is dying."[126] That cry comes from . . . *elsewhere.* One cannot help but the note the reversal of roles in this account: the child becomes the comforter of the father. In the ontological assault on Jewish being it is not enough simply to murder the father. The killing of his body must be preceded by the annihilation of his image, for in his image lies the Jewish being that the father symbolizes.

> They were waiting for the command to set out. And the rain kept falling—it didn't stop for one minute that night, a night that those who survived will remember as the Night of the Old Men. Because those who stood in those groups of four were old.
>
> —Ida Fink, "*****"

The Night of the Old Men is the night of the onset of the Kingdom of Night, the night of the annihilation of the father, of memory, truth, thought, and world. How, then, are we to understand the title of Ida Fink's (1921–2011) short story, "*****," a tale that opens with the annihilation of the father? What does this title tell us about the Night of the Old Men, the night of the extermination of the old men, of the memory harbored by the old men, of their teaching and their testimony, as old men? "*****" signifies the non-signifiable, the nonrepresentable. Hence, the five asterisks refer the reader to something elsewhere—that is the function of the asterisk, of the six-pointed star, here suggesting five Jewish stars of ashes that refer to an elsewhere nowhere to be found.

Could the five stars perhaps conjure up the annihilation of the five levels of the soul that issue from the Father (see *Zohar* II, 94b)? The five levels of the soul are *nefesh,* the physical aspect of the soul shoved into the gas chambers; *ruach,* the emotional aspect of the soul subjected to the devastation of all emotions; *neshamah,* the intellect and understanding that collides with all that surpasses understanding; *chayah,* the life of soul snuffed out wherever Jews were forbidden to pray or to observe the Sabbath; and *yechidah,* the point of contact between the soul and God, annihilated in the annihilation of the Eternal. Then there are the five worlds of creation as taught in the Jewish tradition and transmitted through the memory of old men: *Olam Asiyah,* the World of Action, where good and evil are concretely determined; *Olam Yetzirah,* the World of Formation, where the longing for good over evil is decided; *Olam Beriah,* the World of Creation, where it is determined that the work of creation is "very good"; *Olam Atzilut,* the World of Emanation, where the nonrepresentable revelation of the Good and of the assault on the Good comes to bear; and then the *Adam Kadmon,* from which the immemorial image and likeness of the human being emanates, the emanation that the Nazis set out to extinguish.[127]

In Hebrew an "old man" is a *zaken*; *zakan,* the word for "beard," is a cognate. The word summons veneration for the wisdom associated with a gray beard. Hence, the Torah teaches that we must rise in the presence of our elders (Leviticus 19:32). And in the Midrash it is written, "Like a diadem which belongs to the head of the king, so are the gray hairs beauty and glory to old men" (*Pirke de Rabbi Eliezer* 52). Three times a day we say a special blessing "on the elders of Your people of the House of Israel," *al zikenei amkha beit Yisrael.* As the vessels of wisdom, they are the vessels of teaching and tradition, of history and memory. Even when they have lost their memory, says the Talmud, we must revere them, for the broken tablets, too, were placed inside the Holy Ark (*Berakhot* 8b). Describing an *Aktion* in the Lvov Ghetto, Rabbi David Kahane writes, "First they seized old men with beards and sidelocks. Not even a work card could save a bearded Jew."[128] The Talmud transmitted by Jewish elders teaches that the beard is the glory of the face (*hadrat panim*) (*Shabbat* 152a). If it is the *glory* of the face, then it makes the face into a sign of the Infinite One, who sanctifies the life of the human being. Just as that sanctification transcends representation, so does its annihilation exceed any representation of the Night of the Old Men. Perhaps that is the reason for the title "*****."

What Levinas says about glory eluding all representation applies to this epiphanic moment in Fink's "*****," a moment that "breaks up themes," emerging "from a past that has never been represented": "This glory [of the face] could not appear, for appearing and presence would belie it by circumscribing it as a theme, by assigning it a beginning in the present of representation, whereas, as infinition of infinity, it comes from a past more distant than that which is within the reach of memory. . . . It comes from a past that has never been represented, has never been present. . . . Glory . . . breaks up themes."[129] Instead of themes, in the literary transcendence of Holocaust representation we have traces. The very phrase *the Night of the Old Men* is just such a trace, the trace of the archetypical Father come under a radical assault: like the glory of the Infinite, the assault on the glory is nonrepresentable. Encountering such a phrase in a post-Holocaust context, the reader reads as an orphan, as one bereft of the father and of the limit that the father signifies. So how do you represent the orphaned reader?

> There is no limit to what's "worse." The limit was in his father.
>
> —Arnošt Lustig, "The Lemon," in *Diamonds of the Night*

These lines are from Arnošt Lustig's tale of a boy named Ervin, who was left to fend for himself in the ghetto after his father's death. If there is an afterlife, Ervin reflects, then his "*father must be able to see him. Where do you suppose he really is,* Ervin wondered, *and where am I*?"[130] The two questions are of a piece. The longing for the father is a longing for a sign of who I am, which lies in the ethical limit revealed through the father, the sign of the covenantal law that establishes the presence of the father and the identity of the son. Ervin seeks the sign of a limiting principle, which is the principle of an infinite responsibility that devolves upon the son. The infinite responsibility to and for the other human being is revealed in the limiting of the self's capacity to usurp the place of the other. Ultimately, Levinas states, "the important question of the meaning of being is not: why is there something rather than nothing . . . but: do I not kill by being?"[131] In Judaism, too, this is the question, as we see from the teaching that, even if it means our own death, we must refuse to murder the other person (*Talmud Bavli*, *Sanhedrin* 74a). The glory of the Infinite is manifest precisely in such a *tzimtzum,* to use the Hebrew term, in a "withdrawal," or what Levinas calls "an exasperated contracting,"[132] of the self for the sake of the other. This contracting is the limit that is revealed through the father.

As the figure of the law, the father is the figure of the limit, the one who establishes the difference between good and evil, holy and profane, life and death. When the father is obliterated, the human being is turned over to the limitless, where the only limit is the will to power and the power of the imagination. That is where violence becomes murderous. "Violence," says Levinas, "does not aim simply at disposing of the other as one disposes of a thing, but, already at the limit of murder, it proceeds from unlimited negation. . . . Violence can aim only at a face."[133] So we come to the realization that in the revelation of the limit signified by the father lies the epiphany of the face.

The epiphany here is that what the Nazis did was not unimaginable—it was everything imaginable. "Everything is normal here," writes Ka-tzetnik in *House of Dolls*. "The wildest absurdity—the soberest reality. Anything goes here, anything is possible, the way anything goes and is possible in insanity. Death and life dwell together here. Blood and wine are drunk from the same flask. The Carrion Shed and the SS rooms are one. Borders erased. Boundaries lost."[134] In the time of the Holocaust there was for the Nazis no "going too far." If Améry asserted that "torture was not an accidental quality of this Third Reich, but its essence,"[135] and Fackenheim argued that "the murder camp was not an accidental by-product of the Nazi empire" but "was its pure essence,"[136] it is because every limiting principle was obliterated in the annihilation of the father.

Ervin seeks a sign amid the Nazis' slaughter of signs. He seeks the father, to whom he may answer, "*Hineni*—Here I am *for you!*" This is the word of the father that lives only in response to the limiting principle of the covenantal law and the outcry of the father. For Ervin the only hope of finding what it means to be a Jew is to answer, "Here I am," to the father and the limiting principle that the father represents. The summons to answer, "Here I am," devolves not only upon the orphan left to the ghetto but also upon those who come after, of whom the father asks, "What have you made of me?"

> I ask him where he is going, and he does not answer; I ask him whence he comes, he does not answer. . . . [He asks], "What have you made of me?" And my collection of poems is my answer.
>
> —Elie Wiesel, *The Testament*

In Elie Wiesel's novel *The Testament* the main character Paltiel Kossover relates "a lyrical, mystical vision" in which he sees his father leading a funeral procession. Significantly, in the French text the father's question, "What have you made of me?" is preceded by the phrase *il me fait signe et me demande*, that is, "he makes a sign unto me and demands of me."[137] The father is the giver of signs and demands the return of a sign from the son. Just so, the witness who emerges from the mass grave of Europe, like Moishe the Beadle, makes a sign unto us and demands something of us. The literary response to the Holocaust, therefore, is just such a sign: to write a Holocaust novel is to respond to the summons from the other side of a mountain of ashes, as it comes from one who asks, "What have you made of me?" Those of us who encounter such a response are in turn summoned to answer the question that the witness puts to us: "What have you made of me?" How, then, shall we answer? By indulging in ruminations on Holocaust representation?

As a medic during World War II, Paltiel "felt lost. Abandoned. . . . I was climbing a mountain of ashes. On the other side an old man was waiting. And he was saying, 'Come, my son, come.' "[138] Just as the father calls forth his son, so the father calls forth the novelist and the poet, the dramatist and the memoirist. When we consider the suicides among the authors of Holocaust literature—for example, Tadeusz Borowski, Piotr Rawicz, Paul Celan, Jean Améry, Jerzy Kozinski, Primo Levi—we realize the life-and-death stake in the response to the call of the father. If the messenger transforms us into a witness—if the testimony comes with an ethical demand—are we not also turned over to a life-and-death situation, returned to Albert Camus's famous assertion that "there is but one truly serious philosophical problem, and that is suicide"?[139]

And yet, being transformed into a witness is precisely what saves us, as Wiesel understood. In his novel *The Oath*, an old man saves a young man bent on suicide by relating to him a tale and thus turning him into a messenger: "I'll transmit my experience to him and he, in turn, will be compelled to do the same. He in turn will become a messenger. And once a messenger, he has no alternative. He must stay alive until he has transmitted his message."[140] Entrusted with a testimony to the sanctity of human life, we lose the luxury of suicide. Wherever a *for the sake of* arises, life is instilled with a future and therefore with the meaning that lies in the transcendent, in the invisible, and in the dimension of height. The voice that calls forth Paltiel's poetry appears as a beckoning sign. It "signifies an order," as Levinas states. "It orders me . . . as when one says: 'Someone's asking for you.' "[141] Asking for me, the father asks for the fullness of my word. This is where "substitution," as Levinas says, is a "giving of signs, giving a sign of this giving of signs."[142] This is where poetry happens.

The Obliteration of the Mother

Mama!

—Isaballa Leitner, *Fragments of Isabella*
—Ka-tzetnik 135633, *Shivitti: A Vision*
—Sara Nomberg-Przytyk, *Auschwitz: True Tales from a Grotesque Land*
—Donna Rubinstein, *I Am the Only Survivor of Krasnostav*
—Peretz Opoczynski, "Warsaw Ghetto Chronicle—September 1942"
—Livia E. Bitton Jackson, *Elli: Coming of Age in the Holocaust*
—Josef Katz, *One Who Came Back: The Diary of a Jewish Survivor*
—Anna Langfus, *The Whole Land Brimstone*
—Olga Lengyel, Five Chimneys

In Part One, we explored the obliteration of the mother as a distinguishing feature of the Holocaust, already drawing upon moments of epiphany from the writings of authors such as Ka-tzetnik, Charlotte Delbo, Sara Zyskind, Ana Vinocur, and others. We also explained the millennial Jewish teaching on women, the mothers and the daughters of Israel, which should be kept in mind in what follows. The Jewish teaching on the House of Jacob profoundly informs all that must be said about the Nazis' systematic targeting of Jewish mothers, as well as all that is absent from many studies of Holocaust representation.

Near the end of her novel *The Whole Land Brimstone*, Anna Langfus's (1920–1966) first-person narrator encounters a little girl in the streets of her Polish hometown immediately after the war. The child is crying, "Mama, mama, mama!" and yet, "for some reason I started running so as not to hear her."[143] To be sure, anyone who takes up an inquiry into these matters is tempted to run and hide, as Adam hid. The epiphanic Voice reverberates in the primordial plea for the murdered Jewish mother: from the depths of the cry of "Mama!" the Ultimate seizes anyone who undergoes the collisions with these texts. The cry of "Mama!" is the cry of one who longs for the transcendent maternal love and who is slipping into the abyss of meaninglessness. In the end, we seek not the firm ground but loving kindness, without which there is no meaning. The Nazis' obliteration of the Jewish mother was central to a systematic obliteration of ***kindness.***

In the diary that he kept during the war years in Germany Victor Klemperer (1881–1960) notes on 11 December 1943 the Gestapo's practice of disguising themselves as Jews and then arresting anyone who showed them any kindness.[144] They prohibited all non-Jews in the vicinity of the ghettos and camps from showing any kindness toward the Jews. In the words of Primo Levi, this was all part of the Nazis' creation of realms in which "everything is hostile,"[145] from the hiding place, to the ghetto, to the camp. *Everything* was hostile, and every Jew was homeless—there you have the anti-world. In that realm there is no kindness, no caress. Like the act of loving kindness performed "for nothing," the caress, says Levinas, "consists in seizing upon nothing, in soliciting what ceaselessly escapes its form toward a future never future enough, in soliciting what slips away as though *it were not yet*. It *searches*."[146]

The two words at the very center of the Torah are *darosh darash* (Leviticus 10:16), which translates as "search diligently" but which literally means "search and search again." Thus, the Torah ends its first half with searching and begins again with searching: the Torah, like the mother's caress, is about searching. Hence, it is through women, through the House of Jacob, that Israel receives the Torah. Torah, the manifestation of the love of the Supernal Mother, is revealed in the caress. The cry of "Mama!" is a cry for the caress, for the truth of the divine love that commands loving kindness, a seeking after what eternally slips away, an eternal search for the eternally *hidden* signified by woman. Thus, says the Midrash, woman is created from the side of man because, even when he stands naked, his side is hidden (*Bereshit Rabbah* 80:5). And it is woman—the mother—who manifests the hidden *as hidden*. There, too, lies the literary task: to "represent" the hidden as hidden. Approaching the one who cries out for her mother in the aftermath of the obliteration of the mother, we discover the meaning of the approach, of the caress, and with it a variation on the meaning of the glory of the infinite couched in the cry of "Mama!"

> Mother was stroking my sister's hair, as if to protect her.
>
> —Elie Wiesel, *Night*

Here we realize something more about the caress obliterated in the obliteration of the mother. The caress of the mother says, "It's all right. I'm right here," reassuring her child in the dead of night, as the little one cries out, "Mama!" from an all-too-real nightmare. But this is no nightmare. The mother trapped in the gullet of *this* night is not stroking her daughter's hair, not in her little girl's bedroom but in the midst of the nonrepresentable wasteland known as Birkenau. This caress happens by the light of the flames consuming the body of Israel, calculated to consume both mother and daughter, the mother stroking the hair about to be harvested as raw material for textiles and insulation. We understand more profoundly Charlotte Delbo's realization that "here mothers are no longer mothers to their children."[147] Mothers have been obliterated before they have been gassed and burned, before their ashes rained down on those condemned to survive in the abyss of Auschwitz. "The scent was the smell of burning flesh," Isabella Leitner's words haunt us. "The burning flesh was your mother."[148] This single epiphanic moment announces the folly of reflection on the representation of trauma, of "working through," of the empathetic knowing of what it was like, of the purely academic inquiry.

The one who witnesses this moment of the last caress is drawn into the condition of a child who has been warned, like Eliezer, not to be a child. Immediately after seeing his mother's caress of his sister, a prisoner unloading the transport asks Eliezer, "How old are you?" He says, "Fifteen." The answer: "No. You're eighteen." When Eliezer replies, "But I'm not," the rejoinder of the one trying to save his life is: "Fool. Listen to what I say."[149] Fool, you are not a child. Fool, you have no mother. Here, mothers are no longer mothers to their children, and *children are no longer children to their mothers*. A cry went up from Auschwitz. It was the children weeping for their mothers. And they would not be comforted. For their mothers were not mothers. Thus, they were not.

> A young girl whose mother was assigned to the gas did not want to be separated from her. She wanted to die with her mother. They tore her from her mother by force.
>
> —Sara Nomberg-Przytyk, *Auschwitz: True Tales from a Grotesque Land*

They tear the mother from herself by force, assaulting the caress and the meaning of the mother, in a tearing of meaning from the very word *mother*. Here, the child is no longer a child to her mother, precisely because the mother is no longer a mother to her child; the only way she can remain a child to her mother is to be murdered with her mother. In order for mother and child to *be* who they are, they must *not be*. Hence the anti-world that calls forth the literary transcendence of representation.

Slated for obliteration, mother and child heed the summons to a love that transcends the boundaries of time and death: if they die together in the gas chambers, they die as mother and daughter in a realm where there is no living as mother and daughter. What, then, can the relation between mother and daughter mean? Here, the obliteration of the mother takes the form of an assault on the love for the mother, even unto death: You love your mother? Then be murdered with her. Neither the narratives of history nor the representations of literature, neither systems of signs nor theories of trauma, can convey this overturning of creation that defines the Holocaust. Not only are the mother and child consigned to death, but the love between them is also subject to annihilation through the elimination of the embrace that arises *between* them: to obliterate the mother is to obliterate this *between* space. The Holocaust *is* the obliteration of this between space; it exceeds the "history of the Holocaust." It can be conveyed only in the epiphanic flash that penetrates the literary testimony.

"She wanted to die *with* her mother": the obliteration of the mother is the obliteration of the proximity indicated by this *with*. This space signified by the mother is the space of a proximity that can never be close enough, even unto death, the space of "maternity, vulnerability, responsibility, proximity, contact," to borrow again from Levinas.[150] This proximity between mother and child is the proximity Levinas explains when he writes, "Proximity is . . . a restlessness. . . . Never close enough, proximity does not congeal into a structure. . . . It attains its *superlative* as *my* incessant restlessness . . . forgets reciprocity, as in a love that does not expect to be shared."[151] The maternal is this restlessness, this proximity, manifested not through epistemological deduction but through a moment of epiphany. Says Levinas, "The 'never enough' of proximity, the restlessness of this peace, is the acute uniqueness of subjectivity."[152] Seeking to die with her mother, she seeks a certain peace, a *shalom,* that is a wholeness or *shelem* of subjectivity and therefore of identity. If she can die with her mother, not only will the mother remain a mother, but her death will remain a death.

> For this Aurelia, Barbara felt ready to do everything. The idea of sacrifice took possession of her; never imagined clearly yet ever present, it lent her days the sense of ascent toward a towering peak. Upon this peak a transformation would occur. She, her whole being, would be suspended, someone else would take her place for that instant, and at

> once she would be brought back to kneel at Aurelia's side, to whisper, "I for you—everything."
>
> —Ilona Karmel, *An Estate of Memory*

Ilona Karmel's novel *An Estate of Memory* revolves around a group of women in a concentration camp. Barbara is the "camp daughter" to Aurelia, whom she regards as a mother. To have a mother or a father or a child is to have someone for whom we would joyfully offer up all for the sake of the other, for the sake of the very offering, and thus open up a dimension of height, the dimension of the sanctity of the other human being—everything *for nothing.* Even in the "normal" world this offering constitutes a breach of being. In the anti-world, where everyone is either an enemy or a rival, as Primo Levi says,[153] it is inexplicable. The "everything for nothing" situates this moment of epiphany from Karmel's novel in the realm of the nonrepresentable, in the realm of what Levinas calls a "pre-original language": "Does not disinterestedness, without compensation, without eternal life, without the pleasingness of happiness, complete gratuity, indicate an extreme gravity and not the fallacious frivolity of play? . . . Does not this gravity, where being's *esse* is inverted, refer to this pre-original language, the responsibility of one for the other, the substitution of one for the other, and the condition (or the uncondition) of being hostage which thus takes form?"[154] The inversion of the *esse* is an inversion of self-interest, of the *conatus essendi* or persistence in one's own being; it is the pre-original condition for the ethical in human relation. It is therefore anarchic, in Levinas's sense of the word, beyond essence, and prior to any talk of Holocaust or Holocaust representation.

Barbara's ascent to "a towering peak" is the transformation of the human being into who she is *in truth,* who seeks her humanity despite an anti-world in which everything conspires to undermine that humanity. In so doing, she lends flesh and blood reality to Levinas's philosophical insight: "The subjectivity of subjection of the self is the suffering of suffering, the ultimate offering oneself. . . . An exposure to the other, it is signification, is signification itself, the-one-for-the-other to the point of substitution."[155] How is it that in her transformation "someone else would take her place"? Here, too, Levinas sheds light: "Signification is the-one-for-the-other which characterizes an identity that does not coincide with itself. This is in fact all the gravity of an animate body, that is, one offered to another, expressed or opened up!"[156] In Barbara's "I for you—everything," therefore, we touch upon an Ultimate: it is the transformation of meaninglessness into meaning, through the ultimate act of signification, in a saying of "Here I am for you, I for you—everything." Levinas elaborates further with regard to why such a movement belongs to the otherwise than being and therefore to the otherwise than representation: "Subjectivity of flesh and blood in matter—the signifyingness of sensibility, the-one-for-the-other itself—is the preoriginal signifyingness that gives sense, because it gives. Not because, as preoriginal, it would be more originary than the origin, but because the diachrony of sensibility, which cannot be assembled in a representational present, refers to an irrecuperable pre-ontological past, that of *maternity*."[157] As pre-ontological, maternity is otherwise than representation, which is necessarily ontological: maternity belongs to the immemorial. Ascending "toward a towering peak," Barbara ascends toward the maternal, not for comfort but for meaning.

And so we understand on yet another level why these lines from Karmel's novel constitute a moment of epiphany and thus take us beyond representation to a "pre-original" relation, to an immemorial, that provides the foundation for an estate of memory. Memory of what? Of the one-for-the-other that makes everything *matter*. And where is the "preoriginal signifyingness" situated (or unsituated)? Not in systems of signs or theories of representation, not in "traumatic realism" or "empathetic unsettlement," but in maternity. "In maternity what signifies is a responsibility for others, to the point of substitution for others and suffering both from the effect of persecution and from the persecuting itself."[158] Consequently, Levinas explains further, meaning happens "in nourishing, clothing, lodging, in maternal relations"—everything of which the denizens of the anti-world were systematically deprived. "It is because subjectivity is sensibility—an exposure to others, a vulnerability and a responsibility in the proximity of the others, the-one-for-the-other, that is, signification—and because matter is the very locus of the for-the-other, the way that signification signifies *before* showing itself as a said in the system of synchronism, the linguistic system, that a subject is of flesh and blood, a man that is hungry and eats, entrails in a skin, and thus capable of giving the bread out of his mouth, or giving his skin."[159] Taken in the context of the concentration camp, these words bear staggering implications. "The Lager *is* hunger," declares Levi. "We ourselves are hunger, living hunger."[160] In that realm, the "idea of sacrifice" is as intangible as the skin; it lies in the movement of ascent that characterizes snatching the bread from one's own mouth and offering it to another, a movement that in the concentrationary universe might indeed amount to dying for another.

Barbara's "I for you—everything," then, concretely has meaning "as a 'taking care of the other's need . . . as a giving. But giving has meaning only as a tearing from oneself despite oneself. . . . And to be torn from oneself despite oneself has meaning only as . . . snatching the bread from one's mouth. Only a subject that eats can be for-the-other, or can signify. Signification, the-one-for-the-other, has meaning only among beings of flesh and blood."[161] The idea of sacrifice that takes possession of Barbara is the idea of a *Kiddush HaShem*, a "Sanctification of the Name"—in this case, the name of the mother, in a realm where mothers did not die. No, they were murdered.

> Oh, Mommy! Oh, God, they are killing my mother!
>
> —Livia E. Bitton Jackson, *Elli: Coming of Age in the Holocaust*

To whom is this cry of horror addressed? Does she scream "Mommy!" to the obliterated mother? And to whom does she scream, "Oh, God, they are killing my mother!"? Perhaps in the "Oh, God" she screams a prayer that transcends all prayer to the *Avi Yetomim*, the "Father of Orphans" (as in Psalms 68:6, for example). If so, this casts the outcry of this literary response to the Holocaust in the mode of prayer, which is a transcendence of anything that can be represented. "Oh, Mommy! Oh, God!" suggests a confluence of the two: Here, the outcry to God and to anyone who comes across the outcry is, to use Levinas's terms, an "excession of transcendence, of the beyond,"[162] even beyond "Holocaust": *excession, the epiphany of the Ultimate.* That is why it must be asked: If she cries out to God, does she not cry out to any reader who has a mother? Mikhail Bakhtin suggests just such a juxtaposition of responsibility of the reader toward the text, saying, "What I must be for the other, God is for me,"[163] precisely because, we realize in an epiphanic flash, *my fellow human being has a mother.* The other in this case is the orphaned witness who exposes herself through the literary outcry to an orphaned world in a movement of transcendence. That is why this passage is so moving.

The outcry is addressed simultaneously to God and to humanity. It is, therefore, addressed to *me,* not as one who must muster some empathetic identification with the author in order to know how it feels, but as one who must answer as Adam and Cain were summoned to answer to the questions "Where are you?" and "Where is your brother?" That is what marks the moment of epiphany: from a time—or an eternity—immemorial, it is addressed to *me,* as to one already accused. Therefore, epiphany is the epiphany of the *already*: I am already accused, already called, and late for the appointment. "All revelation is a calling and a mission," as Buber maintains,[164] and, as a moment of revelation, epiphany is a moment of ethical calling and ethical mission. The flash of epiphany is an instant not of knowing "how it feels" but of knowing what must be done. Indeed, the impetus to know "how it feels" can become a flight from the ethical demand. The literary outcry, moreover, is addressed not only to me but also to God in a reversal of the primal question put to the first man, now turned back on the God of the Covenant Himself: Where are *You*? Unlike Adam, the first murderer, who would murder all of humanity in the murder of his brother, had a mother who came from the hand of God, the mother of all humanity. Every Nazi bent on the obliteration of the mother had a mother. And so we collide with the horror of: Why? *Why?*

Stepping before this *why* we are bankrupt, beggared by the abundance of our theories of trauma and representation, of representation and remembrance, of imagination and aesthetics, of identity and interpretation, of language and culture, of race and gender—all the intellectual fashions and fads that obscure the obliteration of the mother in the Shoah. No excursion into systems of signs, no reflection on the representation of trauma, no semiotics of signs and signifiers is adequate to this *why* that attends the epiphanic moment of "Oh, Mommy! Oh, God!" Placed alongside "Oh, Mommy," the "Oh, God!" is no ordinary "Oh, God!" No. It bears no resemblance to the "Oh, God" that permeates everything from pedestrian prattle to homiletic injunction. It eludes the scholarly inquiry that is scandalized by any mention of God, an inquiry characterized by a concomitant flight from the cry of "Mama!" Why the flight? Because "Oh, God, they are killing my mother!" means they are killing God. Maternal love is not part of the fabric of being—it is a divine breach of being. It is the *chesed,* the loving kindness, that emanates from the Supernal Mother (see *Zohar* I, 22b). Through that love the mother opens up a small portal through which the divine reveals itself from beyond the mute neutrality of all there is. "Mothers," writes Ana Vinocur in her memoir, "were sublime, special beings, divine!"[165] We realize, therefore, that what we have here is something otherwise than representation. It lies in the capacity of the mute printed page to emit such a scream, to seize me by the throat and announce my paralysis, as I struggle both to flee from and to fight my way into the next line.

There is no turning away: I am the one called to listen, the one whom her scream singles out—that is the meaning of the epiphanic moment. The concept of epiphany is no mere analytical device; it is irreducible to any critical method. Indeed, the reach of the outcry extends beyond such artifice, beyond ontological determinations of "authenticity" to penetrate into the soul of anyone who has ever had a mother. In that reach, we have the epiphany of a transcendence. Otherwise than representation, this transcendence is always effected on the plane of the flesh-and-blood, of the concrete, and not in the ethereal realm of abstraction: the literary transcendence of the Holocaust is ever manifest in flesh and blood, in the blood that bleeds from the womb in a moment of birth, in the milk of the mother's breast, in the blood of the mother spilled in Auschwitz experiments. And in the blood of the woman sent to the gas chambers, *precisely because she is a mother*: Oh, God, they are killing my mother! They are gassing my mother! They are burning my mother! The line from Isabella's memoir returns to haunt us: "The scent was the smell of burning flesh. The burning flesh was your mother."[166] *Your* mother.

> We . . . could not even succeed in raising a trace of compassion. That was how it remained until Liza started singing a song about a Jewish mother, and we, who had lost our mothers so cruelly, could not keep ourselves from crying.
>
> —Sara Nomberg-Przytyk, *Auschwitz: True Tales form a Grotesque Land*

These orphaned Jewish women did not "lose" their mothers—their mothers were murdered in the Nazis' obliteration of the mother. All that remains of their mothers is a song that breaks through the silence of a realm calculated to obliterate song and compassion, all that makes the human being human. Franz Rosenzweig asserts that he who has not written poetry is not human.[167] Just so, he who has not sung a song is not human. The rhythm of song and poetry constitutes the heartbeat of humanity, offered always in love and often in lamentation. Song is poetry, and poetry is epiphany, even now, Adorno notwithstanding; to write poetry after Auschwitz may be barbaric, but in that anti-world poetry and song were the only measures left to counter a barbarism that exceeded mere barbarism. In these lines Sara Nomberg-Przytyk bequeaths to us a testimony in the mode of song where there should be no song, relating the tale of a song that no one will hear, a silent song offered up to silence. And so we touch upon an Ultimate.

A song. About a Jewish mother. Heard by women systematically orphaned in the obliteration of their mothers, who could find not a trace of compassion, not a trace of *rachamim,* not a trace of *rechem,* neither word nor caress . . . only a song about a Jewish mother that echoes off the mute rafters of a block buried in the shadows of Stutthof. Can we hear it? Listen carefully.

The emptiness into which the words of these women fade is the emptiness of the loss of the mother and of the love that makes the mother who she is. The song about a Jewish mother is, after all, a song about love in its most sacred form. What does the song contain that no words of comfort can? It contains an epiphany. Epiphany is song, and song is epiphany. Says Nachman of Breslov, music and song originate not from this world but from "the source of sanctity" in the upper worlds.[168] It comes to us both from within and from beyond the Holocaust. How to transmit the song that transforms us into witnesses? How to sing the song now? How to represent it?

"We could not keep from crying." But the ethical imperative is not to weep. It is to help, to *be good.* In the epiphanic encounter we live through a moment in the life of the witness; contrary to a *re-present*ing of the moment, we are in the moment, moving as we do into the dimension of the eternal by way of a song we cannot hear: the hearing of the song lies in the testimony to the song. The literary transcendence of representation comes not in a moment of empathy but in a moment of implication, not in a cry of pain but in a cry of "Here I am," precisely because the mother is *not* here. But perhaps a trace of her love, a trace of her weeping, abides in the song and in the poem.

> Aspen tree your leaves glance white into the dark.
> My mother's hair was never white.
> Dandelion, so green is the Ukraine.
> My yellow-haired mother did not come home.
> Rain cloud, above the well do you hover?
> My quiet mother weeps for everyone.
> Round star, you wind the golden loop.
> My mother's heart was ripped by lead.

> Oaken door, who lifted you off your hinges?
> My gentle mother cannot return.
>
> —Paul Celan, "Aspen Tree"

Dominating this poem about the obliteration of the mother is the link between the metaphysical and the mundane, between the pre-originary and the ontological, articulated through images of the dimension of height and images of nature: the "rain cloud" and the "round star" above, the "aspen tree" and the "dandelion," even the "oaken door," below. The mother connects the two, so that the obliteration of the mother is the obliteration of a connection, not only between mother and child but also between above and below, without which nothing and no one has meaning; thus, the "mother weeps for everyone," as she hovers in the heavens like the spirit hovering over the face of the deep, over a world returned to a primal chaos and to which the mother cannot return. Set against the backdrop of nature, the images from the sky impart meaning to an otherwise indifferent nature, and the images of nature impart a non-indifference within the difference. There we have the tension and the epiphany in this poem: epiphany happens in the realization of a connection that exceeds ontological categories.

Nature, of course, is the great mother, the mother who weeps for everyone, like Rachel weeping for her children (see Jeremiah 31:15). This mother weeps, however, not from within nature but from above nature, over a creation undone, over what Levi calls "the mystique of barrenness,"[169] its womb grown cold like a frog in winter, the aspen tree and dandelion notwithstanding. The human connection with nature passes through the Creator, who is the Supernal Mother of humanity. Bearing in mind the association between the Supernal Mother and the House of Jacob, we recall a teaching from the Midrash: "The Holy One, blessed be He, said to His world: 'O My world, My world! Shall I tell thee who created thee, who formed thee? Jacob has created thee, Jacob has formed thee' " (*Vayikra Rabbah* 36:4). For the House of Jacob signifies the mother of creation. From the depths of the mother's compassion human life itself begins to stir. Thus, the mother links us to the Creator, to the absolute origin of all things.

The Nazis were known for their glorification, even deification, of nature, particularly in the writings of ideologues such as Richard Walther Darré (1895–1953), who in 1930 declared that the challenge facing the German people was the restoration of "the unity of blood and soil,"[170] of *Blut und Boden*. Then there was Ernst Lehmann (1880–1957), who asserted, "This striving toward connectedness with the totality of life, with nature itself, a nature into which we are born, is the deepest meaning and the true essence of National Socialist thought."[171] Blood and soil came to mean the spilling of Jewish blood into the soil, and connectedness with nature came to mean the radical disconnect between mother and child.

As the Nazis deify nature, they defy the Supernal Mother and set about the project of the obliteration of the Jewish mother. Once nature is deified, it must have its sacrificial offerings, and those placed on the altar are precisely those who are created in the image and likeness of the God of Abraham: in the time of the Nazis, the earth, the air, and the water were saturated not just with sulfides, acids, and other pollutants, but with the ashen remains of Jewish mothers. In contrast to the star wreathed in a halo of gold is the heart of the mother, who loves with all her heart, ripped with lead. In the contrast between the warm gentleness of the mother and the cold leaden bullet we have an epiphany of what the Holocaust is; the divergence of the tenderness of the caress from the tearing of the bullet could not be more extreme.

And so the mother weeps for everyone. John Felsteiner compares the mother's weeping for everyone to Rachel's weeping for her children, as she cries out in a longing for the Messiah.[172] And yet the coming of the Messiah can happen only with the return of the mother who cannot return: the obliteration of the mother signifies the obliteration of the Messiah. Recall the prophet's pronouncement: "Behold, a young woman will conceive and give birth" (Isaiah 7:14). Each day in the liturgy we recite the Thirteen Principles of Judaism outlined by Maimonides in his commentary on the Mishnah (*Sanhedrin* 10); the Twelfth Principle is: "I believe with complete faith in the coming of the Messiah; even if he may tarry, no matter what, I shall await his coming every day." But what if the Messiah cannot come because the mother cannot return? "The true object of hope," writes Levinas, "is the Messiah, or salvation."[173] Where does salvation lie? In the relationship to the other human being, beginning with the mother.

The time of our lives, of striving to be who we are in our own unique being there for the sake of another, is rooted in the interminable waiting and working for the coming of the Messiah. "The awaiting of the Messiah," says Levinas, "is the duration of time itself—waiting for God—but here the waiting no longer attests to the absence of Godot, who will never come, but rather to a relationship with that which is not able to enter the present, since the present is too small to contain the Infinite."[174] The awaiting is awaiting the return of the mother: this primal relationship is the key. So understood, time is the drawing nigh unto the Holy One that Levinas describes when he says, " 'Going towards God' is meaningless unless seen in terms of my primary going towards the other person. I can only go towards God by being ethically concerned by and for the other person."[175] Indeed, we find such an understanding of the Messiah in Holocaust literature. In his novel *The Gates of the Forest,* Elie Wiesel writes, "The Messiah is that which makes man more human . . . which stretches his soul toward others."[176] In this going toward God by going toward the other person we ignite the messianic aspect of the soul. Though the mother cannot return, yet shall we make this movement toward the other person that defines the very human relation laid low during the Holocaust.

The Collapse of Human Relation

> Here there is no such thing as father, brother, friend. Each of us lives and dies alone.
>
> —Elie Wiesel, *Night*

> Everyone is desperately and ferociously alone.
>
> —Primo Levi, *Survival in Auschwitz*

In Part One, we saw that the Nazis did not want the Jews to be alive; nor did they want them to be dead. They did not want them to *be* anything. And so they set out to remove every predicate, every remnant of identity, from the Jew, whose identity as a Jew is fundamentally determined by the Torah and by the mother through whom the Torah enters the world. Equally fundamental to the identity of the Jew—and to any human being—is human relation. The identity that emerges within human relation lies in a "non-indifference to others, a sign given to the others,"[177] as Levinas has said. "There is no I as such but only the I of the basic word I-You and the I of the basic word I-It," Buber makes this point,[178] and "the basic word I-You establishes the world of relation."[179] In order to bring about the annihilation of the identity of the Jew as a Jew, the Nazis had to bring about the collapse of human relation. They had to bring about the collapse of the "I for you—everything," the sign of an infinite responsibility given to another and the one thing that could overcome the infinite isolation of being ferociously alone.

To bring about the collapse of the "I for you—everything" is to turn the human being over to "useless suffering," as Levinas describes it, in an "explosion and most profound articulation of absurdity."[180] The human relation collapses in the suffering *for nothing*, in the utter abrogation of the injunction found in Wiesel's novel *The Town beyond the Wall*, where Pedro says to Michael: "To say 'I suffer therefore I am' is to become the enemy of man. What you must say is 'I suffer, therefore you are.' "[181] The suffering borne in the Holocaust is more than the suffering of cold, hunger, and hardship. It makes no sense because it has no cause, no purpose, no explanation. It cannot be situated in the world because it is the suffering that ensues upon the destruction of the world: here, there is no suffering for another, because here there is no such thing as father, brother, friend. There is nothing to represent.

Wherever there is a *human* relation there is the relation of the one for the other characterized by an infinite responsibility through which the divine enters this realm in an epiphanic moment to announce who I am in the depths of my identity, an identity for which I am already chosen, and there is no system of signs and signifiers that can represent that relation; the relation is *prior to* all such systems. "The for-the-other of responsibility for the other," Levinas explains, "does not proceed from any free commitment, any present, in which its origin would germinate, or in which an identity identifying itself would catch its breath. . . . Responsibility without a prior commitment, without a present, without an origin, anarchic, is thus an infinite responsibility of the one for the other who is abandoned to me without anyone being able to take my place as the one responsible for him."[182] To be thus irreplaceable is to be who I am. It is to be overwhelmed by a singularity that eludes every theme, eludes essence itself, which makes it nonrepresentable. Because the defining substance of human relation thus exceeds representation, Holocaust literature's transmission of the collapse of human relation happens only in an epiphanic moment of transcendence.

The Nazis' systematic effort to bring about a collapse of human relation was an effort to obliterate every trace of a commandment fundamental to Judaism: "*Veahavta lereakha k'mokha*—You shall love your neighbor as yourself" (Leviticus 19:18). According to the Baal Shem Tov, this commandment—this relationship—is the basis of the entire Torah (*Toledot Yaakov Yosef*, *Korach* 2). If we examine the Hebrew word *k'mokha*, "as yourself," as well as the *le-* in *lereakha*, "your neighbor," a better translation would be: "You shall show love *toward* your neighbor, for that loving relation *is* who you are," as it is written (*Toledot Yaakov Yosef*, *Veetchanan* 5). The commandment is followed by the phrase "I am the Lord," indicating that the human relation and the higher relation are of a piece. With the engineered collapse of the human relation comes the collapse of the higher relation, the commanding dimension of height targeted by the Nazis in the extermination of the eternal. Because the humanity of the human being resides in both relations, the Torah declares that "it is not good for the human being to be alone" (Genesis 2:18); hence, the Nazis' determination that the human being would be ferociously alone, without father or son, friend or brother, and thus rendered inhuman. Only within human relation, says Sforno in his commentary on Genesis 2:18, can the purpose of our being created in the image and likeness of the Holy One be realized: to live in that image is to live in relation to another, for the sake of another. Ultimately, it is to make our dying part of our living, by dying for the sake of another. In the relation to our fellow human being we have life; therefore it is good. What is *lo-tov*, "not good," is being alone in the isolation of our illusory ego: alone, the human being has no identity, no name, and—what is the same thing—no love to offer.

A literary transcendence of Holocaust representation is required for the transmission of the ineffable assault on the love that makes human relation human. And because this transcendence comes in a literary testimony to the collapse of human relation, it bears ethical implications for the relation between author and reader. The reader's "understanding bears an actively responsive character,"[183] writes Bakhtin, so that "the event in the life of the text—that is, its genuine essence—develops *along the boundary between two consciousnesses, two subjects*."[184] The boundary is defined as a being-for-the-other. Elsewhere, he adds, "The text never appears as a dead thing. Beginning with any text, we always arrive . . . at the human voice, which is to say we come up against the human being."[185] The response to the literary testimony to the collapse of human relation, therefore, comes with an ethical demand that devolves upon the reader in relation to the human voice of the author. "Why does one write," asks Elie Wiesel, "if it is not to break out of this solitude?"[186] And the reader has an ethical role in the witness's breaking free from a place where he or she is ferociously alone. Nowhere is the witness more ferociously alone than in the sealed train.

Here in this carload
I am Eve
With my son Abel
If you see my older boy
Cain son of Adam
Tell him that I

—Dan Pagis, "Written in Pencil in the Sealed Freightcar"

Holocaust survivor Dan Pagis (1930–1986) was born in Bukovina, Romania. Soon after the war he immigrated to Israel, where he became a scholar of medieval poetry at the Hebrew University in Jerusalem. In this poem, the mother of humanity is in a freightcar, sealed off from all human relation. This poem is not about a single human being—it is about humankind and the maternal love that lies at the heart of human relation. That is why it is iconic in Holocaust literature. Written "in pencil," *b'ifaron*, it is written in the *afar*, or the "dust," of which the human being is made, as taught in the Torah: "*V'yitzer HaShem Elohim et-ha-adam, afar min-ha-adamah*—The Lord God made the human being from the dust of the earth" (Genesis 2:7). The word *afar*, spelled *ayin-peh-resh*, brings to mind the word *efer*, or "ash," which is *alef-peh-resh*. These lines in pencil, which fade like dust and ashes, emerge upon the collapse of human relation and in an eclipse of the higher relation.

The "sealed" freight car, the car that is *chatum*, reminds us of the greeting Jews extend to each other at Rosh Hashanah, the Day of Judgment: *gmar chatimah tovah*, "may you be sealed in the Book of Life." Here, of course, mother and child are sealed in a train of death, consigned to an anti-judgment, for to stand before a judgment is to nonetheless stand within a relationship. Sealed inside the freight car, the Jew is sealed inside a realm of horror, in which there is no judge and no judgment; she is *b'shloach*, "in a carload," which more literally means "among those who are sent," *shaloach*. It is also a word for "messenger." Any time we come before the other human being, we encounter a messenger who summons us. In this case the voice bears a message and a summons in her very name: "I am Eve," *Chavah*, a word that means "experienced" or "lived through"; its cognate *chivah* is to "pronounce" or "state." Pronouncing her name, she declares, "Here I am," to the reader in an utterance that harbors the question put to Adam: "Where are you?" (Genesis 3:9). She is "here," however, in a non-place with her son Abel, *Hevel*, whose name means "vanity" or "nonsense," the name of the murdered child of the first mother, now on his way to be murdered with his mother in an "overflowing of meaning by nonsense,"[187] inasmuch as the human relation here obtains only in their being murdered together.

Enter the archetypical murderer, her "older boy" Cain, the one exiled to the Land of Nod, literally the Land of Wandering, the Land of Exile (Genesis 4:16), a land that we all inhabit; that is why we may well see him. He is Cain, son of Adam, or son of the "human being," who brings about the collapse of human relation, marked with a death's head on his cap, like a frontlet between his eyes. His name, *Kayin*, means "acquisition" or "appropriation" and is a cognate of *kiynah,* a word that translates as "lament." There is no more profound appropriation of "the other by the same," as Levinas puts it, than in his act of murder.[188] And so the questions put to Cain are here put to us: "Where is your brother?" (Genesis 4:9) and "What have you done?" (Genesis 4:10). Tacitly asked, "Where is Cain?" we are asked, "Where are you?" and we are commanded: "Tell him," that is, *tegidu lo,* "relate to him" the tale, where *tegidu* has the same root as *aggadah,* or "tale." Transformed into witnesses, we are summoned to a human relation by relating the tale of the collapse of human relation, a collapse that transcends representation.

Finally, it must be noted that the poem returns us to the Torah that affirms the infinite responsibility at the heart of human relation, as well as a higher relation, the Torah targeted for annihilation through the collapse of both relations. To be sure, wherever we encounter a moment of epiphany in the literary transcendence of the Holocaust, we come up against the Torah, whether implicitly or explicitly, inasmuch as we stand before an absolute commandment regarding the ethical, outside of which there is no human relation but only a radically dehumanizing isolation.

> With a smile on her lips, she wondered, Who can feel more alone than children without parents, than parents without children, husbands without wives, and wives without husbands? She continued to smile. She would never be able to say it to anyone.
>
> —Arnošt Lustig, *Dita Saxova*

Lustig says what his character wonders but is unable to say. An eighteen-year-old survivor, she is unable to say it because it exceeds all utterance and therefore all representation. That is the literary task: to say what one is unable to utter, to give voice to what robs us of our voice. All of the relationships evoked here—child to parent, parent to child, husband to wife, wife to husband—form the foundation of human relation as such. We are reminded that the vast majority of Holocaust survivors were orphaned children, bereaved parents, and widowed husbands and wives. This is no accident. Dita Saxova cannot say it to anyone because it cannot be said, cannot be transmitted, cannot be understood. If it can be voiced at all, it can be so only through the literary transcendence of representation in a movement of saying, and not in the said. This very analysis of these lines from Lustig's text lapses into the said, into the thematizable and therefore the representable, a risk that Levinas has identified: "Art is the pre-eminent exhibition in which the said is reduced to a pure theme, to absolute exposition, even to shamelessness capable of holding all looks for which it is exclusively destined."[189] Holocaust literature's transcendence of representation, however, may avoid this slippage into the said, into the effable, avoid the absorption of the speaking subject into the said precisely by addressing that slippage: "She would never be able to say it to anyone."

Dita's inability to speak comes not through incapacity but through a refusal to betray the ones of whom the literary text speaks. "The correlation of the saying and the said, that is, the subordination of the saying to the said," writes Levinas, "to the linguistic system and to ontology, is the price that manifestation demands. In language qua said everything is conveyed before us, be it at the price of a betrayal."[190] Thus, we see in Dita the conundrum facing her author: Does Lustig betray the ones for whose sake he bears witness in the offering of his literary testimony? *Navigare necesse est,* we recall Piotr Rawicz's assertion: one *has* to write, to bear witness, even as the character Dita has been made into a witness. Although there is no way out, "the saying in the said of the witness born signifies in a plot other than that which is spread out in a theme," as Levinas has indicated, "other than that which attaches a noesis to a noema, a cause to an effect, the memorable past to the present. This plot connects to what detaches itself absolutely, to the Absolute."[191] Dita's inability to speak points toward this detachment. The connection to the Absolute in Lustig's text lies in the epiphany of an absolute demand abiding in the face, which penetrates the plot by means of an image: "With a smile on her lips"—lips that could not speak—"she wondered. . . ."

And as she pondered the horror of this isolation, "she continued to smile" a kind of anti-smile: whereas in the world a smile is welcoming and inviting—a word beyond words offered to another in an affirmation of human relation—this smile that comes as a remnant of the anti-world is radically isolating. It denotes only the silence that signifies the collapse of human relation. Because of this smile, the incongruity between the said and the unsayable in these lines is staggering. The literary saying irreducible to the said is an attempt to surpass that radical isolation of the incongruous smile attendant upon the collapse of human relation. It is an attempt to recover a caress exchanged between parent and child, husband and wife. The caress of love eludes the said, and the collapse of the caress of love makes it impossible for Dita to say anything. Yet we have the saying despite the said in Lustig's literary text, and this "despite" makes the text an open wound, like Dita's smile, "even if it can take refuge in the said," as Levinas says, "finding again in a wound the caress."[192] The phrase "finding *again*" reminds us that—like the author searching for the word that might transmit the ineffable, the word that might touch the reader—the caress searches for what eludes both the word and the touch fundamental to human relation, fundamental because only the word and the touch can liberate us from the isolation that undermines human relation. In this case, through the literary text we enter into a relation with a character who is incapable of relation. There lies the literary transcendence of representation.

> A new system of human relationships operated in the camp; a different scale of sensibilities and obligations had been established, different from the one in the Five Books of Moses or in the writings of socialist scholars or even in sociology textbooks.
>
> —Arnošt Lustig, *A Prayer for Katerina Horovitzova*

Turning once again to Lustig's novel, we discover that if "a new system of human relationships operated in the camp," it is a system of antihuman relationships devoid of the feminine. That is why Lustig situates his character Katerina, who embodies the feminine, in the midst of the collapse of human relation. "The feminine," Levinas writes, "is described as the *of itself other*, as the origin of the very concept of alterity,"[193] and therefore at the very origin of human relation. As the origin of alterity, the feminine makes possible the establishment of a difference from which all issues of meaning and morality, the stuff of human relation, might arise, a difference transformed into a non-indifference. The feminine represents the mystery of what is forever yet to be born, yet to be revealed, and yet to be consummated. The relationship with the feminine is a relationship "with the future, with what (in a world where there is everything) is never there, with what cannot be there when everything else is there—not with a being that is not there, but with the very dimension of alterity."[194] The alterity of the feminine, then, is not an otherness already contained in being; it is the otherness of what is *better* than being and beyond representation, so that something better is yet to be revealed, something *meaningful* that can manifest itself only within human relation. Thus, meaning belongs to the future designated by the feminine, so that the collapse of human relation in the anti-relationship of the anti-world is a collapse of future. Here we have a key to understanding Katerina Horovitzova.

This absence of future, which is an absence of relation, is an absence of any *ought* conveyed in the commandments of the Five Books of Moses or even of the socialists in their attempts to usurp the absolute. The feminine embodied in the young Katerina, by contrast, announces the ethical summons that defines a human relation consummated in dying for another. Without the feminine, argues Levinas, the human being knows "nothing which transforms his natural life into ethics, nothing which permits living a life, not even the death that one dies for another."[195] Hence, the feminine lies at the core of the human relation that collapses in the camps. Woman, and with her the mystery of humanity and divinity, becomes one more item to be bartered and conquered, possessed and crushed. What can be represented can be bartered or conquered within the systems of signs and signifiers. Here, we realize how the project of representation—whether of trauma or atrocity—can play into the collapse of human relation. Through the testimony of Lustig's literary text, however, woman becomes more than an item to be bartered and conquered.

Lustig's telling of the tale of this collapse of human relation retains the remnants of the Jewish testimony to human relation that the Nazis set out to annihilate through the annihilation of the feminine presence. In the Jewish tradition targeted for annihilation the feminine is represented by the *Shekhinah,* as discussed in Part One. Like the *Shekhinah* accompanying Israel into exile, Katerina accompanies the American Jewish businessmen sent to the camp, where "a new system of human relationship operated," a system calculated to undermine human relation. What is the sign of this accompaniment? It is the Torah itself, the Five Books of Moses that in the anti-world have been obviated. Hence, we see that the Nazis' assault on the Torah is tied to an assault on the feminine, on Katerina Horovitzova.

> I look at my friend Pinni and see him . . . throwing himself at the barracks chief's feet: "Oh merciful Chief, sweet Chief, grant me the flogging instead of my father!" And his father, sentenced to be flogged to death, screams at his son, "Pinni, away from here! For my sake—honor thy father! Away! Away! Away!"
>
> —Ka-tzetnik 135633, *Shivitti: A Vision*

If in the world dying for another is the ultimate testimony to the sanctity of the human life manifest in human relation, in the anti-world it plays into the collapse of that relation. The "soul," the *neshamah,* draws its "breath," its *neshimah,* in the midst of human relation; outside of human relation the soul suffocates, as the Nazis understood perfectly well. This drawing of the breath of the soul happens most profoundly in the movement of substitution: "The other in the same is my substitution for the other through responsibility, for which I am summoned as someone irreplaceable."[196] Such is the case in the world. But is there anything to be learned from the collapse of human relation in the very act of substitution in the anti-world? Perhaps even in the anti-world alienation might be overcome by substitution: "Oh merciful Chief, sweet Chief, grant me the flogging instead of my father!" Does the Fifth Commandment, to honor father and mother, require this dying for the sake of the father, who will nonetheless be murdered? Or does it require heeding the word of the father, who now chooses to die in the place of his son, thanks to his son's begging to die in his place? This is the ultimate of "choiceless choices,"[197] and here we touch upon an Ultimate in a moment of epiphany. Thus, we ask: What are we to do with this? How are we to analyze it? Is there not something blasphemous about this sort of analysis?

At the heart of Levinas's understanding of substitution is an understanding of expiation for the sake of the other: "Signification is the ethical deliverance of the self through substitution for the other. It is . . . an expiation for the other."[198] Not simply by dying but by dying *for the sake of* does the soul take on its substance. But what can this mean in a realm where death itself is undone? And how can Pinni's act be construed as ethical? What does he have to expiate *for*? For the sins of his father? No. For his own sins? Absolutely not. The radical incongruity is underscored by the words "merciful Chief, sweet Chief," the chief who is nothing more than a depraved murderer, the opposite of sweet and merciful, as this act of substitution is the opposite of expiation. Here, we realize an important point about the literary transcendence of Holocaust representation: the transcendence lies not in the comprehension but in the incomprehension of the Holocaust, in the beyond "Holocaust."

If "irreducible to being's essence is the substitution in responsibility, signification or the one-for-another,"[199] Pinni's act of substitution, irreducible to any "essence," is also irreducible to anything that can be represented. Here, as Levinas says, substitution is "the otherwise than being,"[200] and is therefore otherwise than representation. Still, if Levinas's insights apply, they apply only on the hither side of the event: they bring us no closer to the inside of this son's dying for the sake of his father. That is why only an epiphany, and not a philosophical deduction, opens up a pathway into this passage and into the pathos of a devastating question: Is Pinni a good son? In the very question we have the Nazis' inversion of human relation that is a collapse of human relation. In substitution, says Levinas, "the self is goodness, or under the exigency for an abandon of all having, of all *one's own* . . . to the point of substitution. . . . Goodness invests me in my obedience to the hidden Good."[201] Obedience to the hidden Good is obedience to the divine commandment and obedience to the word of the father. But is this obedience? In the world, yes. But in the anti-world, where nothing is hidden, where there are no fathers, no sons? Only a literary transcendence of the representation of the Holocaust can approach this moment from the Holocaust by restoring a trace of the hidden. Perhaps in the end Levinas can be of help after all, understanding as he does that substitution is a negation of representation,[202] here more radically than anywhere else. If substitution is otherwise than being, this instance of substitution from Holocaust literature is beyond representation.

One last thing that comes to mind here. It is the story of another choiceless choice, a story told to me by a friend and survivor of Auschwitz, Rabbi Murray Kohn, scholar and author of *Is the Holocaust Vanishing?*[203] It is a kind of inversion of Ka-tzetnik's tale. When the Nazis arrived in Rabbi Kohn's hometown in Poland, they prohibited all study of Torah. Three men were caught in a violation of the prohibition and sentenced to be hanged before an assembly of the entire village. Two men were summarily hanged, as per the decree. The third was brought to the gallows, an elderly man, with grown sons devoted to Torah. The Nazi in charge brought him to the top of the gallows. But rather than hang him, the Nazi pronounced the following: "I am not going to hang you. Your son is going to hang you. Or else I will murder your entire family before your eyes." The son was brought to the gallows and forced to place the noose around his father's neck. He was screaming and crying, "No! No!" And his father was screaming and crying, "Yes! Yes!" Unlike Pinni, he obeyed his father. Like Pinni, he . . . what? Dishonored his father by killing him? Or honored him by obeying him? Did Pinni dishonor his father by disobeying him? Or did he honor him by dying for him? How are we to indulge in the academic disputations on representation in the light of this nonrepresentable?

The Disintegration of Knowledge

> The axes of its traditional frames of reference then shattered. Beauty: that was an illusion. Knowledge: that turned out to be a game with ideas. . . .
>
> —Jean Améry, *At the Mind's Limits*

> I have attained a level of knowledge I had despaired of reaching.
>
> —Elie Wiesel, *The Testament*

In its most ill-conceived, most popular form, the epistemological problem of the Holocaust revolves around the question of knowing "what it was like" or "how it felt," as if feeling were the same as knowing. If knowing what it was like means somehow going through the experience, do those of us who teach the Holocaust really want our students or anyone else to know "what it was like" in the sealed trains, where the dead had no room to drop, the living had no place to relieve themselves, and people went insane from thirst and heat and hunger? Do we want anyone to know the starvation and brutality of the camps, the humiliation and dehumanization, the excremental assault on the soul, the murder of children before their mothers' eyes, the vision of babies burned alive, the suffocation of Zyklon-B, and on and on and on? Does anyone suppose that the survivors want others to know "what it was like"? Is that the point of testimony? No.

When it comes to the transcendence of Holocaust representation, there is another, more profound question to be addressed. It is the question of how we are to know—or are afraid to know—exactly what happened and what, if anything, it could possibly mean. Some scholars turn not only to the German archives but also to the memoirs, diaries, and chronicles of the Jews who were there in order to attain some sense of "that which happened," to repeat Celan's phrase. Such a move, however, runs the risk of avoiding what might be known. From an epistemological standpoint, James Young, for instance, argues that the diarists "necessarily convert experience into an organized, often ritualized, *memory* of experience."[204] Hence, says Young, "As raw as they may have been at the moment, the ghetto and camp experiences were immediately refined and organized by witnesses within the terms of their *Weltanschauungen*."[205] The epistemological problem of the

Holocaust, however, is not that the witnesses may have understood their experiences "within the terms of their *Weltanschauungen*." No, it is that they could not understand their experiences at all. If the collisions with the Holocaust turn into philosophical questions of epistemology, they are questions that are rather different from any that philosophy has ever had to deal with. With the disintegration of knowledge comes a shattering of philosophy, or at least a *novum,* to use Emil Fackenheim's word, in the philosophical inquiry: with the Holocaust, he says, "philosophers must face a *novum* within a question as old as Socrates: what does it mean to be human?"[206] The disintegration of knowledge is a disintegration of the knowledge of what it means to be human.

There's the rub: for the philosopher, the speculative ontological tradition is incapable of accommodating any *novum,* any singularity, that might exceed the parameters of the syllogistic universals that have defined philosophy since the time of Aristotle. In his Holocaust memoir, Samuel Pisar (b. 1929) makes a statement that undercuts all philosophical inquiry into the Event: "For sheer demented horror, Treblinka, Maidanek, and Auschwitz were in a class of their own: the end of the world, the end of creation,"[207] and the disintegration of knowledge. And so Améry recalls "the philosopher from the Sorbonne," who "gave monosyllabic, mechanical answers and finally grew silent entirely."[208] Wherever reality exceeds possibility in a *dementing* of the possible, what remains is an empty silence. Thus, says Améry, "Existence as such became definitively a totally abstract and thus empty concept. To reach out beyond concrete reality with words became before our very eyes a game that was not only worthless and an impermissible luxury but also mocking and evil."[209] The problem does not lie with the imagination; indeed, the *images* are all too indelibly imprinted on the soul, like the number tattooed into the flesh.

The difficulty is that neither the possible nor the impossible can be *thought* in the anti-world of Auschwitz; it is *demented.* "Everything for us was unreal and insubstantial," Wiesenthal recalls.[210] Does this mean that nothing was felt or experienced? No, on the contrary, what was felt and experienced surpassed all measure and proportion, and that is just the point: it was impossible and yet it was real. "Nowhere else in the world," says Améry, "did reality have such effective power as in the camp, nowhere else was reality so real."[211] There is no knowing apart from a transcendence of what is known; the reality that is "so real" is a reality in which there is nothing to be understood. There is no representing, no prosaic accounting or portraying, of what cannot be known. "The Holocaust," writes Fackenheim, "was a *world* of evil—an *Unwelt* or antiworld—that was previously unthought and unthinkable. It ruptures philosophical thought. It also ruptures . . . art and literature."[212] Because in the Holocaust the world experiences such a rupture, we can approach the unknowable of the Holocaust—what eludes any appropriation of the anti-world—not through the representations of philosophy, art, or history but only, if at all, through a literary transcendence of representation.

The mind strains for a word: this must be hell. But not even the word *hell* applies. Consider this passage from Leon Wells's account of those who dug up bodies and burned them: "The *Untersturmführer* . . . orders the three leather craftsmen in the brigade to make the fire chief and his assistant two hats with horns, like those of a devil. From then on, we march to work with the fire chief and his assistant leading us, wearing their horns and carrying their hooks they used to stir the fire."[213] A scene from Dante's *Inferno*? Hell? No. Hell is about justice. " 'Abandon hope,' are the words greeting those entering Dante's hell," Fackenheim reminds us. "Even so it cannot touch the innocent. The Holocaust would touch *none but* the innocent."[214] The bodies are piled high. The flames ascend on high. But there is no "high." For the Nazis set out to obliterate every dimension of height in the burning and obliteration of the bodies of mothers and fathers who call out to their children from beyond the mass grave. "Many bodies," Wells relates, "are lying around with open mouths. Could they be trying to say: 'We are your own mothers, fathers, who raised you and took care of you. Now you are burning us . . .'? Maybe they would forgive us."[215] Once again we find that the difficulty in approaching the borders of this Kingdom lies not in the lack of imagination but in the disintegration of knowledge. The Nazis' imagination was at work, full blown, without limits. There lies the epistemological problem: Nazi imagination eclipsed human reason.

> Try to grasp the essence of this pattern of daily events, discarding your sense of horror and loathing and contempt, and find for it all a philosophic formula. . . . What is this mystery? This strange power of one man over another?
>
> —Tadeusz Borowski, "Auschwitz, Our Home (A Letter)," in *This Way to the Gas, Ladies and Gentlemen*

In these lines, Tadeusz Borowski poses a literary challenge to the Western philosophical tradition: try to grasp. Try to grasp what? The utter abrogation of the prohibition against murder, the utter annihilation of divine commandment and human relation, the disintegration of all knowledge, including any knowledge of oneself. In short, try to grasp the complete appropriation of one man by another, the appropriation of what cannot be appropriated. What escapes the grasp is precisely what stirs the horror, loathing, and contempt. And yet, if some sense of horror remains, it is because there is a remnant of the ethical sensibility that can respond to the face of another human being. Listen to Levinas: "The face resists possession, resists my powers. In its epiphany, in expression, the sensible, still graspable, turns into total resistance to the grasp. . . . This means concretely: the face speaks to me and thereby invites me to a relation incommensurate with a power exercised, be it enjoyment or knowledge. . . . The depth that opens in this sensibility modifies the very nature of power, which henceforth can no longer take, but can kill. . . . Murder exercises a power over what escapes power."[216] Thus, Levinas gives voice to Borowski's mystery, to the power of one human being over another: it is the power of annihilation, not to kill but to annihilate even the death of the other, to annihilate every predicate attached to the other. There lies the strangeness of the strange power of one man over another.

Knowledge is about predicates. Borowski's predicates have vanished, even before he puts his pen to paper, so that his ability to grasp a reality all too real disintegrates. And that is precisely why it cannot be represented: what would be represented here eludes both thought and power, eludes thought because it eludes power. It eludes *comprehension,* in the literal sense of the word: to comprehend is to "grasp," as the Latin *comprehendere* suggests. To "grasp" is to possess, which has been the project of the Western speculative tradition of knowing, over against the Hebraic tradition of relating.

Knowledge reduces good and evil to *concepts,* nothing more than the understanding and ultimately the will of the knowing ego. In Hebrew "knowledge" is *daat,* which is a "joining together" into a sameness, so that, once the categories are reduced to a human concept and not a divine commandment, there is no distinction between good and evil because there is no absolute. Hence, the biblical warning: on the day you eat of the fruit from of the Tree of Knowledge of Good and Evil, you will surely die (Genesis 2:17). You die because on that day you collapse good and evil into a self-serving sameness in a vain attempt to become "like god" (Genesis 3:5), as the Gerer Rebbe, Rabbi Yehudah Leib Alter (1847–1905), taught.[217] The god we would resemble, however, is not the God of Abraham, who is loving and compassionate, slow to anger and quick to forgive (see Exodus 34:5–7), but is the self-styled god of the speculative ego, the god of power. Therefore, says Fackenheim, the ego's implicit denial of the God of Abraham, from whom the soul emanates, "is self-destruction or rebellion."[218] That is why we die—die as Cain's soul died, by murder—when we eat the fruit of speculative ontological philosophy.

In "Auschwitz Our Home (A Letter)," Borowski describes the SS as "those raised on Luther, Fichte, Hegel, Nietzsche,"[219] so that his short story poses not only a challenge but also an indictment of a line of philosophical thought that culminates in Martin Heidegger, who, under the spell of Nietzschean shibboleths, avowed, "The expression 'will to power' designates the basic character of beings; any being which is, insofar as it is, is will to power."[220] What, then, is this mystery, this strange power of one man over another? It is the mystery and the power first of Athens and then of Auschwitz over Jerusalem. It is the power of the will to power, manifest in stealing gold from human mouths and reducing human beings to numbers.

In the speculative tradition that stems from Athens and leads to Auschwitz, the epistemological question is a question of the power of one man over another; in the Hebraic tradition of a commanded ethical relation to another—the tradition that the Nazis sought to obliterate—it is a matter of one man's relinquishing his power over another. Where the ethical relation obtains, as Levinas has understood, "I have no *power*" over the other person.[221] How is it that in the world I can have no power over the other human being? Levinas answers: "If I can no longer have power over him it is because he overflows absolutely every *idea* I can have of him."[222] In the case of Borowski's literary reply, then, it turns out that the disintegration of knowledge is a disintegration not of knowledge but of this overflow, so that we see not the disintegration of knowledge so much as the disintegration of all ethical understanding. And yet the Western project of knowing leads to just such a disintegration, since "ontology as first philosophy is a philosophy of power,"[223] and a philosophy of power is a philosophy of power over the other human being. Borowski's literary insight shows that once humanity undergoes such a disintegration, so does reality.

> Reality is like an urn that's cracked
> and cannot hold its shape; and very soon
> its rotten shards will shatter like a storm.
> What is his fate who, while he breathes, will so
> speak of what *is* in measure and in form,
> and only thus know he teaches how to know?
>
> —Miklós Radnóti, "O Ancient Prisons"
> (March 27, 1944), in *Foamy Sky*

Miklós Radnóti (1909–1944) was among the greatest Hungarian poets of the twentieth century. An assimilated Jew, he was conscripted in the fall of 1940 to work in the infamous Hungarian labor battalions; after being discharged in December of that year, he was ordered to report again in July 1942 to undergo an ordeal that would last until May 1943. A year later, in May 1944, he was drafted yet again, sent first to the Ukrainian front and then to the copper mines of Bor in Serbia. In September his group of 3,200 prisoners was forced to march to central Hungary; on that march most of them perished, including Radnóti, who was murdered on 9 November 1944. Eighteen months later, his body was exhumed from a mass grave. A notebook of poetry he had written up to the very end of his life was found in his overcoat: here we have a poet whose words have literally risen from the dead.

Composed in the form of a Shakespearean sonnet, "O Ancient Prisons" is the first poem Radnóti wrote after the German invasion of Hungary on 17 March 1944. Noting a parallel between this poem and some of the poetry of William Butler Yeats (1865–1939), for whom "the shaky center pointed toward war," Zsuzsanna Ozsváth comments: "Insisting on the tension between formal elegance and explosive content, the poem suggests the failure of the present age to produce anything enduring, anything dignified," so that for Radnóti, the urn "points toward murder."[224] The epiphany noted above repeats itself in this poetic transcendence: as it goes with reality, so it goes with humanity. More than murder, the breakup of the urn of reality points toward the extermination of a half-million Hungarian Jews. Thus, in these few lines Radnóti conveys the culmination of Western civilization in the present age, as it comes to an end upon the disintegration of a knowledge that, like the serpent of old, failed to fulfill its promises. The cracking of the urn is the fracture of all Grecian measure, of all aesthetic form, so that it contains nothing more than a reality turned to ashes and cast to the winds of a storm. If there had ever been a connection between aesthetics and ethics, it now collapses, and with that collapse comes the disintegration of knowledge. How, then, are we to know how to teach the way of knowledge? Here, in a moment of epiphany, arises the realization of the erasure of all limitation and delineation, all definition and distinction. The horror is not that what we had thought to be possible turned out to be impossible, but that what we had thought to be impossible turned out to be possible.

Trapped in an ancient prison, humanity was locked inside an illusion. Radnóti himself had been an inmate in just such a prison, as his ethical outcry is couched in the trappings of aesthetic beauty, cast in the very conventions that have undergone a radical collapse. And yet we have the poem. And in the poem we have a moment of literary transcendence of convention and representation. The poem itself is a remnant of a broken urn, a shard upon which is inscribed a divinely commanded absolute: Thou shalt not murder. Recall the talmudic tale of the shard that King David cast upon the rising waters to keep the deep at bay, the shard with the Divine Name inscribed upon it (*Makkot* 11a). Perhaps this poem may serve as just such a shard.

> Here in the Lager there are no criminals nor madmen.
>
> —Primo Levi, *Survival in Auschwitz*

Here in the Lager there is no measure, no form, no rule, no law. Words such as *good* and *evil, just* and *unjust,* Levi demonstrates, have no meaning.[225] What enables humanity to distinguish criminals and madmen? It is knowledge. The marker of the disintegration of knowledge? The disintegration of good and evil, not just in the camps but as part of a process that paved the way to the camps. From the outset, the Nazis had no concept of an unjust law, because anything one could will, beyond measure and form, was lawful. Indeed, every action taken against the Jews of Nazi-occupied Europe was *legal.* And so at the Wannsee Conference Reinhard Heydrich was very careful to stipulate that "the aim of all this was to cleanse German living space of Jews *in a legal manner.*"[226] Were the fourteen men seated around a lavish table, sipping cognac and smoking cigars, eight of whom had doctorate degrees, convened to plan the logistics of the extermination of the Jewish people—criminals? Were they madmen? The very question subverts all knowledge.

Primo Levi is not alone in his observation; other memoir writers attempt to transmit a sense of the anti-world as realm void of criminals or madmen. Fania Fénelon asserts that "death, life, tears, laughter, everything was multiplied, disproportionate, beyond the limits of the credible. All was madness."[227] To declare, however, that *all* was madness is to say that there was no measure that could distinguish sanity from insanity. Olga Lengyel recalls that "the mad rulers of the camp dictated that, while normal people were sent to death, lunatics were kept alive."[228] But, again, when *all* is madness, what can it mean to say "normal" people? Indeed, when Lengyel arrived at Auschwitz and had her first look at the women behind the electrified fence, she thought to herself, "Was this the courtyard of a madhouse?"[229] Sara Zyskind has the same memory: " 'It must be a lunatic asylum we've been brought to,' I said to myself."[230] Soon the image she encounters in the faces of these others, however, is imposed upon herself. After being shaved and disinfected, outfitted and humiliated, she recalls, "We would ourselves be taken for lunatics by those arriving after us. Perhaps we *were* all lunatics and Auschwitz an asylum from which we would never escape."[231] And where does she perceive the image of madness that threatens her? In the face of the other, of her friend Surtcha. Staring at each other, they broke into laughter, but, she remembers, "Our laughter lasted barely a few seconds, coming to an abrupt end as we looked at one another with eyes filled with horror. Was it possible that we had both gone mad?"[232] Was it possible that they had *not* gone mad?

"Why do I write?" Wiesel asks. And he answers: "Perhaps in order not to go mad. Or, on the contrary, to touch the bottom of madness."[233] What can he mean by this? If we are to touch the bottom of madness by venturing into a realm void of criminals and madmen, we can do so only in a moment of epiphany, a moment of conveying the disintegration of knowledge that eludes knowledge. Leon Wells notes that it was forbidden for "anybody to see the faces of inmates who have seen the 'sands,' "[234] those pits where bodies retrieved from mass graves were stacked and burned. Why forbidden? Because these are faces ravaged by the madness that follows upon the disintegration of knowledge. Forbidden to be seen, they are the Medusa-like faces that the literary response to the Holocaust would have us see, the faces that silently bring us face to face with a transcendence of the knowable—faces that do not know the difference between life and death.

> I have no fear of dying—nor of living. What frightens me is not to be able to distinguish between life and death.
>
> —Elie Wiesel, *The Oath*

In order to fathom Wiesel's fear, as expressed through his character, we need only recall Primo Levi's discussion of the Muselmann in Part One, where he writes of the Muselmänner, those definitive denizens of Auschwitz who formed "the backbone of the camp," that "one hesitates to call their death death."[235] So why would the witness be afraid of being unable to *know* how to make this distinction? What is at stake? And what do we distinguish when we are able to distinguish between life and death?

Ka-tzetnik offers a clue in *House of Dolls*, when Harry remarks to his sister Daniella, "These days a man has no way of knowing if he's already in the hereafter, or if he still has to wait for death. Everything is mixed up. Life and death in one brew. A hereafter that's not here, not after."[236] Since there is neither a here nor an after, there is no "after the Holocaust." There lies the problem of the knowledge of the difference between life and death. Anyone who spends "every night there," as Fania Fénelon did,[237] has experienced the disintegration of such knowledge. Hence, peering into the heart of the anti-world, we find a group of rabbinical students engaged in study and prayer in Ka-tzetnik's *Sunrise over Hell*; they are searching for "the borderline separating life from death."[238] The difference between life and death decides everything. We fear to ask how anyone could fear to lose the knowledge needed to distinguish between the two. The realization of such a fear comes in a moment of epiphany that transcends representation and knowledge itself.

So what is the knowledge that enables us to distinguish life from death? It is a knowledge of the good that engenders the responsibility for life and for the evil that undermines that responsibility. When good and evil collapse into a sameness, there is no distinction to be made. Where there is no distinction between life and death, there is no knowledge of world or reality. The disintegration of such knowledge begins with the calculated infliction of terror, with the hate-filled shriek of *Juden 'raus!* as the Nazis forced Jews from their homes into the ghettos, from the ghettos onto the trains, from the trains into the gas chambers. Those who were selected to "live" were selected for additional, systematic torture, which is neither life nor death, a life of immortal horror, where one is unable to die. Indeed, the Jew selected to live is turned over not to a concentration camp but to a torture camp, where one is tortured at every turn.

One thing that characterizes this realm of torture is silence.[239] Here, the word, which is the substance of the soul of the human being as a speaking being—the word that enables one to distinguish life from death—is snatched from the mouth. "Even where the torturers do not permanently eliminate the voice through mutilation or murder," writes Scarry, "they mime the work of pain by temporarily breaking off the voice, making it their own, making it speak their words, making it cry out when they want it to cry, be silent when they want its silence."[240] If De-Nur could not say what Auschwitz is, it is because the tearing of the Jew from the word results in the disintegration of the knowledge of the distinction between life and death. And if, as Primo Levi says, there is no word for the "demolition of a man,"[241] it is because there is no word for the torture that is a disintegration of that knowledge. In torture the difference between life and death collapses: the victim is not alive and therefore cannot die. Torture devastates the word, as the torturer takes over the word, transforming it into a scream in a devastation of the word. How does the literary word articulate that devastation?

The Devastation of the Word

> Please try to understand: the Word is everything. Through the Word we elevate ourselves or debase ourselves. . . . How would we pray without it? How would we live without it?
>
> —Elie Wiesel, *Twilight*

> They stole away the meaning words used to have. It's like learning a whole new language in a strange new world.
>
> —Arnošt Lustig, *Darkness Casts No Shadow*

Recalling that the human being is a "speaking being," a *medaber*, we realize that the devastation of the word at the hands of the Nazis was a devastation of the very humanity of the human being, which transcends semiotic systems and ontological categories. It is not that words such as *gas* and *selection* signify nothing; rather, they signify nothing that belongs to the language and therefore to the world of humanity. They signify the nothingness of anti-world and anti-humanity, of anti-word and anti-meaning. "Words are no more," Ka-tzetnik cries out,[242] or, as the Hebrew texts reads, *chadalah sfat-adam,* "human language has ceased."[243] And when human language ceases, the human being is no more. If the human being is a breach of being, as I maintain, then the phenomenon of the word belongs to the transcendent revealed in Holocaust literature. The literary word is what Rosenzweig calls "a bridge" between being and what exceeds being, a bridge made of *mitzvot,* of commandments. The very appearance of the word is a manifestation of the transcendent within the immanent, of the higher relation within the human relation. The word is the hallmark of the human being not merely because the human being speaks; rather, the human being speaks because he or she is created in the image of the Holy One and speaks in response to the summons of the Holy One. That speaking is what the Nazis set out to silence in the devastation of the word.

Because human relation is rooted in the word, the collapse of human relation is driven by the devastation of the word. "Spirit is word," writes Buber. "Spirit is not in the I but between I and You. It is not like the blood that circulates in you but like the air in which you breathe."[244] The devastation of the word amounts to a suffocation of the human being. Therefore, Michael's cellmate Menachem in Wiesel's novel *The Town beyond the Wall* declares to him, "What binds one word to another is no less mysterious than what binds one human being to another."[245] Where the word of one is bound to the word of another, the word of each binds the soul to the other. The soul lives in that between space, so that the devastation of the word is central to the assault on the soul, for the assault on the soul is an assault on the word—a point that becomes clear when we recall that the Targum of Onkelos renders God's breathing a soul into the human being as God's breathing the word the word into the human being (Genesis 2:7). This is the basis of a teaching handed down by the Chasidic master Menachem Mendel of Vitebsk (1730–1788): "Man is the language of God."[246] If man is the language of God, then the devastation of the word is a devastation of God. As always, what befalls humanity befalls God, and what befalls the word befalls both.

The creation of an anti-world demands the devastation of the word. The death, and not just the absence, of the word is graphically portrayed in the Muselmann, as we have seen. The word dies because, recalling Rudolf Vrba, the flesh of the denizen of Auschwitz has fled, and his blood has turned to water.[247] The devastation of the word is as concrete as the look of the human eye, the feel of the human touch, and the sound of the human voice—all of which were radically absent from Auschwitz. The task of Holocaust literature is to convey that absence of the word through the literary word. Like the workers who, according to the Talmud, would occasionally descend in *tevot,* or boxes, to make repairs inside the Holy of Holies (*Midot* 37a), these authors also descend in *tevot,* which also means "words," to mend the word by means of the word. Indeed, the very presence of the literature is a mending of the word. Because the word to be mended defines the human being as a breach of being, the mending comes not as a representation but as a revelation of a nonrepresentable devastation of the word. The literary response, then, is a response not to a trauma suffered so much as to a voice heard. Who calls? It is the very word, the very Name, under assault. And it calls the witness, as well as anyone who receives the testimony of the witness, *by name.*

Here, we realize on a deeper level the link between the memory and the name, between the *yad* and the *shem,* between the memory and the word. When the word is lost, memory is lost; the war against memory, as Wiesel and Levi identified the Holocaust,[248] is a war against the word transmitted *ledor vador,* "from generation to generation": none of us is the first to disturb the silence of the universe, and each of us bears a name already borne by others. In our mouths reverberate the words and the names of generations of testimony, words that in the world appear in the most mundane of phrases laden with the most mystical of meanings, such as "After you,"[249] *unheard of in the anti-world*: where the devastation of the word happens, the expression "After you" becomes either absurd or dangerous. There lies the failure of the word, as when Fania Fénelon writes, "Words failed me then and they fail me now."[250] This fundamental failing does not lie in the evil or trauma that defies depiction, in the paucity of the powers that fall short of description, or in the unprecedented parameters that exceed convention. No, it lies in the devastation of something so simple and profound as the *after you.* Words fail her. And yet she writes. She finds the words to speak of the devastation of the word and the devastation of memory and humanity, reflected in the devastation of the *after you.* The phenomenon of her writing is, in and of itself, an epiphany.

> One by one, words—all the words of the human language—wilt and grow too weak to bear a meaning.
>
> —Piotr Rawicz, *Blood from the Sky*

The wilting of one word leads to the weakening of all others. If the word here is too weak to bear a meaning, however, it is not because the meaning is too heavy or too extreme. Where words take on an extremity of meaning, life becomes heavy with meaning, and a life heavy with meaning is elevating. Where words wilt and are drained of meaning, life collapses under the weight of emptiness. Recall the teaching from the Baal Shem Tov mentioned in Part One, namely, that the letter *alef* abides in every word (*Keter Shem Tov* 45): the word too weak to bear a meaning is a word that has lost its *alef,* the silent reverberation of the Divine Name, which is the tie that binds above to below and human to human.

When considering the literary word that struggles to convey the wilting of words too weak to bear a meaning, we find that passages such as this one from Primo Levi come to mind: "Just as our hunger is not that feeling of missing a meal, so our way of being cold has need of a new word. We say 'hunger', we say 'tiredness', 'fear', 'pain', we say 'winter' and they are different things."[251] When reading such lines, we must note that a word too wilted to bear a meaning does not lie in the degree of hunger, pain, cold, or other suffering. It lies, rather, in the *uselessness* of the suffering, in the suffering *for nothing and for no one,* in the radical *isolation* of the suffering of "hunger," "fear," and "pain." Therefore, other words of the anti-world, such as "left," "right," "gas," "oven," "selection," and "special treatment," were "different things." What, then, did it mean to say "mother," "father," or "child," "good," "evil," or "human being"—or "God?" And what is the author whose medium is words to do with these words? How are words to be used to convey the devastation of words?

This tearing of word from meaning is a definitive aspect of the Event, inasmuch as it is a definitive aspect of the assault on the soul breathed into the human being as word. It is a tearing of husband from wife, of father from son, of human from human, all of which go into the disintegration of human relation: words like *father* and *brother* are turned over to the distant rumbling of emptiness. With the wilting of the word, we are left only with a scream that haunts this rumbling—the scream of the Jew and the scream of the Holy One Himself. "It is a marvel," writes the Rebbe Kalonymos Kalmish Shapira from the depths of the Warsaw Ghetto, "how the world exists after so much screaming."[252] This screaming includes the screaming of God, who "roars, howling over His city" (Jeremiah 25:30). It is a marvel how the world exists in the midst of the divine screaming; it is a marvel that such a devastation can be conveyed through the word of the witness. And yet, unlike any other body of literature, this literature sounds the depths of the word in order to somehow convey the devastation of the word, both human and divine.

Rawicz might have known the talmudic teaching that God suffers with the Jew even more profoundly than the Jew experiences his or her suffering (*Chagigah* 15b; *Sanhedrin* 46a), a suffering that is rooted in the devastation of the word. How does God scream in His suffering? Silently. Here we realize, in a moment of epiphany, that because the Nazis' devastation of the word is also a devastation of silence, it is central to their extermination of the Eternal. When words wilt God screams, shut mouthed.

> Two actors emerge heads facing each other, their eyes conducting a horror-dialogue as their feet climb a staircase of air. Queer, mute gesticulations. Speaking shut-mouthed. Towards them come floating two others, announcing something in an esoteric eye-dialect, not moving lips or hands. Their feet do not seem to be touching the ground. Everything here is happening as though not in the world of man, not even in the world of Auschwitz, but somewhere in primordial space between Chaos and Creation.
>
> —Ka-tzetnik 135633, *Atrocity*

This scene from Ka-tzetnik's novel *Atrocity* is a wordless play performed in a barracks unlike any barracks in the world of words. Two singers from the world of words, Bergson and Hayim-Idl, volunteered to perform in the anti-world, only to be told that the play is a mime, a mute performance that they would play out in the midst of the devastation of the word, "speaking shut-mouthed." They must sing without a sound, scream without a sound, "not in the world of man, not even in the world of Auschwitz." The "world of man" is the world of the word, the world of voice and memory. The "world of Auschwitz" is the world of the devastation of the word; it is an anti-world "between Chaos and Creation," emptied of the word that enables us to distinguish between the two. The word is prior to both chaos and creation, prior to the world of Auschwitz and the world of humanity, transcendent and transmitted only in a moment of epiphany, as though in a dream—a dream such as Jacob's, when he saw angels ascending to the heavens on a staircase of air (Genesis 28:12).

The Talmud raises a question concerning the angels ascending the staircase: Where do they come from? The answer: they are the angels, the messengers (which is the meaning of *malakhim* or "angels"), whom we have created with our thoughts, our actions, and, above all, with our words (*Avot* 4:11; *Chagigah* 41a). The angels we create with our words go out into the world and ascend into the upper realms to do their work, for good or for evil. The actors in this case ascend not just a staircase "of air," but, in the Hebrew, they climb *b'halal,* "in the void"[253] that haunts this literary transcendence of representation. Their hands motionless, the mimes do not even mime. Yet what sort of angels do we create not through words but through the devastation of the word? With the devastation of the word, we create no angels, but only the primordial void between Chaos and Creation.

Thus, we have the two actors engaged in a wordless "horror-dialogue"—a horror because it is wordless, not a dialogue at all, but an anti-dialogue that announces the devastation of dialogue attendant upon the devastation of the word. For the word that bears meaning is dialogical through and through.

The silence of this horror-dialogue is the terrible silence that refuses representation and therefore interpretation; it is the silence that, as Levinas says, "is not a simple absence of speech; speech lies in the depths of silence like a laughter perfidiously held back. It is the inverse of language: the interlocutor has given a sign, but has declined every interpretation; this is the silence that terrifies."[254] The "sign" that refuses interpretation is the "esoteric eye-dialect," the "dialect" not of the listening eye but of the eye no longer capable of listening or reading, hearing or interpreting, the dialect of one struck deaf, mute, and blind.

In Ka-tzetnik's novel, this scene is anticipated by a moment of epiphany earlier in the novel. It happens upon the entry of the boy Moni into an Auschwitz barracks full of shadows who were once men, now slipping into the abyss of the Muselmänner.

> Moni climbed amongst them. The smell of Mussulman bones overwhelmed him. . . . He crawled amongst them. They received him the way the pile behind the block receives a skeleton dumped by the block orderlies. Here no one utters a word. Here speech is extinct.
>
> —Ka-tzetnik 135633, *Atrocity*

Not only is speech extinct but, in the Hebrew, *kol lashon,*[255] "every tongue," that might give utterance to speech has vanished. One is tempted to say that the entry of Moni into the block is the entry of the dead into the company of the dead. There are skeletons stacked in a pile outside the block and the skeletons arranged on the straw bunks inside. But for the occasional trace of movement inside the block, one pile is indistinguishable from the other. Like the dead, the "living" utter not a word, hence the erasure of difference. To be sure, the Midrash teaches that the only difference between the righteous who are living and the righteous who are dead is the faculty of speech (*Midrash Tehillim* 1:30:2). Drained of the faculty of speech, the "living" are neither dead nor alive, as the words *life* and *death* have lost all meaning. Life and death become indistinguishable when speech becomes extinct: the devastation of the word is the devastation of the distinction. If here "there is no such thing as father, brother, friend,"[256] as Wiesel says in his memoir, it is because here speech is extinct.

The vanishing of difference in the anti-world happens in a transformation of difference into indifference. Each skeleton is like the other, all are interchangeable, poured into a silent, nameless, faceless morass. Indeed, where speech is extinct, the face is extinct, for the face is the origin of speech and the revelation of difference as non-indifference, as Levinas has explained.[257] The author who, through the literary word, gives utterance to this scene of the devastation of the word takes up a re-creation of the immemorial beginning, which is the creation of the word itself, the word from which all that is derives its being. As always, the moment of epiphany is more than a moment of realization or revelation; it is a moment of implication and reckoning. The faculty of speech implies the obligation of testimony that devolves upon the human community. Where speech is extinct, testimony, *edah,* which is also "community," is extinct—at least until the witness attests to its extinction.

What, then, becomes extinct where speech is no more? A teaching from the Jewish mystical tradition in which Yehiel De-Nur was educated may shed some light here. According to that tradition, speech comes about through the entry of the Shekhinah, or the Divine Presence, into this "kingdom," which is known as *Malkhut.* Like the Temple, speech is a kind of sanctuary for the Shekhinah. In the Midrash, Rabbi Chiya teaches that the Temple's sanctuary is called *debir* because from it *dibur* or "speech" enters the world; Rabbi Yannai said it is because from the sanctuary we have commandments or "utterances," *dibrot,* that connect this world with the upper worlds (*Shir Hashirim Rabbah* 4:4:9). Both sages, of course, are right. Just as the Divine Light shines through the Temple's windows and into the world (see *Bamidbar Rabbah* 15:2), so is the Divine Presence revealed through speech to reverberate throughout the world. But when speech is extinct, so is the Divine Presence. She no longer follows her children into exile. She is lost in her own exile, in the exile of the word.

> "I can't agree when people who weren't there say it's impossible to put into words, to give it meaning," Dita said. She could not give up the hope that everything people have done—even the most perverse things—could be described. "The sense of a word may shift, but I'm

> not afraid that reality will evaporate like mist. Every reality . . . can be put into words. And one day not only will words get their meaning back, but things will too."
>
> —Arnošt Lustig, *Dita Saxova*

In these lines we have a literary expression of the fundamental problem—and the desperate hope—of Holocaust representation: the hope that words will get their meaning back. Surely, we try to assure ourselves, everything that people have done, every trauma that people have endured, can be related, described, and narrated. Surely every reality, no matter how horrific, can be put into words, told, narrated, and transmitted. Or perhaps, as some maintain,[258] it is the other way around: it is not that every reality can be put into words, but rather that words and narrative generate every reality. If it cannot be represented or narrated, then it did not happen. Words form a kind of event horizon for thought, the parameters of the possible, and if it cannot be thought, then it cannot be real. It did not happen.

The Nazis' methodical devastation of the word in the concentrationary universe demonstrates the bankruptcy of this view of language, word, and reality. For in the time of the Shoah, humanity collided with a reality that exceeds possibility and with an ontological condition that exceeds thought. There are realities that cannot be put into words, not because they are too horrible but because they are too transcendent, accessible only in moments of the revelation of the transcendent Good that exceeds representation and that elevates words to poetry and prayer, to Holy Scripture and salient silence. This transcendent Good—the ground of meaning that *exceeds* words—is revealed not only as the otherwise than being who sanctifies being, but also as the One targeted for annihilation in the extermination of the Jews.

The Good revealed in these moments of epiphany, in the words of Levinas, is revealed as "the trace of the excession, the excessive, of what could not be contained, of the non-content, disproportionate to all measure and all capacity, the trace of the infinite."[259] Where is the trace of the infinite to be found? In the disturbance of the witness, as Levinas has said,[260] in the apperception of "infinity as the Desire for infinity,"[261] so that the infinite is not "an immense object, exceeding the horizons of the look. It is Desire that measures the infinity of the infinite, for it is a measure through the very impossibility of measure . . . it is revelation."[262] And it seeps through these literary lines in a moment of epiphany. Dita's desire for the mending of word and meaning is just such a metaphysical desire: the hope that she refused to give up is the frantic longing for the ineffable Good that came under a radical assault.

To draw again on Levinas, "the metaphysical desire" of someone like Dita Saxova "tends toward *something else entirely,* toward the *absolutely other*."[263] Her longing for the bond between word and meaning is a longing for the bond between human and human; as we have seen, the devastation of the one is the collapse of the other. "For Desire," Levinas elaborates, "this alterity [of the other human being], non-adequate to the idea, has a meaning. It is understood as the alterity of the Other and of the Most High. The very dimension of height is opened up by metaphysical Desire."[264] Non-adequate to the idea, it is non-adequate to representation: in the metaphysical desire that drives the witness's literary response we glimpse the nonrepresentable Good targeted for annihilation. Because it is nonrepresentable, it is invisible and eludes all semiotic systems. Because in its excession the Good exceeds representation, it cannot be possessed, contained, or otherwise comprehended; rather, it *commands* and thus lays claim to me. And the commanding Voice of the Good finds its way into the world through the Jew.

> Across the brow of Shlamek's father they branded *Jude.* Blood gave from the seared word. And the word was as clear as the blood oozing from it. As though it were quite natural that the word *Jude* should give blood.
>
> —Ka-tzetnik 135633, *House of Dolls*

So it is written in Ka-tzetnik's novel *House of Dolls*, a tale based on the story of his murdered sister Daniella. When Daniella is forced into a camp brothel and sees women branded with the word *Feld-Hure* ("field whore"), this image of an old man from the Kraków Ghetto flashes through her memory. These lines harbor a profoundly epiphanic moment, a moment of clarity with regard to how we might understand the demolition of *this* word. The Hebrew word translated as "clear" is *muvenet,*[265] a cognate of *lehavin,* to "understand." Here, the incomprehensible is "understood," as the word *Jude* becomes incomprehensible, not because it surpasses understanding but because it surpasses representation. One realizes that the Nazis' demolition of the word is central to the demolition of the *Jew.* And so the word for "Jew" bleeds Jewish blood: it is as natural for the word *Jude* to bleed as it is natural for the Jew to bleed in a draining of meaning from the word.

As the word of Torah is engraved into the heart, so is the word *Jude* branded into the forehead, like a bleeding frontlet between the eyes, where the head tefillin, the *tefillin shel rosh,* is placed. Its four inner compartments contain words from the Torah that makes the Jew a Jew; as the word *Jude* bleeds, the Torah bleeds from the four inner compartments. The word *Jude* takes on even greater meaning when it bleeds Jewish blood. Bleeding Jewish blood, the word *Jude* bleeds the *dam* of the *adam,* the "blood" of the "human being," the blood that *is* the human being, the blood in which the *nefesh* or "soul" of the human being abides, as it is written (Leviticus 17:11).

A disciple of the great mystic Isaac Luria (1534–1572) known simply as Rabbi Avraham teaches that tefillin are called "the face of the human being."[266] Recall the teaching noted in Part One that one may lay tefillin only when it is light enough to recognize the face of the other human being (*Kitzur Shulchan Arukh* 10:2). To lay tefillin is to affirm that there is no Torah without the face of the other human being, no face without the Torah. The thing that makes the Jew a Jew is the humanity that makes the human being human. Therefore, as Wiesel has written, "there comes a time when one cannot be a man without assuming the Jewish condition."[267] In the particularity of his or her condition the Jew announces the human condition as a condition of infinite responsibility to and for the other human being. As the soul of the Jew bleeds from the word *Jude,* humanity itself bleeds away.

If, as Levinas has said, "the soul is the other in me,"[268] and if the Jew is "the other," as is often affirmed, then the soul is the Jew in me. The Torah transmitted to humanity through the Jews cries out to us, "Where is your brother? And what have you done?" In that outcry we hear the voice of our own soul summoning us to become who we are *in truth.* Thus, Ka-tzetnik enables us to see what bleeds away when the word *Jude* branded into the forehead of an elderly Jew oozes blood. He enables us to see that such a scene is about far more than this single victim. He enables us to see that the meaning of the word *Jude* is the meaning of meaning. For the meaning of the word *Jude* is the meaning of a humanity that needs meaning as the lungs need air, a humanity suffocated upon the devastation of the word and the ensuing demolition of meaning.

The Demolition of Meaning

Meaning is the face of the Other.

—Emmanuel Levinas, *Totality and Infinity*

Give some meaning to the life of Your servant.

—Moshe Flinker, *Young Moshe's Diary*

We have seen how the word comes under a radical assault during the Holocaust. In order to understand how meaning might come under a similar assault, we must first have a sense of what is meant by "meaning." Meaning is not in the word; rather, meaning emanates from a preoriginary silence to give birth to relationship, both higher and human, through the word. "All recourse to words," Levinas makes this point, "takes place *already* within the primordial face to face of language,"[269] which is the silent, immemorial ground of meaning. Prior to all utterance, meaning issues from this nonrepresentable, invisible, immemorial *already*. That is why it eludes representation, why it summons again and ever again the effort to utter the ineffable and to represent the nonrepresentable.

According to the Jewish tradition targeted for annihilation in the Shoah, meaning springs from the silent letter *alef* that precedes the *beit*; the *beit* is the first letter of the alphabet that has a sound, the first letter of the Torah, the letter of the beginning. In the beginning, meaning emerges from silence to become utterance, as the *beit* emerges from the *alef*. The Midrash teaches that when the *beit* is asked who created it, the letter answers, "He who is above created me." When asked, "What is His name?" the *beit* points with the extension of its base back to the *alef*, which signifies the Divine Name (*Pesikta Rabbati* 21:21). As the seat of meaning, says the Baal Shem, "the letter *alef* is Wisdom"; thus, "He created light from the letter *alef*" (*Keter Shem Tov* 355). According to such a view, we do not "make meaning"; in a sense, meaning "makes" us, as it emanates from the divine light that is prior to all the luminaries of the heavens, prior to the heavens themselves: in the beginning God creates the *heavens* and the earth.

"To have meaning," says Levinas, "is to be situated relative to an absolute,"[270] relative to "the Good," which "is before being."[271] The Good is the *alef* before the *beit* of creation; thus, says the mystic sage Jacob ben Jacob ha-Kohen (d. ca. 1270), the *alef* "acts as a witness to the name of the Holy One, blessed be He."[272] If we understand meaning in these Jewish terms, then we see that the Nazis' demolition of meaning has a transcendent, metaphysical, and therefore nonrepresentable aspect that attends the concrete assault on the Jews. If the word is a bridge, it bridges the *alef* with the *beit,* the transcendent, metaphysical meaning with the immediate, ontological reality that lends itself to expression. In the time of the Shoah, the transcendent came under assault in the assault on the flesh-and-blood body of Israel. Epiphany itself came under assault. The demolition of meaning, then, came as an assault on the *alef.* And with the obliteration of the *alef,* there is no *beit,* no world, no Torah, no meaning.

If the word is relational, meaning is axiological. If "meaning is the face of the Other,"[273] it is because "the epiphany of the face is ethical," as Levinas insists,[274] and *absolutely* so, bearing as it does all the "exigency of the holy."[275] Thus, Levinas argues, "a face *enters* into our world from an absolutely foreign sphere, that is, precisely from an absolute."[276] This entry of the face into our world is a *revelation.* The demolition of meaning is the demolition of the absolute ethical exigency, a demolition of the revelation that comes in the epiphany of the face: from the face resounds a commanding Voice, even when nothing is said. If meaning is *heard,* as the Hebrew word for "meaning," *mashmaut,* suggests, it is heard as a summons to reckoning. This is the reason for Levinas's assertion that "it is commandment rather than narration which marks the first step towards human understanding."[277] The postmodern view that all meaning and reality are reducible to narrative here proves to be totally bankrupt with regard to responding to the Nazis' demolition of meaning. The Holocaust author's narrative expression of the nonrepresentable proceeds from an immemorial commandment, which bears an immemorial meaning, even—or especially—when it is dealing with the demolition of meaning. Once again, we realize that "Holocaust representation" is much more an ethical matter than an aesthetic one.

As the transcendent merges with the immanent in the epiphany of the face, meaning merges with word to make heard a commanding Voice: meaning *addresses* us. Meaning is *voiced* in a question that demands a response: Where are you? The demolition of meaning is the demolition of this primordial, perennial question. And the commandment that issues most fundamentally, most insistently, from the merging of word and meaning in the epiphany of the face is: Thou shalt not murder. The demolition of meaning is the demolition of the prohibition. Of all the Scriptures that Levinas deems "the primary foundation of meaning,"[278] this one is most primary: Thou shalt not murder (Exodus 20:13). It is the "Scripture whereby each soul is called to exegesis, which is regulated both by the rigorous reading of the text and by the unicity—unique in all eternity—of its own contribution, which is also its discovery, the soul's share."[279] Inasmuch as we encounter moments of epiphany in Holocaust literature's response to the demolition of meaning, that literature bears a similar call to exegesis and a reckoning of "the soul's share" on the part of the reader. Why? Because, as an epiphany of meaning, this is an epiphany of the face, and "the epiphany of the face qua face opens humanity,"[280] which implicates us in our own humanity. Without such an implication there is no recovery from the demolition of meaning.

The demolition of meaning is the demolition of the meaning *revealed* through the face of the other human being: meaning is the meaning of the other human being. Contrary to almost every notion of representation, signification, language, and meaning, wherever meaning is revealed through the face, it is *without context,* as Levinas explains: "The face is signification, and signification without context. I mean that the Other, in the rectitude of his face, is not a character within a context. . . . All signification in the usual sense of the term is relative to such a context. . . . Here, to the contrary, the face is meaning all by itself."[281] Thus, when Paltiel in Wiesel's novel *The Testament* writes, "The hungry child, / The thirsty stranger, / The frightened old man, / All ask for me,"[282] we do not have to ask, "Which child, which stranger, which old man?" in order to make sense of what we read. Without this "meaning all by itself," life is not life, and death is not death. Without its desperate struggle to recover a trace of meaning, Holocaust literature is not Holocaust literature, even if that recovery amounts to nothing more than an account of the demolition of meaning that characterized the Nazis' assault on the body and soul of Israel.

If there is a single word that has its meaning demolished in the anti-world of the Holocaust, it is the word *You.* Recall the teaching from the Zohar: instead of reading *Bereshit bara Elokim et ha- . . .* as "In the beginning God created the . . . ," we should read it as "In the beginning God created the *alef, tav, hey* of *atah*: You" (*Zohar* I, 15b). The word *atah* is the word of the beginning, whose meaning dispels the darkness over the face of the deep. It is not exactly the opposite of nothingness; rather, it is a category that is beyond the distinctions of being and nothingness. This transcendent meaning of the word *atah* underscores the transcendence—the *height*—of meaning itself: the demolition of meaning is the demolition of height. Note that in the opening line of Genesis, the word that comes after *Bereshit bara Elokim et ha- . . .* is *shamayim,* the "heavens." God began with the heavens and then created the earth, says the Midrash, in order to introduce the dimension of height or meaning to creation before proceeding with the creation of this world (*Tanchuma Bereshit* 1). Without this dimension of meaning—this dimension of transcendent height—that belongs to the anarchic beginning, the soul cannot endure. As long as the preoriginary dimension of height abides, however, the Nazis cannot endure. And the Nazis knew it.

> But they do not know the beginning,
> not the eternal beginning—
> and that's why they hate us.
>
> —Nelly Sachs, *Eli: A Mystery Play of the Sufferings of Israel*

These lines are from Nelly Sachs's mystical drama about one of the *Tzaddikim Nistarim,* the thirty-six righteous individuals who are hidden, but thanks to whom, according to Jewish tradition, the world continues to endure.[283] The Righteous One in the play is a shoemaker named Michael, and he sets out to identify the Nazi who was responsible for the murder of a child named Eli. The lines are spoken by a *dayan,* a judge, in the Jewish community. The "they," of course, refers to the Nazis, and the "us" designates the Jews. So what is the "eternal beginning?" Why would not knowing it lead anyone to hate the Jews? And what does it have to do with the Nazis' demolition of meaning?

From what has been said, we see that the eternal beginning lies in the immemorial meaning attached to the eternal. It accompanies every instant and every utterance, as affirmed in the morning liturgy, when Jews praise God, who "renews the actions of the creation continuously every day." If "time is the presence of God in the world of space," as Heschel has said,[284] the eternal beginning is the presence of meaning—and all that it demands of us—in time. Like the morning blessing on the Holy One, it is the ongoing affirmation of the beginning, the affirmation of "Here I am for you"—"Here I am the *You*" that the Nazis would annihilate in the demolition of meaning. The You is the Yea that Rosenzweig invokes when he says, "Yea is the beginning. . . . The first Yea in God establishes the divine essence for all infinity. And this first Yea is 'in the beginning.' "[285] In the mystical tradition that informs Sachs's drama the Yea is tied to the Hebrew word *kinui,* which means "name of God" and whose root is *ken,* the word for "yes" (see, for example, *Toledot Yaakov Yosef, Emor* 16).[286] The affirming Yea calls forth our affirmation of "Here I am for you," through a movement into a radical vulnerability for the sake of the other human being, to the point of "a denuding beyond the skin, to the wounds one dies from, denuding to death, being as vulnerability," as Levinas has said.[287] If, to recall Buber's insight, "in every You we address the eternal You,"[288] we must add that in every You we are *addressed* by the eternal You: in every You we are faced with the demands of meaning, the demands of this radical vulnerability. And so the Jews are hated for announcing to the nations this revelation of the eternal beginning.

The annihilation of the Jews is tied to the demolition of the meaning that springs from the eternal beginning, from the eternal You. According to Levi Yitzchak of Berditchev, "All the hatred of the Jews" comes "from our constant defense of You,"[289] which is a defense of the eternal You as well as the You of flesh and blood, both of whom announce an infinite responsibility that can be neither fulfilled nor abrogated. In Brian Percival's film *The Book Thief* (2013), based on the novel by Markus Zusak,[290] the question is raised as to why "they" hate the Jews and anyone who helps the Jews. The answer: because the Jews remind them of their humanity. Which is to say: the Jews remind them of the absolute demand of meaning, which emanates from the eternal beginning. The epiphany that comes from the depths of this scene from Sachs's play is this: "they hate us," as the *dayan* says, not because they do not know the eternal beginning but because, on some level, they know it all too well—well enough to wage war against the Eternal.

If Auschwitz signifies anything, it is the systematic demolition of meaning that characterizes this relentless war against the Eternal. And so Levi remembers that his first days in the Lager were filled with a "sound and fury signifying nothing: a hubbub of people without names or faces drowned in a continuous, deafening background noise from which, however, the human word did not surface."[291] The demolition of meaning makes it impossible for the human word to surface, the word that is a saying of "Here I am for you."

> The new set of meanings provided the best evidence of the devastation that Auschwitz created in the psyche of every human being. . . . All of us were drawn into a bizarre transformation of reality.
>
> —Sara Nomberg-Przytyk, *Auschwitz*

New set of meanings? What does *that* mean?

If meaning is *mashmaut,* something that entails hearing a message or a summons, the new set of meanings entails hearing nothing but a sound and a fury signifying nothing, signifying not even nothingness. It is simply *there,* like the "there is," neither something nor nothing, sheer horror and no more, a horror that strips consciousness of its subjectivity "not in lulling it into unconsciousness," as Levinas says, "but in throwing it into an *impersonal vigilance*,"[292] where, "anything can count for anything else."[293] It is the reason why Yehiel De-Nur cannot say what Auschwitz is. Yet how can the demolition of meaning be evidence of anything in any meaningful way?

The new set of meanings is the best evidence of the devastation of meaning, which is the devastation of the meaning of devastation. Do we not have here the devastation of representation as well? Such devastation is consigned to the nonrepresentable, not because of the severity of the suffering and the trauma but because of the very meaning of suffering and trauma. Hence, there can be no "traumatic realism," no "literature of atrocity."

Nomberg-Przytyk invokes the devastation that Auschwitz created in the psyche. In the psyche? No, not in the psyche, at least not as the term is used now. Not in the psyche but *in the soul.* In the soul of every human being, in the assault on the human in the human being. There lies the transformation of reality. Reality is the reality of the human being, the reality of the soul, the reality of the relation in the midst of which reality and the soul unfold. Neither something nor nothing, the unreal is the inhuman. Here, we realize that the worn out phrase "man's inhumanity to man" is in this instance man's unreality to man, where the word *man,* the *ben adam,* loses its meaning to the point of being unreal. Hence, there is no word "to express this offense, the demolition of a man,"[294] because the demolition of a man is the demolition of meaning and reality.

A bizarre transformation of reality? Not exactly: not a transformation but a demolition of reality with the demolition of meaning and humanity, of the soul and the sanctity of the human being. It is a transformation of meaning into meaninglessness, which is the realm of the bizarre. It is a transformation of distinction into the nondescript, so that there is no scripting, no writing the disaster. Here the sun turns to darkness, and the moon turns to blood. What can such a transformation mean? Elsewhere Nomberg-Przytyk gives us a hint.

"In Auschwitz," she writes, "the pigs liked to feast on good people."[295] If the demolition of meaning lies in the demolition of the soul, it lies in the demolition of the Good. Just as the Good is nonrepresentable, so is its demolition. The new set of meanings that provide the best evidence of the destruction that was Auschwitz provide the best evidence of the destruction of the Good. Meaning is itself the category of the ethical, of the nonrepresentable Good that makes meaning matter. The question that remains is: Can the literary account of the transformation of meaning and reality, of the Good and humanity, reverse the transformation? Can it bespeak the ineffable Good in such a way as to transcend the issue of representation?

> *Hier ist kein Warum.*
>
> —Promo Levi, *Survival in Auschwitz*

"Here there is no why." Where there is no Why, there is no meaning, because where there is no Why, there is no Who, no human relation, and therefore no human being. Where there is no humanity, there is no meaning. Where there is no Who, there is no Why: there is simply what is, the "there is," neutral, mute, deaf, and indifferent. Hence, the original title of Levi's memoir: *Se questo è un uomo* (If this is a man, or Is this a man?). Paradoxically, the Why that haunts all of Holocaust literature arises from an obliterated Who. Like a prayer, the Why is a question that has no answer other than itself, put to the Holy One, to the ultimate Who, who is ultimately targeted for obliteration; the question, therefore, is put to the ultimate Why, who haunts the question itself, like the *el* in *shelah.*

Reading these four words from Levi's literary response to the Holocaust alongside the words from the opening pages of the Zohar, the flash of an epiphany illuminates our understanding of both (yes, Levi and Zohar, an unlikely pair):

> When the most Mysterious wished to reveal Himself, He first produced a single point which was transmuted into a thought, and in this He executed innumerable designs, and engraved innumerable engravings. He further engraved with the sacred and mystic lamp a mystic and most holy design, which was a wondrous edifice issuing from the midst of thought. This is called *Mi,* or "Who," and was the beginning of the edifice, existent and non-existent, deep buried, unknowable by name. It was only called *Mi.* It desired to become manifest and to be called by name. It therefore clothed itself in a refulgent and precious garment and created *eleh,* or "These," and . . . the letters of the two words intermingled, forming the complete name *E-l-o-h-i-m* [God]. (*Zohar* I, 2a)

If the *Who* created the heavens and the earth and the human being, then all of creation harbors an elusive, ineffable, yet ineluctable *Why*. If the watchword of the anti-world is *Hier ist kein Warum,* as Levi astutely realized, then the concentrationary universe comes about in an anti-creation.[296] The assault on the Why—the demolition of meaning—is an assault on the Holy One, Creator of heaven and earth.

As the dimension of meaning, the Why is also the dimension of the future, which, as Levinas realized, is a *Who*: "The other is the future."[297] The Who is the future, the one to whom and for whom we have *yet* to fulfill an infinite responsibility, as commanded by the Infinite Who. Meaning is the future. Where there is a sense of meaning, there is an answering to the call of *someone* who summons us to a horizon that we have *yet* to reach. With the demolition of meaning, therefore, comes the demolition of time itself, the demolition of the *after,* as Wiesel has noted: "After? Did you say: after? Meaning what?"[298] What does it mean to speak of trauma and aftermath amid the demolition of the *after*? And yet this *after,* the future, the Why and the Who—all of it—form the matrix of the literary response to the Holocaust. The Why emerges with the remembrance of the declaration of *Hier ist kein Warum.* In other words, the literary response to the Holocaust requires and at times restores the very categories that have been obliterated in the event. That is why the literary response to the Holocaust constitutes a transcendence that is otherwise than representation. It is a kind of resurrection of the soul, mounted by the soul, in the *after*math of the desolation of the soul. For the soul is made of meaning.

The Desolation of the Soul

> The Lord God formed the human being of the dust of the ground and breathed into his nostrils the breath of life; and the human being became a living soul.
>
> —Genesis 2:7

> For this reason was man created alone, to teach that whoever destroys a single soul [*nefesh*]. . . . Scripture imputes to him as though he has destroyed a whole world.
>
> —*Talmud Bavli, Sanhedrin* 37a

The Nazis systematically murdered not only Jewish bodies but also Jewish souls, indeed, the human soul itself. Whereas Torquemada burned and tortured bodies in order to save souls, Fackenheim reminds us, Eichmann set out "to destroy souls before he destroyed bodies."[299] Or perhaps better: they destroyed souls precisely by destroying bodies, limb by limb, cell by cell, thought by thought, word by word. From a Jewish point of view, the body/soul dichotomy of Greek and then Christian thinking is misleading, if not wrongheaded. "The Bible," Heschel observes, "knows neither the dichotomy of body and soul nor the trichotomy of body, soul, spirit."[300] The desolation of the soul that distinguishes the Holocaust comes with the obliteration of this flesh-and-blood givenness of body and soul: the soul is not an abstraction.

When we speak of soul, we speak of *nefesh,* the soul that is in the blood. The *nefesh* is the soul's body, so that the body does not have a soul, but rather the soul has a body. Hence, the desolation of the soul entails a humiliation and desolation of the body. To my knowledge, only Jewish thought entertains the notion of a physical dimension of the metaphysical soul, what is called *nefesh*. The Talmud teaches, for example, that not only the soul but also the body is made of Torah: of the 613 commandments that constitute the Torah, 248 correspond to the bones of the body, and 365 to the sinews of the body (*Makkot* 24a). With the fleeing of the flesh there is a fleeing of Torah and draining of life from the blood itself. Empty of the light of life, the eyes are drained of the light of Torah. Those empty eyes announce our own emptiness.

The assault on human relation and higher relation, on word and meaning, is a radical assault on the soul in its flesh-and-blood reality. In Part One we noted the profound significance of the assault on the name and the teaching from Jewish tradition that says the name and the soul are of a piece.[301] Eclipsing the name, the Nazis forced a number into the body, under the skin, as a first step toward draining the body of its soul and its flesh. Thus, as we have seen in Part One, the memory of the assault on the soul through the flesh-and-blood assault on the name is central to the testimony of many camp survivors. Reducing the person to nothing more than an object to be disposed of, the number is the first weapon drawn in the ontological war on body and soul and the creation of what Fackenheim calls the Nazis' "most characteristic, most original product": the Muselmann.[302]

> All the muselmanns . . . have the same story, or more exactly, have no story; they followed the slope down to the bottom, like streams

> that run down to the sea. . . . [T]hey, the *Muselmänner* . . . form the backbone of the camp, an anonymous mass, continually renewed and always identical, of non-men who march and labour in silence, the divine spark dead within them. . . . One hesitates to call them living: one hesitates to call their death death, in the face of which they have no fear, as they are too tired to understand.
>
> —Primo Levi, *Survival in Auschwitz*

In Part One we went into some detail on the Muselmann, citing various analyses of this phenomenon unique to the Holocaust. Here, we cite Levi's profound insight more fully to discover how his literary genius transcends the representable and offers us an epiphanic glimpse into those eyes in which "not a trace of a thought is to be seen."[303] They are the "shufflers," as Isabella Leitner once described them to me, who do not walk and have no path, both of which are indicators of the desolation of the soul. Because they have no story, Levi tells their story, outside the time and space of representation, for their "faceless presences" embody "all the evil of our time,"[304] and the Evil, like the Good, is nonrepresentable. Telling a tale that cannot be told, Levi speaks not in their place but apart from any "place," from any *makom,* in Hebrew, which is one of the names for God. When the divine spark is gone, the story is gone, as is their place: a trace of the nonrepresentable God is manifest as a story that transcends representation. "The divine image in man *can* be destroyed," says Fackenheim. "No more threatening proof to this effect can be found than the so-called *Muselmann* in the Nazi death camp."[305] Far more than an emaciated human being, the Muselmann announces the ultimate in the Nazi evil, incarnate in a creature whose voice has been silenced and whose death is no longer death.

These lines from Levi's literary response to the Nazi evil reveal that, in a very important sense, the Nazi does not set out to murder the Jew, since only a human being can be murdered. The Nazi perpetrates something other than murder, something more than murder: he transforms the Jew into a Muselmann, who lies outside the categories of human life and death, murder and salvation: if his death is not death, you cannot murder a Muselmann. That is why Levi sees embodied in the Muselmann "all the evil of our time in one image,"[306] the image emptied of the divine image. If Auschwitz signifies the Holocaust, the Muselmann signifies Auschwitz. The Nazis' transformation of man into Muselmann is a singular phenomenon that constitutes the singularity of the Holocaust; it is a transformation situated in the transcendent, and its literary expression transcends representation. For the Muselmann is not merely the calculated outcome of torture, exposure, and deprivation. Far more than the victim of starvation and brutality, the Muselmann is *the Jew* whose very existence was deemed criminal, whose prayers were regarded as an act of sedition, whose holy days were subject to desecration. He is *the Jew* for whom marriage and childbirth were forbidden, for whom schooling was a crime, for whom there was no protection under the law. He is *the Jew,* both widowed and orphaned, forced to witness the murder of his family, and rendered ferociously alone before being rendered ferociously faceless. Aware of the transcendent nature of the phenomenon, Fackenheim describes the Muselmann as "a *novum,*"[307] a singularity that the ontological categories cannot accommodate. And yet Levi wonders whether it is a way of *human* being at all: "non-men" he calls them. Not non-Jews, from a Nazi standpoint, but *precisely Jews*, whom they deemed "non-men."

A non-man, the Muselmann Jew has neither a story nor a death. Neither mortal nor immortal, he cannot speak; stranded outside the realm of mortality, he has nothing inside him to express or convey: drained of the divine image, the he is drained of the word. Without a word, he is without a soul; and yet, he is not absent. On the contrary: he is all too present, overwhelmingly so. The Muselmann, one recalls Levi's words, is part of a *silent,* "anonymous mass" of "non-men," who say nothing not because they have nothing to say but because their words have been reduced to non-words. Strictly speaking, they are not even silent—they are silence itself, a nefarious, unprecedented silence. This mute and faceless mass is not a crowd or even a herd; it is not a body of anything that pertains to "the masses." It is a skeletal river of non-being that flows into an abysmal ocean of ashes. Having reached what Levi calls "the bottom," this river flows upward, through the chimneys, where the silent, anonymous mass ascends into the silence of the heavens. Indeed, the silence of the heavens is precisely the silence of this anonymous mass.

Levi describes the Muselmann as one "in whose eyes not a trace of a thought is to be seen."[308] Where there is no thought, there is no word, nothing that might suggest that *this* is a human being. As a *medaber,* a human being may transcend the blank rumbling of the anonymous mass. Rendered wordless, the man becomes soulless: not a word is to be heard from the parched lips of the Muselmann, and that is why his vacant eyes are empty of thought. Having the capacity neither for speech nor for thought, the Jew made Muselmann is bled of what defines him or her as a human being. The point bears repeating: his silence is not the silence of one who does not speak. Nor is it the silence of a mute who cannot speak. The soul dead within him, the silence of the Muselmann's body is a *dead* silence.

> One of the ugliest sights to a man is that of another man sleeping in his tiny portion of the bunk . . . *because he has a body*—a body that has been exploited to the utmost: with a number tattooed on it . . . with just enough sleep at night to work during the day, and just enough time to eat. . . . If you die . . . your body is burned and your ashes are used to fertilize the fields or fill in the ponds. . . . But elsewhere they make soap out of people, and lampshades out of human skin, and jewelry out of the bones.
>
> —Tadeusz Borowski, "Auschwitz, Our Home (A Letter)"

In these lines that drive home the sheer physical horror of the Holocaust we have one of the most metaphysical, most transcendent passages in all of Borowski's literature. The epiphany lies in the realization that the desolation of the soul is ridden with a radical assault on the concrete space-time existence of the body. The images convey the shattering reality of the bond between body and soul. The body's space undergoes a constant usurpation. The body is too much for the soul, and the soul is too much for the body. That is why this is one of the ugliest sights to a man, and it is the task of literature to transmit this ugliness, in all of its aesthetic power: Holocaust literature is not about unwanted beauty, nor even about trauma—it is about ugliness. More than an aesthetic ugliness, it is an ethical ugliness. If Wiesel's friend once described Auschwitz as "a spectacle of terrifying beauty,"[309] it is due to this ethical ugliness. "It is to be feared," writes Jean-François Lyotard, "that word representations (books, interviews) and thing representations (films, photographs) of the extermination of the Jews, and of 'the jews,' by the Nazis bring back the very thing against which they work unceasingly."[310] Indeed. Here, they work against the flesh-and-blood assault on the soul, in which Holocaust "representation" runs the risk of becoming complicit. If beauty is tied to the Good, ugliness is tied to the Evil, the evil of our time, the evil that eludes representation and at times enlists it. With the Nazis comes the horrifying realization that aesthetics and evil may merge.

"Another man sleeping . . . ," we read. Except no one is sleeping. "One wakes up at every moment," we recall Levi's remark, "frozen with terror, shaking in every limb,"[311] shaking in the confined space of a tiny portion of a bunk, the one space left to the "ordinary" prisoner, the space that both promises and withdraws the respite of the night, denied to the one whose soul is undergoing a systematic demolition. In its demolition, the body is robbed of its *bed,* where at the end of the day the human being speaks within his heart and then falls silent. The demolition of the soul is the demolition of the nocturnal space otherwise promised to the body, cramped and enclosed by other bodies undergoing a similar demolition, bodies that from time to time die next to you during the night without respite: death, too, is forced into this cramped space. In the winter, bodies frozen with ice and terror have to be chipped away from the planks.

In the Nazis' assault on the soul one can see the logical outcome of a strictly material, "scientific" view of the human being, the view that declares the human being to be an animal—or less. One can see how the body is "exploited to the utmost," like an animal, where "to the utmost" defines the demolition of the soul. In the demolition of the soul the body is made into raw material, with Jewish hair made into textiles, Jewish bones into fertilizer, and Jewish skin into lampshades. Like animals. Body parts were even known to turn up in the soup which the body was given just enough time to consume.[312] Like animals. There is the soap, and there is the soup, each perfectly consistent with the other, both integral to the demolition of the soul. Body and soul are robbed of all capacity of being-for-the-other, as the soul is assumed, appropriated, and consumed by the other. There is no suffering for the sake of another, and that is what makes this suffering the suffering of the demolition of the soul.

Suddenly the soul-shattering irony of the title of Borowski's tale, "Auschwitz, Our Home," dawns on us, as we recall another line from Levinas: "The body is not only what is steeped in the element, but what *dwells*."[313] And: "The body is my possession according as my being maintains itself in a home at the limit of interiority and exteriority. The extraterritoriality of a home conditions the very possession of my body."[314] We see the relation between the demolition of the soul and the rendering homeless of the Jew, the Jew and anyone else in Auschwitz (Borowski was not a Jew) turned over to the anti-home of the concentrationary universe. The anti-home is realized in the demolition of the soul. And the perpetrators are just as homeless as their victims, dehumanized in their dehumanization of the other. Hence, the disquieting meaning of the parenthetical title ("A Letter"), brilliantly added (parenthetically). Letters are written from home, not from the anti-world, the anti-home. They are written in a realm in which word and meaning are still interlocked, a realm in which human beings, as speaking beings, as letter-writing beings, still have some sort of bond, created in the image.

> No, no: they definitely were
> Human beings: uniforms, boots.
> How to explain? They were created
> In the image. . . .
> And he in his mercy left nothing of me that would die.
> And I fled to him, rose weightless, blue,
> forgiving—I would even say: apologizing—
> smoke to omnipotent smoke
> without image or likeness.
>
> —Dan Pagis, "Testimony"

These lines reveal the depths of the demolition of the soul. They reveal the depths of the assault on the revelation of the Jewish testimony to the soul that was targeted for a demolition most extreme, a demolition that leaves not a trace, scattered to the heavens transformed into a cemetery. It is a testimony that radically undermines the ideological categories of the National Socialists who, quite perspicaciously, understood that the demolition of the soul was central to the extermination of the Jews and Judaism. Judaism itself is rendered weightless and blue, the color of the sea, which reminds us of the sky, which reminds us of the Creator. Just one thing escaped their calculation: the soul suffers what it inflicts, as Dan Pagis understood very well.

According to Jewish teaching, as the souls of humanity come into being upon the utterance of "Let there be light," each soul is metaphysically tied to the other. And since every human being emerges from a single origin—the body and soul of Adam—each soul is physically tied to the other. Thus, a man's demolition of the soul of his fellow man results in the demolition of his own soul. "We, the master race, are your destroyers," the murderers of the soul announce to the Jew, "but you are no better than we are; if we so wish, and we do so wish, we can destroy not only your bodies but also your souls, just as we have destroyed ours."[315] This is the "Testimony" of Dan Pagis.

It must be insisted: the Nazis were most certainly human beings. For only a man can become a monster. No creature of nature is a monster. An animal is what it is. Only a human being can become inhumane in the dehumanization of another human being; no animal becomes "inanimal." Only one who is a living soul can undertake the demolition of a soul—and in the process undergo the demolition of his own soul. Recall here an incident that Ringelblum relates in his *Notes from the Warsaw Ghetto*: "A police chief came to the apartment of a Jewish family, wanted to take some things away. The woman cried out that she was a widow with a child. The chief said he'd take nothing if she could guess which of his eyes was the artificial one. She guessed the left eye. She was asked how she knew. 'Because that one,' she answered, 'has a human look.' "[316]

Forgiving? Apologizing? Why? For what? Ka-tzetnik perhaps gives us a clue in *Shivitti*: "Oh, Lord, merciful and compassionate Lord, am I the one who's created Auschwitz? It's much worse than that he—the German facing me with the death's skull insignia on his cap, his hands deep in the pockets of his black S.S. coat—could have been in my place. It's that I—and this is the paralyzing horror—I could have been there in his place!"[317] And *I* could have been in his place: Pagis's epiphany is our own. Each soul, we realize, is tied to the other because each soul is tied to the Creator. The Creator Himself ascends, weightless and blue, unforgiving, omnipotent, emptied of image and likeness, demolished in the demolition of the soul. To whom, then, does the poet apologize?

> Black milk of daybreak we drink you at night
> we drink you at noon in the morning we drink you
> at sundown
> we drink and we drink you
> a man lives in the house your golden hair Margarete
> your ashen hair Shulamith he plays with the serpents
> He calls out more sweetly play death death is a master
> from Germany
> he calls out more darkly now stroke your strings then
> as smoke you will rise into air
> then a grave you will have in the clouds there one
> lies unconfined
>
> —Paul Celan, "Death Fugue"

If Germany loses its soul in the demolition of the soul of Israel, we see it here in these lines from Celan's most famous poem, perhaps the most famous poem in all of Holocaust literature. "Death Fugue," like any fugue, plays on a variety of themes, a variety of levels of insight and expression, each resonating against the other because only in their opposition does the ineffable break through. There are many levels of death in this fugue: death of the Jew, death of the Jewish soul, death of the German soul, death of redemption, death of death.

The ultimate grave, unconfined, is the grave that is not a grave. It is the grave that haunts the skies transformed into a cemetery and curdles in the ashen black milk that humanity now harvests from an ashen earth, drinking it in a grim Eucharist, in a forbidding Kiddush, morning, noon, and night. We drink what rains down upon us, and Margarete, unable to redeem the presumption that man has made of man, is now turned over to the bankruptcy of a Western civilization that has surpassed the wildest, unimagined dreams and fears of Faust and Kohelet, both of whom glimpsed far more than they could see: "Learning and knowledge have sickened me," said Faust,[318] who had his Margarete, echoing Kohelet's "in much knowledge is much sorrow" (Ecclesiastes 1:18)—yes, Kohelet, also known as King Solomon, the wisest of men, who had his Shulamith (Song of Songs 7:1). We have played with the serpent who promised that we shall be like God, knowing good and evil, determining good and evil, knowing the infinite. Like Faust, we set out to know and to experience everything, including the infinite, and so we have: "We may not know if the human capacity for good is infinite," Fackenheim once said to me, "but we know full well that we have an infinite capacity for evil." The serpent has kept his promise: we have become like God, dead like God. We are unconfined, without any limiting principle: more is real than is possible. And so we are left with neither forgiveness nor redemption. The golden hair of Margarete is not so golden, and the ashen hair of Shulamith, the Shekhinah who accompanies Israel into exile, her soul demolished, drapes over humanity.

No metaphor here, as John Felstiner points out.[319] But the metaphor is the vehicle of the ineffable. Do we have here, then, an epiphany of the bankruptcy of epiphany? Does the power of this poem lie in its undermining of poetry, of any literary response to *das, was geschah*? And yet we have the poem, a metaphor for the collapse of metaphor. We have the impetus to speak, despite and even against the will of the speaker who knows that he can say nothing, represent nothing, inspire nothing, except, perhaps, despair and desperation—the speaker who ends by drowning himself in the River Seine, the river that flows through the world's center of postmodern sophistication, literary theory, philosophical speculation, the experimental, the avant garde, and the utterly obscene, now a hotbed of Jew hatred that even Celan could neither comprehend nor curtail. Celan "blights" the traditional association in German art between music and death, as Felsteiner astutely observes.[320] He does so by confronting art with history, the representable with the now nonrepresentable, music with what has no place in music. No sublime here. No metaphor for playing death.

"Play *death death*," we read. And we recall another line from another witness: "One hesitates to call their *death death*."[321] *Death death*. The automatic correction function indicates an error in the combination of *death death*. An error indeed. If death is a master that comes from Germany, the master is a new Angel of Death, the Angel with a Thousand Eyes, colored golden yellow like the hair of Margarete, the Angel who is "a figure of yellowish fire,"[322] the yellowish fire of Margarete and the dark ash of Shulamith. Death is a master from Germany who slays death itself.

The Death of Death

> For death in its literary, philosophic, or musical form there was no place in Auschwitz.
>
> —Jean Améry, *At the Mind's Limits*

> Even death is too good for a Jew?
>
> —Isabella Leitner, *Fragments of Isabella*

"Mass death," writes Michael Rothberg, "destroys not just the individual but individual death. . . . The death of death, of course, does not leave life in its wake, but rather lifeless survival."[323] Still, the death of death? It makes no sense, unless, perhaps we take it to mean the denial of the deaths of the Six Million, as when Elie Wiesel asserts, "Nothing is or could be as ugly, as inhuman as the wish to deprive the dead victims of their death."[324] Here we see how the Nazis' war against memory entails, in one sense, the death of death. In this section, however, we confront a slightly different question: How do the Nazis kill death, not in the aftermath of the survivor's trauma, but in the midst of the whirlwind itself?

The Zohar teaches that on the site where Jacob had his dream, the site he named Beth El (Genesis 28: 10–22), was erected the city of Luz, over which death has no power (*Zohar* II, 151b). But that is not what is meant here by the death of death. This city, the city where death dies, is not the city of Luz but the anti-city of Auschwitz, populated by *Muselmänner*. It is not the site where no one dies; it is the site where one hesitates to call their death death. Here, the death of death is beyond representation, spoken only in a moment of literary transcendence, glimpsed only in a moment of epiphany. The death of death is beyond representation for the same reason that there is no word for the demolition of a man: the demolition of a man is the demolition of the word, and the demolition of the word is the demolition of death. How, then, is the witness to give literary voice to the death of death?

The Torah enjoins us to choose life (Deuteronomy 30:19), but making this choice does not mean that we no longer pass away from this earth; it does not entail the removal of death from the world. Rather, it means that in choosing life we understand death to be part of the process of sanctifying life through Torah study, religious observance, and deeds of loving kindness. Understood in terms of the sacred, death is the culmination, not the negation, of life. It is not opposed to life as darkness is opposed to light; it is a task that confronts us in the course of life. Murder is evil; in itself, death is not. Standing by while people die is evil; in itself, dying is not. But the unthinkable evil—the evil that surpasses evil and paralyzes thought, the evil that is ultimate—is the death that is no longer death. The death that is no longer death comes to a life that is no longer life; it comes at a time when good is no longer good and evil is no longer evil. It comes in the time of the Shoah.

For a human being, death is not a natural phenomenon that befalls someone after three score and ten years; rather, it is part of the task that one is summoned to engage from the moment the soul is called into being. For an animal, death is not a task—it is a natural phenomenon, part of a natural cycle in which nature takes its course. An animal does not die the death, so that for an animal neither living nor dying is a matter of testimony. Therefore, Joseph Albo (1380–1444) reminds us, the "perfection" of an animal lies in existence itself, whereas for a human being it lies in fulfilling a purpose or a destiny—*unto death* (*Sefer HaIkkarim* 3:2). The injunction to choose the Good by living the Good makes death an issue for a human being. And it makes death otherwise than a natural phenomenon.

"Death," says Levinas, "is *present* only in the Other, and only in him does it summon me urgently to my final essence, to my responsibility."[325] Getting rid of God, the Nazis get rid of the other; getting rid of the other, they get rid of death. Only others lie in the cemeteries. But during the Holocaust even those who lay in their graves were under attack. For eliminating the "others"—the Jews—was the Nazis' aim, and this they did, in part, by eliminating Jewish cemeteries. In the Talmud it is written: as God buried the dead, so must we bury the dead (*Sotah* 14a). Usurping God, the Nazis are literally grave robbers: they rob the Jews of their graves and thus unbury the dead. Thus, David Kahane comments on "the wanton, barbaric profanation of the Jewish cemetery" in Lvov. "The Nazis," he says, "were not content with tormenting the living Jews; they also vented their spleen upon the dead. A special labor battalion of Jewish workers from the camp was ordered to uproot and smash all the tombstones on the cemetery."[326] Not only do the Nazis undertake the task of desecrating the dead and removing death from Jewish life, but they force Jewish hands to engage the task of destroying the graves where they once said the Kaddish over their mothers and fathers and, God forbid, their children.

The witnesses of this transformation of life into anti-life grope for a metaphor. They look around, and, seeing nothing but darkness, they invoke the Angel of Death, who no longer puts to them the question concerning their name but is as mute as the very heavens. In the image of the death of the Angel of Death we have the antithesis of the image of the *El Molei Rachamim,* as we pray, "O God, full of compassion, who dwells on high, grant the true rest of the wings of the Shekhinah. . . ." Where such prayers are outlawed, so are the dead. To live as a human being is to die as a human being. And to die as a human being is to affirm even in death that life is very good, speaking the Name of the Holy One in a declaration of "Shema Yisrael!" This utterance of "Hear, O Israel" is itself an offering of life to all who hear it.

And so we begin to fathom what "the death of death" might mean. It is central to the collapse of human relationship and the demolition of the soul. During the Shoah, not only was Jewish life consigned to the flames of the ovens but also Jewish death. For living as a Jew entails dying as a Jew. And to die as a Jew is to choose life even in death. What transpires in the Nazi's imposition of death upon the Jew is not only the end of Jewish life but also the end of the *Shema Yisrael* that makes death the death of a Jew. Hence, the Nazi *has* to eliminate the Shema: to stifle the prayer's holy word is to strangle the man's holy image, the *meod* in the *tov,* the *more* in the *good*: it is the death of death.

Wiesel relates in *Night* that, as the Jews approached the flames of the pits where bodies were burned, they began saying the Kaddish *upon themselves.* "I don't know," he writes, "whether during the history of the Jewish people, men have ever before recited Kaddish for themselves."[327] *Jews do not say Kaddish upon themselves.* Nor do they forget to say Kaddish for another, as when Eliezer and his comrades forget to say Kaddish for Akiba Drumer.[328] On the death march out of Auschwitz "sons abandoned the remains of their fathers without a tear,"[329] something equally unthinkable, for in the world Jews do not abandon the bodies of the dead. This absence of another to say Kaddish, this abandonment of the bodies, is a facet of the absence of death: a man has not died—rather, another denizen of the anti-world has expired, without meaning or value. The horror is that with this death of the Angel of Death there is neither evil nor death in the world, that there is nothing but the exile in the midst of a mute cosmos, where every Who is reduced to an It that cannot die, any more than a stone can die.

> From the depths of the mirror a corpse was contemplating me.
>
> —Elie Wiesel, *Night*

The corpse in this mirror is the image not of death but of the death of death. The death of death is the death we "live through," like Moishe the Beadle in Wiesel's *Night*, the mystic who returned to Sighet to relate the story of his own death.[330] Colliding with this corpse at the end of his memoir, we realize that, like Moishe the Beadle, Elie Wiesel, too, crawled out of the mass grave that was Europe to tell the tale of his own death. It is the tale of a black fire that consumed his soul in a dying that was not a death: the death of death attends the death of the soul. It is the tale of a double dying, in the end conveyed through the double image of a corpse and its reflection, the image of a non-man and his *Doppelgänger*. Could Wiesel's memoir be a kind of Kaddish on himself? Or is it an epitaph inscribed over a grave without a monument and a cemetery without a grave? I doubt that in the millennial history of the Jewish people, anyone has ever before written the tale of a corpse staring back at itself from the darkened depths of a mirror.

It can happen that a great poet may transmit to the reader a portion of his or her soul; in this case, the poet transmits to us a measure of his death. Encountering this death of death that marks the Holocaust, something inside of us dies. Experiencing the moment of epiphany, we experience a moment of trauma. As the corpse contemplates the mirror, the mirror contemplates the corpse. Just so, we contemplate the text, the words, and the silence between the words. Suddenly, in a moment of epiphanic horror, we realize that, gazing upon the page before us, the text itself is a mirror held up to us, in which we behold ourselves and the corpse of humanity, individual and collective. "If they had the courage to write it," Wiesel once told me, "we must have the courage to read it." Now we begin to have a sense of why courage would be required to read something: courage is required to undergo the transformation of reader into witness by the testimony of one who has lived through his own death, one who cannot die because his death has been taken away from him, one who continually dies the death, *mot tamut,* six million times over. Moishe had warned Eliezer of the dangers of entering the orchard of hidden wisdom.[331] The young Wiesel entered against his will through the gate marked *Arbeit Macht Frei*; against his will he ate from the poisonous tree of that knowledge. On that day he did not die, but every day thereafter he died the death that is the death of death.

The corpse staring back at Eliezer is a corpse for whom death is no longer a respite. One may now better understand the story that Wiesel tells in *A Beggar in Jerusalem* about a survivor who threw himself on top of a mass grave and begged the dead not to reject him.[332] He cannot crawl into that grave—it has crawled into him. "You are outside," writes Ka-tzetnik. "You weren't buried in the pit. Somebody else was. Who now is the free one?"[333] Thus, the scope of the Nazi's crime against the Jew: the one who accused the Jew of the crime of being alive has now imposed on the Jew the guilt of not dying—not only then but afterward. And yet there is no *after* in the aftermath of the death of death. For the death of death is the death of time, the death of future; it is the desolation of the soul and the demolition of meaning. That is why it eludes the framework of representation. As in *The Book Thief*—but with a difference—death is the omniscient narrator, but here the narrator has died: here, there is neither narration nor omniscience, neither relation nor understanding. Here there is only the epiphany of horror.

> I fell beside him and his corpse turned over,
> Tight already as a snapping string.
> Shot in the neck. "And that's how you'll end too,"
> I whispered to myself; "lie still; no moving.
> Now patience flowers in death." Then I could hear
> "Der springt noch auf," above, and very near.
> Blood mixed with mud was drying on my ear.
>
> —Miklós Radnóti, the fourth of the *Razglednicas* (postcards)

These lines were literally resurrected from the maw of death, discovered in the coat pocket of Miklós Radnóti when he was exhumed from a mass grave in Szentkirályszabadja in May 1946. Like Moishe the Beadle, like Elie Wiesel—but, again, with a difference—he returns from the dead, by way of a poem into which he poured his ravaged soul, to tell the tale of his own death. Contrary to Ludwig Wittgenstein (1889–1951), who once noted that "death is not an event in life, death is not lived through,"[334] Radnóti lived—and died—through his own death. Yet the death that the poet lives through is no longer death; it is the death of death. The poem is the voice of the poet who relates the story of his death, written on 31 October 1944, the day of the death of his death.

Just as he fell beside a corpse to make it stir, we fall beside his falling, reeling as we retrieve the tale of his fall long after his fall, too late. Zsuzsanna Ozsváth notes the poem's reversal of the Hungarian proverb "patience bears roses" in the line "Now patience flowers in death."[335] The outcome of patience in this case is not the roses' sweet scent of success but the stench of one's own rotting corpse: where the death of death occurs, you inhale the stink of your own carcass. It is the death that exceeds the eternity of dying the death, a death lived and died through the inscription of these lines written on the brink of the black hole of a mass grave that is by definition an anti-grave in an anti-world, unmarked and unremembered.

"Lie still." A Muselmann may lie motionless, but he does not lie still. Only the living can lie still, feigning the anti-death, the death of death, lie still and languish in the death that belies death itself. It buries the reader beneath the unbearable weight of the weightless death of Six Million. Then there is the clarion call that the poet hears *from above,* above and *very near.* A new dimension of height, an anti-dimension of an anti-height, opens up with Radnóti's *from above,* every bit as transcendent and nonrepresentable as the dimension of height that Levinas invokes when he writes, "Because being is ordained to height the human body is placed in a space in which the high and the low are distinguished and the sky is discovered."[336] Here, with the death of death, the human body is placed in the inhuman position of lying next to another body. As though seeking a dimension of height, and yet announcing an eclipse of the dimension of height and the advent of a new master of the horizontal, the poet writes, *Der springt noch auf,* where the *auf* is "up." What is the epiphany here? It is that the erasure of the dimension of height, the obliteration of the *auf,* amounts to the death of death.

Just one more thing about *Der springt noch auf:* Radnóti's murderers were Hungarian, not German. My friend and world authority on Radnóti, Zsuzsanna Ozsváth, thinks the poet was simply trying to protect the Hungarians, so great was his national allegiance to Hungary. But I think there may be more to it than that. Reading this line in German, we realize that

Celan's master from Germany is not death but the death of death. *Der springt noch auf*: the dead man stirs, springing up, jumping up, crying out. The dead man springs upward from these lines, *Der springt noch auf*, rises up from between these lines, and gazes upon us from the depths of a mirror in a testimony to the death of death.

> . . . a death undreamed by Death itself.
>
> —Ka-tzetnik 135633, *Kaddish*

This is the terse description of what Auschwitz is, offered up by Yehiel De-Nur, the man who collapsed at the Eichmann trial when asked to say what Auschwitz is. Searching for a metaphor, he summons a personified Death who dreams but cannot dream the dream of its own death. Auschwitz is the dream undreamed by Death itself because it is the dream of the unreality of the death of death, which eludes the unreality of dreams. Indeed, it is neither real nor unreal—hence its transcendence of every representation. What are we to imagine in the effort to imagine a Death that dreams? We can dream about our own death. We can dream about the death of others. But can we dream the death of Death? Can we dream that Death dreams?

In the dream undreamed by Death, the word *death* grows meaningless. Even—or especially—in phrases such as "death camp" and "death factory." It becomes a euphemism that veils the truth of the Nazis' project. "Throughout the era of Hitler," Yitzhak Katznelson raises his cry, "not a single Jew died, they were just murdered, murdered."[337] That is why the Nazis targeted the old and the ailing for murder, as they flooded the earth with death undreamed by Death itself: refusing to simply wait for them to expire, they were determined to see to it that no Jew would die, that the new Nazi god would eliminate Jewish death itself from the world. For this erasure of Jewish death from existence was a key to the elimination of the significance of Jewish existence, an existence made of life and death.

Ka-tzetnik's description of Auschwitz as a death undreamed by Death itself extends beyond the extermination camp. Throughout the ghettos, bodies were not consigned for burial; like trash, they were collected for disposal. Here, death is not a rite of passage; neither rite nor passage, it simply is. Which amounts to saying: it is *nothing*. Hence, death dies. Or rather, it is obliterated. For in the Shoah the conditions and contexts that would make death matter are not just absent; they are annihilated. Fackenheim explains: "In Ezekiel's image [of the dry bones], the dead have fallen in battle. The dead of the Holocaust were denied battle. . . . Denied the peace even of the bones, they were denied also the honour of graves. . . . To apply Ezekiel's image of Jewish death to the Holocaust, then, is impossible."[338] To be sure, the Torah addresses the sanctification of death; as God breathes life into Adam, so does He reclaim the breath of life in the kiss that He places on the mouth of Moses. But in the Holocaust Kingdom there is no divine kiss of death. When the graves and the prayers over them are obliterated, the world and the life that constitute it are also obliterated. And so we have the death that is not death and the birth that is not birth. And so we have the birth that is death.

> Most of us are born to live—to die, but to live first. You, dear darling, you are being born only to die. How good of you to come before roll call though. . . .
>
> And now that you are born, your mother begs to see you, to hold you. But we know that if we give you to her, there will be a struggle to take you away again, so we cannot let her see you because you don't belong to her. You belong to the gas chamber. Your mother . . . is not a mother. . . .
>
> —Isabella Leitner, *Fragments of Isabella*

When a mother is not a mother, birth is not birth. And when birth is not birth, death is not death. In the concentrationary universe, both are obliterated: that is what defines that anti-universe. This assault on the relation that constitutes the mother as mother entails not only dealing out death; it also entails displacing birth with death. It entails a *confusion* of birth and death, so that where there should be birth, there is only death. The womb goes dark. And where it manages to bear life, it bears only more death: the epiphany in these lines is that we behold the death of death in the birth of death. The Angel of Death is rendered obsolete, left with nothing to do. For the Angel of Death can come only to someone who has been born to live before dying.

Emil Fackenheim understood one implication of this radical confusion. "The very concept of holiness," he writes, "must be altered in response to the conjunction, unprecedented in the annals of history, of 'birth' and 'crime.' "[339] Of course, the little one born here is born not to die but to be murdered; in the case of the infant whose birth is a capital crime, the murder is the murder of death. Not just birth and crime, therefore, but birth and *capital crime,* birth and death penalty for being born, come to bear: "You are being born only to die. . . . You belong to the gas chamber." Inasmuch as holiness, at least in the Jewish tradition, is attached to birth, it is undone not in death but in the collapse of the distinction between birth and death, which is the death of death—and the death of holiness. At last, we understand the rabbinic teaching noted in Part One that the *meod* of *tov meod* is death: it is holiness. To give birth is to give life, a life that might be given in the cause of holiness, thus giving meaning to death. Death is the *meod,* the "more," that enables us to give more and more until we have given all. But with the death of death, there is no giving, therefore no holiness and no loving: there is no soul.

The singular horror, the ethical and metaphysical horror, is that these women are led to kill not to destroy but to save, to kill out of love, both for the mother and for the child. "I took the warm little body in my hands, kissed the smooth face," writes Dr. Gisella Perl, "then strangled him and buried his body under a mountain of corpses waiting to be cremated."[340] The incongruity of the caress of love coupled with the touch of death before a life has been lived is staggering. The loving embrace of the child consecrates the higher relation that imparts humanity to the human being. But in a realm where the higher relation is expressed by killing the child, both the relation and the meaning it consecrates are turned on end. She who strangles the child wrings her own heart and soul to the point where she longs for a death that will not come. Hence, the death of death upon the death of the child.

The Eradication of the Child

> Thus says the Lord: A voice was heard in Ramah, lamentation, and bitter weeping; Rachel weeping for her children refused to be comforted for her children, because they were not.
>
> —Jeremiah 31:15

> Suddenly, the stillness was broken by the screaming of children.
>
> —Sara Nomberg-Przytyk, *Auschwitz: True Tales from a Grotesque Land*

Thus says the Lord. That is why, in the words of Emmanuel Levinas, "Neither the categories of power nor those of knowledge describe my relation with the child."[341] *Thus says the Lord.* My relation with the child is a relation with the transcendent, with the holy and the exigency it brings to bear. Not every human being is a mother or father, brother or sister, son or daughter. But every human being is a child. The *more* that is within us, the image and likeness of the Holy One, is the child within us, the child who seeks a child in everyone he or she meets. Here, we glimpse yet another aspect of Levinas's assertion that "the soul is the other in me":[342] the soul is the child in me. *Thus says the Lord.*

Emil Fackenheim observes that "once Moses offered his life in behalf of the children and succeeded. Adam Czerniaków did not merely offer but gave his life for the children. However, unlike Moses he failed. The enemy was more sleepless and slumberless than the God of Israel."[343] Fackenheim is referring to Czerniaków's suicide note of 23 July 1942, in which he cried out to whoever might find his note, to God Himself, that the SS wanted him to kill Jewish children with his own hands.[344] The children were among those first targeted for extermination, not only to annihilate the Jewish future that they represent but also to destroy the Jewish tradition that they sustain. Indeed, the Nazis and their accomplices systematically created realms emptied of Jewish children. Recall the brief but chilling line from the diary of Hélène Berr dated 13 January 1944: "French gendarmes *went to fetch the children at school.*"[345] No commentary is necessary.

Many texts from the Jewish tradition attest to the importance of the child both to the life of the tradition and to presence of the Holy One. In the Midrash it is written: "R. Judah said: Come and see how beloved are the children by the Holy One, blessed be He. The Sanhedrin were exiled but the *Shekhinah* did not go into exile with them. When, however, the children were exiled, the *Shekhinah* went into exile with them" (*Eichah Rabbah* 1:6:33). And in the Zohar we read, "Who is it that upholds the world and causes the patriarchs to appear? It is the voice of tender children studying the Torah; and for their sake the world is saved" (*Zohar* I, 1b). The Torah cannot be eradicated from creation without the eradication of Jewish children from creation, for the voice of tender children is the voice of Torah. As the Jewish people bear the Torah into the world, so a Jewish woman bears a Jewish child into the world. And the Nazis knew it, as Issachar's wife knew it, the woman in Wiesel's *A Jew Today* who sees dead children everywhere. "They are God's memory," she repeated over and over.[346] What is the Torah if not God's memory? Even where children remained, they were transformed into non-children.

"When I saw them with toys in their hands," Wiesenthal remembers, "they looked unfamiliar, uncanny, like old men playing with childish things."[347] Here, we collide with a progeria of the soul. "Children were old, and old men were as helpless as children," Wiesel once put it.[348] The child is no longer the flower of youth but the broken shoot of old age, and so forced into a category robbed of all meaning. The Eternal One whose presence traces the horizon of a future time is erased in this erasure of time. Through the child, the Promise from a past goes out to meet us in the future. But when the child collapses into old age, time and eternity collapse, and the Word of the Promise is lost. Thus "little Bina," says Leon Wells of his younger sister, "would neither talk nor laugh nor play."[349] In the play of the child lies the movement of life, the celebration of life and meaning signified by the child. When that play ceases, life loses its significance. Says Alexander Donat of his three-year-old son: "The lively child whose nature had been movement and playfulness now sat for hours at a time without moving. Whenever I seemed to be leaving him, his only reaction was to tighten his grip on me, uttering only the single word: '*Daddy.*' "[350] This single word not only undoes the father; it announces the undoing of being, for it is a word that both demands a response and makes all response impossible. And yet where response is impossible, literature happens.

The nightmares of survivors such as Donat are made of the literary transcendence of Holocaust representation. Nightmares are about the nonrepresentable, about the desperate pursuit of the symbols that elude all categories. Nightmares are literary. Like all dreams, nightmares are intended to transmit to the soul an epiphany from beyond. That is how we are to read Wiesenthal's nightmare about a ghetto child named Eli: "His father brought him to me in his arms. As he approached he covered his eyes with his hands. Behind the two figures raged a sea of flames from which they were fleeing."[351] And Sim Kessel's nightmare followed him from the anti-world back into the world: "I still dream of the children at Drancy, clutching at their mothers' skirts and crying incessantly."[352] The dreams that invade the nights of Wiesenthal and Kessel form the anti-reality of the Kingdom of Night, night after night. It is the stuff not only of their nights and nightmares but also of their literature.

Primo Levi offers a variation on this theme in his memory of a three-year-old boy called "Hurbinek" (they did not know his real name, perhaps a play on *Churban*), whom he met in Auschwitz after the Russians entered the camp on 27 January 1945. "Hurbinek, the nameless," Levi describes him, "died in the first days of March 1945, free but not redeemed. Nothing remains of him: he bears witness through these words of mine."[353] In the outcry of the literary testimony the namelessness of the child parallels the namelessness of the nonrepresentable. The child remains nameless, but the ineffable Name speaks through the words of the witness, often despite the witness.

> The death of a child is the death of innocence, the death of God in the heart of man. And he who does not drink deeply of this truth, who does not shout it from the rooftops, is a man devoid of heart, of God, he has not seen the misty eyes of a child expiring without a whimper.
>
> —Elie Wiesel, *A Beggar in Jerusalem*

The death of a child? No, the murder of a child. Shout it from the rooftops? No, scream it from the citadels of what passes for modern civilization. The death of God in the heart of man is the death—if one may utter such words—of Torah. For the Torah ends with the letter *lamed* and begins with the letter *beit*. As the end eternally circles back to the beginning we have the *lamed-beit* of the word *lev*, which is "heart." In Judaism the heart is God's dwelling place, the seat of insight and understanding (see *Talmud Bavli, Sanhedrin* 106b), the realm of *ruach* or spirit,[354] the spirit that hovered over the face of the deep in the beginning (Genesis 1:2). With the eradication of the child, therefore, we have the eradication of Creation, a return to the chaos and the void, the *tohu vevohu,* overcome in the movement of Creation: the death of God in the heart.

And so the world does not end with a bang, or even with a whimper. Adorno's fear comes to mind: "Everything has been destroyed without realizing it; humankind continues to vegetate, creeping along after events that even the survivors cannot really survive, on a rubbish heap that has made even reflection on one's own damaged state useless."[355] Can it be that the Holocaust resulted in the collapse of creation, and we did not even notice it? After all, the mystics teach that if the *ki tov*—the Divine assertion that "it is very good"—is removed from the world, then "the whole world is destroyed and *tov* [the good] is not to be found in the world."[356] This surely seems to be the case with the eradication of the child that defines the Shoah.

For these reasons, the Talmud teaches that all of Creation endures thanks to the breath of little children (*Shabbat* 119b), and not by the pillars of power, as invoked by the Greek image of Atlas holding up the world on his shoulders. If the child sustains creation, the murder of the child is central to the war against the Creator. And in the death of the child we see Him in the throes of death. Wiesel drives home this point with devastating pathos in *Night*, where we encounter one of the most harrowing, most haunting passages in all of Holocaust literature. It is a most dreadful memory that continues to haunt all of Jewish memory: the memory of the hanging of a child.

> The SS seemed more preoccupied, more worried, than usual. To hang a child in front of thousands of onlookers was not a small matter. . . . All eyes were on the child. . . .
>
> "Where is merciful God, where is He?" someone behind me was asking. . . .
>
> The two men were no longer alive. . . . But the third rope was still moving: the child, too light, was still breathing . . .
>
> And so he remained for half an hour . . . writhing before our eyes. . . .
>
> Behind me I heard the same man asking:
>
> "For God's sake, where is God?"
>
> And from within me, I heard a voice answer:
>
> "Where is He? This is where—hanging here from this gallows." (Elie Wiesel, *Night*)

It is not for nothing that this horrific scene appears at the center of Wiesel's memoir: it is pivotal to the Churban itself. Eliezer was himself a child who saw his own soul die with the little one on the gallows. The God we beseech to heed the cries of the children is reduced to their unanswered outcry. Wiesel's statement cited in Part One returns to haunt us: "At Auschwitz God was afraid—afraid of Himself."[357] He was afraid of the question put to Him from the lips of a child: "Where is God?" Such a question belongs to the nonrepresentable.

Wiesel refers to the child as "the sad-eyed angel."[358] An angel in Hebrew, as we have noted, is a *malakh*, or "messenger." What could this angel's message be? Perhaps it is his silence, the silence of those sad Jewish eyes that peer into the soul from the depths of these pages. How do we find the arrogance to engage in a "literary analysis" of this text, delving into the usual aesthetics of character, plot, symbol, and scene? How are we to undertake a discussion of the "subtleties of representation" and the "subtext of trauma," when all eyes are on the child? Are we to use such phrases as "writing trauma," "deconstruction of memory," or "postmemory?" With all eyes on the child, are we to indulge in empty neologisms, with their metas- and posts-, or metametas- or postmetas- or metaposts-? Very often we who pretend to be scholars seek in these ploys various ways to elude the outcry of a murdered God silently screaming from the depths of the eyes of a murdered child. We flee to the comfort and the confines of theoretical fashion and fad. And we have no hint of the shame we bring upon ourselves.

The most difficult lecture of the hundreds I have given on the Holocaust was not for a group of scholars or even for a class of graduate students. No, it was for a third grade class at a Jewish day school. How, you ask, could anyone presume to speak of the Holocaust before a class of third graders? For one thing, many in this class of Jewish eight-year-olds had grandparents with numbers on their arms. And they are not stupid. They wanted to know. But who was I to teach them? As I stood in front of the children whose souls were even now under assault, as I looked into their wide, innocent eyes, I grew afraid: Why, oh why, did these babies have to know *this* about their world? And yet they had to know. All of them had seen police security present at Jewish events, even at the synagogue where they went to pray: *the police must protect them if they want to gather to pray as Jews.* Understand? For them the daily threat to Jewish lives is a mundane reality. Thus, even now the Shoah reaches into the lives of Jewish children, if no longer through the numbers on their grandparents' arms, then now through the police protection where they pray.

As I lamely related the story of a Jewish child whose life went from normal to miserable when he and his family were forced into a ghetto, I faltered at every turn and then came to a halt: Any questions?

An eight-year-old Jewish child, eyes as wide as saucers, put up his hand and asked: "Where was God?!!?"

We're back in Buna! the thought raced through my mind. This eight-year-old is Elie Wiesel!

The Talmud teaches that every Jewish soul, living, dead, and yet to be born, was gathered for the revelation at Mount Sinai (*Shabbat* 146a). The epiphany that overwhelms us upon reading this passage from *Night* is this: the souls not just of the Jewish people but of all humanity are gathered in the assembly at Buna for a different revelation, passing by the child who is too light to die at the end of a rope, still breathing even as we gasp for air. Forced to stare at his purple tongue, we cry out, "Where the hell is God?"

Where the hell? Here in . . . no, not in hell. Can the Creator of hell be in hell? No, not in hell: in hell a principle of justice reigns.

Neither the historians nor the social scientists pose such a question. There is no answer in the archives. It is neither scientific nor systematic. Even the SS were preoccupied, shaken from their grim routine and their grisly methods. Even they were at a loss. For they, too, were men.

> If she [Rosa] tried to pick up the sticks of Magda's body they would shoot, and if she let the wolf's screech ascending now through the ladder of her skeleton break out, they would shoot; so she took Magda's shawl and filled her own mouth with it, stuffed it in and stuffed it in, until she was swallowing up the wolf's screech and tasting the cinnamon and almond depth of Magda's saliva; and Rosa drank Magda's shawl until it dried.
>
> —Cynthia Ozick, *The Shawl*

This harrowing scene is from Cynthia Ozick's (b. 1928) tale of a woman who had a baby named Magda in Auschwitz—the worst possible offense against the Nazis' landscape of a *Judenrein* world. Before long the infant Magda was discovered during an *Appell,* a "roll call," and thrown against the electric fence as her mother Rosa looked on. At that moment the mother went insane. The Shoah does not traumatize the mother who is not a mother and the child who is not a child—it renders one insane and the other nonexistent. Insanity is not trauma. We speak of the representation of trauma, but not of the representation of insanity, because there is no representing insanity to a sane world. Trauma requires the retention of some shred of sanity. And for Rosa there remained no trace of sanity upon the murder of Madga—if we can even call it murder. There lies the problem of the literary testimony to the eradication of the child. Murder happens in a world where life is life and death is death, where children are children and old men old men. The eradication of the child in the anti-world is not murder. It is something else. Something transcendent and beyond representation.

In Hebrew, Magda means "from the tower," where "tower" is *migdal. Migdal* shares a root with *gadol,* which is "great," as in the phrase from the daily prayer known as the Amidah, *ha-El ha-Gadol,* "God, the One who is Great," words uttered when a Jew is wrapped in a prayer shawl. To be wrapped in the prayer shawl is to be wrapped in God's light: it corresponds to the *or makif,* or the soul's "surrounding light." The prayer binds together the *or pnimi* and the *or makif,* the "internal light" and the "surrounding light," of the soul. This is why Jews utter the highest of the prayers, the Amidah, both silently and aloud: the silence pertains to the inner light, the words spoken aloud to the surrounding light. The blessing for wrapping oneself in the shawl is upon God, the eternal King, who has sanctified us by His commandments and has commanded us to wrap ourselves in *tzitzit*—not in the shawl but in "fringes." Why? Because the fringes signify Torah. The word *tzitzit* has a numerical value of 600. To this value is added the five knots and eight threads of the *tzitzit,* for a total of 613, the number of commandments in the Torah.

But Magda is made of sticks; she is hardly great. As for Rosa, her breasts have long since dried up. Magda's mother is not a mother, and Magda is not a child. She is lighter than air and can rise higher than a tower, higher even than the Tower of Babel, beyond the confusion of tongues that often characterizes analyses such as this one. Her mother's body made into an anti-body in the anti-world—ravished by all the brutality, hunger, hatred, and exhaustion foisted upon the Jew—is itself a skeletal ladder to the heavens, like the ladder in Jacob's dream. Ka-tzetnik's vision of the SS murderers of children ascending and descending the Jacob-like ladder of the watchtowers comes to mind.[359] Now the SS are crawling up and down the ladder of Rosa's ravaged body. And now the sad-eyed angels ascend and descend the ladder, angels without mothers, treading upon the emaciated remains of a people devastated in the eradication of Jewish children. The angels ascend and descend the ladder in a nightmare unparalleled by Jacob's dream. They transform the worlds below and the worlds above, bespeaking worlds undreamed by Death, incomprehensible to the Creator Himself, the anti-world below with its corresponding anti-world above.

How can such radical evil exist in the same space and time as the universe itself? Without the child, not only is there infinite room for evil but there is no room for a world—at least not for any world as humanity has long understood the term. The Hebrew word *olam* means not only "world" but also "humanity" and "community," both of which are eradicated upon the eradication of the child. Has the eradication of the child not rendered us blind to humanity and community?

The angels ascending and descending the ladder of Rosa's skeletal body have a name. Their name is Magda, and they sing out, in a high pitched, electrical hum, through her tiny, writhing stick-body, "*Ha-El ha-Gadol,*" as she fries on the barbed wire of the electric fence, and, as she burns, the scent of a world devoured by fire sweeps over the face of the earth—without a whimper. The shawl that Rosa suckles is the shawl that Madga suckled when there was no breast to suckle. It has no fringes, no

Torah, no name of God—in short, no mother's milk, which would contain everything that the *tallit* contains. Rosa tastes the taste of almonds, a taste associated with cyanide, as it is associated with prophecy (see Jeremiah 1:11); it tastes of cinnamon, a taste associated with the holy anointing of the priest (see Exodus 30:23). The crowns of prophecy and priesthood and even death are undone, mutated into a radical antithesis to prophecy and priesthood and even death, to everything that Judaism and the Jewish child might remotely signify. And yet Rosa suckles the remnants of centuries of unanswered prayers through the fabric of the shawl that her child suckled, a shawl without fringes.

Suddenly, Rosa becomes the child in search of solace, the soul devastated in the eradication and electrocution of the child. And we realize that the eradication of the child is indeed the eradication of the soul, beyond trauma, beyond the representations of trauma, something that peeks through a tear in the veil of reality in a literary transcendence of representation. What does Rosa swallow up in the swallowing up of the "wolf's screech" that displaces all prayer? Is it the wolf that embodies the sheer animal, ontological, pagan, valueless, stark, void, and utterly empty shriek of the horror over the fact that there is no horror? Indeed, the eradication of the child is the eradication of horror within the very nests of horror.

> O the night of weeping children!
> O the night of children branded for death . . . !
> Terrible nursemaids
> Have usurped the place of mothers,
> Have tautened their tendons with the false death,
> Sown it on the walls and into the beams—
> Everywhere it is hatched in the nests of horror.
> Instead of mother's milk, panic suckles those little ones.
>
> —Nelly Sachs, "O the night of the weeping children," in *O the Chimneys*

Reading these lines, we are once again inundated with the screams of "Mama!" reverberating in the silence between the lines and swallowed up in a weeping unlike any other weeping. Once again, we see that where death is no longer death, children are no longer children, and mothers are no longer mothers. Indeed, weeping is no longer weeping. "Instead of mother's milk, panic suckles those little ones," as it suckles the usurped mother sucking on a shawl. "Everywhere it is hatched in the nests of horror." What, exactly, is hatched? And what are the nests of horror?

The night of weeping children is hatched, the night that is no longer night, no longer part of the cycles of day and night, as in the time of the *Mabul*, the Great Flood and the Great Confusion, that consumed Noah's world, when, says Rashi, day was not day and night was not night (Rashi, commentary on Genesis 8:22). Nelly Sachs knows Rashi very well, just as she knows very well the kabbalistic commentaries on the bird's nest, here transformed into nests of horror. Those teachings handed down by the mystics derive from the Torah: "If you come across a bird's nest in any tree or on the ground, with young ones or eggs and the mother sitting on the young or on the eggs, you shall not take the mother with the young. You shall let the mother go, but the young you may take for yourself, that it may go well with you, and that you may live long" (Deuteronomy 22:6–7). Already we can see the inversion of the Torah's teaching. If the young are taken, there is no life for the mother, whose place has been usurped. And there is no living long, either for the mother or for the child. There lies the horror hatched in the nests of horror, the horror of the devastation of the nest and the eradication of the children.

According to the Zohar, the nest in the verses from the Torah is "the hidden abode of the Messiah," and the mother bird is the Shekhinah, the maternal Presence of the Holy One who abides in the midst of humanity. As the Zohar tells the tale, the Messiah weeps like a child over Rachel's loss and her refusal to be consoled (see *Zohar* II: 8a–9a). Indeed, the Messiah often disguises himself as a child, as it is written: "A little child will lead them" (Isaiah 11:6). But there is no such consolation here. The night of the weeping children is the night of the weeping Messiah, for Nazi nursemaids, with the talons of wolves and leopards, have usurped the place of the mothers; they suckle the weeping children on the black milk of Margarete, the black nothingness of the false death that is no longer death. It is something else, something sown into the walls and the beams to undermine every trace of the security we seek in the fashioning of our hiding place into a home. So we turn to the epiphany of poetry such as this. We turn and we turn, until our head spins. Insanity haunts us. "I have the feeling," says Elie Wiesel, "I am haunted by . . . madness."[360] He is haunted by the night of weeping children.

Already embraced by the arm of heavenly solace
The insane mother stands
With the tatters of her torn mind
With the charred tinders of her burnt mind
Burying her dead child.
Burying her lost light,
Twisting her hands into urns.
Filling them with the body of her child from the air.
Filling them with his eyes, his hair from the air,
And with his fluttering heart—
Then she kisses the air-born being
And dies!

—Nelly Sachs, "Already embraced by the arm of heavenly solace," in *O the Chimneys*

The eradication of the child is the eradication of sanity. Many of the texts to emerge from the anti-world attest to this grim fact. Recall these lines from Wiesel:

The death of the child
Fails to save the others. . . .
But I saw the mother.
I saw her gaze fill with madness.[361]

Then there is the episode that Emmanuel Ringelblum relates about a woman who tried to save her three-year-old child after a guard had thrown him out of a truck headed for the Warsaw Ghetto. As she was about to jump off the truck and go to her child, the Nazi threatened to shoot all the Jews on the truck if she should make a move. "The mother arrived in Warsaw," Ringelblum finishes this terrible tale, "and here went out of her mind."[362] How could it be otherwise?

"If sanity is not of the spirit only," says Fackenheim, "but rather contact with the world (and with God *in* and *through* the world), then such sanity, when the world is Auschwitz, is destroyed by madness. And if sanity consists of flight from the world (and to gods who have themselves fled from the world), then such flight, when the world is the Nazi Holocaust, is necessary if even a shred of sanity is to remain."[363] Such flight—the flight that is madness—is, paradoxically, necessary to sanity. The world that is Auschwitz is the world of the eradication of the child, who is the very ground of sanity. Do our children not reveal to us what there is to love, what there is to fear and to fear for, what is real and what is unreal? Do they not, therefore, keep us sane?

Looking at the German text of Sachs's poem, we notice that the phrase translated as "her torn mind" is *ihres zerrissenen Verstandes*, more literally, "her understanding" or "her capacity for thought ripped to shreds,"[364] something that can be conveyed, if conveyed at all, only through the epiphany of poetry. There is a loss of capacity here, a destruction of judgment and faculty, a devastation therefore of what can be represented; it is transmitted only in a moment of transcendence that takes the reader into the heavens, where the eradicated child is buried. But what can it mean to bury a child in the heavens, in the air? There is a complete inversion of reality, of above and below, of high and low. This shattering of the understanding, of all capacity for comprehension, upon the eradication of the child transcends what Jean Améry describes when he writes, "So it was that in Auschwitz everything intellectual gradually took on a doubly new form: on the one hand, psychologically, it becomes something completely unreal, and on the other hand, to the extent that one defines it in social terms, a kind of forbidden luxury,"[365] so that "not only was rational analytic thinking in the camp of no help, but it led straight to a tragic dialectic of self-destruction."[366] The madness of the mother in this case is not about the loss of "rational analytical thinking." It is about the utter devastation of the soul upon the eradication of the child who, in a profound sense, *is* the soul and all the love, understanding, and devotion that sustain the soul.

In the image of the mother's cupped hands receiving the ashes of her child floating down from the sky—the ashes that could not find a burial in the sky—we have something that goes far beyond the intellectual, the analytical, and therefore the representable. Jews do not have urns. Jews do not cremate. Jews do not bury their dead in the sky. Hence, the mother's light is lost. She cannot see or comprehend, for she cannot catch the ashes of her baby's eyes in her cupped hands of offering and receiving. And so to be embraced in the arms of heavenly solace is precisely to die—of madness.

> At the edge of the sidewalk lay a small, bloody rag. . . . He [the father] walked over. . . . He bent down, picked up the child, stroked the tangle of blonde hair.
>
> "Deine?"
>
> "*Ja, meine.*" And then softly, to her, "Forgive me."

> He stood there with the child in his arms and waited for a second shot. But all he heard was a shout and he understood . . . he had to keep on walking, carrying his dead child. . . .
>
> —Ida Fink, "A Spring Morning," in *A Scrap of Time and Other Stories*

Ida Fink's short story "A Spring Morning" is about a father, a mother, and their five-year-old little girl walking to a train with a group of Jews marked for deportation. In a desperate attempt to somehow save his child, the father sends her running from the doomed procession toward a group of Christians standing outside a church, in the hope that one of them would take her before she is spotted. He is the protector, the father, the one who says, "It's all right, I am right here," whenever she is frightened, the one who now can only beg forgiveness. The father is the figure of the law, the figure of the limit, of truth and justice. And so he apologizes not only because he cannot save his little girl, but also because truth, justice, good and evil, cannot save her. He apologizes for the utter collapse of civilization upon the eradication of the child, which is the reduction of the child—of Western civilization—to a bloody rag. Once the Nazi has shot her, she is no longer a child; she is a "bloody rag." What is a rag? It is something torn, like the torn mind, something not human, something for wiping up the remains of the day, a remnant of a people—that is what makes it a "bloody" rag. "Is this rag yours?" The father who is no longer a father, who cannot protect his child, answers, "Yes, this bloody rag is my rag." It is the bloody rag of the soul of humanity.

For the Christians who ruled Christian civilization, as the Jews were slaughtered in the heart of Christendom, stand idly by. They stand next to the church, founded upon Peter, the Rock, the Church that proclaimed this Jewish child to be a deicide, a murderer of God Himself, in the shadow of God's silent scream. And they stare at the father with the dead child in his arms, in a grisly reversal of the Pietà, the image of the anti-Pietà, as he marches off to the anti-world defined by the eradication of the child, not to his death but to his anti-death. The second shot that he longs for, in a longing for death before he went insane, does not come. And so he walks, but not as the righteous who, since the time of Noah and the Great Flood, are known for their walk (see Genesis 6:9). No. He walks and strokes her blonde hair on his way to a universe of ashes. All on a spring morning, the season of rebirth and resurrection, of liberation and revelation. Should he break into a run? Should we break into a run?

Part Three

The Photographic Transcendence of Holocaust Representation

Revealing the Invisible

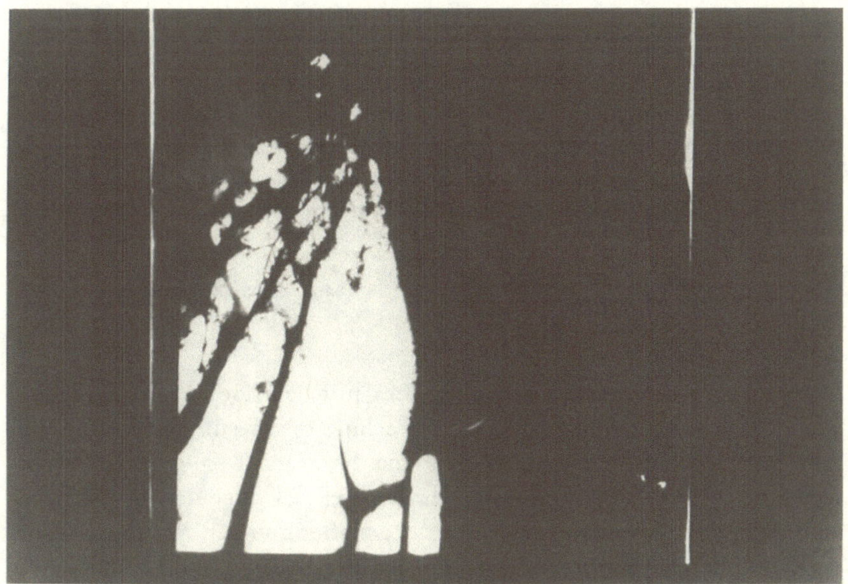

FIGURE 3.1. The fourth Sonderkommando Photograph. The four Sonderkommando photographs are in the public domain, because, according to Article 3 of the copyright law of March 29, 1926, of the Republic of Poland and Article 2 of the copyright law of July 10, 1952, of the People's Republic of Poland, all photographs by Polish photographers (or published for the first time in Poland or simultaneously in Poland and abroad) published without a clear copyright notice before the law was changed on May 23, 1994, are assumed public domain.

The Legacy of Lot's Wife

> And it came to pass, when they had brought them forth abroad, that he said, Escape for thy life; look not behind thee, neither stay thou in all the plain; escape to the mountain, lest thou be consumed. . . . Then the Lord rained upon Sodom and upon Gomorrah brimstone and fire from the Lord out of heaven; and he overthrew those cities, and all the plain, and all the inhabitants of the cities. . . . But his wife looked back from behind him, and she became a pillar of salt.
>
> —Genesis 19: 17–26

> "We'll give you evidence right now," said Perseus.
> "Protect your eyes!" He raised Medusa's face
> Up to the king's and turned him to stone.
>
> —Ovid, *Metamorphoses* (350)

> Leontius son of Aglaion . . . perceived corpses laid out near the gallows. He wanted to look, and at the same time he was disgusted with himself and turned away; he fought with himself for awhile and covered his face, but, overcome by the desire, he held his eyes wide open and ran up to the corpses and said, "Look, damn you. Take your fill of the lovely sight!"
>
> —Plato, *Republic* (439e–440a)

In Part Two we proceeded according to a principle found in the Talmud: whenever the sages would open up a teaching or a testimony to transmit, they would begin by saying, "Come and hear." And so, passage by passage, line by line, we struggled to hear what eludes utterance, in the words and between the words of one literary text after another. We sounded the epiphanic depths of what lay in the silence between the lines and in the margins, hovering over author and reader in a position of transcendence. Here, gazing upon just a few photographs (more would be unbearable), we take the approach adopted in the Zohar, a text devoted to what eludes the eye of understanding; indeed, it is one of the major texts of the *chakhmah nistarah,* the "hidden wisdom," otherwise known as Kabbalah. Whenever the sages of the Zohar would open up a teaching or a testimony to hold up to the initiate, they would begin by saying, "Come and see," as though the eye might somehow glimpse the invisible, hidden, most profound mysteries of creation. Georges Didi-Huberman affirms that in Holocaust (non-) representation the two media, literature and photographs, are interwoven: "For in each testimonial production, in each act of memory, language and image are absolutely bound to one another, never ceasing to exchange their reciprocal lacunae."[1] The literature is essential to any intelligible viewing of the photographs: the photographs are not only seen, but they are heard. They are worth a thousand words only if we have the words of the literature, the words of testimony, at our disposal.

I have argued that in Auschwitz everything was stark, that nothing was hidden, and that the Shoah was, among other things, as assault on the hidden. Perhaps this is what underlies Maurice Blanchot's assertion that Auschwitz was the "invisible forever *rendered visible*"[2] and therefore meaningless. For the hidden is the dimension of meaning, the dimension of the *future*. A search for the photographic rendering of the invisible might approach a restoration of the invisible, of the hidden, in a flash of something that penetrates the stark image of the photograph, something that does not meet the eye, in such a way that the photograph emerges as a ghost not only of the past but also of the future—there lies the urgency of this investigation. Roland Barthes sensed this truth: gazing upon the photograph, he writes, "I read at the same time: *This will be* and *This has been*; I observe with horror an anterior future of which death is the stake."[3] Looking at these photographic images of the Holocaust, we struggle to catch sight of the invisible mystery of the anti-creation that devolves upon us.

The fundamental question to be addressed, then, is: What do these photographic images reveal about the invisible core of the Holocaust that transcends representation? Recall Yehiel De-Nur's insistence that he *saw* everything—everything and more than a photograph can capture—and yet he could not say what Auschwitz *is*. With regard to the photographic representation of Auschwitz, Dan Stone observes: "Ever since the first photos of Auschwitz, the meaning imputed to it has been encompassed in the symbolic framework of the barbed wire, the ramp, or the famous entrance gate. These things are of course important parts of the camp, yet they are not the camp but only how we wish to keep seeing it."[4] Indeed, it can happen that we turn to the photograph in order *not* to see it, to behold only the veil.

Here, however, we shall attempt to penetrate the veil. Just as certain literary passages open up a glimpse of the transcendent "essence" of the Holocaust, so do these photographs reveal what eludes the eyes: they enable us to "see" what we are forbidden to see, what we fear to see, what we cannot see—at least not without being destroyed by what we see. This "at least" lies not in the trauma suffered from gazing upon the destruction (although these images are indeed traumatizing) but in the ethical implication of what gazes *back* at us from the depths of the image, which is a trace of the Holy One who came under this concrete radical assault. If the photographs attest to anything, it is the *concrete* nature of that assault on the sanctity of person affirmed by the millennial tradition of Judaism. If we speak, as Susan Sontag does, of "an ethics of seeing,"[5] it is because these photographs reveal something about the radical evil that targets the Good for annihilation. "One can feel obliged," says Sontag, "to look at photographs that record great cruelties and crimes. One should feel obliged to think about what it means to look at them, about the capacity to actually assimilate what they show."[6] One should also feel obliged to consider the price of the gaze, even if we seek the ethical absolute that eludes the gaze. No one can confront radical evil and come out unscathed.

Regarding the matter of looking back, Elie Wiesel once said to me that the transgression that transformed Lot's wife into a pillar of salt was to rob the victims of the privacy of their suffering and humiliation, and therefore of their dignity as human beings. If the Nazis set out to murder souls before they destroyed bodies—if they systematically tortured and humiliated the Jews before murdering them—then we must not add to the crime by gazing upon the victims. Wiesel made this remark knowing very well what I knew (and far more) about the question of why Lot's wife was transformed into a pillar of salt and the associations with salt in the Jewish tradition. And he surely knew the implications of those associations (much better than I).

In the Torah, for example, one of the more mysterious of the expressions of a covenant with God is the "covenant of salt," which is associated with the offerings brought to God; the heave offerings, for example, affirm "a statute forever . . . a covenant of salt for ever before the Lord unto thee and to thy seed with thee" (Numbers 18:19). The meaning of this covenant that affirms a higher relation is manifest in the ancient custom of dipping bread three times in salt prior to eating it after the blessing on bread. In Hebrew "salt" is *melach,* which (with a numerical value of 78) is three times the value of the Divine Name (26), the Name of the One with whom we enter into the covenant of salt and the covenant of Torah. Is gazing upon these images akin to looking upon the devastation of the Name or the ravishing of the Shekhinah? Perhaps so, since, as we have seen, that is what the Nazis set out to annihilate in the annihilation of the Jews. The letters that form *melach* also form the word *lechem,* which is "bread," the symbol of all that sustains life; the Nazis transformed it into "the holy grey slab,"[7] the antithesis of bread, the stuff that destroyed both body and soul. Is that transformation of bread into anti-bread forbidden to look upon? After all, when bread is not bread, Primo Levi has demonstrated, the human being is not a human being, so it may indeed be questionable to gaze upon such a transformation. And yet the letters of *melach* also form the word *machal,* which is "forgiveness." If we turn to look, seeking a glimpse of the invisible slated for annihilation, can we possibly be forgiven? Or do we run the risk of bringing strange fire to the vision of those flames, the likes of which there have never been?

The words of Torah surrounding the incident with Lot's wife take on a special significance and provide a lens through which to consider the risk we run here: "Escape for thy life; look not behind thee, neither stay thou in all the plain . . . lest thou be consumed." There are, however, important differences. Lot's wife looked upon the destruction of the guilty, while we turn our glances toward the humiliation and murder of the innocent. She saw the fire of retribution rain down, while the Jews endured the flames of destruction rising up. In a word, the people of Sodom and Gomorrah were punished, while the Jews of Europe were murdered.

This point is especially salient when the photographs in question were taken by their murderers. In *Der gelbe Stern* (*The Yellow Star*, 1960), one of the earliest collections of Holocaust photographs, Gerhard Schoenberner reminds us: "The Nazis photographed themselves at work. . . . The [victims] had no choice but to have their photographs taken. As they went to certain death . . . they saw the enemy's camera turned on them. Their eyes, as they look into the camera lens, meet ours as we look upon their photographs decades later, putting us in the position of the murderers."[8] These photographs embody what Isabel Wollaston calls "a Nazi gaze," one that "objectifies, humiliates and violates those photographed. Collectively such photographs embody a desire to record and/or flaunt the deed, staging then recording state-sanctioned murder as spectacle."[9] Perhaps all Holocaust photographs have "a Nazi gaze," whether photographed by Nazis or not; perhaps there is something "Nazi" about our own gaze. If Lot's wife paid a price for gazing upon the destruction of the guilty as she fled to Zoar, how much greater is the price exacted from us for looking back at the innocent as we seek our own refuge? Does it ultimately render us as numb, mute, and lifeless as a pillar of salt? And where shall we flee?

Hence, the imperative to move "beyond the mere authentication of horror," as Barbie Zelizer observes, to "the act of bearing witness, by which we assume responsibility for the events of our times."[10] Both the photographs taken by Nazis documenting the events and the few photos taken by Jews may assume the status of evidence. However, when two Jews, Henryk Rozencwajg-Ross and Mordechaj Mendel Grossman, secretly took photos of the Łódź Ghetto at the risk of their lives,[11] their images transcended the status of evidence to become summons and outcry, and thus to implicate the viewer. The photo below, for example, is the scene of a deportation from the Łódź Ghetto take by Grossman (Figure 3.2).[12] Transcending evidence, in these photographs we have, in the words of Roland Barthes, "that rather terrible thing which is there in every photograph: the return of the dead,"[13] who summon us to a reckoning. The dead Jews stand in crowds and crowd the soul with traces of their lives, a Jewish policeman standing in for the Angel of Death, perhaps in the illusion that he will not be among them. Most striking of all, this is a photograph of a Jewish photographer taking a photograph, an image of the attempt to capture a trace of the diurnal horror from the anti-world for an unlikely, nameless viewer. Sebald confirms this intuition: "Photographs have 'an uncanny ability' to suggest that 'there is another world where the departed are.' They are documents of absence and in some way 'curiously metaphysical. . . . They represent a

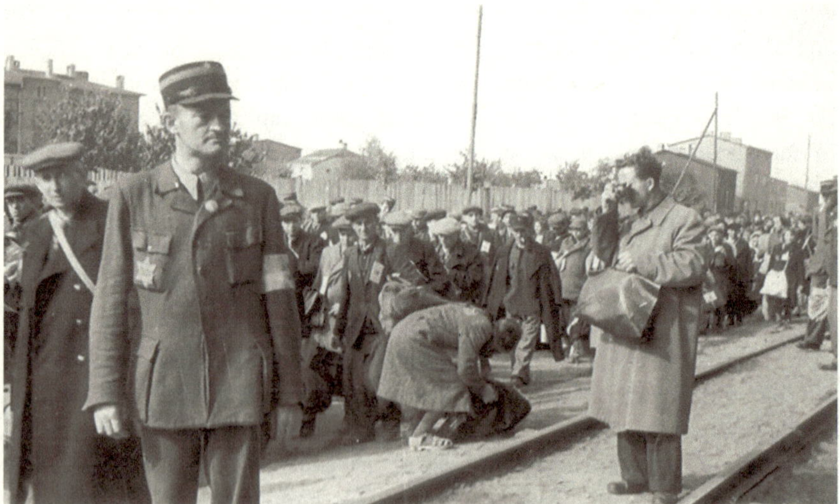

FIGURE 3.2. "Photographs from Łódź Ghetto—Litzmannstadt—Fotografowie getta," public domain.

sense of otherness.' The figures in photographs 'stare at you as if they were asking for a chance to say something.' "[14] Once again, we collide with a new horror, in the realization that we bear a resemblance to the Medusa that gazes back at us.

"In 1945," Didi-Huberman reminds us, "what may be called a period of *visual evidence,* or *visual proof,* began, when the administrative staff of the allies accumulated photographic testimonies of war crimes."[15] Polydectes, King of Seriphos, comes to mind: when he asked Perseus for proof of the evil he had encountered, Perseus pulled out the head of the Medusa, and the king was turned to stone; we pull out a photograph, with the supposition that now we *know* what cannot be known, cannot be appropriated, and we are turned to stone, having long ignored the warning to cover our eyes. The way of knowing as appropriation is as much embodied in the photographic project as it is in the Western ontological project; it is, indeed, a manifestation of the totalizing nature of the Western ontological tradition that led to the Holocaust itself. "To photograph," notes Sontag, "is to appropriate the thing photographed. It means putting oneself into a certain relation to the world that feels like knowledge—and, therefore, like power."[16] Therefore, "there is something predatory in the act of taking a picture."[17] Yes: it is good to be King. We long to be King, and more: we long to be God, all-knowing and all-powerful. And that is why we murder the Jews, who proclaim to us that we are not God.

Levinas makes a point similar to Sontag's when he writes, "In knowledge or vision the object seen can indeed determine an act, but it is an act that in some way appropriates the 'seen' to itself, integrates it into a world by endowing it with a signification, and, in the last analysis, constitutes it."[18] Where Levinas writes "seen," read "photographed." The project of Holocaust representation seeks this power of appropriation and control, the godlike power to assign significance; it is a totalizing power that abets the evil photographed, wittingly or otherwise. In the instant of that complicity we are stone deaf to the outcry of the one who summons us to an infinite responsibility that undermines all knowledge, all appropriation—everything that meets the eye. If there is an ethical imperative underlying the viewing of these photographs, it is to seek in the photographs the ethical absolute that does not meet the eye, the Commanding Voice that the Nazis set out to silence and that they and others nonetheless photographed. Yes: the Commanding Voice of Auschwitz was *photographed.* If not, then we are lost, turned over to the trappings of knowledge and power. Hence the warning concerning the Tree of Knowledge of Good and Evil.

There is one more risk that we run in taking up this consideration of the photographic transcendence of Holocaust representation. Many of us have experienced this when teaching courses on the Holocaust and wrestling with the matter of how much to "show." Years ago, when I was showing graphic images of the horrors of the camps to students in my Holocaust course, something happened that changed my entire outlook on how to teach it: a student asked to see more. Ever since then I have shown no images of the horror to my classes. I had aired what is known as the "Hitchcock film" of the camps, from the time when Alfred Hitchcock worked for the British army, but it was nothing like the voyeurism of Hitchcock's *Rear Window* (1955). No, we are not dealing with mere voyeurism here. I realized that the student's interest in seeing more was neither prurient nor voyeuristic but something else. If we assume the Nazi's point of view when viewing these photographs, we take on the Nazi's temptation to look, which is a temptation to seize, comprehend, and appropriate.

Janina Struk notes that, among the Nazis, taking photos of murdered Jews in the East soon became so widespread that the German command had to restrict it.[19] Just so, "as conditions in the ghetto grew worse, the number of visits by soldier-tourists and camera crews increased."[20] When Sergeant Heinrich Jöst went into the Warsaw Ghetto on his birthday on 19 September 1941 (Figure 3.3),[21] he photographed corpses at the cemetery, "as did photographer Albert Cusian, who commented . . . : 'The subject matter was so interesting. I took pictures in the morgue and at the Jewish cemetery. Bodies of Jews who had died during the night were laid out on the pavements for collection in the morning. I'd wait until the collectors came and then take pictures of them.' "[22] In every instance, the Nazi photographers were "overcome by the desire," their "eyes wide open," as they "ran up to the corpses" to "take their fill of the lovely sight." Of course, looking closer, we see that Jöst photographed more than the murdered child: he photographed the onlookers, images of you and me, the dead who cannot bury the dead. None of this is reducible to mere voyeurism. So what is it? Sontag gives us a hint: "The feeling of being exempt from calamity stimulates interest in looking at painful pictures, and looking at them suggests and strengthens the feeling that one is exempt."[23] Levinas calls it "the temptation of temptation," and it should be kept in mind as we proceed with this investigation.

Levinas explains: "The evil . . . threatens to destroy everything, but the tempted ego is still outside. It can listen to the song of the sirens without compromising the return to its island. It can brush past evil, know

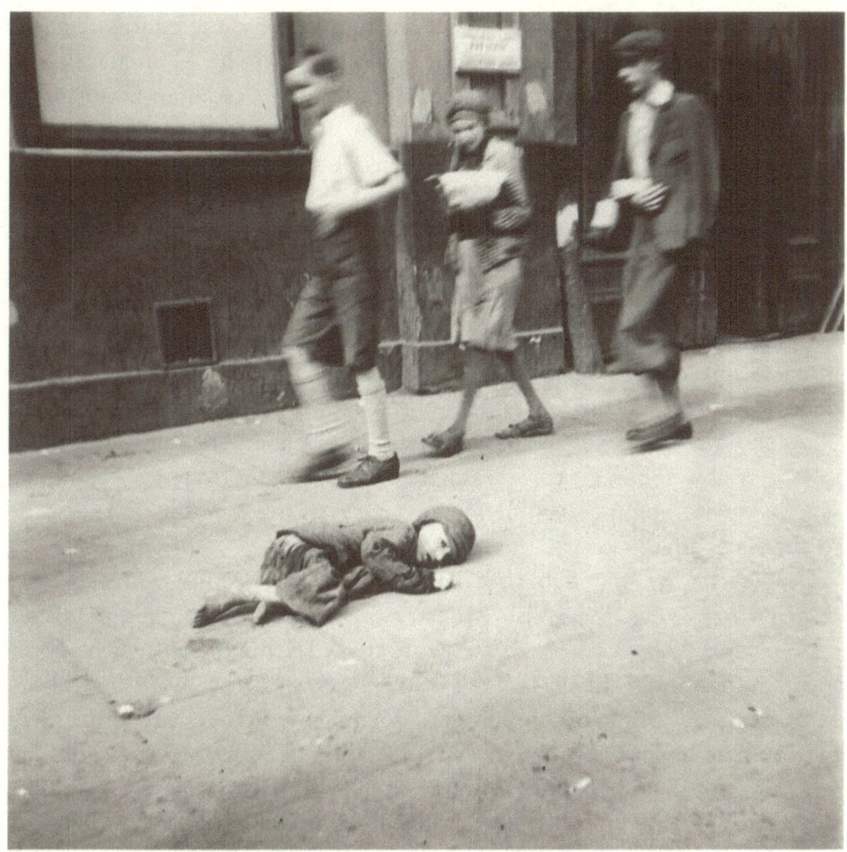

FIGURE 3.3. "A destitute young boy lies on the pavement in the Warsaw ghetto as other children walk by." United States Holocaust Memorial Museum Photo Archives, Desig #481.203, W/S #69946, CD # 0634, with permission of the United States Holocaust Memorial Museum.

it without succumbing to it, experience it without experiencing it, try it without living it, take risks in security. What is tempting is this purity in the midst of total compromise or this compromise which leaves you pure. Or, if you wish, the temptation of temptation *is the temptation of knowledge*."[24] Marianne Hirsch sees the very repetition of these photographs "in books and exhibitions" as "a form of protection and a refusal to confront the trauma of the past."[25] But the trauma is not the trauma of suffering but of the assault on *why it matters* that suffering is inflicted upon human beings—that is where we seek protection from the absolute ethical demand. The temptation of knowledge is the temptation of the photograph, and even more so of the Holocaust photograph. Thus, we recall an insight from Barthes: "Not only is the photograph never, in essence, a memory (whose grammatical expression would be the perfect tense, whereas the tense of the Photograph is the aorist), but it actually blocks memory, quickly becomes counter-memory."[26] We see why the Holocaust photograph is the temptation of representation, the temptation of dealing with trauma rather than what is truly traumatizing, the temptation of having a good cry, getting it over with, protected from having to deal with the invisible questions that lurk in these images: Where are you? Where is your brother? What have you done? And so we realize that these photographs *are not illustrations*: if the photographic transcendence of the Holocaust is about revealing the invisible, it is also about making heard the silent. For the response to human sanctity, to the absolute commandment that tests my response, is a response to the silent invisible.

One of the first published volumes of photographic evidence came out in 1942, when the Polish Ministry of Information in exile published *The German New Order in Poland* with about six hundred pages of documents and photos. In 1943, *The Black Book of Polish Jewry* had about three hundred pages of photos and documents.[27] There are more than two million Holocaust photographs in public archives.[28] Yad Vashem has 130,000, the Ghetto Fighters' House 60,000, Auschwitz-Birkenau 40,000, the United States Holocaust Memorial Museum 70,000, and the Majdanek State Museum 20,000; Yad Vashem has an additional 80,000 in the Hall of Names.[29] All of these zeroes form an abyss, a black hole, that yawns in each and every photograph. One cannot step before these zeroes of images without stepping before the Countenance, before a judgment most severe. In an effort to cling to the handrail of the at-hand—in an effort to keep from tumbling into the infinity of responsibility, more real than the images themselves—here, we shall consider only a few that may be counted among the icons of Holocaust imagery. In doing so, we recall one of the meanings of the Greek word *eikon*: more than an image, it is an "image in the mirror," a mirror held up to the soul, reminding us yet again of the transcendent truth of Elie Wiesel's insight: "The ultimate mystery of the Holocaust is that whatever happened took place in the soul."[30]

In order to establish a method for viewing these photographs, we turn to Ida Fink's short story about a photograph: it is called "Traces." "Traces" is the tale of a woman who was the sole survivor of an Aktion, when the Jews of a ghetto in Poland were rounded up to be shot into a mass grave. She is presented with a photograph from the Aktion of footprints in the snow, the last traces of the lives of the murdered Jews, among whom, as always, were children: She "looks at it for a long time, and says, 'You can still see the traces of footprints. . . .' That's the direction they walked in. From the *Judenrat* down Miesna Street. She looks at the footprints, the snow. . . . 'I wonder who photographed it? And when? Probably right afterwards: the footprints are clear here, but when they shot them in the afternoon it was snowing again.' The people are gone—their footprints remain."[31] Gazing upon these photographs, we gaze upon footprints in the snow. The snow, like time, covers the traces, but there is a trace beneath the snow.

Marianne Hirsch comments on this passage, saying, "The photograph of the footprint is the index par excellence, pointing to the presence, the having-been-there, of the past. . . . More than just evocative and representational power, images also quickly assume symbolic power—the *trace* in the story becomes not just a footprint in the snow but a *trace* of the children who were killed."[32] With such a trace there emerges, in a moment of epiphany, the trace of an ethical absolute that belongs to an absolute past. "A trace qua trace," writes Levinas, "does not simply lead to the past, but is the very passing toward a past more remote than any past and any future which still are set in my time—the past of the other, in which eternity takes form, an absolute past which unites all times."[33] Where eternity takes form, so does a pre-originary ethical absolute find its echo in the present, as "the trace of a past which declines the present and representation, the trace of an immemorial past."[34] Transmitting the invisible, these photographs transmit the immemorial.

Elsewhere, Hirsch refers to this photograph in Fink's tale—an invisible photograph—as a "meta-picture."[35] That is why this invisible photograph serves as a paradigm for the investigation that follows. The footprints in the ephemeral snow are, in one sense, the footprints of no one: their faces, their souls—the souls that came under a radical assault—elude the photograph, lost to oblivion. "A trace can, to be sure, become a sign," Levinas elucidates this point. "But in a face before signifying as a sign it is the very emptiness of an irrecuperable absence. The gaping open of emptiness is not only the sign of an absence. A mark traced on sand [or snow] is not a part of a path, but the very emptiness of a passage. And what has withdrawn is not evoked, does not return to presence, not even to an indicated presence."[36] The footprints in the snow, like these photographs, are "the trace of a beyond borne by a time different from that in which the overflowings of the present flow back to this present across memory and hope."[37] They are the footprints of every Jew, the footprints of the souls that came under a radical assault: they are the footprints of God, of "a presence of that which properly speaking has never been there, of what is always past,"[38] now gazing upon us from the depths of these images, putting to us the pre-originary question, the Jewish Question: Where are you?

Footprints

The wheels hurry onward, onward.
What do they carry?
They carry a cartload
Of shivering shoes.
. . .
I should not ask
But something tears at my tongue
Shoes, tell me the truth
Where are they, the feet?
. . .
Where is the child
To fill those shoes
Why has the bride
Gone barefoot?

—Avraham Sutzkever, "A Cartload of Shoes,"
in *Holocaust Poetry*

Taken in Auschwitz in 1945, this photograph shows a massive pile of shoes from the last transports of murdered Jews (Figure 3.4).[39] It is a photograph of the transcendence of the photograph, a photograph of Holocaust photography's trace of an absence, a trace through which, as Dorota Glowacka has astutely observed, "representation is undone" by the photographic transcendence.[40] It is not a photograph of anything that belongs to this world; it is a photograph of . . . what? Made from a negative, it is made of a negation, of nothingness. One might observe that these are the shoes that made the footprints in the snow and that trudged through the "omnipresent Polish mud," in the words of Primo Levi, "whose monotonous horror fills our days."[41] Indeed, Susan Sontag compares a photograph to a footprint, saying that it is "a trace, something directly stenciled off the real, like a footprint

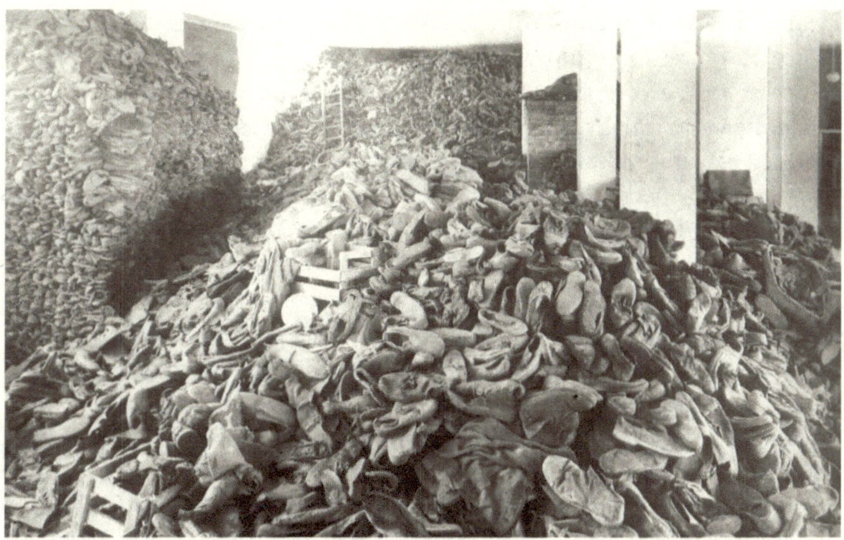

FIGURE 3.4. "Auschwitz, Poland, A pile of shoes," Yad Vashem Photo Archive, Jerusalem, Item ID 102153, Archive Signature 9CO1, with permission of Yad Vashem.

or a death mask."[42] But it is the footprint of a humanity to whom the earth was denied even in death, the death mask of a humanity whose face was obliterated. Perhaps it is indeed like a death mask—the death mask of post-Holocaust humanity.

Gazing upon this image, we are immediately numbed by the numbers, as Aharon Appelfeld's remark returns to haunt us: "We have been taught to speak about the Holocaust in the language of big numbers, and no language distances you from contact more than such a language."[43] The closer the shoes in the foreground of the photograph, the more distant the souls that filled them, turned to ash and cast to the wind, leaving behind a sea of shoes worn to work and to weddings, worn for the Sabbath and for celebrations. "And here, where is the body?" Sutzkever asks. "And there, where is the bride?"[44] Yes, more than numbers, the shoes take on the image of an ocean about to swallow up the viewer, like the *yam Talmud*, the "ocean of Talmud," but with a rather different teaching, not an oral Torah but a silent Torah that undermines Torah. Or is this ocean of shoes better described as a mountain of shoes? The viewer stands at the base of this mountain in a way that reminds us of the Israelites who stood at the base of Mount Sinai, but with a rather different revelation. Emil Fackenheim invokes a "Commanding Voice of Auschwitz" that summons the Jewish people to refuse the murderers a posthumous victory, a revelation that he compares to the revelation at Mount Sinai.[45] If we should wonder about which mountain might have been the site of the revelation, this photograph provides us with one answer, if any answer can be provided.

Looking up at the mountain of shoes, a teaching from the Talmud comes to mind, where it is written that God held a mountain over the Israelites gathered at Sinai and warned them that they would be buried under the mountain if they did not accept the Covenant of Torah (*Shabbat* 88a; *Avodah Zarah* 2b). The point, however, is not that God threatened the Jews, saying, "Accept the Torah, or else I'll crush you." No, it is that without the Torah, humanity is buried under the crushing weight of a strictly material world, lost in a hopeless struggle that no one can win because no one gets out alive, where power is the only reality and weakness the only sin. We may have a choice, but it is, in a sense, a choiceless choice. As Emmanuel Levinas has rightly said, "The Good is good precisely because it chooses you and grips you before you have had the time to raise your eyes to it."[46] So it is with the Covenant. The mountain that compels us to choose *HaEl HaTov,* "the God who is the Good," is not the mountain of might; it is the mountain of the Good itself, the alternative to which is this mountain of shoes. If there is no Mount Sinai and the Covenant is voluntary, then it is also voluntary for God, so that our outcry, our outrage, and our questioning of God are rendered as meaningless as they are groundless. But does this mountain of shoes bury Mount Sinai? Is the Good buried somewhere beneath this mountain of shoes? If so, can the image resurrect the Good in a revelation of an absolute, divine ethical imperative?

In Nelly Sachs's *Eli: A Mystery Play of the Sufferings of Israel,* the Just Man Michael cries out near the end of the play,

> Footprints of Israel,
> gather yourselves together!
> Last earthly moments of Israel,
> gather yourselves together![47]

The footprints could not be more tightly gathered together than in this photograph placed before us, in this image that forces us to make a choice. "I have placed before you life and death," it is written, "therefore choose life" (Deuteronomy 30:19). And "death," says Levi, "begins with the shoes."[48] Yet, as we look closer, we wonder and then look closer still, leaning into the image: Are *those* shoes? And then: Are those ladders? Jacob dreamed of a ladder connecting heaven and earth (Genesis 28:10–22). The shoes ascend into the heavens, outside the frame of the photograph, like traces of the angels ascending the ladder in Jacob's dream, angels that, according to the Talmud, we have created, angels who go out into this world and ascend into the upper worlds to do their work (see *Avot* 4:11; *Chagigah* 41a). How, then, are we now to choose life? How? The shoes overflow the soul the way they overflow the photograph, covering us with their footprints. And we are beggared by their abundance.

The Glory under Assault

> And I will betroth you unto Me forever; and I will betroth you unto Me in righteousness, and in judgment, and in loving-kindness, and in compassion. And I will betroth you unto Me in faithfulness and you shall know the Lord.
>
> —Hosea 2:21–22, words spoken when wrapping tefillin around the fingers

The Nazis in this photograph are wearing boots. The Jew is barefoot, his shoes already consigned to a cart. He has no shoes, but he has a name, a name that has here left a footprint. He is Rabbi Moshe Hagerman, the Dayan of Olkusz, Poland. His photograph was taken on 31 July 1940, on what would become known as Bloody Wednesday (Figure 3.5 on page 208).[49] Yehiel De-Nur kept this photograph on the wall overlooking his writing desk, the rabbi looking down upon him, like a *dayan,* a judge. The passage below is what De-Nur has to say about the photograph in his memoir of five therapy sessions he endured in Holland in order to rid himself of thirty years of nightmares. The memoir's English title is *Shivitti,* from Psalms 16:8, where it is written, *Shivitti Adonai lenegdi tamid,* "I have set the Lord before me always." Just as the psalmist set the Lord before him, so De-Nur set this image of the glory of the Lord before him, the glory that emanated from the hidden light, the light of hiddenness, emanating from Rabbi Hagerman's face crowned with the tefillin:

> I couldn't tear my eyes away . . . from the face of the Jew in his tallith and tefillin who had been posed against a background of

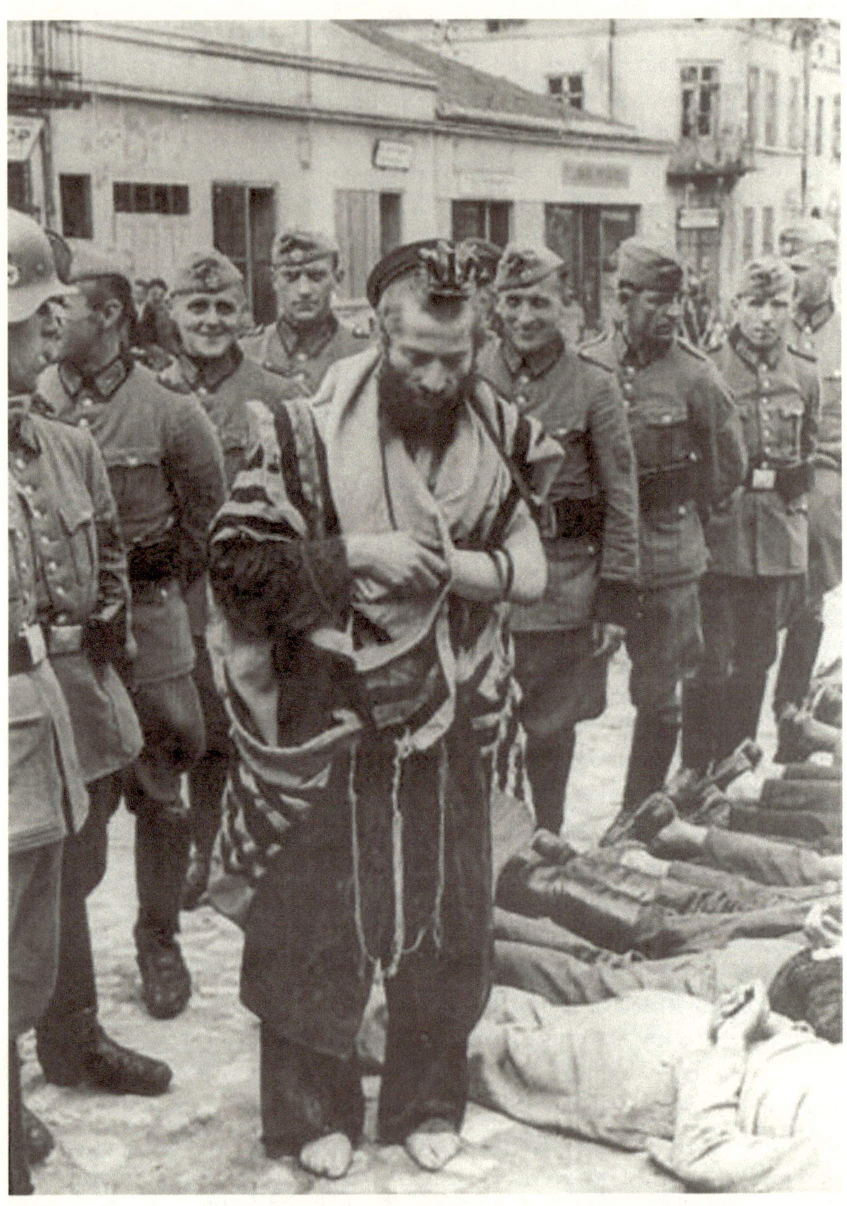

Figure 3.5. "Poland, 31/07/1941, Humiliating a Jew wrapped in a prayer shawl on 'Bloody Wednesday,'" Yad Vashem Photo Archive, Jerusalem, Item ID 56308, Archive Signature 1878, Album Number FA214/133, with permission of Yad Vashem.

> guffawing German soldiers. . . . I took note that the normally square case of the head tefillin was spread into three peaks, like three strokes in the Hebrew letter *shin,* and was placed like a crown on the head of the Jew. . . . Any moment now a bullet would dispatch him to join the row of corpses. . . . But it was not the moment of shooting that was of significance here. Anyone could see this, once in touch with the hidden light radiating from the face of the Jew. . . . It was in the eyes of the Rabbi of Shilev, as we waited our turn for the crematorium, that I saw this same hidden light. I couldn't tear my eyes away from the Jew on the wall. . . . [N]ever had I attained such a state of transcendence.[50]

This is, indeed, a photographic image of transcendence, as it embodies the nonrepresentable essence of the Holocaust. Viewed from the perspective of the Jewish mystical tradition that the Nazis would obliterate, the details of the photograph run deep.

When a Jew wraps himself in a *tallit,* he pronounces a blessing upon God, who commands Jews to wrap themselves not in a *tallit,* precisely, but in *tzitzit,* in fringes. The word *tzitzit* has a numerical value of 600; when the eight threads and five knots of the fringes are added, it comes to 613, the number of commandments in the Torah, so that the Jew wraps himself in the commandments. With four fringes of eight threads, moreover, he is wrapped in thirty-two threads, the numerical value of *lamed-beit,* the letters with which the Torah begins and ends, as well as the number of the pathways that form creation itself, as it is written (*Sefer Yetzirah* 1:1), so that the Jew wraps himself in the Torah. With the five knots, he is wrapped in fifty-two threads and knots, which is one of the numerical values of the Divine Name, the name constituted by the Torah itself,[51] so that the Jew is wrapped in the glory of the Holy One. Wrapped in the *tallit,* then, the Rabbi is wrapped in the glory of Covenant, God, and Torah, like Rabbi Chananiah ben Teradyon, who, at the hands of the Romans, was wrapped in Torah scrolls and burned at the stake (*Talmud Bavli, Avodah Zarah* 18a). This time, however, the Rabbi would be shot before he was burned.

The Rabbi's head tefillin, as De-Nur notes, is not the usual box of four compartments but is splayed like the letter *shin,* forming a kind of crown of thorns, with the accusers of the Jews now acting as deicides, lined up behind him ready to crucify him. In the kabbalistic array of the ten *sefirot* or avenues of divine manifestation, the *shin* is associated with the *sefirah* of Binah, where the Throne of Glory, the *Kise Kavod* (see Isaiah 6:1–3) is situated (*Pardes Rimonim* 27:24). Its three branches correspond to the three pillars that hold up creation, the pillars of Torah study, prayer, and deeds of loving kindness (cf. *Pardes Rimonim* 15:1)—all of which were slated for annihilation in the Nazis' undoing of creation. With the undoing of creation comes the undoing of the human being created in the image and likeness of the Holy One; according to the *Tikkunei HaZohar*, as long as we wear tefillin, we embody what it means to be created in that image and likeness, "rising through the upper realms of the Ophanim, Seraphim, and other angels" (*Tikkunei HaZohar* 83b). There lies the transcendence of which De-Nur speaks. It lies also in the teaching that the letter *alef*, the letter signifying the silence within every word (see *Keter Shem Tov* 45), is made of a *yud* above, a *yud* below, and a *vav* linking the two,[52] and that when a man puts on his tefillin he is transformed into an *alef*, with the head and arm tefillin boxes corresponding to the two *yuds* and his body corresponding to the *vav*. The numerical value of *yud* (10) plus *vav* (6) plus *yud* (10) is twenty-six, which is the value of the Tetragrammaton, the Name of God. Thus, transformed into an embodiment of the Name, Rabbi Hagerman radiates the divine glory.

One of the names of God in the Jewish tradition is the *Ziv HaOlam*, or the "Glory of the World." The word *ziv* or "glory" in this phrase signifies the authority of righteousness and goodness; it signifies an ethical height revealed through a commandment from on high. What is understood as "glory," therefore, is neither the object of contemplation nor a theme that might be postulated. Surpassing human utterance and eloquence, it is an afterimage that shows itself in this photograph not as a shadow but as a light. Recalling that *ziv* also means "light," "luster," or "brilliance," we understand the glory of God to be the radiance of the testimony borne in every act of loving kindness, a testimony that implicates us even as it enlightens us. "The debt," Levinas explains, "increases in the measures that it is paid. This divergency perhaps deserves the name glory. The positivity of the infinite is the conversion of the response to the infinite into responsibility, into approach of the other. The Infinite is non-thematizable, gloriously exceeds every capacity, and manifests, as it were in reverse, its exorbitance in the approach of a neighbor, obedient to its measure."[53] To be thus implicated is to have opened up before us the path to the Glory of the World. Each time we encounter an ethical truth—each time we witness the example of the righteous—we stand accused, just as De-Nur felt himself accused whenever he gazed upon this photograph. For to know this truth is to know we have fallen short of the truth.

Here, we recall Levinas's assertion that "the glory of the Infinite reveals itself through what it is capable of doing in the witness."[54] In this photograph we collide with a dramatic display of that truth, in the image of the witnessing—of the martyrdom—of Rabbi Moshe Hagerman. We collide, in other words, with what the glory of the Infinite is capable of doing to the witness. It is, to borrow further from Levinas, an image of "the transcendence of the Infinite" that "arises in glory,"[55] in "a surplus of the Infinite,"[56] which is a surplus of the Good, or the Good understood precisely *as* such a surplus. The glory of God, as Abraham Joshua Heschel says, "is equated with the goodness of God."[57] There we have the surplus that eclipses the Nazis' grisly grins and overflows the borders of the photograph; it spills onto De-Nur's pages and washes over attempts such as this one to bring to light what eludes the light.

And so, as we come before the photograph, we step before the *Kise Kavod,* the divine "Throne of Glory." The hidden light radiating from the rabbi's face is the light of the *kavod,* a light that is *kaved* or "heavy." It weighs down upon the viewer to make "life heavier," as Martin Buber says, "but heavy with meaning."[58] Suddenly, we realize what this photograph of Rabbi Hagerman is a photograph *of*: it is a photograph of the glory under assault, a photograph of the radical assault on "the glory of transcendence,"[59] a photograph of the Nazi assault on transcendence itself. As such, it is a photograph of the nonrepresentable, unspeakable, invisible "essence" of the Holocaust. As a photograph of such a transcendence—a photograph of the invisible—it "interrupt[s] its own demonstration. Its voice has to be silent as soon as one listens for its message."[60] Indeed, this photograph, like all Holocaust photographs, is not only silent—it is a photograph of silence. As Levinas says, "to bear witness to God is precisely not to state this extraordinary word, as though glory would be lodged in a theme and be posited as a thesis," so that the photograph bears witness to the glory of God by its very silence. It is "a sign given to the other of this very signification, the 'here I am' . . . in the name of God."[61] Indeed, this photograph of the assault on the glory is a photograph of the assault on the "Here I am" so profoundly proclaimed by the rabbi, a "Here I am" that drowns out the guffaws of the murderers.

So now we perhaps have a better sense of what this photograph reveals about the Nazis' invisible assault on the glory. How do the Nazis assault the glory? They stand up a Jew wrapped in *tallit* and *tefillin,* barefoot, ascending through his prayer into the upper realms, reciting the *Shema,* the "Hear, O Israel" prayer, refusing to abandon the millennial teaching, tradition, and testimony to the glory of the Infinite. They guffaw words of mockery calculated to eclipse the words of prayer, of *tefillah,* of *naftolin* or "wrestling," as Jacob wrestled with the Angel of Death. And yet Rabbi Hagerman is surrounded not by the wings of the Angel of Death but by those who would obliterate the Angel of Death, the Angel of a Thousand Eyes, who is also an emanation of the glory of the Infinite. As we gaze upon this image, the Angel leaves us with a new set of eyes: turning away from the photograph, we turn to look upon a world that will never look the same.

The Mothers of Israel

> Suddenly, the stillness was broken by the screaming of children . . . a scream repeated a thousand times in a single word, "Mama," a scream that increased in intensity every second, enveloping the whole camp. Our lips parted without our being conscious of what we were doing, and a scream of despair tore out of our throats. . . . At the end everything was enveloped in death and silence.
>
> —Sara Nomberg-Przytyk, *Auschwitz: True Tales from a Grotesque Land*

In the mystical tradition we have a teaching that says the letter *shin* on the head tefillin that we saw in the previous photograph signifies the Upper Mother, who gives birth to creation through her mother's love and through that love imparts meaning to life (*Tikkunei HaZohar* 26a). And so we step before this photograph. Whoever has seen this image taken in the Ukraine in 1942 has been transformed by it. It is an iconic photograph of a Jewish mother holding her child in her arms, with the Nazi's rifle aimed at the back of her head (Figure 3.6),[62] iconic because this single image captures the evil of the Third Reich and its systematic assault on the mothers of Israel. In this Jewish mother are gathered all the Jewish mothers who could not save their children but who nevertheless held them close, in their arms. Just so, the photograph captures the infinite extent to which a mother is prepared to be with her little one. De-Nur's realization that the key to Auschwitz lies in the murder of the mother comes to mind; indeed, it is emblematic of the Shoah itself. In Parts One and Two we examined at length the significance

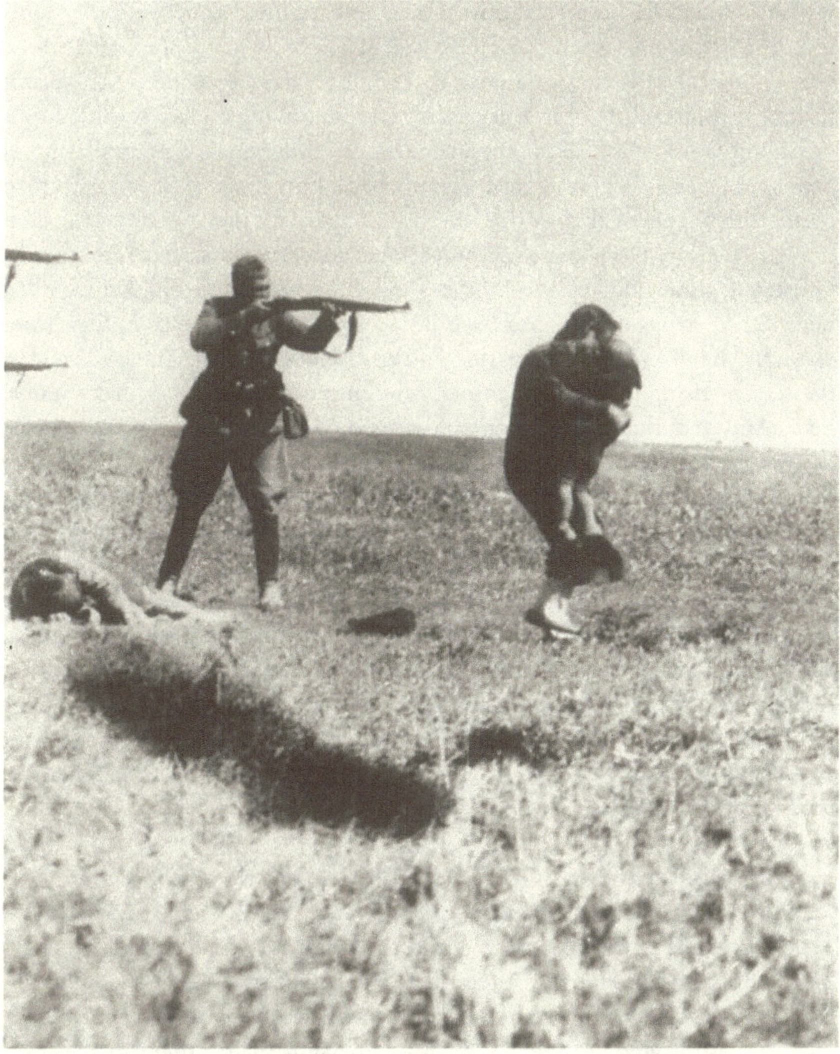

FIGURE 3.6. Member of Einsatzgruppe D shooting mother and child, Photo taken in the Ukraine in 1942, public domain.

of the mother in Jewish tradition. No need to repeat that investigation here. Still, keeping all of that in mind, let us examine the image before our eyes.

There are no faces visible here. The murderer's face, like his humanity, is obscured by the murderer's weapon: the weapon renders him faceless. The

Jewish mother's face is turned downward, perhaps looking to regain her footing on this barren, ashen piece of earth; it is obscured by the child whose life—whose death—she is desperately trying to save. And the child's face is turned away, certainly oblivious to the camera, seeking a place to hide in his or her mother's arms. Recall the image of the children in Ka-tzetnik's novel *Star of Ashes*, as they struggle to climb back into their mother's womb to escape the horror of this world. The little ones, he writes, "push again their mother's belly, as if seeking to get inside once more. Their scream, embryonic, unuttered, howls out of the mother's eyes."[63] This Jewish child, too, filled with terror, struggles to climb back inside somewhere, his face hidden from view, his howl encompassing the universe. Gazing at this image, we feel the scream rising in our own throats, choking us. There are no faces visible here. And yet, this is a photograph of the obliteration of the face as the obliteration of the divine, absolute prohibition against murder (much more about the face below). In that prohibition that howls from the depths of this image lies the photographic transcendence of Holocaust representation.

Like the screams that flooded the women's camp in Auschwitz, this photograph shatters any stillness we or the world might experience from the horrific moment that we lay eyes on it. The child shatters that stillness. The child is screaming, "Mama!" You can hear it even now, rising up from the depths of the black and white. It haunts us. Or is it the screams of the mother? The two merge into a cosmic scream. The Jewish mother's arms are wrapped around the Jewish child, like the wings of the Shekhinah in the prayer *El molei rakhamim*:

> *El molei rakhamim*—God filled with compassion—who dwells in the heights, bring proper rest to the soul of [this one] beneath the wings of the *Shekhinah,* amid the heights of the holy and the pure, illuminating like the brilliance of the firmament the souls of our beloved and our holy ones, who went to their eternity. May You who are the source of compassion shelter them in the shade of your wings eternally, and bind their souls in the bonds of the living. The Lord is his/her heritage. May he/she find rest and peace. And let us say: Amen. (My translation)

But there is no saying amen to this image. Unlike the Shekhinah, this Jewish mother is unable to protect her Jewish child. And the *El molei rakhamim* was never said for this mother and child.

Never has there ever been such a transcendent image of the *embrace.* It gives new, devastating meaning to Levinas's insight: "Proximity is not a state, a repose, but, a restlessness, null site, outside of the place of rest. . . . No site then, is ever sufficiently a proximity, like an embrace. Never close enough, proximity does not congeal into a structure. . . . Proximity, as the 'closer and closer,' becomes the subject. It attains its *superlative* as *my* incessant restlessness, becomes unique, then one, forgets reciprocity, as in a love that does not expect to be shared."[64] The restlessness ignited by this photograph is the restlessness of an ethical demand that can never be met; it is as incessant as it is unrelenting. It allows no sleep. This Jewish mother's embrace conveys the meaning of "proximity," which Levinas describes as "transcendence itself,"[65] the proximity that can never be close enough. It is the infinite closeness, the unbridgeable closeness of what is very nigh unto thee, the closeness of the transcendent ethical demand, which insists that the death which concerns me is the death of the other—the death of the child.

Oblivious to the photographer and the photograph, this Jewish mother about to be cast into oblivion can think only of her Jewish child. She is a mother. She struggles to keep her footing on the shifting ground of a homeland transformed into a wasteland, the ground of a creation now reeling under the trauma of an anti-creation. Is she trying to run? She wants to run. But run where? The lines from Wiesel's *Ani Maamin* return to us:

> I run . . .
> And while I run,
> I am thinking:
> This is insane,
> This Jewish child
> Will not be spared. . . .
> I perceive a whisper . . . :
> I believe in you.[66]

She and the child are about to be shot before she can take a step. The two possibilities normally allowed a victim are denied to these two: neither submission nor flight is an option for them. Only a death that is not death, as the image of this mother and child brings to mind these lines dated 20 October 1941 from the diary of Sarra Gleikh, who survived a similar action in the Ukraine, near her town of Mariupol: "Somewhere above the corpses children were crying. Most of them, especially the babies whose mothers held them in their arms to protect them (they shot us in the back), had fallen, now buried under the bodies of their mothers; buried alive under the corpses, they were smothering."[67] Those who are smothering beneath this iconic image of the Shoah are the invisible aspect of the photograph, the transcendence that opens our eyes and steals our breath.

Who is this man who takes aim at the grim image of a horrifying Madonna? What is his rifle for? Self-defense? Defense against the Jewish contagion that threatens the soul of all humanity? What is he trying to kill? He is killing the soul of the mother. It is one thing to shoot a woman, but quite another to shoot a woman trying to protect her child from being shot. It is a categorical, metaphysical, transcendent distinction conveyed by this photograph. Does the Nazi murderer know that as soon as he fires he has lost his own soul? What does his one open eye focus on, as it stares down the sights of his rifle? Is this something that those sights were designed to sight? Does he have a mother? Did his mother ever offer him the embrace with which this Jewish mother embraces her child? No, never. Never did his mother embrace him to protect him from a murderer who would nonetheless murder him. Does he write home to his mother? What does he say? Does his mother write to her son APO *Einsatzgruppe D*? Does she sign her letters, "Love, Mutti?" We can only question. We cannot comment. This photographic image of the transcendent exceeds analysis and commentary. There are other questions: Who is the photographer? What is he trying to document? For whose eyes has he taken the photograph? Not for our eyes. And yet the image stubbornly demands our gaze. Once again we collide with the question put to the first human being, the question that decides our humanity and the dearness of the *other* human being: Where are you?

The Child

> And a little child shall lead them.
>
> —Isaiah 11:6

On 8 May 1943, after twenty days of fighting, the Nazis finally succeeded in crushing the uprising in the Warsaw Ghetto. On that day they discovered the ghetto fighters' headquarters at Mila 18, where they killed the leader of the uprising, Mordecai Anielewicz (1919–1943), along with many others. With the assistance of the Poles, the Germans spent the next

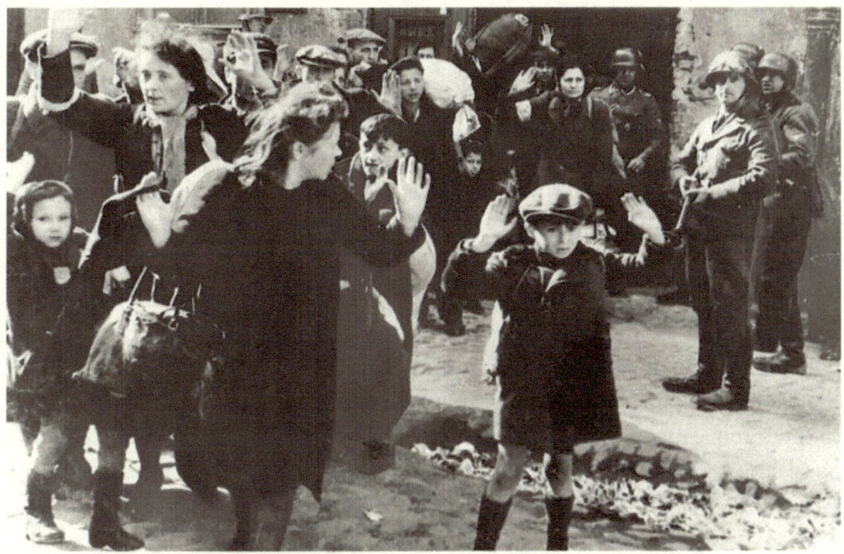

FIGURE 3.7. "Jews captured by SS and SD troops during the suppression of the Warsaw ghetto uprising are forced to leave their shelter and marched to the Umschlagplatz for deportation," United States Holocaust Memorial Museum Photo Archives, Photograph 2654, public domain.

eight days flushing out the Jews who were still hiding in the ghetto. This photograph, one of the most infamous to surface from the depths of the Shoah, was taken on 16 May 1943.[68] It originally appeared in *The Stroop Report*, an album prepared by SS Major General Jürgen Stroop, commander of the German forces in charge of liquidating the ghetto; with such photos, Stroop intended to demonstrate the "heroism" of the 1,200 SS, Wehrmacht, and police troops who emerged victorious over approximately 220 poorly armed, starving Jews, who, according to Stroop, were fighting on behalf of more than 50,000 Jews in hiding. Of those who survived, 7,000 were sent to Treblinka and another 22,000 to Majdanek. Some 15,000 were sent to the concentration camp at Poniatowa, and another 6,000, including the Rebbe of the Warsaw Ghetto Rabbi Kalonymos Kalmish Shapira, to the camp at Trawniki. Stroop's report was presented to Heinrich Himmler as a souvenir in celebration of the great German victory. In the report the caption reads, "Jews captured by SS and SD troops during the suppression of the Warsaw Ghetto Uprising are forced to leave their shelter and march to the Umschlagplatz for deportation."[69]

Several figures in the photograph have been identified. The German on the right holding the machine gun on this helpless crowd of Jews is SS-Rottenführer Josef Blösche, who was tried for war crimes by a Polish court in 1969 and executed in July of that year. The little girl on the far left is Hanka Lamet, who was murdered at Majdanek. And the little boy with hands raised? One survivor of Bergan-Belsen, Tsvi Nussbaum (1935–2012), has claimed that this is a photo of him at the age of seven. After the war, Nussbaum moved to Israel, and then to the United States, where he became a physician in New York City. It is generally accepted that the child in the photograph is indeed Dr. Nussbaum. Although this point is of extreme importance, of more importance for our purpose here is the matter of Holocaust iconography. Evidence for the iconic status of the photograph can be found in Samuel Bak's series of canvases featuring this child, many of which portray him in a manner suggesting a crucifixion, his face stamped with the terror of *Eli, Eli, lama azavtani*? "My God, my God, why have you forsaken me?" (Psalms 22:2; Matthew 27:46). That is perhaps why the volume featuring these paintings is titled *Icon of Loss: The Haunting Child of Samuel Bak*.[70] Of course, Bak's painting came long after Franklin Littell's *Crucifixion of the Jews*,[71] a book whose title, like Bak's work, places the cruciform image of the Jewish—of the Jewish *child*—in the realm of the transcendent. Once consigned to the canvas as the Suffering Servant of the Holy One, the image takes on a transcendence through which the hidden is revealed *as* hidden—or as removed—and therefore as non-thematizable, which is to say, nonrepresentable. In a word, the iconographic image situates the systematic assault on the Jewish child—and with the child, the Jewish people—in the realm of sacred history.

The previous photograph of mother and child has in the background a barren wasteland turned into a killing field—the background of modern inhumanity. This photograph is set in an urban wasteland turned into an instrument of extermination—the scene of modern brutality and blatant monstrosity. The Warsaw Ghetto was, indeed, an instrument of torture and extermination, and the children were among the first to fall prey to its systematically murderous conditions. With a legal ration of only 220 calories per person per day, the Jews of the Warsaw Ghetto could stay alive only by becoming criminals.[72] "Whatever we do," writes Chaim Kaplan in his ghetto diary, "we do illegally; legally we don't even have the right to exist."[73] This dictum applied most fundamentally to the children of the ghetto, such as this child in this image. Here, we have a hint of the invisible, of the history—or the sacred history—that Marianne Hirsch invokes when she complains, "The picture's well-known history, however, mostly remains invisible in its contemporary representations, representations that actually enable viewers to forget or ignore its troubling source."[74] Indeed, whenever we attempt to represent the nonrepresentable we run the risk of turning memory over to the formulaic and thus "enable viewers to forget or ignore its troubling source." Confronting this image, we would slip into the temptation to ignore its "troubling source," troubling because of the absolute, transcendent ethical demand that stems from the invisible history that overshadows the image. So what is the transcendent lens of the invisible through which we might view this photograph?

First of all, in the context of its iconography, as well as the photo's historical contexts, this is not just a child whose Jewishness threatens the Nazis wielding their weapons, as they escort him to the trains. Shedding ourselves of our armor, we peer into the abject fear of this child, *the terror of a Jewish child,* that horrifies any human being who has ever been a child or who has ever had a child. In the time of the Holocaust, the Jewish child is the one whose very being is wrapped not in wings of an angel but in abject fear, with "death as a cradle and the curse of death as a cradle song," as Edmond Jabès (1912–1991) expresses it.[75] And his mother? Where is she? Is she already dead? Like almost all survivors, like all of humanity, this Jewish child is in all likelihood an orphan with hands raised, cruciform, whose Father has indeed forsaken him and all of humanity, whose image accuses a world bereft of all redemption, all revelation, all salvation.

In the ghetto, the pervasive cradle song of death is the cry of starvation: the fear etched into this Jewish child's face is the fear of a starving child. Starvation, indeed, defines the ontological condition of the Jewish child in the ghetto, and the Warsaw Ghetto diarists repeatedly point this out. "They are living skeletons from the ranks of street beggars," writes Adam Czerniaków, head of the ghetto's Jewish Council. "Some of them came to my office. They talked with me like grown-ups—these eight-year-old citizens. I am ashamed to admit it, but I wept as I have not wept for a long time. . . . Damned be those of us who have enough to eat and drink and forget about these children."[76] Similarly, Emmanuel Ringelblum notes, "Three-year-old children are out begging in the streets. You can't rest nowadays in a Jewish apartment. You hear beggars rapping on doors on either side of your own apartment."[77] Elsewhere, Ringelblum describes a six-year-old boy who "lay gasping all night, too weak to roll over to the piece of bread that had been thrown down to him from the balcony."[78] Soon the starvation of the child rapping at the door and lying below the balcony became a defining feature of the entire ghetto. The starving Jewish child is not part of the landscape—he is the sum of the landscape, from which there is no escape. And that landscape is gathered into the image of the child in the photograph, a child who suppresses the silent scream about to erupt from his throat. In his suppressed scream are gathered all the children's screams heretofore suppressed.

But there is more. "On the streets," writes Ringelblum on 22 November 1941, "one regularly comes across children frozen to death."[79] Taking the invisible framework of the photograph further, we recall an entry from the diary of Janusz Korczak (1878–1942): "The body of a dead boy lies on the sidewalk. Nearby, three boys are playing horses and drivers. At one point they notice the body, move a few steps to the side, go on playing."[80] Shall we, too, having collided with this photograph, go on playing our sanctimonious games? In this image we confront the death before death, the slaughter before the slaughter, which is a slaughter of the innocents in their innocence: it is the waking dream that brings on the nightmare Korczak describes when he says that in his sleep he sees "bodies of dead children. One dead child in a bucket. Another skinned, lying on the boards in the mortuary, clearly still breathing."[81] Still breathing and yet shrouded in death: this is the breath emptied of soul, the *neshimah* drained of *neshamah,* not the last breath but the breath that is continually the last, suffocated before the last breath is drawn. It is the breath of a child, which sustains all of creation, as it is written in the Talmud (*Shabbat* 119b). This is a photograph of the collapse of creation, a photograph of the anti-creation.

As for those children who, like this child before us, were hiding from an open season on their lives, we may refer to the entry in Menahem Kon's diary from the Warsaw Ghetto dated 6 August 1942: "The children are being hidden since they are the most sought after by the murderers. I make up my mind not to go into the cellar, I shall not take up room where some more children could be hidden. The children have preference to be saved."[82] But, of course, they cannot be saved. Or rather, a world that might have saved them has abandoned them. In this photographic image of such an abandonment we have a photographic transcendence of the Holocaust, as we realize when reminded of these lines from Elie Wiesel's character Moshe in his novel *The Oath*: "The Messiah. We seek him, we pursue him. We think he is in heaven; we don't know that he likes to come down as a child. And yet, every man's childhood is messianic in essence."[83] One of the texts from the Jewish tradition that articulates this view of the child as savior is the *Even Sheleimah* of Elijah ben Shlomo Zalman Kremer

(1720–1797), the Vilna Gaon. There he writes, "The child redeems his parent from Gehinom and causes him to be brought to Gan Eden."[84] Hence, the meaning of "a little child will lead them." But where does the little child in this photograph, a Jewish child who treads the edge of annihilation, lead us? The viewer, Dorota Glowacka suggests, "is called upon to take up the labor of memory in imaginative substitution and partake in an act of rescue in which she herself becomes a repository of disappearing traces."[85] The photographic transcendence lies in this disappearance. Thus, the child in the photograph launches us into the transcendence of an ethical absolute that at once demands and refuses rescue.

Commenting on the photograph, Marianne Hirsch raises a question: "Why are the most powerful and resonant among iconic images after the Holocaust images of children?" She answers, wrongly: "Our culture has a great deal invested in the children's innocence and vulnerability, and also, at the same time, in their eroticism and knowledge. Less individualized, less marked by the particularities of identity, moreover, children invite multiple projections, and lend themselves to universalization. Their photographic images elicit an affiliative and identificatory as well as a protective spectorial look marked by these investments."[86] Eroticism? Less marked by the particularities of identity? Why? Because of their vulnerability and innocence? Perhaps because everyone has been a child, everyone lends themselves to universalization. What the "spectorial look marked by these investments" might mean, I am not sure; identity lies in responsibility and implication, not in investments.

Most of the Jews in the photograph are women and children, the men having been killed or already rounded up. "The children have preference to be saved," as Menahem Kon says. But there is no salvation for them and no redemption for us. The woman in the foreground knows this. She looks over her shoulder to see whether the murderers will murder them now or wait until later, an instant teetering on the edge of an abyss. We see the bundles and the bags of these Jews setting out on a long day's journey into the Kingdom of Night, the Kingdom of Nothingness and Darkness that the Light Cannot Comprehend. No young men. No old men. No old women. And in the Germans we discover the iconic image of Amalek: "Remember what the Amalekites did to you along the way when you came out of Egypt. When you were weary and worn out, they met you on your journey and attacked all who were lagging behind; they had no fear of God. When the Lord your God gives you rest from all the enemies around you in the land he is giving you to possess as an inheritance, you shall blot out the name of Amalek from under heaven. Do not forget!" (Deuteronomy 25:17–19). Look at this photograph and do not forget! Remember to wipe out the name—the murderous teaching and testimony—of Amalek, the Am Lak who licks blood in a grim reversal of the blood libel. It is all outlined in this photograph: the Jewish child, hands raised, cruciform, now becomes the embodiment of the Suffering Servant.

In addition to the image before our eyes there is an echo of a refrain that struck terror in the hearts of the hidden Jewish children: it is the dreaded, bestial barking of *Juden 'raus!* In 1946 David Boder (1886–1961), a psychologist from the Illinois Institute of Technology, traveled to Europe to record the first testimonies from Holocaust survivors. Gert Silberbart, a child who hid from the Nazis, related to him, "During these last three days I hid in cellars and sewage holes. I did not eat or drink during these days, just always listened anxiously to the cry of '*Juden raus*'; and when somebody, something moved close to me, when I heard any sound, I immediately grew terrified."[87] In this photograph, all eyes, the eyes of all who have just heard the howl of *Juden 'raus,* are on the murderers. Of course. These Jews are terrified. No one's eyes are turned to the child with hands raised, the child turned over to a radical, horrific isolation, who is sure to be murdered in his radical isolation, with no help, no help, murdered not as a fugitive with hands raised but as a Jewish child who as a Jew must be murdered—murdered, not killed, not someone who dies, *but one who must be murdered from the ideological necessity of* Rassenseele, a defining feature of his non-being (never mind the possible survivor status of Nussbaum). Yes, the eyes . . .

The Face

> The Infinite comes in the signifyingness of the face. The face *signifies* the Infinite. . . . It is the exigency of holiness.
>
> —Emmanuel Levinas, *Ethics and Infinity*

> The face, for its part, is inviolable; those eyes, which are absolutely without protection, the most naked part of the human body, none the less offer an absolute resistance in which the temptation to murder is inscribed: the temptation of absolute negation.
>
> —Emmanuel Levinas, *Difficult Freedom*

The title of this photograph from the Yad Vashem Photo Archives is "Bergen-Belsen, Germany, a survivor inside a barrack, 1945" (Figure 3.8).[88] It is a witness photograph, in contrast to the perpetrator photographs we have seen, although all of these images transform the viewer into a witness.

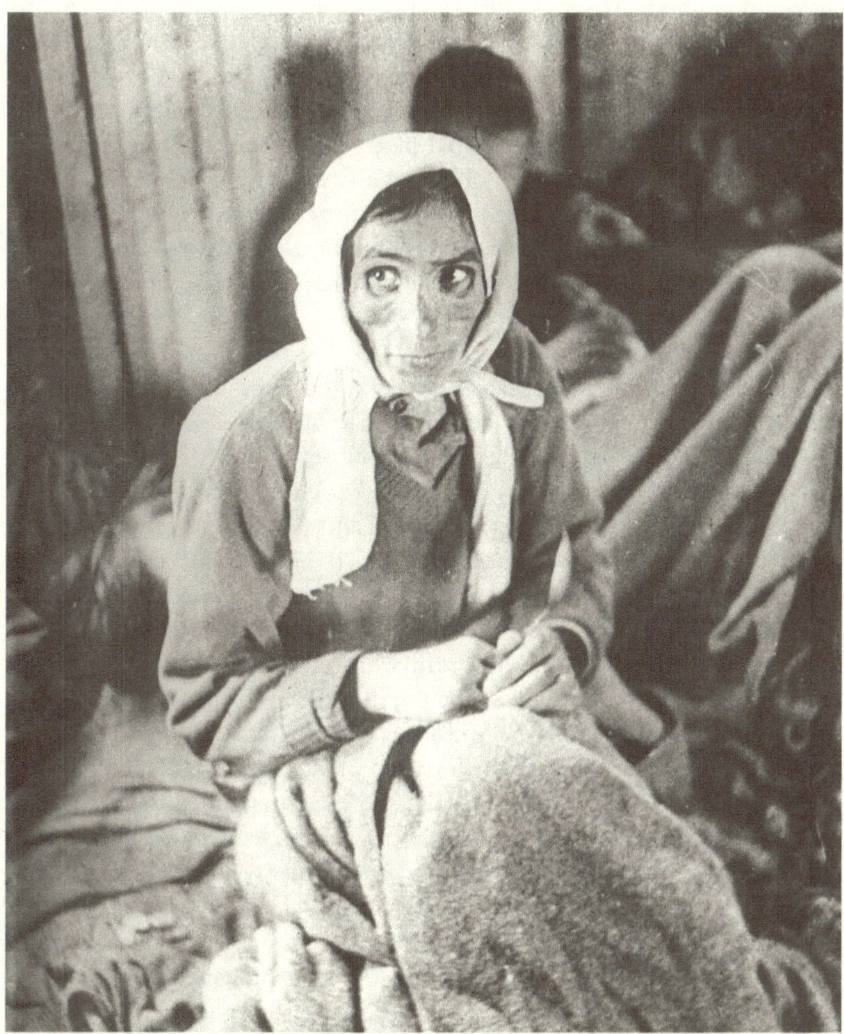

FIGURE 3.8. "Bergen-Belsen, Germany, a survivor inside a barrack, 1945," Yad Vashem Photo Archive, Jerusalem, M.2, ID 50722, Archival Signature 5031/45, with permission of Yad Vashem.

That, in part, is what makes them icons. In its skeletal features, brought on by starvation, brutality, exposure, humiliation, torture, and other forms of the assault on the soul, the frightened Jewish face resembles a *memento mori,* and yet it is the opposite of a *memento mori*: the reminder is not of the truth that "you shall die" but of the absolute commandment, "Thou shalt not murder" (Exodus 20:13). This is the "ab-solute" that Levinas refers to when he writes, "The face *enters* our world from an absolutely foreign sphere, that is, precisely from an ab-solute."[89] Therefore, as a face, although situated in history, it transcendentally and "enigmatically comes from the infinite and its immemorial past"[90] to demonstrate the truth that "the face is what forbids us to kill"[91]—the face, yes, but even more so *the eyes*. What have those eyes seen? What are they looking at? What are they looking out for? Are they about to turn their gaze on us? No one can say, but one thing is certain: neither your eyes nor mine nor the eye of the camera would want to gaze upon the Medusa that those eyes have gazed upon: look what the sight did to her.

This woman has come face to face with the Angel of Death, the Angel with a Thousand Eyes, as described in the Talmud (see *Avodah Zarah*, 20b). In this case the Angel did not take her but left her with new eyes, eyes that overtake the eye of the camera and invade our eyes, even as her eyes look away, still fearful. Or perhaps she wants to protect us from gazing into those eyes: it would be like a gaze into the sun or into the abyss. The Talmud compares the whole of this world and what transcends this world to an eye. "This world," it says, "is likened to a person's eyeball: the white of the eye [corresponds to] the ocean which surrounds the whole world; the iris to the [inhabited] world; the pupil of the eye to Jerusalem; the face in the pupil to the Temple" (*Derekh Eretz Rabbah* 9:13). In this case, the white of the eye corresponds to the abyss of the anti-world and its ocean of ashes that now surround the world; the iris corresponds to the blue of the sky now made gray, transformed into a cemetery inhabited by the dead who look down upon us and demand to know what we have made of them; the pupil of the eye—that circle of darkness through which the infinite that is Jerusalem, the Divine Presence that calls out to us, "Where are you!? How could you!? *Ayeka?!*"—corresponds to Planet Auschwitz, site of a new *Churban,* a different destruction; and the face in the pupil corresponds to the face of the One who hides His face, who comes under a radical assault in the Nazis' assault on the human face, who peers into our eyes from the transcendent depths of this photograph of the *remnant of a face*.

The great sage of the Talmud, Rabbi Akiva, maintains that the humanity and the dignity of the human being are revealed in the face; in the face, he held, lies the image of the Holy One,[92] signifying the exigency of the holy. If that is the case, then in this face we behold the remains of the Nazis' assault on the Holy One and on the absolute ethical demand of the transcendent Infinite, which is an assault on the very meaning of the human being, as the tradition teaches. It is a transcendent, however, that is as concrete as the image in this photograph, with the fleeting flesh and blood of *this* human being, whose name we do not know but who calls out to us by name. Recall in this connection that the Hebrew word for "face," *panim,* is plural because each of us has two faces: the face of Adam, who came from the hand and mouth of God, and our own individual face. Gazing upon this face, therefore, we experience a fundamental link to this other human being, a link that itself came under assault in the assault on the face. If the encounter with the face is an encounter with the Holy One, then it is an encounter with Torah. Through the face, Torah enters this world. Through the face of the other, Torah commands us to be there for the sake of the other. And that is the transcendent that the Nazis set out to obliterate, as Hitler once confided to Hermann Rausching: he declared to Rausching that his mission in life was to destroy the "tyrannical God of the Jews" and His "life-denying Ten Commandments."[93] And the war on God begins with the war on the sixth commandment: Do not murder.

Levinas rightly understands that the primary commandment to arise from the face is the prohibition against murder, which issues from *on high.*[94] Because the face signifies the ethical exigency of the holy, we recall Levinas's insight, "the face is signification, and signification *without context.* I mean that the Other, in the rectitude of his face, is not a character within a context. Ordinarily . . . the meaning of something is in its relation to another thing. Here, to the contrary, the face is meaning all by itself."[95] That is why the Nazis *must* obliterate the face of the Jew in their assault on the soul of the Jew: their aim is to eliminate the meaning couched in the *absolute* prohibition against murder. Indeed, without this meaning, without this absolute, that enters this world through the flesh-and-blood soul embodied in the face, this world has no meaning. Through the face, moreover, Torah commands us not just to refrain from murder but also to be there for the sake of another. It summons from us the response of "Here I am," and "the subject who says 'Here I am,'" Levinas asserts, "*testifies* to the Infinite."[96] The face of the soul testifies to the Infinite because it commands *absolutely*. In the face, the infinite and the finite merge into a commanding voice that speaks in the mode of a silence that in this photograph surpasses utterance.

When the holy within the human comes under assault, as in the Nazi assault on the soul of the Jew in this photograph, the mystery and the meaning of the face are obliterated in a twisting and torturing of the face itself. In the time of the Holocaust, one means of attaining this twisting was to render the Jew *shamefaced,* both in her own eyes and in the eyes of others. Consider an observation from Auschwitz *Sonderkommando* diarist Zalman Lewental (d. 1944). "We were ashamed of one another," he writes, "and dared not look one another in the face. Our eyes swollen with pain, shame, tears and lamentations, each of us burrowed into a hole to avoid meeting one another."[97] The hole these Jews burrow into swallows up their humanity, because what is buried in this hole that resembles a grave is the human face. Does not the viewer of this photograph also want to crawl into a hole? This distance between one human being and another creates a void into which every trace of humanity disappears. For the human image belongs not just to this person or that but rises up where two come together face to face. And to have a face is to be capable of being shamefaced. Having divested themselves of conscience and therefore of shame, the Nazis' pride in the public display of their cruelty is a major part of what links their assault on the human image to a defilement of the human image within themselves. Not only do they spill blood—they wallow it in. Refusing to turn their faces away in shame and insisting upon showing their faces in public, as we have seen in the photograph of Rabbi Hagerman, they show themselves to be without a face: they show themselves to be inhuman. And so we begin to see a progression in this mutilation of the face, from shame to sorrow, from terror to emptiness.

Which brings us to one more question, a question that, like Adam hiding from God, we long to hide from: Who is the one rendered shamefaced in the collision with this photograph? Primo Levi recalls that when the Russians first stumbled across Auschwitz on 27 January 1945, in their faces he saw "the shame that drowned us after the selections, and every time we had to watch, or submit to, some outrage: the shame the Germans did not know."[98] It is the shame that washes over the face of any one of us who comes face to face with the face in this photograph, a shame before the transcendent that cannot be represented. And if it cannot be represented, then there is no "Holocaust representation." The very phrase is rendered shameful. Only where we come face to face with an inherent dearness in the face of the other human being, as in this photograph, do we discover a presence that transcends our thinking and our being and that lays claim to us, rendering us shamefaced. "The face with which the other turns to me," in the words of Levinas, "is not reabsorbed in a representation of the face. To hear his destitution which cries out for justice is not to represent an image to oneself, but is to posit oneself as responsible."[99] But there is no justice. Hence the shame. No analysis. No investigation of representation. Only shame. Abject shame.

Overcome with shame, we see more clearly why the holy is situated in the *panim* that is the face of the soul. Returning to this key word, we recall that it suggests a presence both "within" us and "before" us, both *bifnim* and *bifnei*. To behold the face—especially the face in this photograph—is to behold just what does not meet the eye, the transcendent in the imminent, framed in a makeshift scarf. The cognate term *penim* means "inside" or "interior," and yet it is an interior that *radiates* from the face while remaining hidden: the face is the exposure of the interior without the loss of interiority. The face reveals the hidden *as* hidden, forever pure and inviolate, even in the visage of this ravished human being. Thus, we have yet another view on why the Hebrew word *panim* is plural: it is because the face both exposes and veils the depth dimension of the *inner* being that is nonetheless *distinct* from being and thus *transcends* being. To paraphrase Levinas, the *in* of the Infinite is "both *non-* and *within*," and the face is precisely a manifestation of that Infinite that is "both *non-* and *within*."[100] It is *non-* because it is not part of the mute and indifferent landscape of being; rather, it is an irruption of being. It is a *within* that is also an *above*: the height manifest from within the face is the height that sanctifies being. And being can be "sanctified" only by what is otherwise than being. Therefore, the face is disarming and unsettling. Longing to have matters settled, we seek every possible means of obliterating the face. That is why we come before this photograph shamefaced: voyeuristically gazing upon this woman, we are complicit in the assault on her soul.

There is, of course, an unbridgeable chasm that yawns between us and the image in the photograph, and it is not merely the chasm of the historical—it is the chasm of the immemorial that announces yet a another immeasurable breach, like a gulf that separates two universes, two worlds, the world and the anti-world.

The Edge of the Anti-World

> I had mounted the train of death wearing European clothes, a European man; I alighted at the other end a dazed creature of Auschwitz.
>
> —Eugene Heimler, *Night of the Mist*

> Time there was not like it is here on earth. Every fraction of a minute there passed on a different scale of time. And the inhabitants of this planet had no names, they had no parents nor did they have children. There they did not dress in the way we dress here; they were not born there and they did not give birth; they breathed according to different laws of nature; they did not live—nor did they die—according to the laws of this world. . . .
>
> —Yehiel De-Nur, "The Trial of Adolf Eichmann, Session 68"

The anti-world that emerged within the Nazis' concentrationary universe is something neither imagined nor deduced from the ontological categories that shape human consciousness. An invisible borderline was etched into reality to form a kind of anti-reality. This is a photograph of that invisible borderline (Figure 3.9). Here, we stand before the entrance to Auschwitz

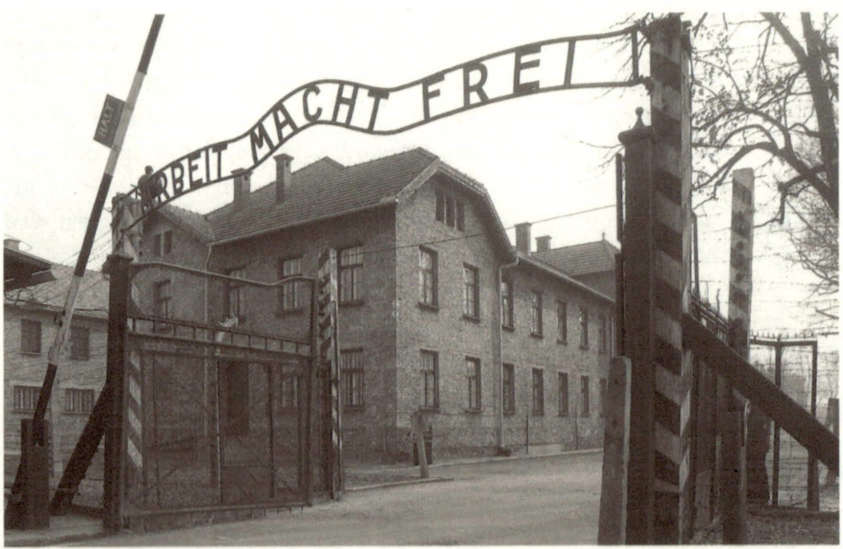

FIGURE 3.9. Auschwitz, Poland: An inscription above the camp's gate: *Arbeit Macht Frei*—"Work Liberates." Dnalor 01, Wikimedia Commons, CC-BY-SA 3.0.

I, an entrance into a non-place and a non-time allocated to the Jews, not as a punishment but as a circle of non-being for non-men, contrived by men who had lost their humanity. The gate in the photograph delineates a gulf that cannot be traversed by anyone who was not there—there lies the problem of Holocaust representation. It unfolds in this very image. It has nothing to do with representing atrocity or trauma. It has, rather, to do with the radical evil that is defined by a radical assault on the Good, by an assault on the very distinction between good and evil, in the creation of the anti-world. It is a photograph of the edge between a realm in which there are borders between good and evil, and a realm in which all borders have collapsed, a realm in which "there are no criminals nor madmen" as Primo Levi has said.[101]

How can an edge be photographed? It is like trying to photograph a geometric line, which, by definition, has only one dimension. And yet this is a photograph of the edge of the anti-world, more alien, more otherwise, more otherworldly than anything devised in the science fiction of alternative universes, worm holes, black holes, or other flights of the fantastic. As a photograph of an ontological and metaphysical edge—razor thin, nearly invisible, no more than a hair's breadth—it is a transcendence of any representation of the Holocaust. It is a photograph of what lies on the other side of what can be represented. Representation traverses boundaries in a world made of boundaries. But how is Holocaust representation to traverse the boundary conveyed in this photograph? It cannot.

The viewer of the photograph looks not *through* the gate but *up* through the gate and toward the sky, so that the *Arbeit Macht Frei* eclipses the height of the One known as the Most High. "Height ordains being," as Levinas says. "Height introduces a sense into being. It is already lived across the experience of the human body. It leads human societies to raise up altars. It is not because men, through their bodies, have an experience of the vertical that the human is placed under the sign of height; because being is ordained to height the human body is placed in a space in which the high and the low are distinguished and the sky is discovered."[102] Here, however, the sky is obliterated in the *Arbeit Macht Frei*'s eclipse of the transcendent height that imparts meaning to humanity. Here is sky is discovered precisely as that which has been obliterated.

One understands, then, how certain memories of the sky might reflect the memory of the collapse of meaning and humanity. "One evening at dusk," Fania Fénelon relates a very telling moment, "Florette commented on the magnificent sunset. But the distant red glow wasn't the sun."[103] No, it was not the sun above: it was the glow of the ditch aflame with the burning bodies of the Hungarian Jews. The smoke and the glow of the Auschwitz sky blot out the sun that sets and the sun that rises, as we note in Kitty Hart's memory of her arrival at Auschwitz: "Dawn was breaking. Or was it really the dawn? A reddish glow through the mist was flickering in the weirdest way, and there was a sickly, fatty, cloying smell."[104] Reality breaks down in the breaking of this dawn, in the realization that the sun is not the sun above but another fire, a flame brought low, where it consumes the earth and the mothers, fathers, and children of the earth. "Around us, everything is hostile," Levi remembers. "Above us the malevolent clouds chase each other to separate us from the sun; on all sides the squalor of the toiling steel closes in on us. We have never seen its boundaries, but we feel all around us its evil."[105] Again, the boundaries have been erased. That is why *everything is hostile,* including the very sky above—that is the meaning of the obliteration of height revealed in this photograph. It is the meaning of the Majdanek Anthem, as remembered by Paul Trepman (1916–1987):

> There has never been,
> Nor will there ever be,
> Anywhere on earth,
> A sun like that which shines
> Upon our Maidanek.[106]

Hence, Rudolf Vrba remembers, "Barracks, barbed wire and beyond that, nothing. Not a tree, not a shrub. Desolation. Maidanek had been set apart from civilization."[107] Trees and shrubs require a sky. So does civilization.

The *Arbeit Macht Frei* announces the obliteration of the sky that sustains civilization. *Arbeit Macht Frei.* "Work makes free?" "Work sets you free?" What does it mean? The *Arbeit* is the *Arbeit* of the Nationalsozialistische Deutsche *Arbeit*erpartei, the National Socialist German Workers' Party, and all that it works for—not the work of the Jews, who are not free until they are worked to death, beaten to death, or burned to death. The work—the *Arbeit*—is the annihilationist work of the Nazi; this is, after all, the entrance to a *Vernichtungslager,* an "annihilation camp." *Macht* is from *machen,* the verb meaning "to do" or "to make." It is also the noun that means "power," as in *der Wille zur Macht,* "the will to power." This entrance to Auschwitz embodies the vaunted triumph of the will to power. On the other side of this gate power is the *only* reality, weakness is the only sin, and the will is the only limit. And *Frei*? It is the *Frei* in the *Freiheit,* in the freedom understood as autonomy and the autonomy understood as being self-legislating. It is the freedom extolled by Dr. Walter Schultze at the June 1939 meeting of the National Socialist Association of University Lecturers: "What the great thinkers of German Idealism dreamed of . . . finally comes alive, assumes reality. . . . Never has the German idea of freedom [as the autonomy of the will to power] been conceived with greater life and greater vigor than in our day."[108] If, indeed, the dream of German Idealism finally comes alive, this is a photograph of the site of its fulfillment.

A tree looms in the background, behind the *Arbeit Macht Frei*. It is the Tree of Knowledge of Good and Evil, where good and evil collapse into a sameness, as the Gerer Rebbe taught.[109] For the Hebrew word *daat,* "knowledge," also means to "join together" into one. Contrary to the Tree of old, however, the day we eat from the fruit of this Tree is not the day we die but the day of the death of death itself. And the angels of fire surrounding the Tree of Life have been vanquished by men, who through the sheer will to power have transformed the Garden of Eden into the Garden of Auschwitz, the anti-paradise of *Arbeit Macht Frei.*

So what does this photograph of the *Arbeit Mach Frei* mean to those of us who now come before it? Marianne Hirsch has a thought: "Could 'Arbeit macht frei' not also be read, by and for us . . . as a reference to the tricks played by memory itself, the illusory promise that one could become free if one could only do the work of memory and mourning that would open the gate, allow one to enter back into the past and then, through work, emerge out again into a new freedom?"[110] I don't think so; as Hirsch says, the promise of freedom for us is an illusory one. If there is a message "for us," it is about an absolute ethical demand that collapsed upon the traversing of this borderline, and not about allowing us to work through anything for "a new freedom." A new freedom for what? What does this new freedom mean? Is it a way of "getting over it" by "working through it," as Dominick LaCapra says?[111] Such a freedom is what Levinas describes as "the freedom that is the identification of the same, not allowing itself to be alienated by the other,"[112] a counterfeit freedom closed in on itself.

Just one more thing, perhaps the most disturbing thing, about the gate in the photograph. According to a talmudic tale, one day the sage Rabbi Yehoshua ben Levi was walking outside the gates of Rome with the prophet Elijah. He asked the prophet when the Messiah would come, whereupon Elijah directed him to a leper sitting outside at the gates binding his wounds: "Ask him yourself," said Elijah to the sage. And so Rabbi Yehoshua went over and put the question to the Messiah: "When will you come? Have we not waited long enough?" And the Messiah answered, "Today"—that is, "Today, if you heed the Voice of HaShem" (*Sanhedrin* 98a).[113] And Yehoshua ben Levi walked away in dismay. It is said that if he had simply helped the Messiah with his wounds, the Messiah would have declared himself, and the age of redemption would have been ushered in. If the advent of the Messiah is at every moment possible, we are the ones who must make it happen. Indeed, according to the Talmud, the question of whether we anticipated and worked for the coming of the Messiah is one of the four questions that God puts to us when we stand before the heavenly tribunal (*Shabbat* 31a).[114] It is a question concerning whether we have kindled the spark of the messianic soul within ourselves. But the Messiah no longer languishes at the gates of Rome. No, he abides within the gates of Auschwitz embossed with the sardonic *Arbeit Macht Frei.* He peers at us through the barbed wire, whose electrified touch is deadly. And he cannot get out. Perhaps that is the true meaning of *Arbeit Macht Frei*: the grim phrase announces the advent of the impossibility of redemption. And so creation collapses.

The Grave without a Cemetery

> They bury them half-alive . . . or half-dead . . . and the soil was moving . . . the soil was moving . . . they bury them half-alive . . . and the soil was moving. . . .
>
> —Judith Dribben, *And Some Shall Live*

In Part One, it was noted that Miklós Nyiszli describes the Planet Auschwitz as a "cemetery of millions, a cemetery without a single grave."[115] In this image of the anti-world that the Nazis imposed on creation we collide with a grave without a cemetery (Figure 3.10). And we realize that the realm delineated by *Arbeit Macht Frei* extends far beyond the compound that lies on the other side of that gate. This is a photograph of the ravine known as Babi Yar, one of the most infamous of all the mass graves that churn beneath the bloodlands of Eastern Europe. It could be Ponary, the Ninth Fort, Katyn, Rumbula, Maly Trostinets, Rava Russka, or Brona Gora—or Citadel "Shtalag-328," Pyatydni, Lysynychi, Bilogorshcha, Chortkiv, or many, many thousands of others—how many, no one knows. "The exact number of these sites is yet to be determined, but we now know of more

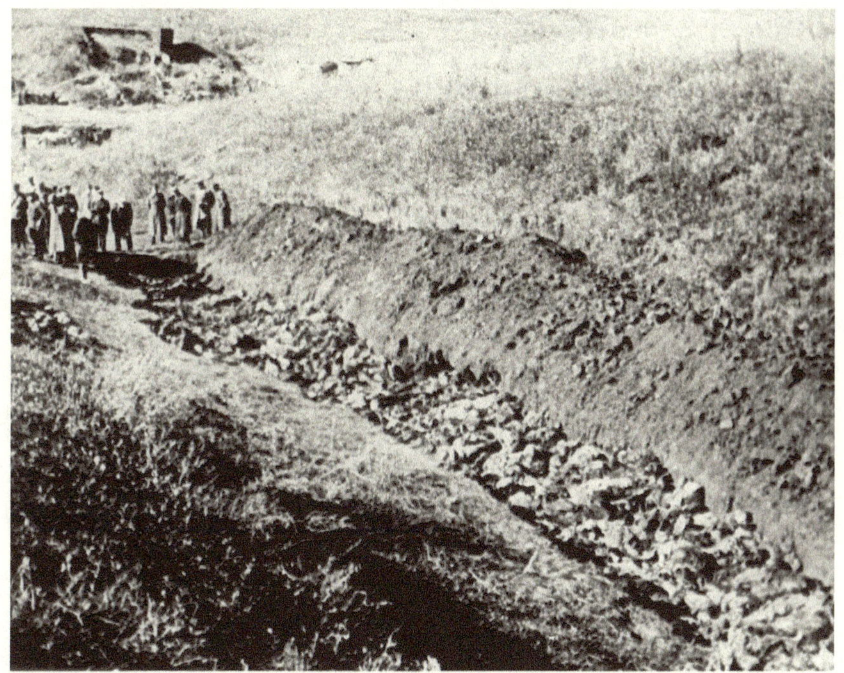

FIGURE 3.10. Babi Yar, Ukraine, Corpses in a mass grave, public domain.

than 2,500 in the Former USSR alone, and there were many hundreds, if not thousands, such mass murder sites in many other countries."[116] Imagine this photograph repeated ten thousand times over. Babi Yar was selected as a site for the murder of the Jews of Kiev because it is a ravine, a ready-made grave without a cemetery, as if the earth itself had opened, ready to swallow up the Jews.

German troops entered Kiev on 19 September 1941. On 22 September there were mass beatings of Jews in the city's streets.[117] On 27 and 28 September, announcements appeared on the walls of the buildings: "Kikes of Kiev! On Monday, 29 September, at 7:00 a.m. you are to appear with your belongings, money, documents, valuables, and warm clothing on Dorogozhitskaya Street next to the Jewish cemetery. Failure to appear is punishable by death. Hiding kikes is punishable by death."[118] In his account of what transpired, the Ukrainian Jewish poet Lev Ozerov (1914–1996) relates that "one Jewish family was hiding in a basement for several days. The mother decided to take her two children and go to the country. Some

Germans stopped them. They cut off the head of one child and killed the other right before the mother's eyes. The woman went out of her mind and held the bodies of her dead children to her bosom. Once the Hitlerites had had their fill of the spectacle, they murdered her too."[119] This, however, "was just the prelude" to the creation of the grave without a cemetery:

> At dawn on 29 September the Jews of Kiev were moving slowly along the streets. . . . Many of them thought they were being sent to provincial towns. Some of them understood that Babi Yar meant death. Therefore on that day there were many suicides. . . .
>
> Old men and women walked along supporting each other. Mothers carried their infants in their arms or pushed them in baby carriages. Children plodded along with their parents. Young people brought nothing with them, but the elderly tried to take everything they could from home. Leading them by the hand, grandchildren walked with old women who were pale and had difficulty breathing. Those who were sick or paralyzed were borne on stretchers, blankets, and sheets. . . .
>
> This death procession continued for three days and three nights. The city had fallen silent. . . . As they approached Babi Yar, a murmur mixed with moans and sobbing grew louder and louder. . . .
>
> Then the Germans ordered everyone, without exception—girls, women, children, and old men—to strip naked. . . . Then the executioners placed the doomed people in rows along the edge of the deep ravine and shot them at pointblank range. The bodies fell over the cliff. Small children were pushed into the ravine alive. Many went insane as they approached the execution site.[120]

Reading this brief account from *The Complete Black Book of Russian Jewry* alongside the photographic image, one feels the onset of the insanity that overcame so many. It is a transcendent insanity brought on by a longing to save what cannot be saved, a longing for what has been not to have been.

The camera angle is looking down, from on high: it is a God's-eye view. Was God among those who went insane at the execution site? "God has gone mad," Wiesel has written. His evidence? The numbers.[121] In the beginning was the word, the word of madness, the madness that empties all words of meaning through sheer numbers. Conveying the transcendent invisible, this is a photograph of the madness of the invisible God, who suffers infinitely over the suffering of just one. It is a photograph of the "execution site," where on 29–30 September 1941, 33,771 Jews were murdered; ultimately more than 100,000 Jewish men, women, and children would lie beneath this stretch of Ukrainian earth.[122] More than 120,000 gallons of blood: the underground lake at Babi Yar. The bodies in the photograph lie not only in the earth but also in an ocean of blood. This grave without a cemetery has the look of a wound cut deep into the earth, deep into the soul, deep into creation, deep into the Creator. It is indeed a wound that bleeds. And, as it is written, the soul is in the blood (Leviticus 17:11).

You have to look closely at the photograph to even recognize those things in the grave without a cemetery as human bodies. You have to look closely, but carefully; otherwise, as you stare into that abyss, it will stare back into you. And the people on the left, looking down into the grave—who are they? Did they, too, go mad? If not, why not?

According to Jewish law, if we should discover the body of a murder victim, bruised and bloodied, and if there is no hope of apprehending the perpetrator, we are to bury the body just as we found it (see *Kitzur Shulchan Arukh* 197:9; based on Deuteronomy 21:1–9), without the usual preparations for burial. The reason? According to one of my teachers, it is to put it in God's face: "Look at what has become of Your creation! We did not do this evil! What are *You* going to do about it?" It is a question about whether the invisible God has grown blind and deaf. Perhaps His invisibility lies in His blindness and deafness. Or in His madness.

This is a photograph of a place from which God—*HaMakom,* "the Place"—seems to have turned His face, His eyes, and His ears. Of course, in Jewish tradition, the worst of all the curses that can fall upon humanity is for God to turn away His face, His revelation, His commandment (see Deuteronomy 28). Turning away His face, He turns away from the suffering that drives His creatures mad, for the pain is too much for Him to bear, as it is taught in the Talmud. Overwhelmed by His infinite suffering—when God's Infinity lies in His infinite suffering—God retreats to a special hiding place that He has reserved for weeping, the place "called *Mistarim* [meaning 'concealment'], in the inner chambers" (*Chagigah* 5b). According to the Midrash, this secret place is the realm of darkness overcome in the act of creation; it is the darkness from which God drew forth the Ninth Plague, the darkness in which "a man could not see his brother" (Exodus 10:23). That is the darkness that makes God weep (*Midrash Tehillim* 1:18:16). For God's pain cannot enter the world without destroying it. This weeping is the outcome not of Jewish sin but of Nazi evil: God is driven into hiding, where He weeps in secret and roars in silence—roars in madness, His insanity manifest in the insanity of those who went insane at the edge of the abysmal ravine. How does the One who witnesses the internment of His children in a grave without a cemetery—without *shivah* or *kaddish,* without bereavement or mourning—continue to sustain His creation? Or—and this is the true horror—has He left us to sustain His creation without Him?

Perhaps He has joined the Jews lying in this mass grave. If so, then what now becomes of the One in whose image and likeness the human being is created? What now becomes of the image and likeness of the human being? Can the camera's image of humanity's handiwork convey the transcendent dimension of such a question? If such a question has an answer, it may lie in what follows.

The Muselmann

> One hesitates to call their death death.
>
> —Primo Levi, *Survival in Auschwitz*

> The Nazi state had no higher aim than to murder souls while bodies were still alive. The *Muselmann* was its most characteristic, most original product. He is a *novum* in human history.
>
> —Emil L. Fackenheim, *To Mend the World*

Ecce homo! Behold the *novum* in human history, the unique creation of National Socialism, fashioned in the image and likeness of the void that is the anti-world!

This is the iconic image of the invisible icon. There are no photographs of the Muselmänner, the consummate denizens of the anti-world, as they "followed the slope down to the bottom, like streams that run down to the sea . . . an anonymous mass, continually renewed and always identical, of non-men."[123] All we have are the disappearing traces, the remnants not of men or women but of the Muselmänner. This photograph, taken by a soldier in the United States Army, is titled "Buchenwald, Germany, 1945, A Muselmann on a wagon, after the liberation" (Figure 3.11).[124] The contrast between the remains of the man or woman in the cart—there is no

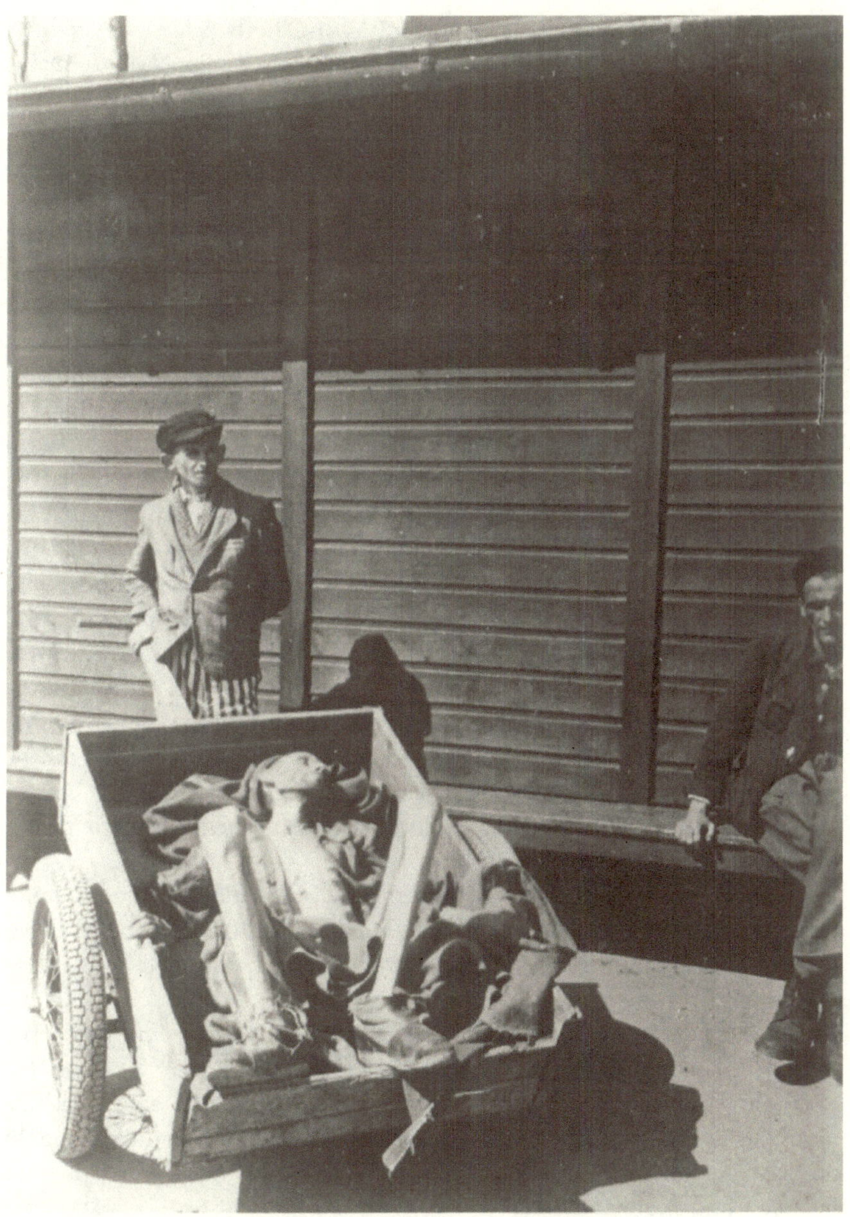

FIGURE 3.11. "Buchenwald, Germany, 1945, A Muselmann on a wagon, after the liberation," Yad Vashem Photo Archive, Jerusalem, ID 102959, Archival Signature 18BO2, with permission of Yad Vashem.

telling which—and the man casually sitting on the bench to the right is staggering. Jews were forbidden to sit on park benches in Nazi Germany. What can be going through his mind? Who is that guiding the cart, still wearing the striped pants of the inmate's garb? Guiding it to where? Did he present his passenger to the soldier for the photograph? Whereas the woman from Bergen-Belsen in photograph of "The Face" looks as though she might say something, not a word is anticipated from the Muselmann. No longer a *medaber,* a "speaking being," he is boxed into his silence, just as he is boxed into his cart, a coffin—or an ossuary—on wheels, except that the Muselmänner had neither coffins nor graves nor even ossuaries.

I have met numerous veterans of World War II, several of whom were among those who were the first to come across the camps, including Dr. Leon Bass (1925–2015), who was at Buchenwald. He was in an African American unit (the troops were segregated during World War II, as the result of a policy previously established by President Woodrow Wilson). They say that the odor itself was overwhelming; indeed, veterans have told me that they could smell the camps for miles, long before they reached them.

Elie Wiesel once told me a story about a black American G.I. who walked into the Buchenwald block where he and dozens of others were lying on their plank beds waiting to die. The soldier paused for a moment in the middle of the block. He stood in the middle of the block, waiting for his eyes to adjust to the dimly lit space. Decked out in battle gear, he was an imposing figure indeed.

"He was a giant," Wiesel told me, "like some mythical hero." Most of these Jews had never seen a black man.

As the soldier began to make out the skeletal shades surrounding him, tears started to run down his cheeks. The ghost-like beings crawled down from their plank bunks and shuffled over to comfort him, their bony hands patting him on the back and shoulders.

"The harder we tried to console him," said Wiesel, "the harder he sobbed. Like a child."

He would not be comforted. Perhaps like the soldier who took this traumatizing photograph of the incarnation of the anti-world. He could not say what he had seen; he could only hold up the photograph that rendered him mute.

If, as Fackenheim has maintained, a Voice commands us to restore the divine image that was extinguished in the Muselmann lying in the cart before us,[125] it commands us to do so by returning to the Torah slated for annihilation, where we receive the teaching concerning the divine image in which the human being is created and sanctified. Those of us who have seen the graphic photos of Union soldiers in Andersonville or of American soldiers in Japanese POW camps may be tempted to think, "They look like the Jews, the skeletal humanoids we have seen in the films and photos of the Nazi camps." But there are differences: (1) The POWs were *soldiers* who had been combatants in war, who bravely risked their lives within the intelligible contexts of society's institutions; not so the Jews. (2) The Jews witnessed the destruction of their homes, the murder of their children, the ravaging of their wives, and the erasure of their names; not so the soldiers, who could declare their name, rank, and serial number. (3) The soldiers who survived the prisoner of war camps returned to their homes, where their families had tied a yellow ribbon around the old oak tree; not so the Jews. (4) The Jews endured an assault on their holy days, their prayers, their synagogues, their Torah, the very essence of their tradition, memory, and identity; not so the soldiers. (5) The families of soldiers who died received letters of condolence from their government; not so the Jews. It was as if their death were not death.

Obliterated during the Shoah was not only Jewish life but also Jewish death, as evidenced by the Muselmann, whose death was not death. Here lies a manifestation of the invisible, transcendent singularity of the Shoah. For to die as a Jew is to choose life even in death, speaking even in death the Name of the One who is the origin of life in a cry of "*Shema Yisrael!*" Can anyone imagine the Jew in this photograph uttering the Shema? Or is the Shema inscribed in his (or her?) emaciated body? If so, then it is a plea not just for Israel to hear but for God to hear: Hear, O Lord!

What transpires in the Nazis' imposition of death upon European Jewry is not only the end of Jewish life but also the end of the *Shema Yisrael* that makes death the death of a Jew. "The Nazi murder machine," we recall Fackenheim's insight, "was systematically designed to stifle this *Shema Yisrael* on Jewish lips before it murdered Jews themselves."[126] And they did so by transforming the Jew into a Muselmann. To stifle the prayer's holy word is to strangle the human's holy image, and that was the Nazis' ultimate aim. If the murder camp was the "pure essence" of the Nazi *Weltanschauung*, as Fackenheim argues,[127] the pure essence of the murder camp was the Nazis' obliteration of the divine essence of the Jew and, by implication, of all humanity through the unique creation of the Muselmann. The proof lies in the cart in this photograph. That is what makes it a photograph of the transcendent invisible: it is a photograph of the destruction of the divine image within the human being.

Once again, Primo Levi's description of the Muselmänner as "the backbone of the camp" leaps to mind, along with his assertion that "one hesitates to call their death death."[128] Says Fackenheim, "This is devastating. If there was one difference one would have thought was absolute, it is the difference between life and death."[129] The collapse of the difference, the erasure of the boundary, unfolds in the viewer's collision with the transcendent invisible in this horrific photograph. Where Fackenheim invokes the divine image, Levi refers to the divine spark. But what is this image or spark of the divine? It is the holiness that inheres in the human being who emerges from the Word of the Holy One. The Nazi, however, extinguishes the divine spark that God breathes into the Jew and thus destroys the trace of the holy Word that makes a human being a human being. The remnant of the human being lying in this cart, the divine spark, was destroyed long before the arrival of the photographer. So what does it mean to photograph a remnant, a trace—indeed, a trace of what? It is a trace of the Jewish testimony to what makes the *other human being* matter, a trace of what impels the viewer of the photograph to reach out to the subject of the photograph, a trace of the invisible that singles out the viewer and transforms him or her into a witness.

Setting out to murder the Jew, the Nazi creates the Muselmann over against the Jew precisely by making the *Jew*—not the communist, homosexual, or Gypsy, not the Jehovah's Witness, Catholic priest, or trade unionist—into a Muselmann. This Nazi creation of the anti-man, of the Muselmann, defines the Nazi, just as the Torah's revelation of the creation of man defines the Jew. The Nazis' transformation of man into Muselmann is a singular phenomenon that characterizes the singularity of the Holocaust, and it makes the Holocaust decisive for all humanity. If what took place at Auschwitz was an "anti-creation," as Levi describes it,[130] it was the anti-creation of the "non-man," of the Muselmann, undertaken through the erasure of his story and the obliteration of his memory. As Levi has said, they have no story.[131] And if they have no story, they have no memory. In the Muselmann, the Nazis attain their most absolute victory, a victory over time itself. For the Jew, the horizons of time are delineated by a memory that exceeds the horizons of birth and death: a memory of the Exodus from Egypt and of the Creation itself, as affirmed in the Sabbath Kiddush, as well as a memory of the messianic future. Which means: the eternal is manifest in memory. Where memory is absent, the eternal is absent, meaning is absent, time is absent. If that time can be restored, perhaps it is restored in the photographic image of the destruction of the life time of the human being.

To be a human being is to have a story. It is a story inscribed in the name, the past in the surname and the future in the given name, as Franz Rosenzweig has suggested.[132] The namelessness of the Muselmann is tied to this absence of a story, of any *yet to be* that might impart meaning and therefore humanity to the human being. As long as this *yet to be* is at work in life, memory exceeds the boundaries of birth and death. When memory exceeds those horizons, death is once again death, and dying is once again a task and a testimony. The one who has no story—the Jew lying in the cart, whom the Nazis transformed into a *Muselmann* in their war against memory—is the one who has no tradition, no heritage, no inheritance. Thus, his death is no longer the death of *someone,* no longer the death of one who dies as a witness to his or her tradition in an act of *Kiddush Hashem,* a "Sanctification of the Name." Catching a glimpse of a transcendent, invisible aspect of the Shoah in this photograph, we discover what a "holy one" looks like. And we shrink in horror.

Selection: No Judge and No Judgment

> He was oppressed, though he humbled himself and opened not his mouth; as a lamb that is led to the slaughter, and as a sheep that before her shearers is dumb; yea, he opened not his mouth.
>
> —Isaiah 53:7

> "Over there. Do you see the chimney over there? Do you see it? And the flames, do you see them?" (Yes, we saw the flames.) "Over there, that's where they will take you. Over there will be your grave. You still don't understand? You sons of bitches. Don't you understand anything? You will be burned! Burned to a cinder! Turned into ashes!"
>
> —Elie Wiesel, *Night*

Shown here is a transport of Hungarian Jews, almost half a million of whom were gassed and burned between May and July 1944. If "the divine image in man *can* be destroyed," as Fackenheim maintains,[133] it was destroyed neither in the *Muselmänner* nor in these Jews lined up for selection but in the SS murderers who lined them up. Those who go like unblemished lambs to the slaughter are not the ones disgraced; no, the shame and humiliation falls upon the ones leading them to slaughter. It falls on us all, particularly the

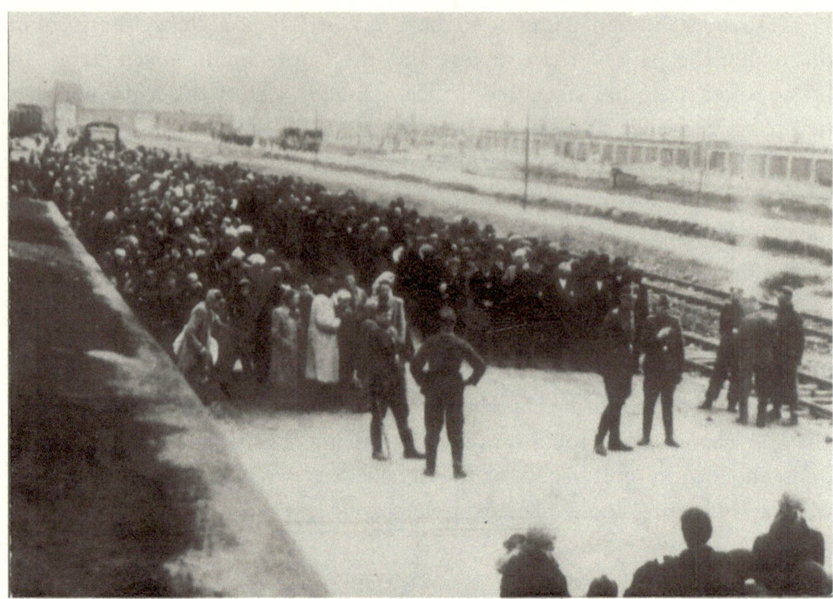

FIGURE 3.12. Birkenau, Poland, SS soldiers performing a selection, public domain.

ones who would blame the victims for their victimhood by saying, "They went"—as did the Suffering Servant—"like sheep to the slaughter."

The photograph is titled "Birkenau, Poland, SS soldiers performing a selection" (Figure 3.12). For centuries, the Jews have been accused of deicide, but these SS murderers—not soldiers but murderers—are the true deicides. They strike a very businesslike pose, one with arms akimbo, ready to usurp the throne of divine judgment and begin processing units, deciding on this day who shall live (just a little while longer) and who shall die (within the hour). The viewer peers through the camera lens to gaze down from the vantage point of this usurped height. Are they waiting for Josef Mengele (1911–1979), the Angel of Death, to make his appearance?

Through an eerie haze of smoke the signature entrance to the extermination camp looms in the background. It is an entrance that allows no exit. To be sure, the only exit for this mass of Jews lined up before the SS murderers is through the entrance to the gas chamber, known as the "Highway to Heaven" or "the Jewish state."[134] The sky is overcast with the remains of the Jewish people. The sun cannot penetrate the haze of human smoke. There are no birds flying overhead. Everything is "as silent as an aquarium,"[135] as silent as the dead who remain inside the train: according to Yehuda Bauer, an average of about 30 percent died in transit.[136] As for the living, they open not their mouths, except to choke on the smoke. They are in no condition to resist.

Elie Wiesel remembers:

> The beloved objects that we had carried with us from place to place were now left behind in the wagon and, with them, finally, our illusions.
>
> An SS came toward us wielding a club. He commanded: "Men to the left! Women to the right!"
>
> Eight words spoken quietly, indifferently, without emotion. Eight simple, short words. Yet that was the moment when I left my mother. There was no time to think, and I already felt my father's hand press against mine: we were alone. In a fraction of a second I could see my mother, my sisters, move to the right. Tzipora was holding Mother's hand. I saw them walking farther and farther away. Mother was stroking my sister's blond hair, as if to protect her. And I walked on with my father, with the men. I didn't know that this was the moment in time and the place where I was leaving my mother and Tzipora forever.[137]

All that was left to them was to say Kaddish for themselves, in a radical inversion of the order of creation, magnifying and sanctifying the Name of the Creator on this platform, reciting the Orphan's Prayer for an orphaned world, the prayer that no one else would recite for them. "I don't know," writes Wiesel, "whether, during the history of the Jewish people, men have ever before recited Kaddish for themselves."[138] Did they choke on the words, as they choked on the smoke? Those who say the Kaddish glorify His Name and bless the world He created according to His will. But is *this* the world He created according to His will? Did they say, "Amen," to *that*? "Oh Lord of Auschwitz heavens," we recall Ka-tzetnik's outcry, "illumine my ignorance of your handiwork,"[139] illumine our ignorance by the light of the terrible pillar of fire looming in the distance. Or should we rather pray for ignorance, so that we may say the Kaddish without reeling at the words?

Look closely in the background on the right, and you will see the women's camp on the other side of the fence, situated across from the unloading platform. Were the women watching when this photograph was taken? Sometimes, Sara Nomberg-Przytyk remembers, the women would try to shout to the newly arrived Jews to tell them what lay in store for them. "When the Jews marched off to the gas after they had arrived at Auschwitz," she writes, "they simply did not know where they were going, and when we told them they did not believe us."[140] Can *we* believe it? They, the women of the women's camp, cry out to us what is about to befall this throng, but do we believe them? We, too, are lined up, lined up before this photograph, before this remnant of anti-time, when the minutes, hours, and days "revolved around the cogwheels of a different time-sphere."[141] All of humanity is lined up here, on the inside, yet looking in from the outside. In this tension between inside and outside lies the tension of photographic transcendence and the representation of the invisible chasm that separated one universe from another.

The Jewish women and the Jewish men in the photograph are lined up separately: men to the left, women to the right, the children with the women. As the Angel of Death, Dr. Josef Mengele, once declared, it would be cruel not to gas the children with their mothers.[142] The Angel of Death is an Angel of Mercy, a merciful usurper of the Throne of Divine Judgment: in the camp there was no way for the children to "develop normally." Nomberg-Przytyk, in fact, recalls a daughter who frantically longed to go with her mother to the gas chambers.[143] If she could die with her mother, they would at least in death remain mother and daughter. In the camp there are no mothers, no daughters. Only in the gas chambers, where they embraced as mother and daughter in the agonizing throes of death by Zykoln-B, could mothers remain mothers to their daughters and daughters to their mothers. Such would surely be the fate of the mother and child in the foreground of the photograph.

This is a photograph of new arrivals to the anti-world. Commenting on the *zugangi,* or the "new arrivals," Nomberg-Przytyk relates that they "made themselves absurd trying to defend their human dignity."[144] Why absurd? For these Jews lined up on the platform, the adjustment to the anti-world was so radical that the many who were not immediately selected to be murdered could not make the adjustment to this reality in which more was real than was possible. Why absurd? Because they failed to realize that the moment they were assembled as we see in this photograph, they had lost the last remnant of humanity left to them.

Why absurd? This is why: "Babies! Yes, I did see this with my own eyes . . . children thrown into the flames. . . . A little further on there was another, larger pit for adults. I pinched myself: Was I still alive? Was I awake?"[145] To "read" this photograph within any framework familiar to us is to be launched into the transcendent, where everything that lends any meaning to the photograph eludes the photograph and belongs to the *elsewhere,* where the absurd and the transcendent intersect. "In Auschwitz," beginning with the selection upon arrival, says Fackenheim, "everything was synthesized, because there was no God, there was no man, there was no history, it was just what he [Ka-tzetnik] called 'the planet.'"[146] This is the reality that exceeds possibility in a *dementing* of the possible, infinitely removing it from the parameters of *mens* or "mind."

Thus, from the moment the men lined up on the left and the women on the right, says Jean Améry, "existence as such became definitively a totally abstract and thus empty concept. To reach out beyond concrete reality with words became before our very eyes a game that was not only worthless and an impermissible luxury but also mocking and evil."[147] The problem does not lie with the imagination; indeed, the *images* are all too indelibly imprinted on the soul, like this image before our eyes. The difficulty is that the possible, as it unfolds in the Shoah, cannot be *thought* in the anti-world of Auschwitz; it is *demented.* "Everything for us was unreal and insubstantial," Simon Wiesenthal recalls.[148] Does this mean that nothing was felt or experienced? No, on the contrary, what was felt and experienced surpassed all measure and proportion, and that is just the point: it was impossible and yet it was real. In order to begin to approach it, we must make ourselves absurd and abandon the project of theorizing about the nuances of Holocaust representation. Indeed, here we realize that there is nothing more absurd, nothing more shameful, nothing more irresponsible than the pretense to theorize about Holocaust representation—not in the attempt to represent the event but in its *theorizing.*

We begin to realize why Debórah Dvork and Robert Jan van Pelt assert that "the process of selection is the core and the moral nadir of the horror of the Holocaust—the selection, and not the gas chambers and crematoria."[149] Not the gas chambers and crematoria—these are merely the murder weapons and the measures taken to cover up the murder. The selection platform in this photograph is the site of the Nazis' radical usurpation of the seat of divine judgment and with it the meaning of God, world, and humanity. That is what makes it the nadir of the horror of the Holocaust.

It is the site of the assault on the family and the remnant of the home, where the human being's name was first uttered with love, compassion, and kindness. It is the site of the systematic assault on the mother, through whom the divine love for humanity enters the world, and on the child, through whom the outcry of humanity is heard on high (if, indeed, it is heard). It is the site where fathers are no longer fathers, where children cry out, "Oh, Daddy . . . ! How could you leave me?"[150] For the father who heard these words, the undoing was absolute. It is the site where Isabella Leitner screamed with every ounce of her being, "Mama! If you don't turn around I'll run after you. But they won't let me. I must stay on the 'life' side. Mama!"[151] Ka-tzetnik told Gideon Hausner, we recall from Part One, "I saw the beatings, the exhaustion, the starvation, the smoke rising from the chimneys, and the ashes raining down. I saw men humiliated and mutilated, reduced to non-men. But that is not Auschwitz. What Auschwitz is, I tried to explain to him, I cannot say." Perhaps this photograph of the arrival of a transport of Hungarian Jews in Birkenau can reveal a disappearing trace of what Auschwitz is.

There exists, however, a set of photographs that take us into the depth dimensions of Planet Birkenau, where the camera became an instrument of a radical resistance, the instrument of the Ultimate, the transcendent, and the invisible. They are known as the "Sonderkommando Photographs."

A View from the Gas Chambers

> Tell them that if your heart should turn to [stone], your brain become a cold thinking machine and your eye transform into a camera, you will not come back to them again. Hold me tightly by the hand, do not tremble . . . because you will have to see even worse.
>
> —Zalman Gradowski, Sonderkommando Diary, quoted in Didi-Huberman, *Images in Spite of All*

> Seeker, dig around everywhere, in every piece of land. Documents, mine and those of other persons, are buried there. . . . We, the *Sonderkommando* workers, distributed them over the entire terrain . . . so that the world might find palpable traces there of the millions murdered.
>
> —Gradowski, Sonderkommando Diary

Seeker, dig. Poet, dig. Reader, dig. Viewer, dig. The traces are palpable. The testimonies are spread not only over the grounds of the ovens and gas chambers. They are spread over the face of the earth. Dig everywhere that the ashes of the Jews have rained down, which is everywhere. Dig in the sky. Dig in your very heart and soul. Lest your heart turn to stone. Lest you lose your humanity. Lest your brain become a cold thinking machine.

Lest you go insane. Dig, so that your eye may be transformed into a *camera lucinda* filled with images that gaze back at you from the margins of the image and invade your dreams, lest you forget just how palpable these disappearing traces are; indeed, the more invisible they are, the more palpable.

In this last section we dig through the images to move ever deeper into the belly of the beast.[152] Here, we wind our way into the lair of the *Sonderkommando,* the "special unit," those caretakers of the Thing-in-Itself: *Sonderkommando,* a distinctively Nazi euphemism for something like "grisly detail of the murderers' minions." But even such a phrase cannot translate the term. And what is untranslatable is nonrepresentable.

The Sonderkommando of Birkenau consisted mostly of Jewish inmates who were forced to do the soul-searing labor of gassing and burning the body of Israel. Like scavengers harvesting the material of human beings reduced to mere matter, they collected clothing and jewelry, hair and gold teeth, from the dead. On occasion they would find members of their own families among the bodies that they dragged naked from the gas chambers and shoved into the ovens of the crematoria, as it happened with Béla Katz in Elie Wiesel's *Night*: he was a Sonderkommando member who fed his own father to the ovens.[153] From May 1942 until October 1944, their numbers grew from about four hundred to more than a thousand men who worked in as many as five crematoria. With the onset of the tidal wave of Hungarian Jewry from 15 May to 9 July 1944, they attended the open pits of flames that Wiesel glimpsed upon his entry into the anti-world.[154]

Every three months or so, the men of the Sonderkommando were themselves gassed and burned,[155] for they were considered *Geheimnisträger,* the "bearers of secrets,"[156] so that there were twelve (some say fourteen) generations of Sonderkommando units in Birkenau.[157] The irony of the designation of *Geheimnisträger* is glaring, as we realize that the Nazis regarded all Jewish people as *Geheimnisträger,* the bearers of the secret truth that sanctifies every human life, the secret of Torah that would undermine the entire totalitarian project of National Socialism. (Perhaps that was the secret that the Gestapo—the *Geheime Staatspolizei,* or "Secret State Police"—was designed to obliterate. It was not that the Gestapo itself operated in secret, but rather that their aim was to root out the secret embodied by the presence of the Jews in the world.) In the photographs shown below we glimpse the nonrepresentable secret for which the Jews and the Sonderkommando members were murdered, a secret that nonetheless emanates from the face of every human being. And, gazing into these images, we ourselves are transformed into *Geheimnisträger.*

Before the Nazis murdered the men of a given Sonderkommando unit, they took one more step in their assault on the Jewish soul, as Primo Levi observes: the SS in charge of the crematoria at Birkenau forced the Sonderkommando Jews to play soccer with them. "You too," Levi mimics the murderers, "like us and like Cain, have killed the brother. Come, we can play together."[158] Thus, in a usurpation of the Creator, the Nazis recreated the Jews after their own image and likeness. How? By making them into murderers. Come, we can murder together.

The photographs below attest to a resistance to that usurpation. It took place in a realm where *everything* conspired to make all resistance impossible: it should not—it *could* not—have taken place in that realm. And yet we have the photographs. Here, as Fackenheim has said, "we touch upon an Ultimate,"[159] which is by definition nonrepresentable. Says Didi-Huberman, "It is in the fold of these two impossibilities—the imminent obliteration of the witness, the certain unrepresentability of the testimony—that the photographic image suddenly appeared."[160] Contrary to Didi-Huberman, however, the power of the photographic appearance lies not in the image on the negative but in the negative of the negative, in the transcendent that eludes the eye of the camera. The very existence of the photographs reveals a reality that exceeds possibility and a transcendence that eludes explication. In that transcendence lies a trace of the secret borne by the *Geheimnisträger*.

Survivors of the Sonderkommando, such as Filip Müller and Shlomo Venezia (1923–2012), were almost without exception part of the last Sonderkommando unit, the unit that staged the Birkenau Uprising of 7 October 1944.[161] Four hundred fifty-one Jews died in the uprising, including the diarists Zalman Lewental and Zalman Gradowski (b. 1910); dozens of others were rounded up, tortured, and executed for their complicity in the uprising, including women such as Ala Gertner (1912–1945) and Roza Robota (1921–1945).[162] One month later, on 7 November, the Nazis destroyed the crematoria and left them in ruins. But, by some miracle, beneath the ruins of this ravishing of the Jewish soul slept a trace of the Sonderkommando's testimony to the radical evil of Auschwitz. In addition to the diaries of Lewental and Gradowski, manuscripts by Leib Langfus (executed 27 November 1944), Chaim Herman, and Marcel Nadjary were discovered in October 1962, when the crematoria sites were excavated and cleaned up to serve as memorial sites, the only *matzevahs* or "gravestones" in a vast cemetery without a single grave.[163] The root of the Hebrew word *matzevah, matzav,* means "condition" or "situation." The cemetery without a single matzevah is the ultimate non-condition exemplified by the anti-world, and the non-condition is ultimately nonrepresentable, beyond every ontological "situation."

Stepping before the photographs below, we inch our way toward the thin periphery of Birkenau inhabited by the Sonderkommando, toward the edges of the anti-world where the only matzevahs consist of the Sonderkommando diaries hidden beneath the crematoria that consumed the body of Israel, the secret matzevahs that bear the secrets of the *Geheimnisträger*. Turning now to these photographs, we tread a metaphysical minefield. The eye of the viewer who gazes upon these images is transformed into the unblinking eye of a camera, unable to turn away, fixed on the Medusa-like image of the annihilation of God, world, and humanity. The blood chills, the bone freezes, and the heart turns to stone: shall we have to behold even worse? Who can fathom it? And yet by now we sense that the worse exceeds, transcends, and obliterates anything that anyone can behold: *the worse* has nothing to do with what meets the eye or forms on the tongue.

The worse is not unimaginable—it is invisible, not because it is microscopic or cosmic but because it transcends all ontological categories and therefore exceeds the categories of the camera in a graphic demonstration of the Levinasian "excession of transcendence, of the beyond."[164] If we have to behold even worse—if we must turn our gaze to the excession—our right hand shall lose its cunning and our tongue shall cleave to the roof of our muted mouth as it is written (Psalms 137:5–6). Our eyes shall be engulfed in shame, pain, and lamentation that far exceed representation. Thus, the collisions with the nonrepresentable—nonrepresentable not because the image is unreal or traumatizing but because it illustrates the dementing truth that more was real than was possible, the truth that transforms the brain into a cold non-thinking machine.

Commenting on the Sonderkommando photographs, Dan Stone writes, "In terms of the visual record, they are unquestionably the most important documents that we have. Photographs taken by members of the SS are today no less horrific to our eyes for the fact of their authorship, but the *Sonderkommando* photographs are especially harrowing, not only because of their content but also because of the extreme difficulties involved in taking them, smuggling the film out of the camp, and having them developed in Kraków."[165] This is not, however, the only reason for the harrowing nature of these images. Yes, these are among the photographs taken under pain of death, like the diaries written in the gullet of the anti-world. More than that, however, they are photographs of the earthquake that shook the soul of the photographer whose eyes saw the soul of Israel, the God of the Covenant, and all truth and meaning consigned to the pit.

In this last section, we must ease into the photographs, like easing into a lake of fire, into a realm devoid of oxygen and truth and humanity and divinity and the living and the dead. Here, the death of death transcends even what we have seen in the Muselmann's death, the death that Levi hesitates to call death. The traces of the death that is not death are indeed palpable, as Zalman Gradowski says—palpable and elusive, at once concrete and transcendent. We soon understand why Stone would assert above that these photographs "are unquestionably the most important documents that we have." But perhaps for even deeper reasons.

The four photographs, numbered 280 to 283, were taken in August 1944 at Crematorium V by Alberto Israel Errera (1913–August 1944), an officer in the Greek Navy known simply as Alex. When the Nazis occupied Greece in April 1941, Errera joined the partisans and was arrested on 25 March 1944; on 2 April, he was deported from Athens to Auschwitz.[166] Alter Fajnzylberg (b. 1910), Shlomo and Josel Dragon, and David Szmulewski assisted Errera in the clandestine task of taking the photographs. Helena Dantón smuggled photos out of the camp in a toothpaste tube.[167]

On 4 September 1944, Polish political prisoners Jósef Cyrankiewicz (1911–1989) and Stanislaw Klodzinski (1918–1990) smuggled out a note to the Polish resistance in Kraków: "Urgent. . . . Sending you photos of Birkenau showing prisoners sent to gas chambers. One photo shows one of the stakes at which bodies were burned when the crematorium could not manage to burn all the bodies."[168] Cropped images from the photographs were first published in 1945. (The matter of cropping the photographs will prove to be crucial.) In 1947, one of the photographs was exhibited at Auschwitz. The others appeared in 1958 in Warsaw in the book *1939–1945: We Have Not Forgotten* edited by Stanisław Wrzos-Glinka, Tadeusz Mazur, and Jerzy Tomaszewski.[169]

Didi-Huberman takes "the very existence and the possibility" of the photographs to be a refutation of "an *unsayable* Auschwitz," adding, "It is to the very core of speech that testimony invites us, compelling us to work there. It is harsh work, since what it concerns is a description of death at work, with the inarticulate cries and the silences that are implied."[170] Without the literary response to the Shoah examined in Part Two, there are no inarticulate cries or silences to be transmitted by these photographs. So this statement provides yet another justification for this project of examining together the literary and photographic nonrepresentations of the

Holocaust. In the photographic transmission of the "inarticulate cries and silences" we encounter the photographic transcendence of the Holocaust. Didi-Huberman argues that "the very existence and form of the testimonies powerfully contradict the dogma of the unimaginable. It is as a tragic experience that the unimaginable calls upon its contradiction, the act of imagining *in spite of all*."[171] But this *in spite of all* is just where the project of Holocaust representation is undone: representation happens not in spite of all but because of all, working as it does within the confines of all there is. The *in spite of all* opens up a trace of more than all there is, a trace of the transcendent. Thus "if we look at the four photographs of Birkenau as *tear-images* rather than *veil-images*," writes Didi-Huberman, "we find ourselves perceiving a *naked horror,* a horror that leaves us all the more devastated as it ceases to bear the hyperbolic mark of the 'unimaginable.' "[172] And so we realize that the task of the one transformed into a witness in the encounter with the literary and photographic transcendence of representation is not about imagination. The nonrepresentable is nonrepresentable not because it is unimaginable but because it belongs to a sanctity that is unassimilable, beyond all appropriation. Indeed, as we have seen, the Nazi evil was not unimaginable—it was everything imaginable. The task that confronts us, rather, is about a recovery of the Good that came under a radical assault.

This is the first of the four photographs, number 280 (Figure 3.13 on page 252). "The *mass of black* that surrounds the sight of the cadavers and the pits," Didi-Huberman observes, "is the space of the gas chamber: the *dark room* into which one had to retreat . . . to give light to the work of the *Sonderkommando*. . . . That mass of black gives us the situation itself . . . the condition of existence of the photographs themselves."[173] The mass of black is the darkness from which the bodies of Jewish men, women, and children were dragged to the pits. It is a darkness that stinks of body fluids and the unearthly screams of the dead still hanging in the air. For the viewer, the black frame forms not a border but a barrier, like "Arbeit Macht Frei," that cannot be traversed. From this dark edge we peer into the abyss of the Shoah. The mass of black is the mass of the anti-world, the mass of the *Churban,* a realm devoid of light. The mass of black is a mass of the void that is the pit of death and the death of death. What Didi-Huberman calls "the situation itself" is unlike any situation on Planet Earth: it is the non-situation, the uncondition, of Planet Auschwitz. The black mass in the photograph is the dark matter that dominates the concentrationary universe. And it *is* the *concentrationary* universe: there is nothing ontological about "the condition of existence of the photographs themselves."

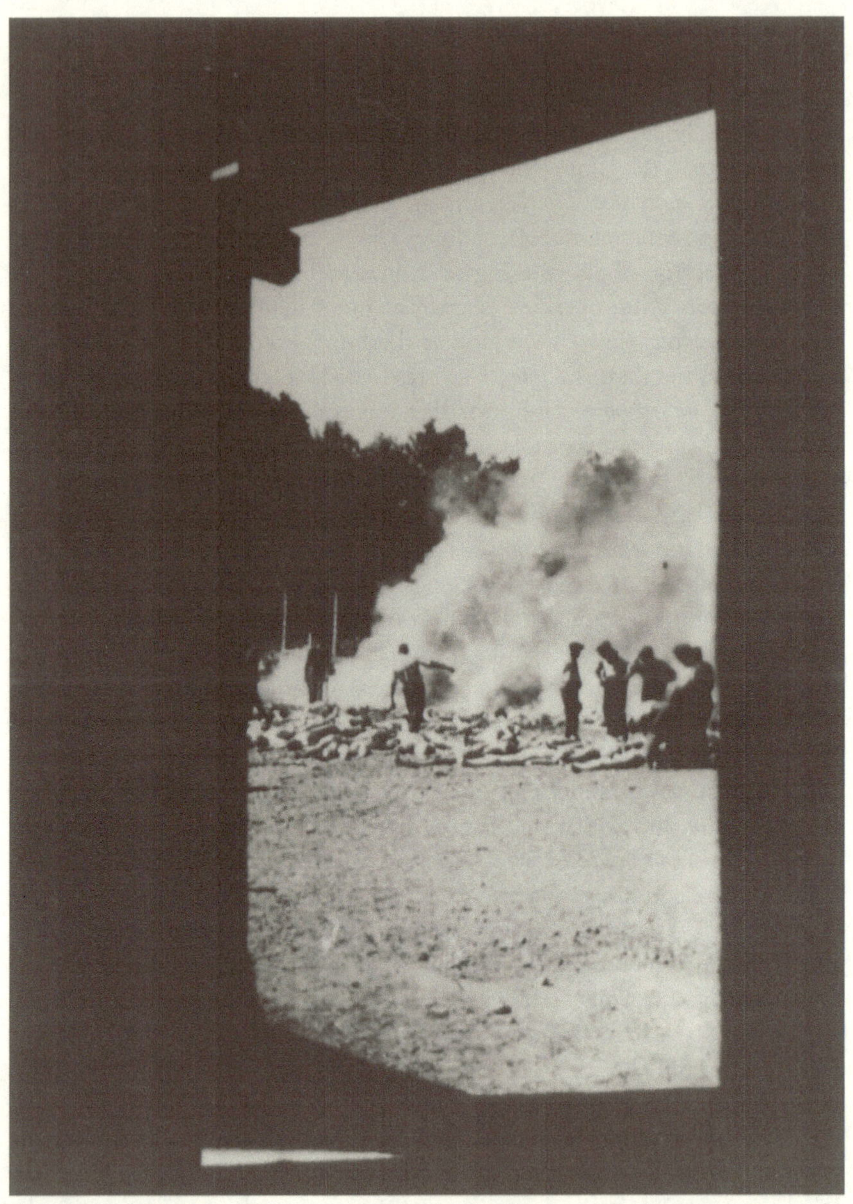

FIGURE 3.13. The first Sonderkommando Photograph, from the archival collection of the State Museum Auschwitz-Birkenau in Oświęcim.

Nicholas Chare elaborates: "The black frame forms part of the noise of the photographs. These images are edged by horror: the blackness is the boundary that permits the photograph to be. To remove this ambiguous edge is to avoid confronting the origin of the horrors portrayed in the pictures."[174] Yes, the *noise* of the photographs. It is the noise of the gas chamber and the roar of the crematorium flames, the hiding place from which Alex takes the photograph. It is the din of the boundary that erases all boundaries between life and death, between good and evil: there lies the horror. The burning of the bodies is not Auschwitz; no, the mass of black is Auschwitz, if anything can be said to be Auschwitz. That is why De-Nur could not say what Auschwitz is: it eludes all light. It is the secret imposed on the *Geheimnisträger*. Chare continues:

> Atrocity photographs initially wound the eye, they cause pain but then—with repeated viewing—the wound becomes cauterized. The darkness, however, is plaintive. It does not shock the spectator. It is registered instead as emptiness. It is felt as a kind of loss in the field of vision. There pictures can be given the appearance of coherence. . . . They can be named, shaped, made into some thing. They can be filled. Yet a part of the darkness will always resist this desire to contour it. It remains rather that out of which contour arises, bordering all interpretations yet resisting being delimited by them. Shape momentarily disappears in this darkness.[175]

As shape disappears in this darkness, so does the word disappear in the silent noise of the photograph, and with it the representable. Here, the photographic image is precisely *not* a representable image: what you see in this photograph *is not* how it was, and yet here it is. *That is the purpose of the edge of black.* To remove the edge, then, is to remove the invisible, nonrepresentable aspect of the event. It is to remove the "there is" of the event, which is neither something nor nothing, a silent rumbling, a noise that transcends everything that is there, a non-place where the bottom has fallen out.

"Transcendence," the words of Levinas come to mind, "is passing over to being's *other,* otherwise than being. Not *to be otherwise,* but *otherwise than being*. . . . Being and not-being illuminate one another, and unfold a speculative dialectic which is a determination of being. Or else the negativity which attempts to repel being is immediately submerged by being. The void that hollows out is immediately filled with the mute and anonymous rustling of the *there is*,"[176] which is "the horrible eternity at the bottom of essence."[177] In this case, however, being's *other* is not the One who commands the Good, but rather the negation of the commanding Voice; what might have been submerged here rises up as the *choshekh,* the "darkness," over the face of the deep that would undo creation. Embodied in the black mass of darkness is the anti-world's attempt to repel the *otherwise than being*: there lies the horrible eternity and the eternal horror of *this* "there is," the horror that takes away the breath and with it the word.

Longing to take away the horror, we take away the darkness. Thus, attempting to restore something to which one might give voice, a cropped version of this image, as well as the others framed in darkness, is often displayed (Figure 3.14). As Blake Remington points out, a cropped version appears, for example, in Alain Renais's *Night and Fog* "in order to provide evidence that fits within the larger narrative of the film."[178] Absent the darkness, the image can be appropriated, known, and thematized; it can be presented as evidence of a crime committed. With the darkness, on the other hand, we behold the assault on the Good that makes the very category of "crime" intelligible.

The smoke rising from what is precisely *not* a funeral pyre occludes nature herself, all of creation, in this most unnatural scene. The trees stand in the background as mute, indifferent fixtures. The sky is a blank, gray, silent canopy, emptied of the sun. No creatures of the air fly overhead; there is no "overhead," no dimension of height, for height itself is here occluded by the smoke made of the ashes of the Jewish people, the ashes that imbue the earth we tread and the bread we eat and that now lurk within us, in our bone and marrow, in our being and matter.

The eye immediately goes to the man trying to make his way through the bodies without stumbling. It is as though he were walking through a mine field that threatens to destroy his dead soul, as though he were about to fall into the growing pile of the dead, treading a tightrope over an abyss that yawns all around him, ready to devour him, as though the ashen earth piled knee-deep with bodies whose dead hands grab at him might at any moment open up and swallow him. His arms are stretched outward: is he trying to keep his balance? Or is he trying to fly away to join the other Jews launched skyward on the cloud of smoke and the pillar of fire?

We see a man with his hands on his hips, as though he were out on a routine job, the foreman perhaps. All of us who have had summer jobs

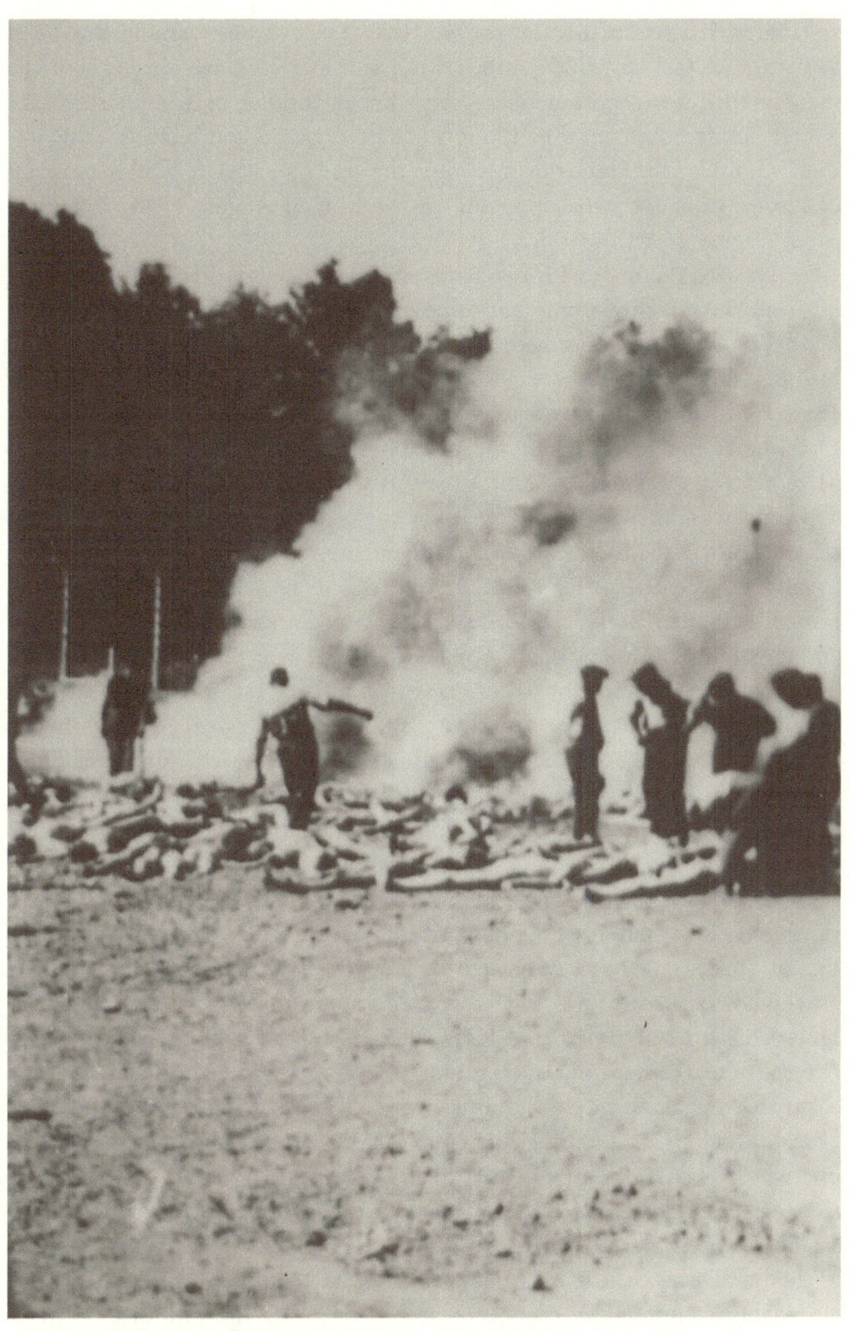

FIGURE 3.14. The first Sonderkommando Photograph cropped.

as laborers have seen this image. We have seen our boss assume this pose, as if to say, "Get to work!" And, on our summer jobs, we obeyed. For the men on this Sonderkommando—who knew nothing of winter, since the winter Sonderkommando had long since been gassed and burned—this was their summer job. Hands on his hips, the foreman tries to find a moment of respite from the exhausting toil in the heat of August 1944. But there is no respite. Not from this.

Next to the man with his hands on his hips is another man scratching his head, as though working out some mundane matter regarding the task at hand. "Do we need more kerosene and timber? How are we going to finish burning this batch? How shall we divide up the goods taken from these Jews? How many more will they send us? When do we break for lunch?" Or is he trying to work out the metaphysical implications of the task? Is he wondering, "Where is God? Where is God now?" Or is he wondering, as we all wonder when we gaze upon these images in our anger and our shame: "What shall I say when I stand before the celestial tribunal?" Or is it simply: "What shall I say to my children?" After all, he is—or is he?—a human being. In all likelihood he gazes upon the cadavers surrounding him and sees himself among them. For he knows he will never leave this place.

Yes, the cadavers: look more closely. You peer into the image and ask, both knowing and afraid to know: "Are those human *bodies*?! Are they *human* bodies?!" The bodies are unlike any human bodies prepared for either burning or for burial. They are the "units" or the "pieces" of the "*Wieviel Stück?*" of Levi's remembrance.[179] This is not how human beings bury the bodies of human beings. Indeed, this is not a burial of bodies—it is a disposal of human remains: the difference is infinite. The difference is the definition of the Holocaust—and it is a nonrepresentable difference. Here we have the radical opposite of bodies prepared by the *Cheverah Kadishah,* the company assembled to prepare one who is created in the image and likeness of the Holy One for a return to the Holy One. Members of the *Cheverah Kadishah* speak to the departed and comfort them as they prepare them, assuring them that their passage to the upper worlds will be a smooth one, careful to observe modesty, and apologizing from any discomfort that might cause the one who has passed. None of that here. What, indeed, could these men say to these dead? Here, we have a death that is not death, a death that is an assault on death, a death that drives away the Angel of Death, the Angel of a Thousand Eyes, whose eyes now gaze back at us through the camera lens.

This is photograph number 281 (Figure 3.15). The field of view twists and turns and recedes into a distance that can never be traversed, as Alex

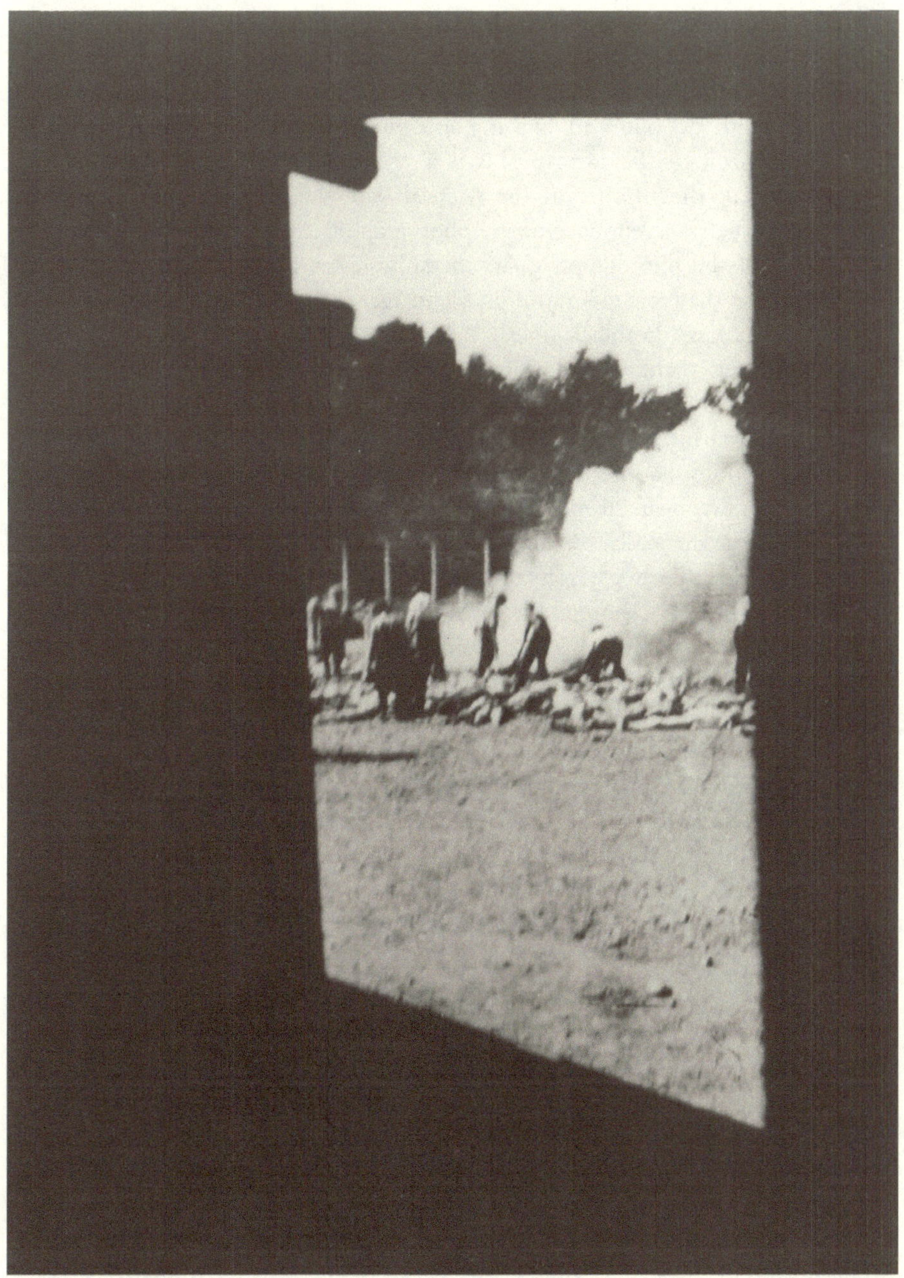

FIGURE 3.15. The second Sonderkommando Photograph, from the archival collection of the State Museum Auschwitz-Birkenau in Oświęcim.

withdraws into the unsoundable depths of the gas chamber for fear of being seen. (Along the left margin is a piece of the subsequent image, the one tied to the other, as we shall see.) Something or someone vanishes to the rear, but with no one and nothing, no promise and no persona, waiting on the horizon of the future. This is a photograph of the obliteration of the future, of the murder of the Messiah who languishes at the gates of Birkenau. The transcendence of the photographic image, from the ontological being of the photograph to its metaphysical otherwise than being, lies in a Promise that remains unfulfilled and recedes as we approach it, just as Alex recedes into the black hole.

And yet, thanks to Alex, from the future we struggle to draw forth this past, in spite of all. His testimony is not limited to a field of vision: his withdrawal into the haunted gas chamber is itself part of his testimony. It is a testimony haunted by the screams and the prayers and the outcries to a God grown deaf, steeped in the dying guttural utterance of the Shema, the clawing at the walls, the clinging to the loved one, all of it flooding the world with its aftershock from this epicenter, the site of the murder of tens of thousands. It is as though one of those who were gassed were clicking the camera's shutter, hoping that no one outside, friend or foe, would hear the click, praying that everyone on the outside, friend and foe, would behold the image snatched from this piece of Planet Auschwitz.

Withdrawing into the unplumbed depths of this darkness, Alex himself tries to become invisible in his attempt to photograph the invisible—not just the burning of bodies but what the burning of these bodies *means,* seeking to retrieve something other than what Charlotte Delbo calls "useless knowledge," useless not because it is not utilitarian but because, for the one who knows it, this knowledge forever obstructs the relationship with other human beings.[180] Only by retrieving the disappearing trace of why it matters can these images ever have the slightest hope of restoring what here comes under a stark assault, namely, the human relationship that constitutes our humanity.

The most prominent part of this photographer's gaze upon an unreality from the depths of a darker unreality is the smoke that continues its ineluctable rise toward the indifferent, valueless vault above. To be sure, in this photograph of a total reversal of reality we have a total reversal of the "cloud of smoke by day" and the "pillar of fire by night" that guided the Israelites from the ancient site of their exile (Exodus 13:21). Is there any way for *this* cloud of smoke to guide us out of our own exile? Here, as during the time of the *Mabul,* the Great Flood, the confusion of values and reality is so radical that there is no day or night (Rashi, commentary on Genesis 8:22)—there is only the cloud of smoke, of flame and ash, not to guide the Jewish people but to consume them. That is the meaning of the black mass, a meaning from which we struggle to flee, as we crop the black mass from the photograph—not to behold the face of the Medusa but to turn away even as we gaze upon it, succumbing to the temptation of temptation.

Most of us know what it means to work hard at manual labor. It is part of growing up and making our way into the world; it is, once again, the proverbial summer job that reminds us of why we are in school. Of course for many people, backbreaking work is all they know, as they toil to make a living and a life, to provide for a family, and to build a legacy—all of which is utterly alien to the image before our eyes (Figure 3.16 on page 260).

Gradowski's prescient words come back to haunt us: "Hold me tightly by the hand, do not tremble . . . for you will have to see even worse."[181] Do not ask: How can it be worse? In the uncropped image of Photograph 281 we have seen even worse. Here we see men hard at work. They tug and they pull; they groan and they grunt, all the while cursing the heat of August and the heat of the flames. We see the incongruity between these hardworking men and the work they work hard at, engaged as they are in backbreaking and soul-breaking labor, laboring with their bare hands, skilled and unskilled, breathing in the smoke of the incinerated Jewish people in the diurnal devastation of the eternal. This is not a photograph of one day but of a hundred days and more in the summer of 1944.

What perhaps in the uncropped photograph appeared to be tree trunks turn out to be the posts of the electrified fence. The fence forms the thin boundary and announces the infinite distance between world and anti-world, between the world of trees and the world of corpses, the unique product manufactured in the death factory. And yet, like the column of smoke riding the winds, the world of corpses spills over the fence and into the world of trees, as we discover in Photograph 282 (Figure 3.17 on page 261).

Looking at this photograph, we sense Alex's desperation, as he rushes through this haunted wood, the paradigm of the survivor desperate to deliver a message that he cannot deliver. He runs not only to avoid getting caught but perhaps also to flee the scene. And yet the scene follows him like his own shadow. He bears the burden of a word and an image in an attempt to somehow save the image and the word, to retrieve them from a realm calculated to undo every word, every image.

In this photograph, nature is turned askew; it is a photograph of creation itself turned askew. Consisting mostly of trees and sky, the photograph

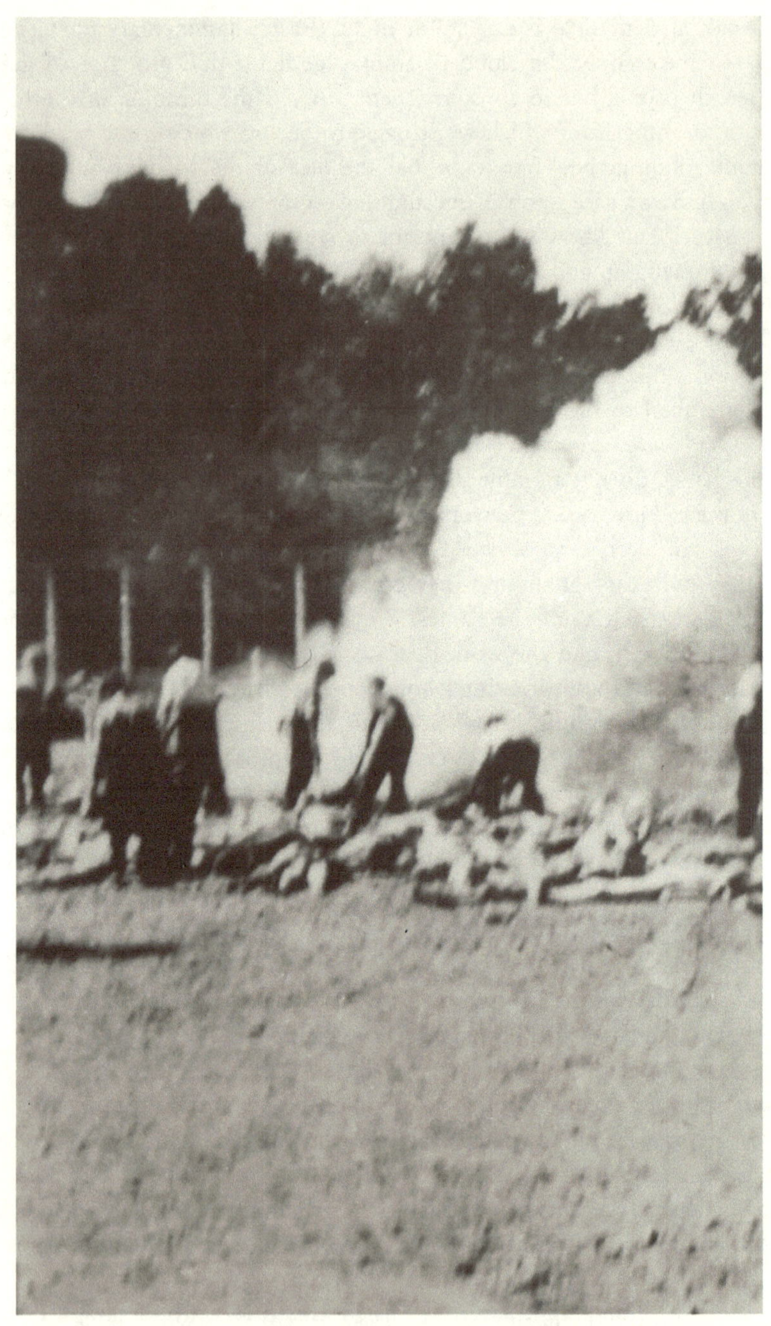

FIGURE 3.16. The second Sonderkommando Photograph cropped.

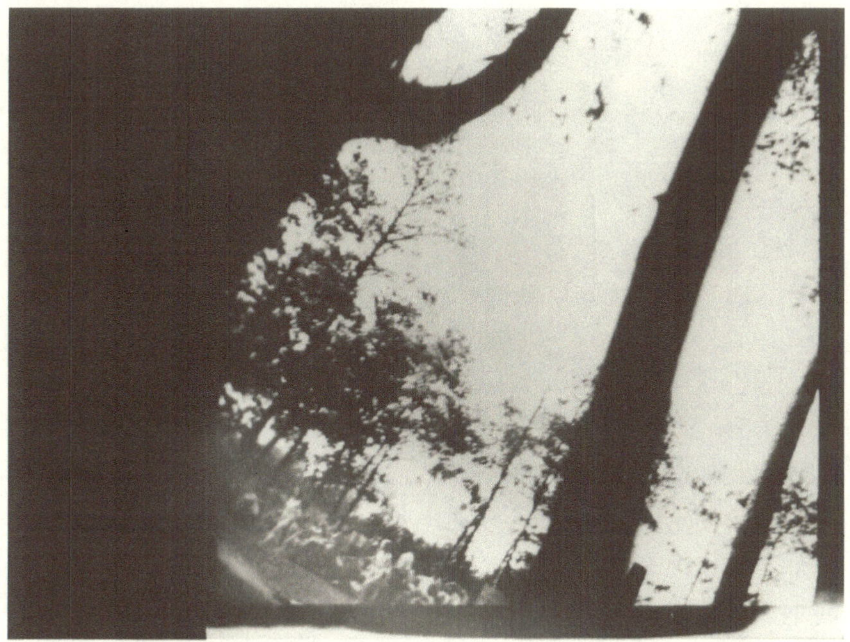

FIGURE 3.17. The third Sonderkommando Photograph, from the archival collection of the State Museum Auschwitz-Birkenau in Oświęcim.

looks upward, like an outcry or a curse hurled to the heavens. Aimed at the smoky gray expanse, the camera has taken a photograph of a Jewish cemetery. With its viewfinder turned to the sky, the camera captures an image of the dimension of height from which the Most High is absent. The heavens are as vast as they are silent, dwarfing the naked humanoid figures on the lower left, so small that they seem to be utterly insignificant to the photograph itself. And yet they are precisely the subject of the photograph, a subject that can be viewed only by looking askance. This is where the corpses piled next to the pit of flames had been just hours before they were photographed. This is what they looked like, naked yet radically unnatural.

The cropped version of Photograph 282 voyeuristically zooms in on them (Figure 3.18 on page 262). Gazing upon it, you can feel yourself starting to turn into a pillar of salt.

Much of the sky and most of the trees are left out of the cropped photograph. It zeros in on a humanity rendered unrecognizable as humans, laid bare, ascending to the left, about to ascend to their invisible graves on

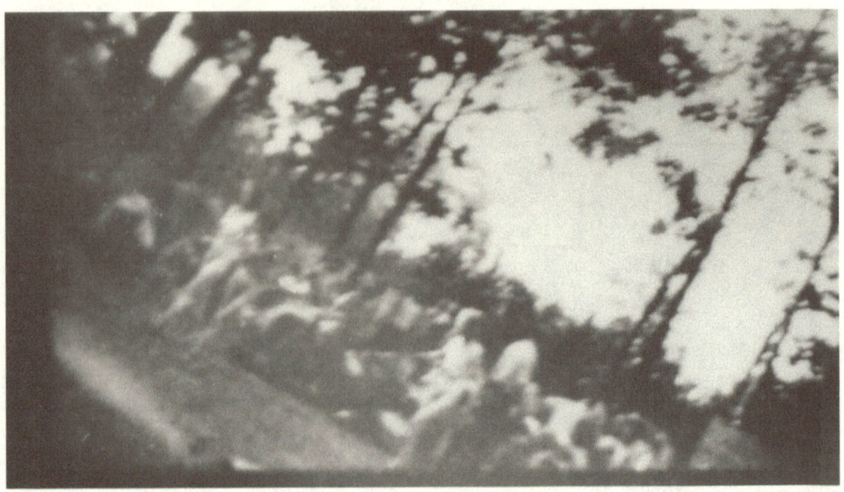

FIGURE 3.18. The third Sonderkommando Photograph cropped.

high. Among the naked women are clothed men, looking as if they were on some sort of crowd control detail, grim guides herding these helpless women to their demise. They are the Sonderkommando members in this Sonderkommando photograph, men exposed far more than their naked victims are exposed. How do these doomed women register what is happening all around them? They surely smell the stench of burning flesh. They surely hear the roar of the flames. They surely see the smoke rising above the trees. They surely are going insane. Or is the Shema rising to their lips?

The ostensible purpose of cropping these first three Sonderkommando photographs is to get a "close-up" of their subject matter, so that it may be "used" as evidence of this history of the Third Germany. And yet, inasmuch as the subject matter is Auschwitz and not burning bodies or naked victims, it is lost in the cropping. In the cropped photographs the transcendent, nonrepresentable, invisible Auschwitz has itself been cropped out.

There is, however, no cropped version of the fourth photograph, number 283. There is nothing to zoom in on, no photographic subject, nothing to *see,* nothing to serve as evidence, nothing of the ontological or the representable, because it *shows* nothing. As Remington points out, the first three images are displayed on the website of the Auschwitz-Birkenau State Museum, but not the fourth.[182] The same is the case in the British Imperial War Museum. And in his *History of the Holocaust* Yehuda Bauer notes that "three photographs of the crematoria compounds" were smuggled out; he makes no mention of the fourth, probably assuming that the fourth photograph is not a photograph of anything.[183] For purposes of history and memory, it is as though there were no fourth photograph. Therefore, he perhaps concluded, it is useless. It is useless because it is un-re-*cognize*-able and therefore represents nothing: it eludes all epistemological appropriation. In the words of Levinas, the truth of the photograph "*is not the truth of representation*, is not *evidence*."[184] The fourth photograph, therefore, could never be entered as evidence of anything. Evidence belongs to the representable, to what can be *shown*.

This photograph shows nothing (Figure 3.19). It is itself made of what was cropped from the others, made of the darkness of the black mass and the immensity of the gray sky. For that reason alone, this fourth photograph is a photograph of the anti-world of Auschwitz. Recall De-Nur's plea with Gideon Hausner not to call him to the stand. "I saw the burning, the beating, the starvation, the torture—but *that is not Auschwitz is*. What Auschwitz is, I cannot say." And so the survivor took the stand at the trial and fainted before he had barely begun his testimony. Perhaps De-Nur could have simply held up the fourth photograph, shown it to

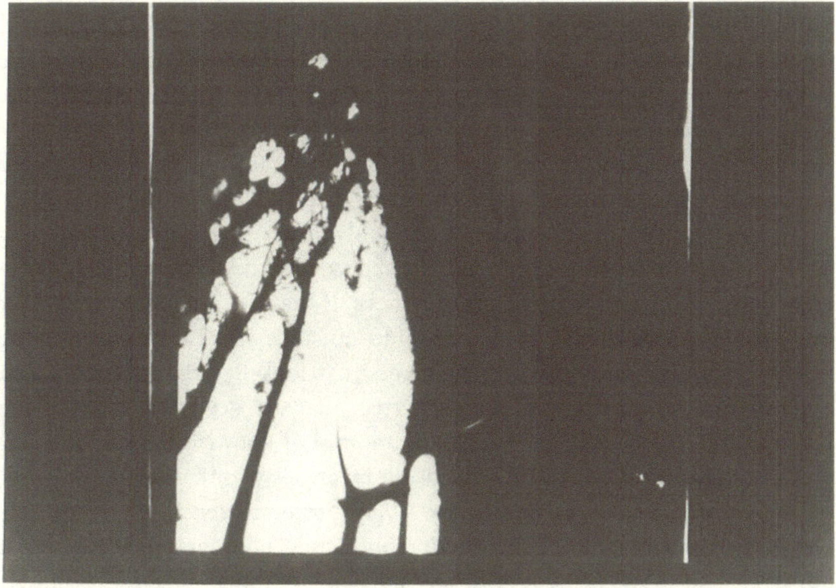

FIGURE 3.19. The fourth Sonderkommando Photograph, from the archival collection of the State Museum Auschwitz-Birkenau in Oświęcim.

the judges, and declare, "This is what Auschwitz was." But that would be as futile as the poetic words he attempted to put together, as futile as his fainting. And yet his fainting was part of his testimony, just as this fourth photograph is part of the set of the Sonderkommando Photographs. It is the photograph of a faint.

Didi-Huberman insists that to say it is useless because it shows nothing "is to forget all that it tells us phenomenologically about the photographer: the impossibility of aiming the camera, the risk undergone, the urgency, the fact that he may have been running, the awkwardness, the sun in his eyes, and perhaps breathlessness too."[185] The photograph tells us much more than that, and it has profound implications as testimony. Testimony belongs to the transcendent, which is why poetry may be part of the testimony to an ineffable aspect of the Shoah. It is true that in a strictly legal sense testimonies were entered into evidence at war crimes trials; poetry about the assault on the soul, however, was not offered as evidence. Evidence belongs to the world of representation. The testimony of poetry, however, is testimony to the assault on the soul, on the Good, on the Holy. It is testimony to the erasure of boundaries, when more was real than was possible. "The final *Sonderkommando* photograph," Nicholas Chare emphasizes, "gestures towards such a dissolution of boundaries. It shows the dissolution of shape. It *shows* the spectator the horror of a world without boundaries."[186] The subject of the fourth photograph, in other words, is the invisible. That is why there is nothing to crop. It is a photograph of a soul and a cosmos gone insane. There lies this photograph's transcendence of the representable. It is as if Auschwitz were saying, "You may not behold my face, for no man may see my face and live. But you may behold my back."

The photograph is made of more darkness than light; it has just enough light to show the grotesquely shaped darkness, the darkness of a mad desperation and a desperate madness. If we did not know that Alex was running through the trees, we would not take those dark forms to be trees at all. Who among us has seen trees that look like that? Rising up in a world that is not a world, they are trees that are not trees, trees of the Knowledge of Good and Evil in a realm devoid of knowledge and good and evil, trees bearing strange fruit, edged not by angels with flaming swords but by men alongside pits of flames. In a very profound sense, therefore, this one is the most graphic of the Sonderkommando photographs, depicting a horror that surpasses depiction. It does not show nothing—it shows nothingness, what Chare calls the "horror of a world without boundaries," which is not only the anti-world of Auschwitz but is also the world that now lives in its shadow. That is why we leave it out of history books and exhibits.

W. H. Auden had a prescient sense of what this photograph conveys. In his testimonial poem "September 1, 1939" he writes:

> Faces along the bar
> Cling to their average day:
> The lights must never go out,
> The music must always play,
> All the conventions conspire
> To make this fort assume
> The furniture of a home;
> Lest we should see where we are,
> Lost in a haunted wood,
> Children afraid of the night
> Who have never been happy or good.[187]

Here before our eyes, through the eye of the Sonderkommando's camera, we behold the haunted wood in which we are lost. We might suppose that the photographic testimony of the Holocaust photographs could help us find our way out of the wood and into the light; we might suppose that is why we undertake investigations of Holocaust representation. But taking the photographs was no help to Alex Errera: three days later, Alex Errera was captured and beaten to death.[188] Thus, the price of the testimony.

So what exactly is the point in examining the photographs that portray the transcendent, invisible aspect of the Event? Above all, it is not to try to imagine "what it was like." Photograph 283 is not a picture of "what it was like." It is an image of what Auschwitz was *about,* of what Auschwitz *meant* (if anything), of what Auschwitz *was*. The same may be said of any of the photographs that we have considered. Worse than vanity, the question of "what it was like" is a diversion, a flight from the accusing transcendent into the reassuring representable. Much more urgent than imagining what it was like is confronting how it implicates me. Imagining what it was like, I do the imagining, the experiencing, the appropriating. I do the *feeling,* curled up in the illusion that if I know what it was like, then I know how it felt, and if I know how it felt, then I know it. Then I can work through it. Then I can control it. Then I can comprehend it. Then I am absolved. Called to a reckoning, however, the event comprehends, apprehends, and lays claim to *me* and thus puts to me from an immemorial time the first question put to the first human being: Where are you?

In all of the images we have encountered, this question lays claim to us, as we behold "what man's presumption made of man," as Primo Levi, once again, so tersely states it.[189] We behold beings created in the image and likeness of the Holy One, human beings like you and me, transformed into murderers and victims. And yet to speak of murderers and victims is to speak the language of the world that can be represented in language, a language undone in the anti-world, where no one took the bread from his own mouth to offer it to another,[190] where bread was not bread but the "holy grey slab" known as "bread-brot-Broid-chleb-pain-lechem-keynér."[191] Human beings murder and are murdered, hence the prohibition against murder, which itself is undone in the undoing of language, which is the undoing of the human being as a speaking being. In the inhuman, nonhuman, antihuman realm of Auschwitz these words, like all words, collapse into the ashes that cover the ground and fill the air. They too are lost in the woods—the only thing that appears in all four of the Sonderkommando photographs.

What, then, is to be done? If Alex Errera had the courage to take these photographs, at the cost of his life, then we must summon the courage to gaze upon the image and offer up a reckoning of our lives. As Fackenheim has said, "The Nazi logic of destruction was irresistible: *it was, nevertheless, being resisted.* This logic is a *novum* in human history, the source of an unprecedented, abiding horror: but resistance to it on the part of the most radically exposed, too, is a *novum* in history, and it is the source of an unprecedented, abiding wonder. *To hear and obey the commanding Voice of Auschwitz is an 'ontological' possibility, here and now, because the hearing and obeying was already an 'ontic' reality, then and there.*"[192] The "commanding Voice of Auschwitz" is the Voice of the transcendent. The Voice is the invisible revealed in the photographic transcendence of the Holocaust that we have seen in these pages. And so we realize that transcendence happens not in a swoon but in a summons.

In Part Three, we have glimpsed a few images from the concentrationary universe. It is, however, a universe that is much closer to us than we may realize. It is closer to us than our own shadows. And it reminds us of what is at stake in our thoughts, words, and deeds. So gaze upon these images, but not too long, lest your soul turn into a pillar of salt. Gaze just long enough to sense that what is infinitely precious, what is profoundly human in the human being, is infinitely fragile. And if we do not watch over it, care for it, and love it, it will be lost. And so shall we.

Notes

Preface

1. Emmanuel Levinas, *Otherwise Than Being or Beyond Essence*, trans. Alphonso Lingis (The Hague: Nijhoff, 1981), 11.

2. Emmanuel Levinas, *Ethics and Infinity*, trans. Richard A. Cohen (Pittsburgh: Duquesne University Press, 1985), 105.

Part One. Reflections on Holocaust Representation and the Nonrepresentable

1. Maurice Blanchot, *The Writing of the Disaster*, trans. Ann Smock (Lincoln: University of Nebraska Press, 1986), 41; italics in the original.

2. Ibid., 40.

3. Dori Laub, "An Event without a Witness: Truth, Testimony, and Survival," in Shoshana Felman and Dori Laub, *Testimony: Crisis of Witnessing in Literature, Psychoanalysis, and History* (London: Routledge, 1992), 78.

4. Ibid., 79.

5. Ibid., 80; emphasis added.

6. Emil L. Fackenheim, *Quest for Past and Future: Essays in Jewish Theology* (Bloomington: Indiana University Press, 1968), 205.

7. Emil L. Fackenheim, *God's Presence in History* (New York: Harper and Row, 1970), 87–88.

8. Eric Kligerman, *Sites of the Uncanny: Paul Celan, Specularity and the Visual Arts* (Berlin: Walter De Gruyter, 2007), 23.

9. Andrea Liss, *Trespassing Through Shadows: Memory, Photography, and the Holocaust* (Minneapolis: University of Minnesota Press, 1998), 25.

10. See Herman Kruk, *The Last Days of the Jerusalem of Lithuania: Chronicles from the Vilna Ghetto and the Camps, 1939–1944*, ed. Benjamin Harshav, trans. Barbara Harshav (New Haven: Yale University Press, 2002), 311.

11. According to Colonel General Franz Halder, Hitler made this remark in a meeting of German commanders on 30 March 1941; see Benjamin Lieberman, *The Holocaust and Genocides in Europe* (London: Bloomsbury Academic, 2013), 32.

12. Paul Celan, "Speech on the Occasion of Receiving the Literature Prize of the Free Hanseatic City of Bremen," in *Collected Prose*, trans. Rosemarie Waldrop (New York: Routledge, 2003), 33.

13. Philippe Lacoue-Labarthe, *Heidegger, Art and Politics: The Fiction of the Political*, trans. Chris Turner (Oxford: Blackwell, 1990), 37.

14. Sidra DeKoven Ezrahi, *By Words Alone: The Holocaust in Literature* (Chicago: University of Chicago Press, 1980), 2.

15. Emil L. Fackenheim, *The Jewish Return into History* (New York: Schocken Books, 1978), 247.

16. Emil L. Fackenheim, "The Rebirth of the Holy Remnant," lecture presented at Yad Vashem, Jerusalem, 17 June 1993.

17. Ibid.

18. Alvin Rosenfeld, *The End of the Holocaust* (Bloomington: Indiana University Press, 2011), 11.

19. Karla Grierson, *Discours d'Auschwitz: Littérarité, représentation, symbolization* (Paris: Honoré Champion Éditeur, 2003), 180; my translation.

20. Camille Touboul, *Un relais d'étoiles* (Montreal: Bibliothèque Nationale du Québec/Les Éditions Julad, 1982), 33; my translation.

21. Primo Levi, *The Reawakening*, trans. Stuart Wolf (Boston: Little, Brown, 1965), 33.

22. Ibid., 128.

23. Elie Wiesel, *Legends of Our Time* (New York: Avon, 1968), 176.

24. Other catastrophes that took place on that date include the Roman massacre of the Jews of Betar in 133 and the expulsions of the Jews from England in 1290 and from Spain in 1492.

25. Dan Cohn-Sherbok, *God and the Holocaust* (Herefordshire: Fowler Wright Books, 1996), 29.

26. Elie Wiesel, *Ani Maamin: A Song Lost and Found Again*, trans. Marion Wiesel (New York: Random House, 1973), 27, 29.

27. Elie Wiesel, *A Jew Today*, trans. Marion Wiesel (New York: Random House, 1978), 178–79.

28. See Kruk, *The Last Days of the Jerusalem of Lithuania*, 311.

29. Cited in Nehemia Polen, *The Holy Fire: The Teachings of Rabbi Kalonymus Kalman Shapira* (Northvale, NJ: Jason Aronson, 1999), 102.

30. Ka-tzetnik 135633, *Kaddish*, trans. Nina De-Nur (New York: Algemeiner Associates, 1998), 30.

31. George Lucius Salton, *The 23rd Psalm: A Holocaust Memoir* (Madison: University of Wisconsin Press, 2002), 218.

32. Quoted in Eliyahu Kitov, *The Book of Our Heritage*, Vol. 1, trans. Nathan Bluman (New York: Feldheim Publishers, 1973), 75–76.

33. See Louis I. Newman, ed., *The Hasidic Anthology* (New York: Schocken Books, 1963), 337.

34. Chaim A. Kaplan, *Scroll of Agony: The Warsaw Diary of Chaim A. Kaplan*, trans. and ed. Abraham I. Katsh (New York: Collier, 1973), 202.

35. The *Pesikta de-Rab Kahana* is a collection of midrashic teachings dating from sometime between the fifth and seventh centuries CE; there were several great sages known as Rav Kahana from the earlier centuries. The *Sifre* is a rabbinic commentary on the Book of Deuteronomy dating from around the year 300 CE.

36. Kaplan, *Scroll of Agony*, 179.

37. See Robert G. Ingram, *Religion, Reform, and Modernity in the Eighteenth Century* (Woodbridge, UK: Bitdell Press, 2007), 176.

38. Quoted in Robert Wistrich, *A Lethal Obsession: Anti-Semitism from Antiquity to the Global Jihad* (New York: Random House, 2010), 110.

39. Elie Wiesel, *Against Silence: The Voice and Vision of Elie Wiesel*, Vol. 3, ed. Irving Abrahamson (New York: Holocaust Library, 1985), 297.

40. Jean-François Lyotard, *Heidegger and "the jews,"* trans. Andreas Michel and Mark S. Roberts (Minneapolis: University of Minneapolis Press, 1990), 22.

41. Ibid., 23.

42. Fackenheim, *God's Presence in History*, 83.

43. Leo Strauss, *Studies in Platonic Political Philosophy* (Chicago: University of Chicago Press, 1985), 147.

44. Leo Strauss, *The Rebirth of Classical Political Rationalism: An Introduction to the Thought of Leo Strauss*, selected by Thomas L. Pangle (Chicago: University of Chicago Press, 1989), 72.

45. Strauss, *Studies in Platonic Political Philosophy*, 150.

46. Brett Ashley Kaplan, *Unwanted Beauty: Aesthetic Pleasure in Holocaust Representation* (Urbana: University of Illinois Press, 2007), 97.

47. Elie Wiesel, *Somewhere a Master: Further Hasidic Portraits and Legends*, trans. Marion Wiesel (New York: Summit Books, 1982), 68.

48. Fabrice Midal, *Auschwitz, l'impossible regard* (Paris: Éditions du Seuil, 2012), 11; my translation.

49. "The Trial of Adolf Eichmann, Session 68," 7 June 1961, State of Israel Ministry of Justice, *The Nizkor Project*, available at http://www.nizkor.org/hweb/people/e/eichmann-adolf/transcripts/Sessions/Session-068-01.html.

50. Saul Friedländer, "The *Shoah* between Memory and History," *Jewish Quarterly* 37, no. 1 (Spring 1990): 10.

51. From David Rousset, *L'Univers concentrationnaire* (Paris: Éditions de Minuit, 1965).

52. Jean Améry, *At the Mind's Limits: Contemplations by a Survivor on Auschwitz and Its Realities*, trans. Sidney Rosenfeld and Stella P. Rosenfeld (New York: Schocken Books, 1986), 19.

53. Levinas, *Otherwise Than Being*, 87.

54. Ka-tzetnik 135633, *Shivitti: A Vision*, trans. Eliyah De-Nur and Lisa Herman (New York: Harper and Row, 1989), xvii.

55. Primo Levi, *Survival in Auschwitz*, trans. Stuart Woolf (New York: Simon and Schuster, 1996), 82–83.

56. Eugene Heimler, *Night of the Mist*, trans. Andre Ungar (New York: Vanguard, 1959), 36.

57. See Paul Trepman, *Among Men and Beasts*, trans. Shoshana Perla and Gertrude Hirschler (New York: Bergen Belsen Memorial Press, 1978), 137.

58. Elie Wiesel, *Night*, trans. Marion Wiesel (New York: Hill and Wang, 2006), 110.

59. Lea Wernick Fridman, *Words and Witness: Narrative and Aesthetic Strategies in the Representation of the Holocaust* (Albany: State University of New York Press, 2000), 72.

60. See, for example, Schneur Zalman, *Likutei Amarim Tanya*, trans. Nissan Mindel et al. (Brooklyn: Kehot, 1981), 183.

61. Ka-tzetnik 135633, *Shivitti*, 15–16.

62. Ka-tzetnik 135633, *Phoenix over the Galilee*, trans. Nina De-Nur (New York: Harper and Row, 1969), 28.

63. Elie Wiesel, *From the Kingdom of Memory: Reminiscences* (New York: Summit Books, 1990), 166.

64. Michael Bernard-Donals, *Forgetful Memory: Representation and Remembrance in the Wake of the Holocaust* (Albany: State University of New York Press, 2009), 28.

65. Levinas, *Otherwise Than Being*, 14.

66. Ka-tzetnik 135633, *Sunrise over Hell*, trans. Nina De-Nur (London: W. H. Allen, 1977), 78.

67. Briefly stated, the Thirteen Principles are: (1) God exists; (2) God is one and unique; (3) God is incorporeal; (4) God is eternal; (5) prayer is to be directed to God alone and to no other; (6) the words of the prophets are true; (7) Moses's prophecies are true, and Moses was the greatest of the prophets; (8) the Written Torah (first five books of the Bible) and Oral Torah (teachings now contained in the Talmud and other writings) were given to Moses; (9) there will be no other Torah; (10) God knows the thoughts and deeds of men; (11) God will reward the good and punish the wicked; (12) the Messiah will come; and (13) the dead will be resurrected. The Mishnah is the oral tradition put into writing in the form of commentary on the Torah, Jewish law, and tales; it forms the core text of the Talmud.

68. Sidra DeKoven Ezrahi, "Considering the Apocalypse: Is the Writing on the Wall Only Graffiti?" in *Writing and the Holocaust*, ed. Berel Lang (New York: Holmes and Meier, 1988), 155.

69. Blanchot, *The Writing of the Disaster*, 13.

70. Michael Rothberg, *Traumatic Realism: The Demands of Holocaust Representation* (Minneapolis: University of Minnesota Press, 2000), 136.

71. Dorota Glowacka, *Disappearing Traces: Holocaust Testimonials, Ethics, and Aesthetics* (Seattle: University of Washington Press, 2012), 98; emphasis added.

72. Daniel R. Schwarz, *Imagining the Holocaust* (New York: St. Martin's, 1999), 77.

73. Levi, *Survival in Auschwitz*, 72–73.

74. The word *nevelah* is from the verb *naval*, which means to "wither," to "perish," or to "be destroyed"; the noun *naval* refers to one who is base and vile; it can also refer to one who is godless, an "unbeliever."

75. Yaakov Culi, *The Torah Anthology: MeAm Lo'ez*, Vol. 1, trans. Aryeh Kaplan (New York: Moznaim, 1977), 420.

76. Levi, *Survival in Auschwitz*, 39.

77. Levinas, *Otherwise Than Being*, 77.

78. Levi, *Survival in Auschwitz*, 160.

79. James E. Young, *Writing and Rewriting the Holocaust: Narrative and the Consequences of Interpretation* (Bloomington: Indiana University Press,1988), 90; emphasis added.

80. Ibid., 92.

81. Zoë Vania Waxman, *Writing the Holocaust: Identity, Testimony, Representation* (New York: Oxford University Press, 2008), 175.

82. David Hirsch, *The Deconstruction of Literature: Criticism after Auschwitz* (Hanover, NH: University Press of New England, 1991), 151.

83. Ibid., 130.

84. Emmanuel Levinas, *Nine Talmudic Readings*, trans. Annette Aronowicz (Bloomington: Indiana University Press, 1990), 111–12.

85. Hirsch, *The Deconstruction of Literature*, 67–68.

86. Wiesel, *Night*, 41.

87. Levinas, *Otherwise Than Being*, 5.

88. Sara Nomberg-Przytyk, *Auschwitz: True Tales from a Grotesque Land*, trans. Roslyn Hirsch (Chapel Hill: University of North Carolina Press, 1985), 72.

89. Yehuda Loeve, *Maharal of Prague: Pirke Avos*, trans. and ed. R. Tuvia Basser (Brooklyn: Mesorah, 1997), 288.

90. Emmanuel Levinas, *Proper Names*, trans. Michael B. Smith (Stanford: Stanford University Press, 1996), 93.

91. Kalonymos Kalmish Shapira, *Sacred Fire: Torah from the Years of Fury 1939–1942*, trans. J. Hershy Worch, ed. Deborah Miller (Northvale, NJ: Jason Aronson, 2000), 46–47.

92. See Yitzchak Ginsburgh, *The Alef-Beit* (Northvale, NJ: Jason Aronson, 1991), 2–3.

93. Abraham Isaac Kook, *Orot*, trans. Bezalel Naor (Northvale, NJ: Jason Aronson, 1993), 93.

94. Georges Didi-Huberman, *Images in Spite of All: Fours Photographs from Auschwitz*, trans. Shane B. Lillis (Chicago: University of Chicago Press, 2003), 20.

95. Aharon Appelfeld, *Essays in the First Person* (Jerusalem: Zionist Library, 1980), 21.

96. Wiesel, *Night*, 42.

97. Miklós Nyiszli, *Auschwitz: A Doctor's Eyewitness Account*, trans. Tibere Kremer and Richard Seaver (New York: Fawcett Crest, 1960), 26.

98. Sara Zyskind, *Stolen Years*, trans. Margarit Inbar (Minneapolis: Lerner, 1981), 211.

99. Alexander Donat, *The Holocaust Kingdom* (New York: Holocaust Library, 1978), 168.

100. Rudolf Vrba and Alan Bestic, *I Cannot Forgive* (New York: Bantam, 1964), 78–79.

101. Nathan Shapell, *Witness to the Truth* (New York: David McKay, 1974), 116.

102. Olga Lengyel, *Five Chimneys* (London: Granada, 1972), 116.

103. Moshe Sandberg, *My Longest Year*, trans. S. C. Hyman (Jerusalem: Yad Vashem, 1968), 55.

104. Nachman of Breslov, *Advice*, trans. Avraham Greenbaum (Brooklyn: Breslov Research Institute, 1983), 301.

105. Primo Levi, *The Drowned and the Saved*, trans. Raymond Rosenthal (New York: Vintage Books, 1988), 119.

106. Levi, *Survival in Auschwitz*, 28.

107. Ibid.

108. Isabella Leitner, *Fragments of Isabella*, ed. Irving Leitner (New York: Thomas Crowell, 1978), 94.

109. Mikhail Bakhtin, *Art and Answerability*, trans. Vadim Liapunov (Austin: University of Texas Press, 1991), 49–50.

110. Martin Buber, *I and Thou*, trans. Walter Kaufmann (New York: Scribner's, 1970), 66.

111. Levinas, *Proper Names*, 22.

112. Charlotte Delbo, *None of Us Will Return*, trans. John Githens (Boston: Beacon Press, 1968), 15.

113. Zyskind, *Stolen Years*, 11.

114. Ibid., 44.

115. Ana Vinocur, *A Book without a Title*, trans. Valentine Isaac and Ricardo Iglesia (New York: Vantage, 1976), 106–107.

116. Ibid., 1.

117. Leitner, *Fragments of Isabella*, 19–20.

118. Ka-tzetnik 135633, *Shivitti*, 103.

119. Levinas, *Otherwise Than Being*, 193.

120. Levinas, *Nine Talmudic Readings*, 183.

121. Yitzhak Katznelson, *Vittel Diary*, trans. Myer Cohn, 2nd ed. (Tel-Aviv: Hakibbutz Hameuchad, 1972), 109.

122. Avraham Tory, *Surviving the Holocaust: The Kovno Ghetto Diary*, trans. Jerzy Michalowicz, ed. Martin Gilbert (Cambridge: Harvard University Press, 1990), 114.

123. Terrence Des Pres, *The Survivor: An Anatomy of Life in the Death Camp* (New York: Oxford University Press, 1976), 33.

124. Nomberg-Przytyk, *Auschwitz*, 81.

125. Blanchot, *The Writing of the Disaster*, 51.

126. "Jerusalem, Israel Leah Michelson's statue 'The Silent Scream,'" Yad Vashem Photo Archive, ID 7084, Archival Signature 5432/15 available at http://collections1.yadvashem.org/notebook.asp?lang=ENG&dlang=ENG&module=search&page=list&rsvr=7¶m=<uppernav>simple</><nob>1</><rsvr_ser>@@7</><search_type>simple</><view>records</><nrsvr>N</><sort>TI</><dispq>z1z Title: z3zLeah Michelson, Literal z1zDatabanks: z3z Photos Archive</><dlang>ENG</><query_name>jaguar50_2624_038775</><quantity>15</><start_entry>1</><num_of_items>1</><query_index>@TI</><thumb>0</><smode>dts</><first_item>1</><last_item>1</><book_id>70684</><mainimage>/arch_srika/5001-5500/5413-5500/5432_15a.jpg</>¶m2=<num_fields>12</><nvf>11</><nvr>3</><search_type>simple</>&site=sapir.

127. Cf. Elie Wiesel, *Souls on Fire: Portraits and Legends of Hasidic Masters*, trans. Marion Wiesel (New York: Vintage Books, 1973), 235.

128. Shapira, *Sacred Fire*, 287–88.

129. Emmanuel Levinas, "Revelation in the Jewish Tradition," trans. Sarah Richmond, in *The Levinas Reader*, ed. Sean Hand (Oxford: Basil Blackwell, 1989), 204.

130. Levi, *The Drowned and the Saved*, 139–40.

131. Levi, *Survival in Auschwitz*, 115.

132. Dante Alighieri, *Inferno*, trans. John Ciardi (New York: Random House, 1996), 71–72.

133. Susan Sontag, *On Photography* (New York: Farrar, Straus and Giroux, 1977), 19–20; emphasis added.

134. Maya Jaggi, "Recovered Memories: Interview with W. G. Sebald," *The Guardian*, 22 September 2001, available at http://www.theguardian.com/books/2001/sep/22/artsandhumanities.highereducation; quoted in Christopher Bigsby, *Remembering and Imagining the Holocaust* (Cambridge: Cambridge University Press, 2006), 69.

135. Thomas A. Kovatch and Martin Walser, *The Burden of the Past: Martin Walser on Modern German Identity: Texts, Contexts, Commentary* (Rochester: Camden House, 2008) 26. I am indebted to Blake Remington for this reference.

136. Didi-Huberman, *Images in Spite of All*, 179–80.

137. Ka-tzetnik 135633, *Sunrise over Hell*, 111.

138. Among the various commanders of the Einsatzgruppen were Dr. Franz Walter Stahlecker (1900–1942), commander of Einsatzgruppe A, Dr. Erich Ehrlinger (1910–2004), commander of Einsatzgruppe B; Dr. Otto Rasch (1891–1948), commander of Einsatzgruppe C; and Dr. Otto Ohlendorf (1907–1951) was commander of Einsatzgruppe D.

139. Those eight were Dr. Alfred Mayer of the Reich Ministry for the Occupied Eastern Territories; Dr. Wilhelm Stuckart of the Reich Ministry for the

Interior; Dr. Erich Neumann, Head of the Four Years Plan Office; Dr. Roland Freisler of the Reich Ministry of Justice; Dr. Josef Bühler, Director General of the Generalgouvernement; Dr. Martin Luther from the Foreign Office; Dr. Karl Eberhard Schöngarth of the Sicherheitsdienst; and Dr. Rudolf Lange of the Sicherheitsdienst.

140. Levi, *Survival in Auschwitz*, 26.

141. Fackenheim, *The Jewish Return into History*, 246.

142. Améry, *At the Mind's Limits*, 24; emphasis added.

143. Elaine Scarry, *The Body in Pain: The Making and Unmaking of the World* (Oxford: Oxford University Press, 1985), 35.

144. Blanchot, *The Writing of the Disaster*, 81.

145. Nicholas Chare, *Auschwitz and Afterimages: Abjection, Witnessing, and Representation* (London: I. B. Tauris, 2011), 111.

146. Emmanuel Levinas, *Totality and Infinity*, trans. Alphonso Lingis (Pittsburgh: Duquesne University Press, 1969), 124.

147. Ibid.; emphasis added.

148. Levinas, *Otherwise Than Being*, 140.

149. Mikhail Bakhtin, *Estetika slovesnogo tvorchestva* (Moscow: State Publishing House, 1979), 117; my translation.

150. Joseph Conrad, *Heart of Darkness* (New York: Penguin Books, 1983), 111.

151. Hélène Berr, *The Journal of Hélène Berr*, trans. David Bellos (New York: Weinstein Books, 2008), 262.

152. Ibid., 6.

153. Ka-tzetnik 135633, *Star of Ashes*, trans. Nina De-Nur (Tel Aviv: Hamenora, 1971), 53.

154. Maimonides, *Guide for the Perplexed*, trans. M. Friedlaender (New York: Dover, 1956), 68.

155. Similarly, Saadia Gaon teaches that through the "luminosity" it received from God, the soul "came to be endowed with the power of speech." See Saadia Gaon, *The Book of Belief and Opinions*, trans. Samuel Rosenblatt (New Haven: Yale University Press, 1976), 242.

156. See, for example, Joseph Gikatilla, *Sha'are Orah: Gates of Light*, trans. Avi Weinstein (San Francisco: Harper Collins, 1994), 337.

157. Ka-tzetnik 135633, *Star of Ashes*, 52.

158. André Neher, *The Exile of the Word: From the Silence of the Bible to the Silence of Auschwitz*, trans. David Maisel (Philadelphia: Jewish Publication Society, 1981), 141.

159. Ibid., 63.

160. Aharon Appelfeld, *Badenheim 1939*, trans. Dalya Bilu (New York: Washington Square, 1980), 70.

161. Heimler, *Night of the Mist*, 188.

162. Alvin Rosenfeld, *A Double Dying: Reflections on Holocaust Literature* (Bloomington: Indiana University Press, 1980), 14–15.

163. Elie Wiesel, *One Generation After*, trans. Lily Edelman and Elie Wiesel (New York: Pocket Books, 1970), 108.

164. Neher, *The Exile of the Word*, 212.

165. Elie Wiesel, *The Testament*, trans. Marion Wiesel (New York: Summit Books, 1981), 207.

166. Emmanuel Levinas, *Time and the Other*, trans. Richard A. Cohen (Pittsburgh: Duquesne University Press, 1987), 46.

167. Neher, *The Exile of the Word*, 10.

168. Franz Rosenzweig, *The Star of Redemption*, trans. William W. Hallo (Boston: Beacon Press, 1972), 80.

169. Wiesel, *Against Silence*, Vol. 2, 119.

170. Wiesel, *Against Silence*, Vol. 3, 267.

171. Quoted in Didi-Huberman, *Images in Spite of All*, 129–30.

172. Jean-François Lyotard, *The Differend: Phrases in Dispute*, trans. Georges Van Den Abbeele (Minneapolis: University of Minnesota Press, 1983), 56–57; see also Liss, *Trespassing Through Shadows*, 30–31.

173. Donat, *The Holocaust Kingdom*, 25.

174. Delbo, *None of Us Will Return*, 37.

175. Ibid., 39.

176. Ka-tzetnik 135633, *Atrocity*, trans. Nina De-Nur (New York: Kensington, 1977), 286.

177. Bigsby, *Remembering and Imagining the Holocaust*, 346.

178. Glowacka, *Disappearing Traces*, 122.

179. Ka-tzetnik 135633, *Pipel* (Tel Aviv: Hakibbutz Hameuchad, 1988), 224.

180. Josef Bor, *The Terezín Requiem*, trans. Edith Pargeter (New York: Avon, 1963), 41–42.

181. Blaise Pascal, *Pensées*, trans. A. J. Krailsheimer (New York: Penguin, 1995), 66.

182. Wiesel, *The Testament*, 210.

183. See Emil L. Fackenheim, *To Mend the World: Foundations of Post-Holocaust Jewish Thought* (New York: Schocken Books, 1989), 316–18.

184. Nomberg-Przytyk, *Auschwitz*, 135–36.

185. Miguel de Unamuno, *The Tragic Sense of Life*, trans. Anthony Kerrigan (Princeton: Princeton University Press, 1972), 199.

186. Blanchot, *Writing the Disaster*, 134–35.

187. Ka-tzetnik 135633, *Shivitti*, 12–13.

188. Ibid., 40–41.

189. Elie Wiesel, *Twilight*, trans. Marion Wiesel (New York: Summit Books, 1998), 11.

190. Wiesel, *Against Silence*, Vol. 3, 309.

191. Levi, *Survival in Auschwitz*, 19.

192. Shapira, *Sacred Fire*, 22.

193. Ibid., 23.

194. Fackenheim, *To Mend the World*, 100.

195. Leon Poliakov, *The Harvest of Hate* (Syracuse: Syracuse University Press, 1954), 222.

196. Vrba and Bestic, *I Cannot Forgive*, 91.

197. Levinas, *Ethics and Infinity*, 86.

198. Levi, *Survival in Auschwitz*, 90; emphasis added.

199. See Martin Heidegger, *Sein und Zeit*, 2nd ed. (Tübingen: Max Niemeyer, 1963), 245, 262–63.

200. Giorgio Agamben, *Remnants of Auschwitz: The Witness of the Archive*, trans. Daniel Heller-Roazen (New York: Zone Books, 2002), 75–76.

201. Levi, *Survival in Auschwitz*, 74.

202. Levinas, *Totality and Infinity*, 75.

203. Levinas, *Otherwise Than Being*, 74.

204. Levi, *Survival in Auschwitz*, 90.

205. Elie Wiesel, *Evil and Exile*, trans. Jon Rothschild (Notre Dame: University of Notre Dame Press, 1990), 25.

206. Emmanuel Levinas, *Collected Philosophical Papers*, trans. Alphonso Lingis (Dordrecht: Martinus Nijhoff, 1987), 138.

207. Ibid., 183.

208. Fackenheim, *To Mend the World*, 250.

209. Fackenheim, *God's Presence in History*, 67; Fackenheim ascribes this tale to Elie Wiesel.

210. Neher, *The Exile of the Word*, 123.

211. Wiesel, *Against Silence*, Vol. 1, 114.

212. Levinas, *Ethics and Infinity*, 109.

213. Elie Wiesel, *The Gates of the Forest*, trans. Frances Frenaye (New York: Holt, 1966), 33.

214. Leitner, *Fragments of Isabella*, 4.

215. Heimler, *Night of the Mist*, 30.

216. Vinocur, *A Book without a Title*, 66.

217. Emmanuel Levinas, *Existence and Existents*, trans. Alphonso Lingis (The Hague: Martinus Nijhoff, 1978), 57–58.

218. Levinas, *Ethics and Infinity*, 52.

219. Ibid.

220. Levi, *Survival in Auschwitz*, 29.

221. I owe this connection between the Who and the Why to the profound insight of my student Karl Sen Gupta.

222. Ann Richardson, "The Ethical Limitations of Holocaust Literary Representation," *ESharp: Borders and Boundaries* 5 (Summer 2005): 2–3.

223. Levinas, *Otherwise Than Being*, 11.

224. Emmanuel Levinas, *Difficult Freedom: Essays on Judaism*, trans. Sean Hand (Baltimore: Johns Hopkins University Press, 1990), 17.

225. Germaine Tillion, *Ravensbrück*, trans. Gerald Satterwhite (Garden City: Doubleday, 1975), 180.

226. Levinas, *Otherwise Than Being*, 18.

227. Levinas, *Totality and Infinity*, 214.

228. Zelizer, *Remembering to Forget*, 111.

229. Levinas, *Otherwise Than Being*, 48.

230. Levinas, *Nine Talmudic Readings*, 135.

231. Levinas, *Otherwise Than Being*, 151.

232. Alfred Rosenberg, *Race and Race History and Other Essays*, ed. Robert Pais (New York: Harper and Row, 1974), 131–32.

233. Quoted in Richard M. Lerner, *Final Solutions: Biology, Prejudice, and Genocide* (University Park: Pennsylvania State University Press, 1992), 39.

234. Uriel Tal, "On the *Study* of the Holocaust and Genocide," *Yad Vashem Studies* 13 (1979): 45; see also Robert Wistrich, *Hitler and the Holocaust* (New York: Modern Library, 2001), 240.

235. See Max Weinreich, *Hitler's Professors: The Part of Scholarship in Germany's Crimes against the Jewish People* (New Haven: Yale University Press, 1999), 78.

236. Rosenberg, *Race and Race History*, 34.

237. Quoted in Weinreich, *Hitler's Professors*, 26.

238. Rosenberg, *Race and Race History*, 183.

239. Steven T. Katz, *The Holocaust in Historical Context*, Vol. 1 (New York: Oxford University Press, 1994), 6; emphasis added.

240. Emil L. Fackenheim, *Jewish-Christian Relations after the Holocaust: Toward Post-Holocaust Theological Thought* (Chicago: The Joseph Cardinal Bernardin Jerusalem Lecture, 1977), 10.

241. Ibid., 14.

242. See Fackenheim, *To Mend the World*, 327–31.

243. Levinas, *Otherwise Than Being*, 43.

244. See Wiesel, *Evil and Exile*, 155; and Levi, *The Drowned and the Saved*, 31.

245. Levinas, *Otherwise Than Being*, 19.

246. Neher, *The Exile of the Word*, 37.

247. Ibid., 141.

248. A. Anatoli (Kuznetsov), *Babi Yar: A Document in the Form of a Novel*, trans. David Floyd (New York: Pocket Books, 1971), 356.

249. Bachya ibn Paquda, *Duties of the Heart*, Vol. 2, trans. Moses Hyamson (New York: Feldheim Publishers, 1970), 389.

250. Hannah Arendt, *The Jewish Writings*, ed. Jerome Kohn and Ron H. Feldman (New York: Schocken Books, 2007), 162.

251. Wiesel, *One Generation After*, 83.

252. Wiesel, *From the Kingdom of Memory*, 239.

253. Levinas, *Totality and Infinity*, 224.

254. Levinas, *Time and the Other*, 77.

255. Levi, *Survival in Auschwitz*, 90.

256. Primo Levi, *Se questo è un uomo* (Torino: Einaudi, 1989), 82.

257. Emmanuel Levinas, *Outside the Subject*, trans. Michael B. Smith (Stanford: Stanford University Press, 1994), 87.

258. Rosenzweig, *The Star of Redemption*, 224.

259. Levinas, *Ethics and Infinity*, 98–99.

260. Abraham ibn Ezra, *The Commentary of Ibn Ezra on Isaiah*, trans. Michael Friedlander (New York: Feldheim, 1943), 287.

261. Abraham Joshua Heschel, *The Sabbath: Its Meaning for Modern Man* (New York: Farrar, Straus, and Giroux, 1981), 100.

262. Emmanuel Levinas, "Dialogue with Emmanuel Levinas (with Richard Kearney)," in Richard A. Cohen, ed., *Face to Face with Lévinas* (Albany: State University of New York Press, 1986), 18.

263. Lyotard, *The Differend*, 101.

264. Leitner, *Fragments of Isabella*, 23.

265. Nyiszli, *Auschwitz*, 151.

266. Wiesel, *Legends of Our Time*, 25.

267. Michael Zylberberg, *A Warsaw Diary* (London: Vallentine Mitchell, 1969), 31.

268. Kaplan, *Scroll of Agony*, 267.

269. Ibid., 275–76.

270. Adam Czerniaków, *The Warsaw Ghetto Diary of Adam Czerniaków*, ed. Raul Hilberg, Stanislaw Staron, Joseph Kermisz, trans. Stanislaw Staron et al. (New York: Stein and Day, 1979), 218.

271. Emmanuel Ringelblum, *Notes from the Warsaw Ghetto*, trans. and ed. Jacob Sloan (New York: Schocken Books, 1974), 196–97.

272. Vladka Meed, *On Both Sides of the Wall*, trans. Benjamin Meed (Tel-Aviv: Hakibbutz Hameuchad, 1973), 334–35.

273. Ringelblum, *Notes from the Warsaw Ghetto*, 267.

274. David Kahane, *Lvov Ghetto Diary*, trans. Jerzy Michalowicz (Amherst: University of Massachusetts Press, 1990), 53.

275. Wiesel, *Legends of Our Time*, 25.

276. Wiesel, *Night*, 7.

277. Charlotte Delbo, *Useless Knowledge*, in *Auschwitz and After*, trans. Rosette Lamont (New Haven: Yale University Press, 1995), 228.

278. Emil Dorian, *The Quality of Witness*, ed. Marguerite Dorian, trans. Mara Soceanu Vamos (Philadelphia: Jewish Publication Society, 1982), 322.

279. Leon Wells, *The Death Brigade* (New York: Holocaust Library, 1978), 244.

280. Donat, *The Holocaust Kingdom*, 293.

281. Zivia Lubetkin, *In the Days of Destruction and Revolt*, trans. I. Tubbin (Tel-Aviv: Hakibbutz Hameuchad, 1981), 246.

282. Elie Wiesel, *The Jews of Silence*, trans. Neal Kozodoy (New York: Holt, Rinehart, and Winston, 1966), 36.

283. Levi, *The Drowned and the Saved*, 224–25.

284. Fania Fénelon, *Playing for Time*, trans. Judith Landry (New York: Atheneum, 1977), ix.

285. Leitner, *Fragments of Isabella*, 51.

286. Kitty Hart, *Return to Auschwitz* (New York: Atheneum, 1982), 163.

287. For a good discussion of this point, see Rosenzweig, *The Star of Redemption*, 155.

288. George Steiner, "The Long Life of Metaphor: An Approach to the 'Shoah,'" in *Writing and the Holocaust*, ed. Berel Lang 170.

289. Omer Bartov, *Murder in Our Midst: The Holocaust, Industrial Killing, and Representation* (New York: Oxford University Press, 1996), 58.

290. Ka-tzetnik 135633, *Shivitti*, 9.

291. Fackenheim, *To Mend the World*, 135.

292. Fackenheim, *Jewish-Christian Relations after the Holocaust*, 20.

293. Rosenberg, *Race and Race History*, 181.

294. Emmanuel Levinas, "Reflections on the Philosophy of Hitlerism," trans. Sean Hand, *Critical Inquiry* 17 (1990): 63; quoted in Josh Cohen, *Interrupting Auschwitz* (New York: Continuum, 2003), 5–6; emphasis in the original.

295. Levinas, *Totality and Infinity*, 46–47.

296. Levinas, *Collected Philosophical Papers*, 52.

297. Immanuel Kant, *Conflict of the Faculties*, trans. Mary J. Gregor (New York: Abaris, 1979), 95.

298. Newman, *The Hasidic Anthology*, 147.

299. Zelig Kalmanovitch, "A Diary of the Nazi Ghetto in Vilna," trans. and ed. Koppel S. Pinson, *YIVO Annual of Jewish Social Studies* 8 (1953): 52.

300. Judith Dribben, *And Some Shall Live* (Jerusalem: Keter, 1969), 24.

301. Levinas, *Otherwise Than Being*, 146; emphasis added.

302. Ibid., 38.

303. Levi, *Survival in Auschwitz*, 27.

304. See, for example, Yehuda HeChasid, *Sefer Chasidim*, trans. Avraham Yaakov Finkel (Northvale, NJ: Jason Aronson, 1997), 244.

305. Menachem M. Schneerson, *Torah Studies*, adapted by Jonathan Sacks, 2nd ed. (London: Lubavitch Foundation, 1986), 45.

306. Ka–tzetnik 135633, *Kaddish*, 97–98.

307. See Elie Wiesel, *Evil and Exile*, 39.

308. Wiesel, *Night*, 25.

309. Des Pres, *The Survivor*, 170.

310. See Zsuzsanna Ozsváth, *When the Danube Ran Red* (Syracuse: Syracuse University Press, 2010).

311. Nelly Sachs, *O the Chimneys: Selected Poems*, trans. Michael Hamberger et al. (New York: Farrar, Straus, and Giroux, 1967), 3.

312. André Schwarz-Bart, *The Last of the Just*, trans. Stephen Becker (New York: Overlook, 2000), 374.

313. Arnošt Lustig, *A Prayer for Katerina Horovitzova*, trans. Jeanne Nemcova (New York: Harper and Row, 1973), 50–51.

314. Emil L. Fackenheim, "Jewish Faith and the Holocaust," in *A Holocaust Reader: Responses to the Nazi Extermination*, ed. Michael L. Morgan (New York: Oxford University Press, 2001), 116.

315. Zelizer, *Remembering to Forget*, 202.

Part Two. The Literary Transcendence of Holocaust Representation

1. Theodor W. Adorno, *Prisms*, trans. Shierry Weber Nicholsen and Samuel Weber (Boston: MIT Press, 1983), 34.

2. Gertrude Kolmar, *My Gaze Is Turned Inward: Letters, 1934–1943*, ed. Johanna Woltmann, trans. Brigitte M. Goldstein (Evanston: Northwestern University Press, 2004), 76.

3. Emil Dorian, *The Quality of Witness*, ed. Marguerite Dorian, trans. Mara Soceanu Vamos (Philadelphia: Jewish Publication Society, 1982), 33.

4. Ibid., 229.

5. "The Trial of Adolf Eichmann, Session 68," 7 June 1961, State of Israel Ministry of Justice, *The Nizkor Project*, available at http://www.nizkor.org/hweb/people/e/eichmann-adolf/transcripts/Sessions/Session-068-01.html.

6. Suzanne Birnbaum, *Une Française juive est revenue: Auschwitz, Belsen, Raguhn* (Maulévrier, France: Éditions Hérault, 1989), 8; my translation.

7. Charles Joyon, *Qu'as-tu fait de ta jeunesse?* (Paris: Éditions Renée Lacoste, 1957), 7; my translation.

8. Hélène Berr, *The Journal of Hélène Berr*, trans. David Bellos (New York: Weinstein Books, 2008), 156.

9. Imre Kertész, "Who Owns Auschwitz?" *The Yale Journal of Criticism*, 14, no. 1 (2001): 268.

10. R. Clifton Spargo, "Introduction: On the Cultural Continuities of Literary Representation," in *After Representation? The Holocaust, Literature, and Culture*, ed. R. Clifton Spargo and Robert M. Ehrenreich (New Brunswick: Rutgers University Press, 2009), 5.

11. Karin Bauer, *Adorno's Nietzschean Narratives: Critiques of Ideology, Readings of Wagner* (Albany: State University of New York Press, 1999), 122.

12. Piotr Rawicz, *Blood from the Sky*, trans. Peter Wiles (New York: Harcourt, 1964), 295.

13. Ibid., 134.

14. Des Pres, *The Survivor*, 51–72.

15. Elie Wiesel, *A Mad Desire to Dance*, trans. Catherine Temerson (New York: Alfred A. Knopf, 2009), 101.

16. Levinas, *Totality and Infinity*, 78.

17. Ibid., 199.

18. Schwarz-Bart, *The Last of the Just*, 370.

19. Paul Celan, *Paul Celan: Poems*, trans. Michael Hamburger (New York: Persea Books, 1980), 143.

20. Ibid., 142.

21. Levi, *Survival in Auschwitz*, 66.

22. Fackenheim, *The Jewish Return into History*, 269.

23. See Fackenheim, *God's Presence in History*, 83.

24. Saul Friedlander, introduction to Saul Friedlander, ed., *Probing the Limits of Representation: Nazism and the "Final Solution"* (Cambridge: Harvard University Press, 1992), 2–3.

25. Blanchot, *The Writing of the Disaster*, 5.

26. Wiesel, *Against Silence*, Vol. 1, 239.

27. Irving Halperin, *Messengers of the Dead: Literature of the Holocaust* (Philadelphia: Westminster Press, 1970), 13–14.

28. Sem Dresden, *Persecution, Extermination, Literature,* trans. Henry G. Schogt (Toronto: University of Toronto Press, Inc., 1995), 58; I owe this source to my student Rebecca Thompson.

29. Wiesel, *From the Kingdom of Memory*, 173.

30. Alvin Rosenfeld, *A Double Dying: Reflections on Holocaust Literature* (Bloomington: Indiana University Press, 1980), 31.

31. Michael Bernard-Donals and Richard Glejzer, *Between Witness and Testimony: The Holocaust and the Limits of Representation* (Albany: State University of New York Press, 2001), ix.

32. Wiesel, *Twilight*, 100.

33. Ruth Franklin, *A Thousand Darknesses: Lies and Truth in Holocaust Fiction* (Oxford: Oxford University Press, 2011), 102.

34. Glowacka, *Disappearing Traces*, 9.

35. Wiesel, *Night*, 25.

36. Arnošt Lustig, *A Prayer for Katerina Horovitzova*, trans. Jeanne Nemcova (New York: Harper and Row, 1973), 50–51.

37. Jonathan Sacks, *Crisis and Covenant: Jewish Thought after the Holocaust* (Manchester: Manchester University Press, 1992), 242.

38. Alon Confino, "Why Did the Nazis Burn the Hebrew Bible? Nazi Germany, Representations of the Past, and the Holocaust," *The Journal of Modern History* 84 (June 2012): 394.

39. Elie Wiesel, *The Town beyond the Wall*, trans. Stephen Becker (New York: Avon, 1964), 103.

40. Pelagia Lewinska, *Twenty Months at Auschwitz*, trans. A. Teichner (New York: Lyle Stuart, 1968), 150.

41. Fackenheim, *To Mend the World*, 218.

42. Lawrence Langer, *The Holocaust and the Literary Imagination* (New Haven, Conn.: Yale University Press, 1975), 8.

43. Glowacka, *Disappearing Traces*, 165.

44. Levinas, *Otherwise Than Being*, 61.

45. Michael Bernard-Donals and Richard Glejzer, "Teaching (after) Auschwitz: Pedagogy between Redemption and Sublimity," in *Witnessing the Disaster: Essays on Representation and the Holocaust*, ed. Michael Bernard-Donals and Richard Glejzer (Madison: University of Wisconsin Press, 2003), 245.

46. Confino, "Why Did the Nazis Burn the Hebrew Bible?": 385.

47. Schwarz-Bart, *The Last of the Just*, 327.

48. Ibid., 366.

49. Sidra DeKoven Ezrahi, *By Words Alone: The Holocaust in Literature* (Chicago: University of Chicago Press, 1980), 2–3.

50. See Wiesel, *Legends of Our Time*, 230.

51. Rosenfeld, *A Double Dying*, 8.

52. Levi, *Survival in Auschwitz*, 26.

53. Ibid., 121–22.

54. Ibid., 121; emphasis added.

55. Ibid., 119.

56. Ibid., 104–105.

57. Fackenheim, *Quest for Past and Future*, 89.

58. Abraham Joshua Heschel, *The Prophets*, Vol. 1 (New York: Harper and Row, 1962), 172.

59. Glowacka, *Disappearing Traces*, 46.

60. Wiesel, *Night*, 7.

61. Ibid.

62. Wiesel, *One Generation After*, 28–29.

63. Wiesel, *Twilight*, 174.

64. Anatoli (Kuznetsov), *Babi Yar*, 365.

65. Emmanuel Levinas, *Is It Righteous to Be? Interviews with Emmanuel Levinas*, ed. Jill Robbins (Stanford: Stanford University Press, 2001), 228.

66. Barbara Vedder, "Translator's Note," in Tadeusz Borowski, *This Way for the Gas, Ladies and Gentlemen*, trans. Barbara Vedder (New York: Penguin Books, 1976), 9.

67. Levinas, *Otherwise Than Being*, 136.

68. Ibid., 15.

69. Levi, *Survival in Auschwitz*, 66.

70. Elie Wiesel, *Somewhere a Master: Further Hasidic Portraits and Legends*, trans. Marion Wiesel (New York: Summit Books, 1982), 201.

71. Levinas, *Otherwise Than Being*, 127.

72. Elie Wiesel, *Paroles d'étranger* (Paris: Éditions du Seuil, 1982), 172.

73. Filip Müller, *Auschwitz Inferno: The Testimony of a Sonderkommando*, trans. Susanna Flatauer (London: Routledge and Kegan Paul, 1979), 66.

74. Livia E. Bitton Jackson, *Elli: Coming of Age in the Holocaust* (New York: Times Books, 1980), 38.

75. Wiesel, *Paroles d'étranger*, 166.

76. Levinas, *Otherwise Than Being*, 11.

77. Jakov Lind, *Landscape in Concrete*, trans. Ralph Manheim (New York: Pocket Books, 1968), 140.

78. Haim Gouri, *The Chocolate Deal*, trans. Seymour Simkes (New York: Holt, 1968), 56.

79. Wiesel, *Legends of Our Time*, 25.

80. Levinas, *Otherwise Than Being*, 169–70.

81. Emmanuel Levinas, *Proper Names*, trans. Michael B. Smith (Stanford: Stanford University Press, 1996), 43; my emphasis.

82. Levi, *Survival in Auschwitz*, 90.

83. André Neher, *The Exile of the Word: From the Silence of the Bible to the Silence of Auschwitz*, trans. David Maisel (Philadelphia: Jewish Publication Society, 1981), 143.

84. Wiesel, *Against Silence*, Vol. 2, 249.

85. See ibid., 82.

86. Karla Grierson, *Discours d'Auschwitz: Littérarité, représentation, symbolization* (Paris: Honoré Champion Éditeur, 2003), 337–38; my translation.

87. Levinas, *Difficult Freedom*, 281.

88. Emmanuel Levinas, *Of God Who Comes to Mind*, trans. Bettina Bergo (Stanford: Stanford University Press, 1998), 148.

89. Ibid.

90. Levinas, *Ethics and Infinity*, 99.

91. Levinas, *Time and the Other*, 77.

92. Levinas, *Proper Names*, 95; emphasis in the original.

93. Levinas, *Time and the Other*, 104.

94. Ibid., 113.

95. Levi, *Survival in Auschwitz*, 29.

96. Fackenheim, *Quest for Past and Future*, 6.

97. Levinas, *Totality and Infinity*, 62.

98. Levinas, *Otherwise Than Being*, 11.

99. Levi, *Survival in Auschwitz*, 16.

100. See Ilya Ehrenburg and Vasily Grossman, *The Complete Black Book of Russian Jewry*, trans. and ed. David Patterson (Piscataway: Transaction Publishers, 2002), 479.

101. Ka-tzetnik 135633, *Star of Ashes*, 179.

102. Ibid., 190.

103. Ibid., 35.

104. Ibid., 191.

105. Ka-tzetnik 135633, *Atrocity*, trans. Nina De-Nur (New York: Kensington, 1977).

106. Levinas, *Otherwise Than Being*, 183–84; emphasis in the original.

107. Elie Wiesel, *Zalman or The Madness of God*, adapted for the stage by Marion Wiesel (New York: Random House, 1974), 88.

108. Ka-tzetnik 135633, *Shivitti*, 12.

109. Wiesel, *A Mad Desire to Dance*, 13.

110. Simon Wiesenthal, *The Sunflower*, trans. H. A. Piehler (New York: Schocken Books, 1976), 14–15.

111. Simon Wiesenthal, *Die Sonnenblume: Von Schuld und Vergebung* (Hamburg: Hoffman and Campe, 1970), 13.

112. Wiesel, *The Town beyond the Wall*, 123.

113. See Martin Buber, *The Legend of the Baal Shem*, trans. Maurice Friedman (New York: Schocken Books, 1969), 27.

114. Louis I. Newman, *The Hasidic Anthology* (New York: Schocken Books, 1963), 147.

115. Buber, *I and Thou*, 57.

116. Abraham Joshua Heschel, *Man's Quest for God: Studies in Prayer and Symbolism* (New York: Charles Scribner's Sons, 1954), 76.

117. Elie Wiesel, *Ani Maamin: A Song Lost and Found Again*, trans. Marion Wiesel (New York: Random House, 1973), 15.

118. Ibid., 107.

119. Wiesel, *Legends of Our Time*, 18.

120. Wiesel, *Twilight*, 141–42.

121. Elie Wiesel, *The Time of the Uprooted*, trans. David Hapgood (New York: Schocken Books, 2005), 80–81.

122. Jackson, *Elli*, 34.

123. Heimler, *Night of the Mist*, 186.

124. Müller, *Auschwitz Inferno*, 1–2.

125. Fénelon, *Playing for Time*, 15.

126. Gerda Weissmann Klein, *All But My Life* (New York: Hill and Wang, 1957), 20.

127. See Chayyim Vital, *The Tree of Life (Ets Chayyim)*, trans. D. W. Menzi and Z. Padeh (Northvale, NJ: Aronson, 1999), xxxii.

128. David Kahane, *Lvov Ghetto Diary*, trans. Jerzy Michalowicz (Amherst: University of Massachusetts Press, 1990), 45.

129. Levinas, *Otherwise Than Being*, 144.

130. Arnošt Lustig, "The Lemon," in *Diamonds of the Night*, trans. Jeanne Nemcova (Washington, DC: Inscape, 1978), 28.

131. Levinas, *Ethics and Infinity*, 120.

132. Levinas, *Otherwise Than Being*, 114.

133. Levinas, *Totality and Infinity*, 225.

134. Ka-tznetik 135633, *House of Dolls*, trans. Moshe M. Kohn (New York: Pyramid, 1958), 212.

135. Améry, *At the Mind's Limits*, 24.

136. Fackenheim, *The Jewish Return into History*, 246.

137. Elie Wiesel, *Le testament d'un poète juif assassin* (Paris: Éditions du Seuil, 1980), 269.

138. Wiesel, *The Testament*, 285.

139. Albert Camus, *The Myth of Sisyphus*, trans. Justin O'Brien (New York: Random House, 1955), 3.

140. Elie Wiesel, *The Oath* (New York: Avon, 1973), 42.

141. Levinas, *Ethics and Infinity*, 98.

142. Levinas, *Otherwise Than Being*, 15.

143. Anna Langfus, *The Whole Land Brimstone*, trans. Peter Wiles (New York: Pantheon, 1962), 305.

144. Victor Klemperer, *I Will Bear Witness: A Diary of the Nazi Years, 1942–1945*, trans. Martin Chalmers (New York: Random House, 1999), 277.

145. Levi, *Survival in Auschwitz*, 42.

146. Levinas, *Totality and Infinity*, 257–58.

147. Delbo, *None of Us Will Return*, 15.

148. Leitner, *Fragments of Isabella*, 94.

149. Wiesel, *Night*, 30.

150. Levinas, *Otherwise Than Being*, 76.

151. Ibid., 82.

152. Ibid., 139.

153. Levi, *Survival in Auschwitz*, 42.

154. Levinas, *Otherwise Than Being*, 6.

155. Ibid., 54.

156. Ibid., 70.

157. Ibid., 78; emphasis added.

158. Ibid., 75.

159. Ibid., 77; emphasis added.

160. Levi, *Survival in Auschwitz*, 74.161. Levinas, *Otherwise Than Being*, 74.

162. Levinas, *Otherwise Than Being*, 151.

163. Bakhtin, *Art and Answerability*, 56.

164. Buber, *I and Thou*, 164.

165. Ana Vinocur, *A Book without a Title*, trans. Valentine Isaac and Ricardo Iglesia (New York: Vantage, 1976), 88.

166. Leitner, *Fragments of Isabella*, 94.

167. See Franz Rosenzweig, *The Star of Redemption*, trans. William W. Hallo (Boston: Beacon Press, 1972), 245–46.

168. Quoted in Milton Aron, *Ideas and Ideals of the Hassidim* (Secaucus: Citadel, 1969),150.

169. Levi, *The Reawakening*, 128.

170. Richard Walther Darré, *Um Blut und Boden: Reden und Aufsätze* (Munich: Zentralverlag der NSDAP, 1940), 28.

171. Ernst Lehmann, *Biologischer Wille: Wege und Ziele biologischer Arbeit im neuen Reich* (Munich: Zentralverlag der NSDAP, 1934), 10–11.

172. John Felsteiner, *Paul Celan: Poet, Survivor, Jew* (New Haven: Yale University Press, 1995), 238.

173. Emmanuel Levinas, *Existence and Existents*, trans. Alphonso Lingis (The Hague: Martinus Nijhoff, 1978), 92.

174. Emmanuel Levinas, "Revelation in the Jewish Tradition," trans. Sarah Richmond, in *The Lévinas Reader*, ed. Sean Hand (Oxford: Basil Blackwell, 1989), 203.

175. Emmanuel Levinas, "Dialogue with Emmanuel Levinas," in *Face to face with Levinas*, ed. Richard A. Cohen (Albany: State University of New York Press, 1986), 23.

176. Wiesel, *The Gates of the Forest*, 33.

177. Levinas, *Otherwise Than Being*, 171.

178. Buber, *I and Thou*, 54.

179. Ibid., 56.

180. Emmanuel Levinas, "Useless Suffering," in *The Provocation of Levinas: Rethinking the Other*, ed. Robert Bernasconi and David Wood (London: Routledge, 1988), 157.

181. Wiesel, *The Town beyond the Wall*, 127.

182. Levinas, *Otherwise Than Being*, 153.

183. Bakhtin, *Estetika slovesnogo tvorchestva*, 246; my translation.

184. Ibid., 285; emphasis in the original; my translation.

185. Mikhail Bakhtin, *The Dialogic Imagination*, trans. Caryl Emerson and Michael Holquist (Austin: University of Texas Press, 1981), 252–53.

186. Wiesel, *Against Silence*, Vol. 3, 197.

187. Levinas, *Otherwise Than Being*, 64.

188. Levinas, *Totality and Infinity*, 170.

189. Levinas, *Otherwise Than Being*, 40.

190. Ibid., 6.

191. Ibid., 147.

192. Ibid., 150.

193. Levinas, *Ethics and Infinity*, 66.

194. Levinas, *Time and the Other*, 88.

195. Levinas, *Difficult Freedom*, 34.

196. Levinas, *Otherwise than Being*, 114.

197. A term used in Lawrence Langer, *Admitting the Holocaust* (Oxford,: Oxford University Press, 1995), 46.

198. Levinas, *Otherwise Than Being*, 164.

199. Ibid., 18.

200. Ibid., 19.

201. Ibid., 118.

202. Ibid., 151.

203. Murray Kohn, *Is the Holocaust Vanishing? A Survivor's Reflections on the Academic Waning of Memory and Jewish Identity in the Post-Auschwitz Era* (Lanham, MD: Hamilton Books, 2005).

204. James E. Young, "Interpreting Literary Testimony: A Preface to Rereading Holocaust Diaries and Memoirs," *New Literary History* 18 (1987): 414.

205. Ibid.

206. Emil L. Fackenheim, *Jewish Philosophers and Jewish Philosophy*, ed. Michael Morgan (Bloomington: Indiana University Press, 1996), 133.

207. Samuel Pisar, *Of Blood and Hope* (Boston: Little, Brown, 1979), 66.

208. Améry, *At the Mind's Limits*, 7.

209. Ibid., 19.

210. Wiesenthal, *The Sunflower*, 41.

211. Améry, *At the Mind's Limits*, 19.

212. Fackenheim, *To Mend the World*, 285.

213. Leon Wells, *The Death Brigade* (New York: Holocaust Library, 1978), 187.

214. Emil L. Fackenheim, *The Jewish Bible after the Holocaust* (Bloomington: Indiana University Press, 1990), 68.

215. Wells, *The Death Brigade*, 141–42.

216. Levinas, *Totality and Infinity*, 197–98.

217. Yehudah Leib Alter, *The Language of Truth: The Torah Commentary of the Sefat Emet*, trans. Arthur Green (Philadelphia: Jewish Publication Society, 1998), 10.

218. Fackenheim, *Quest for Past and Future*, 38.

219. Borowski, *This Way for the Gas, Ladies and Gentlemen*, 105.

220. Martin Heidegger, *Nietzsche*, Vol. 1, trans. D. Krell (San Francisco: Harper and Row, 1979), 18.

221. Levinas, *Totality and Infinity*, 39.

222. Ibid., 87.

223. Ibid., 46.

224. Zsuzsanna Ozsváth, *In the Footsteps of Orpheus: The Life and Times of Miklós Radnóti* (Bloomington: Indiana University Press, 2000), 193.

225. Levi, *Survival in Auschwitz*, 86.

226. "Minutes of the Wannsee Conference," 20 January 1942, available at http://prorev.com/wannsee.htm; emphasis added.

227. Fénelon, *Playing for Time*, 70.

228. Olga Lengyel, *Five Chimneys* (London: Granada, 1972), 198.

229. Ibid., 28.

230. Sara Zyskind, *Stolen Years*, trans. Margarit Inbar (Minneapolis: Lerner, 1981), 185.

231. Ibid., 192.

232. Ibid., 185.

233. Wiesel, *From the Kingdom of Memory*, 13.

234. Wells, *The Death Brigade*, 143.

235. Levi, *Survival in Auschwitz*, 90.

236. Ka-tzetnik 135633, *House of Dolls*, 63.

237. Fénelon, *Playing for Time*, ix.

238. Ka-tzetnik 135633, *Sunrise over Hell*, trans. Nina De-Nur (London: Allen, 1977), 143.

239. See, for example, Levi, *Survival in Auschwitz*, 19.

240. Scarry, *The Body in Pain*, 54.

241. Levi, *Survival in Auschwitz*, 26.

242. Ka-tzetnik 135633, *Star of Ashes*, 69.

243. Ka-tzetnik 135633, *Kokhev ha-efer* (Tel-Aviv: Hamenora, 1971), 69.

244. Buber, *I and Thou*, 90.

245. Wiesel, *The Town beyond the Wall*, 147.

246. Wiesel, *Souls on Fire*, 86.

247. Rudolf Vrba and Alan Bestic, *I Cannot Forgive* (Vancouver: Regent College Publishing, 1997), 91.

248. See Wiesel, *Evil and Exile*, 155; Levi, *The Drowned and the Saved*, 31.

249. See Levinas, *Ethics and Infinity*, 88–89.

250. Fénelon, *Playing for Time*, 181.

251. Levi, *Survival in Auschwitz*, 123.

252. Kalonymos Kalmish Shapira, *Sacred Fire: Torah from the Years of Fury 1939–1942*, trans. J. Hershy Worch, ed. Deborah Miller (Northvale, NJ: Jason Aronson, 2000), 328.

253. Ka-tzetnik 135633, *Pipel* (Tel Aviv: Hakibbutz Hameuchad, 1988), 119.

254. Levinas, *Totality and Infinity*, 91.

255. Ka-tzetnik 135633, *Pipel*, 67.

256. Wiesel, *Night*, 110.

257. See Levinas, *Ethics and Infinity*, 87.

258. See, for example, Robert Eaglestone, *Postmodernism and Holocaust Denial* (Duxford, UK: Icon Books, 2001), 39.

259. Levinas, *Otherwise Than Being*, 91.

260. Levinas, *Ethics and Infinity*, 109.

261. Levinas, *Totality and Infinity*, 292.

262. Ibid., 62.

263. Ibid., 33; emphasis in the original.

264. Ibid., 34–35.

265. Ka-tzetnik 135633, *Beit habubot* (Tel Aviv: Kibbutz Hameuchad, 1987), 131.

266. Rabbi Avraham, *Galya Raza* (Jerusalem: Yirid Hasfarim, 2000), 417–18; my translation.

267. Wiesel, *A Beggar in Jerusalem*, 77.

268. Levinas, *Otherwise than Being*, 193.

269. Levinas, *Totality and Infinity*, 206; emphasis added.

270. Ibid., 97.

271. Levinas, *Otherwise Than Being*, 122.

272. Quoted in Joseph Dan, ed., *The Early Kabbalah*, trans. Ronald C. Kiener (New York: Paulist Press, 1986), 155.

273. Levinas, *Totality and Infinity*, 206.

274. Ibid., 199.

275. Levinas, *Ethics and Infinity*, 105.

276. Levinas, *Collected Philosophical Papers*, 96.

277. Levinas, "Revelation in the Jewish Tradition," 204.

278. See Emmanuel Levinas, *New Talmudic Readings*, trans. Richard A. Cohen (Pittsburgh: Duquesne University Press, 1999), 69–70.

279. Ibid., 75–76.

280. Levinas, *Totality and Infinity*, 213.

281. Levinas, *Ethics and Infinity*, 86.

282. Wiesel, *The Testament*, 38.

283. The tradition is based on a talmudic interpretation of Isaiah 30:18, where it is written, *Ki-elokei mishpat HaShem ashrei kol-chikhei lo*, that is, "For the Lord is a God of justice; blessed are those who await him." The word *him* is a translation of the Hebrew word *lo*, whose letters *lamed* and *vav* have a numerical value of thirty-six; hence, the thirty-six righteous people who sustain the world (*Sukkah* 45b, *Sanhedrin* 97b).

284. Heschel, *The Sabbath*, 100.

285. Rosenzweig, *The Star of Redemption*, 26–27.

286. The association of the word *ken* with the names of God lies in the numerical value of *ken*, which is seventy, and there are seventy names of God (see *Zohar* II, 216a).

287. Levinas, *Otherwise Than Being*, 49.

288. Buber, *I and Thou*, 57.

289. Quoted in Victor Cohen, ed., *The Soul of the Torah: Insights of the Chasidic Masters on the Weekly Torah Portions* (Northvale, NJ: Jason Aronson, 2000), 98.

290. See Markus Zusak, *The Book Thief* (New York: Alfred A. Knopf, 2007).

291. Levi, *The Drowned and the Saved*, 93–94.

292. Levinas, *Existence and Existents*, 60.

293. Ibid., 59.

294. Levi, *Survival in Auschwitz*, 26.

295. Nomberg-Przytyk, *Auschwitz*, 45.

296. Levi, *The Reawakening*, 128.

297. Levinas, *Time and the Other*, 77.

298. Wiesel, *One Generation After*, 72–73.

299. Fackenheim, *God's Presence in History*, 74.

300. Abraham Joshua Heschel, *The Prophets*, Vol. 2 (New York: Harper and Row, 1975), 37.

301. See, for example, the *Sefer Chasidim* (244) of the medieval sage Rabbi Yehuda HeChasid; see also Nachman of Breslov, *Tikkun*, trans. Avraham Greenbaum (Jerusalem: Breslov Research Institute, 1984), 103.

302. Fackenheim, *To Mend the World*, 100.

303. Levi, *Survival in Auschwitz*, 90.

304. Ibid.

305. Fackenheim, *The Jewish Return into History*, 246.

306. Levi, *Survival in Auschwitz*, 90.

307. Fackenheim, *To Mend the World*, 100.

308. Levi, *Survival in Auschwitz*, 90.

309. Wiesel, *Legends of Our Time*, 176.

310. Lyotard, *Heidegger and "the jews,"* 26.

311. Levi, *Survival in Auschwitz*, 62.

312. See Nomberg-Przytyk, *Auschwitz*, 60.

313. Levinas, *Totality and Infinity*, 137.

314. Ibid., 162.

315. Levi, *The Drowned and the Saved*, 53–54.

316. See Ringelblum, *Notes from the Warsaw Ghetto*, 84.

317. Ka-tzetnik 135633, *Shivitti*, 13.

318. Johann Wolfgang von Goethe, *Faust, a Tragedy: Part I*, trans. Martin Greenberg (New Haven: Yale University Press, 1992), 54.

319. John Felstiner, *Paul Celan: Poet, Survivor, Jew* (New Haven: Yale University Press, 1995), 27.

320. Ibid., 33.

321. Levi, *Survival in Auschwitz*, 90.

322. See Saadia Gaon, *The Book of Belief and Opinions*, trans. Samuel Rosenblatt (New Haven: Yale University Press, 1976), 255.

323. Rothberg, *Traumatic Realism*, 86.

324. Elie Wiesel, "The Holocaust as Literary Inspiration," in Elie Wiesel et al., *Dimensions of the Holocaust* (Evanston: Northwestern University Press, 1977), 16.

325. Levinas, *Totality and Infinity*, 179.

326. Kahane, *Lvov Ghetto Diary*, 53.

327. Wiesel, *Night*, 33.

328. Ibid., 77.

329. Ibid., 92.

330. Ibid., 7.

331. Ibid., 5.

332. Wiesel, *A Beggar in Jerusalem*, 80.

333. Ka-tzetnik 135633, *Star of Ashes*, 35.

334. Ludwig Wittgenstein, *Tractatus Logico-Philosophicus*, trans. C. K. Ogden (London: Kegan Paul, Trench, Trubner, 1922), 185.

335. Ozsváth, *In the Footsteps of Orpheus*, 218.

336. Levinas, *Collected Philosophical Papers*, 100.

337. Yitzhak Katznelson, *Vittel Diary*, trans. Myer Cohn, 2nd ed. (Tel-Aviv: Hakibbutz Hameuchad, 1972), 228.

338. Fackenheim, *The Jewish Bible after the Holocaust*, 67.

339. Fackenheim, *The Jewish Bible after the Holocaust*, 87.

340. Gisella Perl, *I Was a Doctor in Auschwitz* (New York: International Universities Press, 1948), 84.

341. Levinas, *Totality and Infinity*, 277.

342. Levinas, *Otherwise Than Being*, 193.

343. Fackenheim, *The Jewish Bible after the Holocaust*, 47.

344. Czerniaków, *The Warsaw Ghetto Diary of Adam Czerniaków*, 70.

345. Berr, *The Journal of Hélène Berr*, 243.

346. Wiesel, *A Jew Today*, 81.

347. Wiesenthal, *The Sunflower*, 47.

348. David Patterson, *In Dialogue and Dilemma with Elie Wiesel* (Wakefield, NH: Longwood Academic, 1991), 21.

349. Wells, *The Death Brigade*, 107.

350. Donat, *The Holocaust Kingdom*, 94.

351. Wiesenthal, *The Sunflower*, 71.

352. Sim Kessel, *Hanged at Auschwitz*, trans. Melville and Delight Wallace (New York: Stein and Day, 1972), 46.

353. Levi, *The Reawakening*, 22–23.

354. See Abraham ibn Ezra, *The Secret of the Torah*, trans. H. Norman Strickman (Northvale, NJ: Jason Aronson, 1995), 96–97.

355. Theodor W. Adorno, *Aesthetic Theory*, trans. R. Hullot-Kentor (Minneapolis: Minnesota University Press, 1997), 153; see also Cohen, *Interrupting Auschwitz*, 65.

356. Joseph Gikatilla, *Sha'are Orah: Gates of Light*, trans. Avi Weinstein (San Francisco: HarperCollins, 1994), 87.

357. Wiesel, *Against Silence*, Vol. 3, 309.

358. Wiesel, *Night*, 64.

359. Ka-tzetnik 135633, *Shivitti*, 59.

360. Quoted in Harry James Cargas, *In Conversation with Elie Wiesel* (New York: Paulist Press, 1976), 2.

361. Wiesel, *Ani Maamin*, 39, 41.

362. Ringelblum, *Notes from the Warsaw Ghetto*, 135.

363. Fackenheim, *God's Presence in History*, 68–69.

364. Nelly Sachs, "Schon vom Arm des himmlischen Trostes umfangen," in Sachs, *O the Chimneys*, 14.

365. Améry, *At the Mind's Limits*, 7.

366. Ibid., 10.

Part Three. The Photographic Transcendence of Holocaust Representation

1. Didi-Huberman, *Images in Spite of All*, 26.

2. Quoted in ibid., 27.

3. Roland Barthes, *Camera Lucida: Reflections on Photography*, trans. Richard Howard (New York: Hill and Wang, 1981), 96.

4. Dan Stone, "Chaos and Continuity: Representations of Auschwitz," in *Representations of Auschwitz: Fifty Years of Photographs, Paintings, and Graphics*, ed. Yasmin Doorsy(Oświęcim: Auschwitz-Birkenau State Museum, 1995), 27.

5. Sontag, *On Photography*, 3.

6. Susan Sontag, *Regarding the Pain of Others* (New York: Farrar, Straus, and Giroux, 2003), 95.

7. Levi, *Survival in Auschwitz*, 39.

8. Gerhard Schoenberner, *The Yellow Star: The Persecution of the Jews in Europe, 1933–1945* (New York: Fordham University Press, 2004), xiii.

9. Isabel Wollaston, "The Absent, the Partial and the Iconic in Archival Photographs of the Holocaust," *Jewish Culture and History* 12, no. 3 (2010): 441.

10. Barbie Zelizer, *Remembering to Forget: Holocaust Memory through the Camera's Eye* (Chicago: The University of Chicago Press, 1998), 10.

11. Janina Struk, *Photographing the Holocaust: Interpretations of the Evidence* (London: I. B. Tauris, 2004), 97.

12. Photo from "Photographs from Łódź Ghetto—Litzmannstadt—Fotografowie getta," accessed at http://jimbaotoday.blogspot.com/2013/03/photographs-from-lodz-ghetto.html.

13. Barthes, *Camera Lucida*, 9.

14. Quoted in Bigsby, *Remembering and Imagining the Holocaust*, 81.

15. Didi-Huberman, *Images in Spite of All*, 68.

16. Sontag, *On Photography*, 4.

17. Ibid., 14.

18. Levinas, *Totality and Infinity*, 195.

19. Struk, *Photographing the Holocaust*, 70.

20. Ibid., 79.

21. A destitute young boy lies on the pavement in the Warsaw ghetto as other children walk by." United States Holocaust Memorial Museum, Photo Archive number 69946; see Günther Schwarberg, *In the Ghetto of Warsaw: Photographs by Heinrich Jöst* (Göttingen: Steidl, 2001).

22. Struk, *Photographing the Holocaust*, 80.

23. Sontag, *On Photography*, 168.

24. Levinas, *Nine Talmudic Readings*, 33; my emphasis.

25. Marianne Hirsch, "Surviving Images: Holocaust Photographs and the Work of Postmemory," in *Visual Culture and the Holocaust*, Barbie Zelizer (New Brunswick: Rutgers University Press, 2001), 237.

26. Barthes, *Camera Lucida*, 91.

27. Struk, *Photographing the Holocaust*, 5–6.

28. Marianne Hirsch, *The Generation of Postmemory: Writing and Visual Culture After the Holocaust* (New York: Columbia University Press, 2012), 107.

29. Struk, *Photographing the Holocaust*, 203.

30. Wiesel, *Against Silence*, Vol. 1, 239.

31. Ida Fink, "Traces," in Ida Fink, *A Scrap of Time and Other Stories*, trans. Madeline Levine and Francine Prose (Evanston: Northwestern University Press, 1995), 136.

32. Marianne Hirsch, "Surviving Images," 224–25.

33. Levinas, *Collected Philosophical Papers*, 106.

34. Ibid., 136.

35. Hirsch, *The Generation of Postmemory*, 110.

36. Levinas, *Collected Philosophical Papers*, 65–66.

37. Ibid., 62.

38. Ibid., 105.

39. Yad Vashem, "Auschwitz, Poland, A pile of shoes," Item ID 102153, Archive Signature 9CO1, available at http://collections1.yadvashem.org/notebook.asp?lang=ENG&dlang=ENG&module=search&page=list&rsvr=7¶m=<uppernav>simple</><nob>1</><rsvr_ser>@@7</><search_type>simple</><view>records</><nrsvr>N</><sort>TI</><dispq>z1zTitle: z3z102153, Literal z1zItem ID: z3z102153, Literal z1zDatabanks: z3z Photos Archive</><dlang>ENG</><query_name>jaguar51_4572_404451</><quantity>15</><start_entry>1</><num_of_items>1</><query_index>@TI@SN</><thumb>0</><smode>dts</><first_item>1</><last_item>1</><book_id>102153</><mainimage>/arch_srika/1A-245G/1A-35G/9CO1_.jpg</>¶m2=<num_fields>12</><nvf>11</><nvr>3</><search_type>simple</>&site=sapir.

40. Glowacka, *Disappearing Traces*, 165.

41. Levi, *Survival in Auschwitz*, 67.

42. Sontag, *On Photography*, 154.

43. Aharon Appelfeld, *Essays in the First Person* (Jerusalem: Zionist Library, 1980), 21.

44. Sutzkever, "A Cartload of Shoes," trans. David G. Roskies, in *Holocaust Poetry*, ed. Hilda Schiff (New York: St. Martin's, 1996) 27.

45. Fackenheim, *God's Presence in History*, 80.

46. Levinas, *Nine Talmudic Readings*, 135.

47. Nelly Sachs, *Eli: A Mystery Play of the Sufferings of Israel*, trans. Christopher Holme, in *Plays of the Holocaust: An International Anthology*, ed. Elinor Fuchs, ed., Elinor Fuchs (New York: Theatre Communications Group, 1987), 51.

48. Levi, *Survival in Auschwitz*, 34.

49. Yad Vashem, Poland, 31/07/1941, Humiliating a Jew wrapped in a prayer shawl on "Bloody Wednesday," Item ID 56308, Archive Signature 1878, Album Number FA214/133, available at http://collections1.yadvashem.org/notebook.asp?lang=ENG&dlang=ENG&module=search&page=list&rsvr=7¶m=<uppernav>simple</><nob>1</><rsvr_ser>@@7</><search_type>simple</><view>records</><nrsvr>N</><sort>TI</><dispq>z1zTitle: z3z56308, Literal z1zItem ID: z3z56308,Literal z1zDatabanks: z3z Photos Archive</><dlang>ENG</><query_name>jaguar51_2496_030984</><quantity>15</><start_entry>1</><num_of_items>1</><query_index>@TI@SN</><thumb>0</><smode>dts</><first_item>1</><last_item>1</><book_id>56308</><mainimage>/arch_srika/Albums/211-245/214_133.JPG</>¶m2=<num_fields>12</><nvf>11</><nvr>3</><search_type>simple</>&site=sapir.

50. Ka-tzetnik 135633, *Shivitti*, xvii–xix.

51. See Eliahu Klein's note in Chayyim Vital, *Kabbalah of Creation: Isaac Luria's Earlier Mysticism*, trans. Eliahu Klein (Northvale, NJ: Aronson, 2000), 279–80.

52. Nehunia ben Hakanah, *Sefer HaTemunah* (Jerusalem: Nezer Sharga, 1998), 2.

53. Levinas, *Otherwise Than Being*, 12.

54. Levinas, *Ethics and Infinity*, 109.

55. Levinas, *Collected Philosophical Papers*, 166.

56. Ibid., 169.

57. Abraham Joshua Heschel, *Between God and Man: An Interpretation of Judaism*, ed. Fritz A. Rothschild (New York: The Free Press, 1959), 56.

58. Buber, *I and Thou*, 158.

59. Levinas, *Otherwise Than Being*, 13.

60. Ibid., 152.

61. Ibid., 149.

62. Photo taken in the Ukraine in 1942, available at http://ohdelaholocaust-project.pbworks.com/w/page/4260207/Einsatzgruppen; see Yitzhak Arad, *The Pictorial History of the Holocaust* (Jerusalem: Yad Vashem, 1990), 200.

63. Ka-tzetnik 135633, *Star of Ashes*, 52.

64. Levinas, *Otherwise Than Being*, 82.

65. Levinas, *Collected Philosophical Papers*, 70.

66. Wiesel, *Ani Maamin*, 89, 91.

67. Sarra Gleikh, "The Diary of Sarra Gleikh," in *The Complete Black Book of Russian Jewry*, ed. Ilya Ehrenburg and Vasily Grossman, English version trans. and ed. David Patterson (New Brunswick, NJ: Transaction Publishers, 2002), 54.

68. "Jews captured by SS and SD troops during the suppression of the Warsaw ghetto uprising are forced to leave their shelter and marched to the Umschlagplatz for deportation," United States Holocaust Memorial Museum Photo Archives, Photograph 26543, available at http://collections.ushmm.org/search/catalog/pa1088110.

69. Jürgen Stroop, *The Stroop Report: The Jewish Quarter of Warsaw Is No More!*, trans. Sybil Milton (New York: Pantheon, 1980), 15.

70. See Danna Nolan Fewell and Gary A. Phillips, *Icon of Loss: The Haunting Child of Samuel Bak* (Syracuse: Syracuse University Press, 2009).

71. See Franklin H. Littell, *The Crucifixion of the Jews* (Macon: Mercer University Press, 1986).

72. See Yehuda Bauer, *A History of the Holocaust*, revised edition (New York: Franklin Watts, 1982), 170.

73. Chaim A. Kaplan, *Scroll of Agony: The Warsaw Diary of Chaim A. Kaplan*, trans. and ed. Abraham I. Katsh (New York: Collier, 1973), 332–33.

74. Hirsch, *The Generation of Postmemory*, 129.

75. Edmond Jabès, *The Book of Yukel and Return to the Book*, trans. Rosemarie Waldrop (Middletown, CT: Wesleyan University Press, 1977), 195.

76. Czerniaków, *The Warsaw Ghetto Diary of Adam Czerniaków*, 366.

77. Ringelblum, *Notes from the Warsaw Ghetto*, 158.

78. Ibid., 204–205.

79. Ibid., 237.

80. Janusz Korczak, *Ghetto Diary*, trans. Jerzy Bachrach and Barbara Krzywicka (New York: Holocaust Library, 1978), 121.

81. Ibid., 146.

82. Menahem Kon, "Fragments of a Diary (August 6, 1942–October 1, 1942)," trans. M. Z. Prives, in *To Live with Honor and Die with Honor: Selected Documents from the Warsaw Ghetto Underground Archives "O.S.,"* ed. Joseph Kermish (Jerusalem: Yad Vashem, 1986), 80.

83. Wiesel, *The Oath*, 132.

84. Elijah ben Shlomo Zalman Kremer, *Even Shleimah*, trans. Yaakov Singer and Chaim David Ackerman (Southfield, MI: Targum Press, 1992), 45.

85. Glowacka, *Disappearing Traces*, 143.

86. Hirsch, *The Generation of Postmemory*, 162.

87. Quoted in Patricia Heberer, *Children during the Holocaust* (Lanham, MD: Rowman and Littlefield, 2011), 379.

88. "Bergen-Belsen, Germany, a survivor inside a barrack, 1945," Yad Vashem Photo Archives M.2, ID 50722, Archival Signature 5031/45, available at

http://collections1.yadvashem.org/notebook.asp?lang=ENG&dlang=ENG&module=search&page=next_list&rsvr=7¶m=<uppernav>simple</><nob>3</><rsvr_ser>@@7</><search_type>simple</><view>records</><nrsvr>N</><sort>TI</><dispq>z1z Title: z3zsurvivor, Literal z1zDatabanks: z3z Photos Archive</><dlang>ENG</><query_name>jaguar50_2852_018721</><quantity>15</><start_entry>46</><num_of_items>294</><query_index>@TI</><thumb>0</><smode>dts</><book_id>50722</><mainimage>/arch_srika/5001-5500/5001-5098/5031_45.JPG</>¶m2=&site=sapir.

89. Emmanuel Levinas, *Humanism of the Other*, trans. Nidra Poller (Urbana: University of Illinois Press, 2006), 32.

90. Levinas, *Collected Philosophical Papers*, 73.

91. Levinas, *Ethics and Infinity*, 86.

92. See Louis Finkelstein, *Akiba: Scholar, Saint and Martyr* (New York: Atheneum, 1981), 103.

93. Quoted in Dennis Prager and Joseph Telushkin, *Why the Jews? The Reason for Antisemitism* (New York: Simon and Schuster, 2003), 16.

94. See Levinas, *Ethics and Infinity*, 86.

95. Ibid., 86–87; emphasis added.

96. Ibid., 106.

97. Zalman Lewental, Manuscript of Sonderkommando Member, trans. Krystyna Michalik, in *Amidst a Nightmare of Crime: Manuscripts of Members of Sonderkommando*, ed. Jadwiga Bezwinska (Oświęcim: State Museum, 1973), 136.

98. Levi, *The Reawakening*, 12.

99. Levinas, *Totality and Infinity*, 214.

100. Emmanuel Levinas, *Of God Who Comes to Mind*, trans. Bettina Bergo (Stanford: Stanford University Press, 1998), 63.

101. Levi, *Survival in Auschwitz*, 98.

102. Levinas, *Collected Philosophical Papers*, 100.

103. Fénelon, *Playing for Time*, 144.

104. Hart, *Return to Auschwitz*, 60.

105. Levi, *Survival in Auschwitz*, 42.

106. Paul Trepman, *Among Men and Beasts*, trans. Shoshana Perla and Gertrude Hirschler (New York: Bergen Belsen Memorial Press, 1978), 137.

107. Rudolf Vrba and Alan Bestic, *I Cannot Forgive* (New York: Bantam, 1964), 58.

108. Quoted in George L. Mosse, *Nazi Culture* (New York: Grosset and Dunlop, 1966), 316.

109. Yehudah Leib Alter, *The Language of Truth: The Torah Commentary of the Sefat Emet*, trans. Arthur Green (Philadelphia: Jewish Publication Society, 1998), 10.

110. Hirsch, *The Generation of Postmemory*, 116.

111. Dominick LaCapra, *Writing History, Writing Trauma* (Baltimore: Johns Hopkins University Press, 2001), 204.

112. Levinas, *Totality and Infinity*, 42.

113. See also Raphael Patai, *The Messiah Texts* (New York: Avon, 1979), 110–11.

114. The other three questions are: Did you try to make time to study Torah? Were you devoted to raising a family? Were you honest in your business affairs?

115. Miklós Nyiszli, *Auschwitz: A Doctor's Eyewitness Account*, trans. Tibere Kremer and Richard Seaver (New York: Fawcett Crest, 1960), 151.

116. Thomas Lutz et al., *Killing Sites: Research and Remembrance* (Berlin: Metropol Verlag, 2015), 15; see also Patrick Desbois, *The Holocaust by Bullets: A Priest's Journey to Uncover the Truth behind the Murder of 1.5 Million Jews* (New York: Palgrave Macmillan, 2008).

117. Lev Ozerov, "Kiev: Babi Yar," in *The Complete Black Book of Russian Jewry*, ed. Ehrenburg and Grossman, 4.

118. Ibid., 5.

119. Ibid., 6.

120. Ibid., 7–8.

121. Wiesel, *Legends of Our Time*, 183.

122. Karel C. Berkhoff, "Dina Pronicheva's Story of Surviving the Babi Yar Massacre: German, Jewish, Soviet, Russian, and Ukrainian Records," in *The Shoah in Ukraine: History, Testimony, Memorialization*, ed. Ray Brandon and Wendy Lower (Bloomington: Indiana University Press, 2008), 292.

123. Levi, *Survival in Auschwitz*, 90.

124. "Buchenwald, Germany, 1945, A Muselmann on a wagon, after the liberation," Yad Vashem Photo Archives, ID 102959, Archival Signature 18BO2, available at http://collections1.yadvashem.org/notebook.asp?lang=ENG&dlang=ENG&module=search&page=list&rsvr=7¶m=<uppernav>simple</><nob>1</><rsvr_ser>@@7</><search_type>simple</><view>records</><nrsvr>N</><sort>TI</><dispq>z1zItem ID: z3z102959, Literal z1zDatabanks: z3z Photos Archive</><dlang>ENG</><query_name>jaguar50_664_756078</><quantity>15</><start_entry>1</><num_of_items>1</><query_index>@SN</><thumb>0</><smode>dts</><first_item>1</><last_item>1</><book_id>102959</><mainimage>/arch_srika/1a-245g/1A-35G/18BO2_.jpg</>¶m2=<num_fields>12</><nvf>11</><nvr>3</><search_type>simple</>&site=sapir.

125. Fackenheim, *The Jewish Return into History*, 251.

126. Fackenheim, *God's Presence in History*, 74.

127. See Fackenheim, *The Jewish Return into History*, 246.

128. Levi, *Survival in Auschwitz*, 90.

129. Emil L. Fackenheim and David Patterson, "Why the Holocaust Is Unique," *Judaism* 50 (Fall 2001): 445–46.

130. Levi, *The Reawakening*, 128.

131. Levi, *Survival in Auschwitz*, 90.

132. See Franz Rosenzweig, *Understanding the Sick and the Healthy*, trans. Nahum Glatzer (Cambridge: Harvard University Press, 1999), 82.

133. Fackenheim, *The Jewish Return into History*, 246.

134. Haim Gouri, *Facing the Glass Booth: The Jerusalem Trial of Adolf Eichmann*, trans. Michael Swirsky (Detroit: Wayne State University Press, 2004), 146.

135. Levi, *Survival in Auschwitz*, 19.

136. Bauer, *A History of the Holocaust*, 240.

137. Wiesel, *Night*, 29.

138. Ibid., 33.

139. Ka-tzetnik 135633, *Shivitti*, 13.

140. Nomberg-Przytyk, *Auschwitz*, 34.

141. Ka-tzetnik 135633, *Shivitti*, xvii.

142. Nomberg-Przytyk, *Auschwitz*, 69.

143. Ibid., 35.

144. Ibid., 13.

145. Wiesel, *Night*, 32.

146. Emil L. Fackenheim, interview at Ben Gurion University, 22 January 2003, unpublished manuscript.

147. Améry, *At the Mind's Limits*, 19.

148. Wiesenthal, *The Sunflower*, 41.

149. Debórah Dvork and Robert Jan van Pelt, *Auschwitz* (New York: W. W. Norton, 1996), 353.

150. Jackson, *Elli: Coming of Age in the Holocaust*, 34.

151. Leitner, *Fragments of Isabella*, 19–20.

152. The photographs are available at "*Sonderkommando* Photographs," Wikipedia, https://en.wikipedia.org/wiki/Sonderkommando_photographs. The photographs are in the public domain, because, according to Article 3 of the copyright law of March 29, 1926, of the Republic of Poland and Article 2 of the copyright law of July 10, 1952, of the People's Republic of Poland, all photographs by Polish photographers (or published for the first time in Poland or simultaneously in Poland and abroad) published without a clear copyright notice before the law was changed on May 23, 1994, are assumed public domain in Poland.

153. Wiesel, *Night*, 35.

154. Ibid., 32.

155. Gideon Greif, *We Wept without Tears: Testimonies of the Jewish Sonderkommando from Auschwitz* (Coral Gables: University of Miami Press, 2005), 327.

156. Ibid., 68–69.

157. Nyiszli, *Auschwitz*, vi.

158. Levi, *The Drowned and the Saved*, 55.

159. Fackenheim, *To Mend the World*, 219.

160. Didi-Huberman, *Images in Spite of All*, 6.

161. See Filip Müller, *Auschwitz Inferno: The Testimony of a Sonderkommando*, trans. Susanna Flatauer (London: Routledge and Kegan Paul, 1979; Shlomo Vene-

zia, *Inside the Gas Chambers: Eight Months inside the Sonderkommando of Auschwitz* (Malden, MA: Polity Press, 2009).

162. See Hermann Langbein, "The Auschwitz Underground," in *Anatomy of the Auschwitz Death Camp*, ed. Yisrael Gutman and Michael Berenbaum (Bloomington: Indiana University Press, 1994), 501.

163. See Ber Mark, *The Scrolls of Auschwitz*, trans. Sharon Neemani, ed. Isaiah Avrech (Tel Aviv: Am Oved, 1985); see also Jadwiga Bezwinska, ed., *Amidst a Nightmare of Crime: Manuscripts of Members of Sonderkommando* (Oświęcim: State Museum, 1973).

164. Levinas, *Otherwise Than Being*, 151.

165. Dan Stone, "The Sonderkommando Photographs," *Jewish Social Studies* 7, no. 3 (2001): 132; quoted in Blake William Remington, *Read, Look, Go: Ethics and Dialogue in Holocaust Memorial Texts*, PhD dissertation, University of Texas at Dallas (Ann Arbor: ProQuest/UMI, 2015, Publication No. AAT 3719454), 213.

166. Greif, *We Wept without Tears*, 375.

167. Didi-Huberman, *Images in Spite of All*, 16.

168. Quoted in ibid., 16.

169. See Stanisław Wrzos-Glinka, Tadeusz Mazur, and Jerzy Tomaszewski, eds., *1939–1945: We Have Not Forgotten* (Warsaw: Polania Publishing, 1960).

170. Didi-Huberman, *Images in Spite of All*, 25.

171. Ibid., 64.

172. Ibid., 81.

173. Ibid., 36.

174. Nicholas Chare, *Auschwitz and Afterimages: Abjection, Witnessing, and Representation* (London: I. B. Tauris, 2011), 143.

175. Ibid.

176. Levinas, *Otherwise Than Being*, 3.

177. Ibid., 176.

178. Remington, *Read, Look, Go*, 216.

179. Levi, *Survival in Auschwitz*, 16.

180. Charlotte Delbo, *Auschwitz and After*, trans. Rosette Lamont (New Haven: Yale University Press, 1995), 254.

181. Quoted in Didi-Huberman, *Images in Spite of All*, 16.

182. Remington, *Read, Look, Go*, 218; see http://auschwitz.org/en/gallery/historical-pictures-and-documents/extermination,11.html.

183. Bauer, *A History of the Holocaust*, 240.

184. Levinas, *Otherwise Than Being*, 146; emphasis added.

185. Didi-Huberman, *Images in Spite of All*, 36–37.

186. Chare, *Auschwitz and Afterimages*, 147.

187. W. H. Auden, "September 1, 1939," in W. H. Auden, *Selected Poems*, ed. Edward Mendelson (New York: Random House, 2007), 96.

188. Steven B. Bowman, *The Agony of Greek Jews, 1940–1945* (Stanford: Stanford University Press, 2009), 95.

189. Levi, *Survival in Auschwitz*, 55.

190. See Levinas, *Otherwise Than Being*, 74.

191. Levi, *Survival in Auschwitz*, 39.

192. Fackenheim, *To Mend the World*, 25.

Bibliography

Abraham ibn Ezra. *The Commentary of Ibn Ezra on Isaiah.* Translated by Michael Friedlander. New York: Feldheim, 1943.

———. *The Secret of the Torah.* Translated by H. Norman Strickman. Northvale, NJ: Jason Aronson, 1995.

Adorno, Theodor W. *Aesthetic Theory.* Translayed by R. Hullot-Kentor. Minneapolis: Minnesota University Press, 1997.

———. *Negative Dialectics.* Translated by E. B. Ashton. New York: Continuum, 1973.

———. *Prisms.* Translated by Shierry Weber Nicholsen and Samuel Weber. Cambridge: MIT Press, 1983.

Agamben, Giorgio. *Remnants of Auschwitz: The Witness of the Archive.* Translated by Daniel Heller-Roazen. New York: Zone Books, 2002.

Albo, Joseph. *Sefer Halkkarim: Book of Principles.* 5 Vols. Translated by Isaac Husik. Philadelphia: Jewish Publication Society, 1946.

Alighieri, Dante. *Inferno.* Translated by John Ciardi. New York: Random House, 1996.

Alter, Yehudah Leib. *The Language of Truth: The Torah Commentary of the Sefat Emet.* Translated by Arthur Green. Philadelphia: Jewish Publication Society, 1998.

Améry, Jean. *At the Mind's Limits: Contemplations by a Survivor on Auschwitz and Its Realities.* Translated by Sidney Rosenfeld and Stella P. Rosenfeld. New York: Schocken Books, 1986.

Anatoli, A. (Kuznetsov). *Babi Yar: A Document in the Form of a Novel.* Translated by David Floyd. New York: Pocket Books, 1971.

Appelfeld, Aharon. *Badenheim 1939.* Translated by Dalya Bilu. New York: Washington Square, 1980.

———. *Essays in the First Person.* Jerusalem: Zionist Library, 1980.

———. *The Story of a Life.* Translated by Aloma Halter. New York: Schocken Books, 2004.

Arad, Yitzhak. *The Pictorial History of the Holocaust.* Jerusalem: Yad Vashem, 1990.

Arendt, Hannah. *The Jewish Writings.* Edited by Jerome Kohn and Ron H. Feldman. New York: Schocken Books, 2007.

Aron, Milton. *Ideas and Ideals of the Hassidim.* Secaucus, NJ: Citadel, 1969.

Auden, W. H. *Selected Poems*. Edited by Edward Mendelson. New York: Random House, 2007.

Avraham, Rabbi. *Galya Raza*. Jerusalem: Yirid Hasfarim, 2000.

Baal HaTurim. *Commentary on the Torah: Bereshis*. Translated by Avie Gold. Brooklyn: Mesorah, 1999.

Bachya ibn Paquda. *Chovot Halevavot: Duties of the Heart*. 2 Vols. Translated by Moses Hyamson. New York: Feldheim, 1970.

Bakhtin, Mikhail. *Art and Answerability*. Translated by Vadim Liapunov. Edited by Michael Holquist and Vadim Liapunov. Austin: University of Texas Press, 1990.

———. *The Dialogic Imagination*. Translated by Caryl Emerson and Michael Holquist. Austin: University of Texas Press, 1981.

———. *Estetika slovesnogo tvorchestva*. Moscow: State Publishing House, 1979.

Barthes, Roland. *Camera Lucida: Reflections on Photography*. Translated by Richard Howard. New York: Hill and Wang, 1981.

Bartov, Omer. *Murder in Our Midst: The Holocaust, Industrial Killing, and Representation*. New York: Oxford University Press, 1996.

Bauer, Karin. *Adorno's Nietzschean Narratives: Critiques of Ideology, Readings of Wagner*. Albany: State University of New York Press, 1999.

Bauer, Yehuda. *A History of the Holocaust*. Revised Ed. New York: Franklin Watts, 2001.

Berkhoff, Karel C. "Dina Pronicheva's Story of Surviving the Babi Yar Massacre: German, Jewish, Soviet, Russian, and Ukrainian Records." In *The Shoah in Ukraine: History, Testimony, Memorialization*, edited by Ray Brandon and Wendy Lower, 291–317. Bloomington: Indiana University Press, 2008.

Bernard-Donals, Michael. *Forgetful Memory: Representation and Remembrance in the Wake of the Holocaust*. Albany: State University of New York Press, 2009.

———, and Richard Glejzer. *Between Witness and Testimony: The Holocaust and the Limits of Representation*. Albany: State University of New York Press, 2001.

———. "Teaching (after) Auschwitz: Pedagogy between Redemption and Sublimity." In *Witnessing the Disaster: Essays on Representation and the Holocaust*, edited by Michael Bernard-Donals and Richard Glejzer, 245–61. Madison: University of Wisconsin Press, 2003.

———, eds. *Witnessing the Disaster: Essays on Representation and the Holocaust*. Madison: University of Wisconsin Press, 2003.

Bernasconi, Robert, and David Wood, eds. *The Provocation of Levinas: Rethinking the Other*. London: Routledge and Kegan Paul, 1988.

Berr, Hélène. *The Journal of Hélène Berr*. Translated by David Bellos. New York: Weinstein Books, 2008.

Bezwinska, Jadwiga, ed. *Amidst a Nightmare of Crime: Manuscripts of Members of Sonderkommando*. Oświęcim: State Museum, 1973.

Bigsby, Christopher. *Remembering and Imagining the Holocaust*. Cambridge: Cambridge University Press, 2006.

Birnbaum, Suzanne. *Une Française juive est revenue: Auschwitz, Belsen, Raguhn.* Maulévrier, France: Editions Hérault, 1989.
Blanchot, Maurice. *The Writing of the Disaster.* Translated by Ann Smock. Lincoln: University of Nebraska Press, 1986.
Bor, Josef. *The Terezín Requiem.* Translated by Edith Pargeter. New York: Avon, 1963.
Borowski, Tadeusz. *This Way to the Gas, Ladies and Gentlemen.* Translated by Barbara Vedder. New York: Penguin Books, 1974.
Bowman, Steven B. *The Agony of Greek Jews, 1940–1945.* Stanford: Stanford University Press, 2009.
Brandon, Ray, and Wendy Lower, eds. *The Shoah in Ukraine: History, Testimony, Memorialization.* Bloomington: Indiana University Press, 2008.
Buber, Martin. *I and Thou.* Translated by Walter Kaufmann. New York: Scribner's, 1970.
———. *The Legend of the Baal Shem.* Translated by Maurice Friedman. New York: Schocken Books, 1969.
Cargas, Harry James. *In Conversation with Elie Wiesel.* New York: Paulist Press, 1976.
Celan, Paul. *Collected Prose.* Translated by Rosemarie Waldrop. New York: Routledge, 2003.
———. *Paul Celan: Poems.* Translated by Michael Hamburger. New York: Persea Books, 1980.
———. *Paul Celan: Selections.* Edited by Pierre Joris. Berkeley: University of California Press, 2005.
Camus, Albert. *The Myth of Sisyphus.* Translated by Justin O'Brien. New York: Random House, 1955.
Chare, Nicholas. *Auschwitz and Afterimages: Abjection, Witnessing, and Representation.* London: I. B. Tauris, 2011.
———, and Dominic Williams, eds. *Representing Auschwitz: At the Margins of Testimony.* London: Palgrave Macmillan, 2013.
Chayim ben Attar. *Or Hachayim.* 5 Vols. Translated by Eliyahu Munk. Jerusalem: Munk, 1995.
Cohen, Josh. *Interrupting Auschwitz.* New York: Continuum, 2003.
Cohen, Richard A., ed. *Face to Face with Levinas.* Albany: State University of New York Press, 1986.
Cohen, Victor, ed. *The Soul of the Torah: Insights of the Chasidic Masters on the Weekly Torah Portions.* Northvale, NJ: Jason Aronson, 2000.
Cohn-Sherbok, Dan. *God and the Holocaust.* Herefordshire: Fowler Wright Books, 1996.
Confino, Alon. "Why Did the Nazis Burn the Hebrew Bible? Nazi Germany, Representations of the Past, and the Holocaust." *The Journal of Modern History* 84 (June 2012): 369–400.
Conrad, Joseph. *Heart of Darkness.* New York: Penguin Books, 1983.
Cordovero, Moses. *Pardes Rimonim.* Jerusalem: Yarid Hasefarim, 2000.

Culi, Yaakov. *The Torah Anthology: MeAm Lo'ez*. Vol. 1. Translated by Aryeh Kaplan. New York: Moznaim, 1977.

Czerniaków, Adam. *The Warsaw Ghetto Diary of Adam Czerniaków*. Edited by Raul Hilberg, Stanislaw Staron, and Joseph Kermisz. Translated by Stanislaw Staron et al. New York: Stein and Day, 1979.

Dan, Joseph, ed. *The Early Kabbalah*. Translated by Ronald C. Kiener. New York: Paulist Press, 1986.

Darré, Richard Walther. *Um Blut und Boden: Reden und Aufsätze*. Munich: Zentralverlag der NSDAP, 1940.

Delbo, Charlotte. *Auschwitz and After*. Translated by Rosette Lamont. New Haven: Yale University Press, 1995.

———. *None of Us Will Return*. Translated by John Githens. Boston: Beacon Press, 1968.

———. *Who Will Carry the Word?* Translated by Cynthia Haft. In *The Theatre of the Holocaust*, Vol. 1, edited by Robert Skloot, 267–325. Madison: University of Wisconsin Press, 1982.

Des Pres, Terrence. *The Survivor: An Anatomy of Life in the Death Camp*. New York: Oxford University Press, 1976.

Desbois, Patrick. *The Holocaust by Bullets: A Priest's Journey to Uncover the Truth behind the Murder of 1.5 Million Jews*. New York: Palgrave Macmillan, 2008.

Didi-Huberman, Georges. *Images in Spite of All: Fours Photographs from Auschwitz*. Translated by Shane B. Lillis. Chicago: University of Chicago Press, 2003.

Donat, Alexander. *The Holocaust Kingdom*. New York: The Holocaust Library, 1978.

Doorsy, Yasmin, ed. *Representations of Auschwitz: Fifty Years of Photographs, Paintings, and Graphics*. Oświęcim: Auschwitz-Birkenau State Museum, 1995.

Dorian, Emil. *The Quality of Witness*. Edited by Marguerite Dorian. Translated by Mara Soceanu Vamos. Philadelphia: Jewish Publication Society, 1982.

Dresden, Sem. *Persecution, Extermination, Literature*. Translated by Henry G. Schogt. Toronto: University of Toronto Press, 1995.

Dribben, Judith. *And Some Shall Live*. Jerusalem: Keter Books, 1969.

Dwork, Debórah, and Robert Jan van Pelt. *Auschwitz*. New York: W. W. Norton, 1996.

Eaglestone, Robert. *Postmodernism and Holocaust Denial*. Duxford, UK: Icon Books, 2001.

Ehrenburg, Ilya, and Vasily Grossman. *The Complete Black Book of Russian Jewry*. Translated and edited by David Patterson. Piscataway, NJ: Transaction Publishers, 2002.

Ezrahi, Sidra DeKoven. *By Words Alone: The Holocaust in Literature*. Chicago: University of Chicago Press, 1980.

———. "Considering the Apocalypse: Is the Writing on the Wall Only Graffiti?" In *Writing and the Holocaust*, edited by Berel Lang, 137–53. New York: Holmes and Meier, 1988.

Fackenheim, Emil L. *Encounters between Judaism and Modern Philosophy.* New York: Basic Books, 1993.

———. *God's Presence in History: Jewish Affirmations and Philosophical Reflections.* New York: Harper and Row, 1970.

———. Interview at Ben Gurion University, 22 January 2003, unpublished manuscript.

———. *The Jewish Bible after the Holocaust.* Bloomington: Indiana University Press, 1990.

———. *Jewish-Christian Relations after the Holocaust: Toward Post-Holocaust Theological Thought.* Chicago: The Joseph Cardinal Bernardin Jerusalem Lecture, 1977.

———. "Jewish Faith and the Holocaust: A Fragment." In *A Holocaust Reader: Responses to the Nazi Extermination*, edited by Michael L. Morgan, 115–21. New York: Oxford University Press, 2001.

———. *Jewish Philosophers and Jewish Philosophy.* Edited by Michael Morgan. Bloomington: Indiana University Press, 1996.

———. *The Jewish Return into History.* New York: Schocken Books, 1978.

———. *Quest for Past and Future: Essays in Jewish Theology.* Bloomington: Indiana University Press, 1968.

———. "The Rebirth of the Holy Remnant." Lecture presented at Yad Vashem, 17 June 1993, unpublished manuscript.

———. *To Mend the World: Foundations of Post-Holocaust Jewish Thought.* New York: Schocken Books, 1989.

———, and David Patterson. "Why the Holocaust Is Unique," *Judaism* 50 (Fall 2001): 438–47.

Felman, Shoshana, and Dori Laub. *Testimony: Crisis of Witnessing in Literature, Psychoanalysis, and History.* London: Routledge, 1992.

Felsteiner, John. *Paul Celan: Poet, Survivor, Jew.* New Haven: Yale University Press, 1995.

Fénelon, Fania. *Playing for Time.* Translated by Judith Landry. New York: Atheneum, 1977.

Fewell, Danna Nolan, and Gary A. Phillips. *Icon of Loss: The Haunting Child of Samuel Bak.* Syracuse: Syracuse University Press, 2009.

Fink, Ida. *A Scrap of Time and Other Stories.* Translated by Madeline Levine and Francine Prose. Evanston: Northwestern University Press, 1995.

Finkelstein, Louis. *Akiba: Scholar, Saint and Martyr.* New York: Atheneum, 1981.

Flinker, Moshe. *Young Moshe's Diary.* Translated by Shaul Esh and Geoffrey Wigoder. Jerusalem: Yad Vashem and Board of Jewish Education, 1971.

Franklin, Ruth. *A Thousand Darknesses: Lies and Truth in Holocaust Fiction.* New York: Oxford University Press, 2011.

Fridman, Lea Wernick. *Words and Witness: Narrative and Aesthetic Strategies in the Representation of the Holocaust.* Albany: State University of New York Press, 2000.

Friedländer, Saul. "The *Shoah* between Memory and History." *Jewish Quarterly* 37, no. 1 (Spring 1990): 5–11.

———, ed. *Probing the Limits of Representation: Nazism and the "Final Solution."* Cambridge: Harvard University Press, 1992.

Fuchs, Elinor, ed. *Plays of the Holocaust: An International Anthology*. New York: Theatre Communications Group, 1987.

Gikatilla, Joseph. *Sha'are Orah: Gates of Light*. Translated by Avi Weinstein. San Francisco: Harper Collins, 1994.

Gilbert, Martin. *Churchill and the Jews: A Lifelong Friendship*. New York: Henry Holt and Company, 2007.

Ginsburgh, Yitzchak. *The Alef-Beit: Jewish Thought Revealed through the Hebrew Letters*. Northvale, NJ: Jason Aronson, 1991.

Gleikh, Sarra. "The Diary of Sarra Gleikh." In *The Complete Black Book of Russian Jewry*, edited by Ilya Ehrenburg and Vasily Grossman. Translated and edited David Patterson, 50–54. New Brunswick, NJ: Transaction Publishers, 2002.

Glowacka, Dorota. *Disappearing Traces: Holocaust Testimonials, Ethics, and Aesthetics*. Seattle: University of Washington Press, 2012.

von Goethe, Johann Wolfgang. *Faust, a Tragedy: Part I*. Translated by Martin Greenberg. New Haven: Yale University Press, 1992.

Gouri, Haim. *The Chocolate Deal*. Translated by Seymour Simkes. New York: Holt, 1968.

———. *Facing the Glass Booth: The Jerusalem Trial of Adolf Eichmann*. Translated by Michael Swirsky. Detroit: Wayne State University Press, 2004.

Greif, Gideon. *We Wept without Tears: Testimonies of the Jewish Sonderkommndo from Auschwitz*. Coral Gables: University of Miami Press, 2005.

Grierson, Karla. *Discours d'Auschwitz: Littérarité, représentation, symbolisation*. Paris: Honoré Champion Éditeur, 2003.

Gutman, Yisrael, and Michael Berenbaum, eds. *Anatomy of the Auschwitz Death Camp*. Bloomington: Indiana University Press, 1994.

Halevi, Judah. *The Kuzari* [*Kitav al khazari*]. Translated by Henry Slonimsky. New York: Schocken Books, 1963.

Halperin, Irving. *Messengers of the Dead: Literature of the Holocaust*. Philadelphia: Westminster Press, 1970.

Hand, Sean, ed. *The Levinas Reader*. Oxford: Basil Blackwell, 1989.

Hart, Kitty. *Return to Auschwitz*. New York: Atheneum, 1982.

Hawthorne, Jeremy. "The Face-to-Face Encounter in Holocaust Narrative." In *After Testimony: The Ethics and Aesthetics of Holocaust Narrative for the Future*, edited by Jakob Lothe, Susan Rubin Suleiman, and Jams Phelan, 143–61. Columbus: The Ohio State University Press, 2012.

Heberer, Patricia. *Children during the Holocaust*. Lanham, MD: Rowman and Littlefield, 2011.

HeChasid, Yehuda. *Sefer Chasidim*. Translated by Avraham Yaakov Finkel. Northvale, NJ: Jason Aronson, 1997.

Heidegger, Martin. *Nietzsche*. 2 Vols. Translated by D. Krell. San Francisco: Harper and Row, 1979.

———. *Sein und Zeit*. 2nd Ed. Tübingen: Max Niemeyer, 1929.

Heimler, Eugene. *Night of the Mist*. Translated by Andre Ungar. New York: Vanguard, 1959.

Heschel, Abraham Joshua. *Between God and Man: An Interpretation of Judaism*. Edited by Fritz A. Rothschild. New York: The Free Press, 1959.

———. *Man's Quest for God: Studies in Prayer and Symbolism*. New York: Charles Scribner's Sons, 1954.

———. *The Prophets*. 2 Vols. New York: Harper and Row, 1962, 1975.

———. *The Sabbath: Its Meaning for Modern Man*. New York: Farrar, Straus, and Giroux, 1981.

Hirsch, David H. *The Deconstruction of Literature: Criticism after Auschwitz*. Hanover, NH: University Press of New England, 1991.

Hirsch, Marianne. *The Generation of Postmemory: Writing and Visual Culture After the Holocaust*. New York: Columbia University Press, 2012.

———. "Surviving Images: Holocaust Photographs and the Work of Postmemory." In *Visual Culture and the Holocaust*, edited by Barbie Zelizer, 214–46. New Brunswick: Rutgers University Press, 2001.

Ingram, Robert G. *Religion, Reform and Modernity in the Eighteenth Century*. Woodbridge, UK: Bitdell Press, 2007.

Jabès, Edmond. *The Book of Yukel and Return to the Book*. Translated by Rosemarie Waldrop. Middletown, CT: Wesleyan University Press, 1977.

Jackson, Livia E. Bitton. *Elli: Coming of Age in the Holocaust*. New York: Times Books, 1980.

Jaggi, Maya. "Recovered Memories: Interview with W. G. Sebald," *The Guardian*, 22 September 2001, available at http://www.theguardian.com/books/2001/sep/22/artsandhumanities.highereducation.

Joyon, Charles. *Qu'as-tu fait de ta jeunesse?* Paris: Éditons Renée Lacoste et Cie, 1957.

Kaes, Anton. "Holocaust and the End of History: Postmodern Historiography in Cinema." In *Probing the Limits of Representation: Nazism and the "Final Solution,"* edited by Saul Friedlander, 206–22. Cambridge: Harvard University Press, 1992.

Kahane, David. *Lvov Ghetto Diary*. Translated by Jerzy Michalowicz. Amherst: University of Massachusetts Press, 1990.

Kalmanovitch, Zelig. "A Diary of the Nazi Ghetto in Vilna." Translated and edited by Koppel S. Pinson. *YIVO Annual of Jewish Social Sciences* 8 (1953): 9–81.

Kant, Immanuel. *The Conflict of the Faculties*. Translated by Mary J. Gregor. New York: Abaris, 1979.

Kaplan, Brett Ashley. *Unwanted Beauty: Aesthetic Pleasure in Holocaust Representation.* Urbana: University of Illinois Press, 2007.

Kaplan, Chaim A. *Scroll of Agony: The Warsaw Diary of Chaim A. Kaplan.* Translated and edited by Abraham I. Katsh. New York: Collier, 1973.

Karmel, Ilona. *An Estate of Memory.* Hartfordshire: Panther, 1973.

Katz, Josef. *One Who Came Back: The Diary of a Jewish Survivor.* Translated by Herzl Reach. New York: Herzl Press and Bergen-Belsen Memorial Press, 1973.

Katz, Steven T. *The Holocaust in Historical Context.* Vol. 1. New York: Oxford University Press, 1994.

Ka-tzetnik 135633. *Atrocity.* Translated by Nina De-Nur. New York: Kensington, 1977.

———. *Beit habubot.* Tel Aviv: Hakibbutz Hameuchad, 1987.

———. *House of Dolls.* Trans. Moshe M. Kohn. New York: Pyramid, 1958.

———. *Kaddish.* Translated by Nina De-Nur. New York: Algemeiner Associates, 1998.

———. *Kokhev ha-efer.* Tel Aviv: Hamenora, 1971.

———. *Phoenix over the Galilee.* Translated by Nina De-Nur. New York: Harper and Row, 1969.

———. *Pipel.* Tel Aviv: Hakibbutz Hameuchad, 1988.

———. *Salamandrah.* Tel Aviv: Kakibbutz Hameuchad, 1987.

———. *Shivitti: A Vision.* Translated by Eliyah De-Nur. New York: Harper, 1989.

———. *Star of Ashes.* Translated by Nina De-Nur. Tel Aviv: Hamenora, 1971.

———. *Sunrise over Hell.* Translated by Nina De-Nur. London: W. H. Allen, 1977.

Katznelson, Yitzhak. *Vittel Diary.* Translated by Myer Cohn. 2nd Ed. Tel Aviv: Hakibbutz Hameuchad, 1972.

Kessel, Sim. *Hanged at Auschwitz.* Translated by Melville and Delight Wallace. New York: Stein and Day, 1972.

Kertész, Imre. "Who Owns Auschwitz?" *The Yale Journal of Criticism* 14, no. 1 (2001): 267–72.

Keter Shem Tov. Brooklyn: Kehot, 1972.

Kitov, Eliyahu. *The Book of Our Heritage.* 3 Vols. Translated by Nathan Bluman. New York: Feldheim, 1973.

Kitzur Shulchan Arukh—Code of Jewish Law. 4 Vols. Compiled by R. Solomon Ganzfried. Translated by Hyman E. Goldin. Rev. Ed. New York: Hebrew Publishing Co., 1961.

Klein, Gerda Weissmann. *All But My Life.* New York: Hill and Wang, 1957.

Klemperer, Victor. *I Will Bear Witness: A Diary of the Nazi Years, 1942–1945.* Translated by Martin Chalmers. New York: Random House, 1999.

Kligerman, Eric. *Sites of the Uncanny: Paul Celan, Specularity, and the Visual Arts.* Berlin: Walter De Gruyter, 2007.

Kohn, Murray. *Is the Holocaust Vanishing? A Survivor's Reflections on the Academic Waning of Memory and Jewish Identity in the Post-Auschwitz Era.* Lanham, MD: Hamilton Books, 2005.

Kolmar, Gertrude. *My Gaze Is Turned Inward: Letters, 1934–1943*. Edited by Johanna Woltmann. Translated by Brigitte M. Goldstein. Evanston: Northwestern University Press, 2004.

Kon, Menahem. "Fragments of a Diary (August 6, 1942-October 1, 1942)." Translated by M. Z. Prives. In *To Live with Honor and Die with Honor: Selected Documents from the Warsaw Ghetto Underground Archives "O.S.,"* edited by Joseph Kermish, 80–86. Jerusalem: Yad Vashem, 1986.

Kook, Abraham Isaac. *Orot*. Translated by Bezalel Naor. Northvale, NJ: Jason Aronson, 1993.

Korczak, Janusz. *Ghetto Diary*. Translated by Jerzy Bachrach and Barbara Krzywicka. New York: Holocaust Library, 1978.

Kovatch, Thomas A., and Martin Walser. *The Burden of the Past: Martin Walser on Modern German Identity: Texts, Contexts, Commentary*. Rochester: Camden House, 2008.

Kremer, Elijah ben Shlomo Zalman. *Even Shleimah*. Translated by Yaakov Singer and Chaim David Ackerman. Southfield, MI: Targum Press, 1992.

Kruk, Herman. *The Last Days of the Jerusalem of Lithuania: Chronicles from the Vilna Ghetto and the Camps, 1939–1944*. Edited by Benjamin Harshav. Translated by Barbara Harshav. New Haven: Yale University Press, 2002.

LaCapra, Dominick. *Representing the Holocaust*. Ithaca: Cornell University Press, 1994.

———. *Writing History, Writing Trauma*. Baltimore and London: Johns Hopkins University Press, 2001.

Lang, Berel. *Writing and the Holocaust*. New York: Holmes and Meier, 1988.

Langbein, Hermann. "The Auschwitz Underground." In *Anatomy of the Auschwitz Death Camp*, edited by Yisrael Gutman and Michael Berenbaum, 485–502. Bloomington: Indiana University Press, 1994.

Langer, Lawrence. *Admitting the Holocaust*. Oxford: Oxford University Press, 1995.

———. *The Holocaust and the Literary Imagination*. New Haven: Yale University Press, 1975.

Langfus, Anna. *The Whole Land Brimstone*. Translated by Peter Wiles. New York: Pantheon, 1962.

Laub, Dori. "An Event without a Witness: Truth, Testimony and Survival." In Shoshana Felman and Dori Laub. *Testimony: Crisis of Witnessing in Literature, Psychoanalysis, and History*, 75–93. London: Routledge, 1992.

Lehmann, Ernst. *Biologischer Wille: Wege und Ziele biologischer Arbeit im neuen Reich*. Munich: Zentralverlag der NSDAP, 1934.

Leitner, Isabella. *Fragments of Isabella*. Edited by Irving Leitner. New York: Thomas Crowell, 1978.

Lengyel, Olga. *Five Chimneys*. London: Granada, 1972.

Lerner, Richard M. *Final Solutions: Biology, Prejudice, and Genocide*. University Park: Pennsylvania State University Press, 1992.

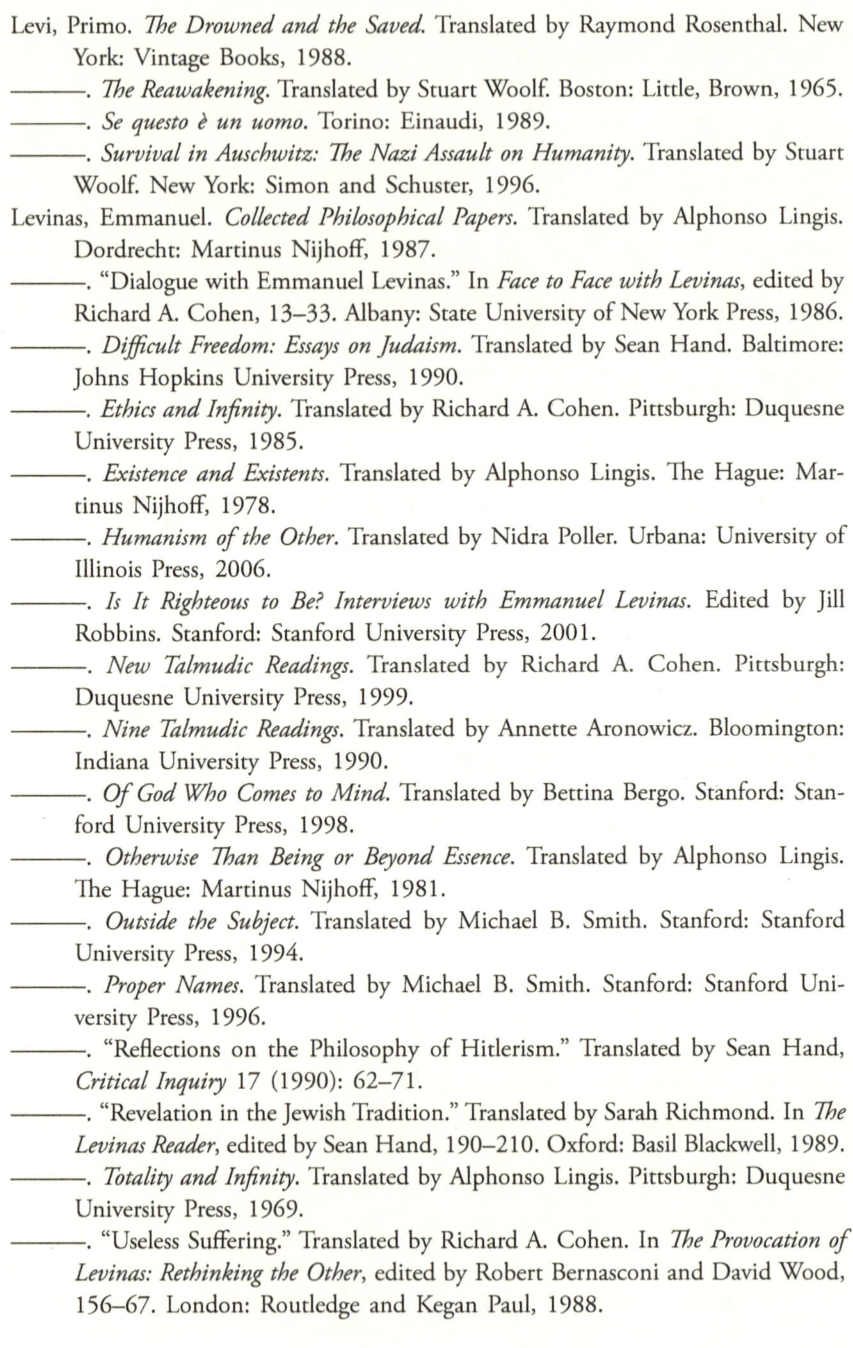

Levi, Primo. *The Drowned and the Saved.* Translated by Raymond Rosenthal. New York: Vintage Books, 1988.

———. *The Reawakening.* Translated by Stuart Woolf. Boston: Little, Brown, 1965.

———. *Se questo è un uomo.* Torino: Einaudi, 1989.

———. *Survival in Auschwitz: The Nazi Assault on Humanity.* Translated by Stuart Woolf. New York: Simon and Schuster, 1996.

Levinas, Emmanuel. *Collected Philosophical Papers.* Translated by Alphonso Lingis. Dordrecht: Martinus Nijhoff, 1987.

———. "Dialogue with Emmanuel Levinas." In *Face to Face with Levinas,* edited by Richard A. Cohen, 13–33. Albany: State University of New York Press, 1986.

———. *Difficult Freedom: Essays on Judaism.* Translated by Sean Hand. Baltimore: Johns Hopkins University Press, 1990.

———. *Ethics and Infinity.* Translated by Richard A. Cohen. Pittsburgh: Duquesne University Press, 1985.

———. *Existence and Existents.* Translated by Alphonso Lingis. The Hague: Martinus Nijhoff, 1978.

———. *Humanism of the Other.* Translated by Nidra Poller. Urbana: University of Illinois Press, 2006.

———. *Is It Righteous to Be? Interviews with Emmanuel Levinas.* Edited by Jill Robbins. Stanford: Stanford University Press, 2001.

———. *New Talmudic Readings.* Translated by Richard A. Cohen. Pittsburgh: Duquesne University Press, 1999.

———. *Nine Talmudic Readings.* Translated by Annette Aronowicz. Bloomington: Indiana University Press, 1990.

———. *Of God Who Comes to Mind.* Translated by Bettina Bergo. Stanford: Stanford University Press, 1998.

———. *Otherwise Than Being or Beyond Essence.* Translated by Alphonso Lingis. The Hague: Martinus Nijhoff, 1981.

———. *Outside the Subject.* Translated by Michael B. Smith. Stanford: Stanford University Press, 1994.

———. *Proper Names.* Translated by Michael B. Smith. Stanford: Stanford University Press, 1996.

———. "Reflections on the Philosophy of Hitlerism." Translated by Sean Hand, *Critical Inquiry* 17 (1990): 62–71.

———. "Revelation in the Jewish Tradition." Translated by Sarah Richmond. In *The Levinas Reader,* edited by Sean Hand, 190–210. Oxford: Basil Blackwell, 1989.

———. *Totality and Infinity.* Translated by Alphonso Lingis. Pittsburgh: Duquesne University Press, 1969.

———. "Useless Suffering." Translated by Richard A. Cohen. In *The Provocation of Levinas: Rethinking the Other,* edited by Robert Bernasconi and David Wood, 156–67. London: Routledge and Kegan Paul, 1988.

Lewental, Zalman. "Manuscript of Sonderkommando Member." Translated by Krystyna Michalik. In *Amidst a Nightmare of Crime: Manuscripts of Members of Sonderkommando*, edited by Jadwiga Bezwinska, 130–78. Oświęcim: State Museum, 1973.

Lewinska, Pelagia. *Twenty Months at Auschwitz.* Translated by A. Teichner. New York: Lyle Stuart, 1968.

Lieberman, Benjamin. *The Holocaust and Genocides in Europe.* London: Bloomsbury Academic, 2013.

Lind, Jakov. *Landscape in Concrete.* Translated by Ralph Manheim. New York: Pocket Books, 1968.

Liss, Andrea. *Trespassing Through Shadows: Memory, Photography, and the Holocaust.* Minneapolis: University of Minnesota Press, 1998.

Littell, Franklin H. *The Crucifixion of the Jews: The Failure of Christians to Understand the Jewish Experience.* Macon: Mercer University Press, 1986.

Loeve, Yehuda. *Maharal of Prague: Pirke Avos.* Translated and edited by R. Tuvia Basser. Brooklyn: Mesorah, 1997.

Lothe, Jakob, Susan Rubin Suleiman, and Jams Phelan, eds. *After Testimony: The Ethics and Aesthetics of Holocaust Narrative for the Future.* Columbus: The Ohio State University Press, 2012.

Lubetkin, Zivia. *In the Days of Destruction and Revolt.* Translated by I. Tubbin. Tel-Aviv: Hakibbutz Hameuchad, 1981.

Lustig, Arnošt. *Darkness Casts No Shadow.* Translated by Jeanne Nemcova. Evanston: Northwestern University Press, 1985.

———. *Diamonds of the Night.* Translated by Jeanne Nemcova. Washington, DC: Inscape, 1978.

———. *Dita Saxova.* Translated by Jeanne Nemcova. New York: Harper and Row, 1979.

———. *A Prayer for Katerina Horovitzova.* Translated by Jeanne Nemcova. New York: Harper and Row, 1973.

Lutz, Thomas, et al. *Killing Sites: Research and Remembrance.* Berlin: Metropol Verlag, 2015.

Lyotard, Jean-François. *The Differend: Phrases in Dispute.* Translated by Georges Van Den Abbeele. Minneapolis: University of Minnesota Press, 1983.

———. *Heidegger and "the jews."* Translated by Andreas Michael and Mark S. Roberts. Minneapolis: University of Minnesota Press, 1990.

Maimonides. *Guide for the Perplexed.* Translated by M. Friedlaender. New York: Dover, 1956.

Mark, Ber. *The Scrolls of Auschwitz.* Translated by Sharon Neemani. Edited by Isaiah Avrech. Tel-Aviv: Am Oved, 1985.

Meed, Vladka. *On Both Sides of the Wall.* Translated by Benjamin Meed. Tel-Aviv: Hakibbutz Hameuchad, 1973.

Mekilta de-Rabbi Ishmael. 3 Vols. Translated by Jacob Z. Lauterbach. Philadelphia: Jewish Publication Society, 1961.

Midal, Fabrice. *Auschwitz, l'impossible regard.* Paris: Éditions du Seuil, 2012.

Midrash on Psalms (Midrash Tehillim). 2 Vols. Translated by William G. Braude. New Haven: Yale University Press, 1959.

Midrash Rabbah. 10 Vols. Translated and edited by H. Friedman, Maurice Simon et al. London: Soncino, 1961.

Midrash Tanchuma. 2 Vols. Jerusalem: Eshkol, 1935.

"Minutes of the Wannsee Conference," 20 January 1942. Available at http://prorev.com/wannsee.htm.

Morgan, Michael L., ed. *A Holocaust Reader: Responses to the Nazi Extermination.* New York: Oxford University Press, 2001.

Mosse, George L. *Nazi Culture.* New York: Grosset and Dunlap, 1966.

Müller, Filip. *Auschwitz Inferno: The Testimony of a Sonderkommando.* Translated by Susanna Flatauer. London: Routledge and Kegan Paul, 1979.

Nachman of Breslov. *Advice.* Translated by Avraham Greenbaum. Brooklyn: Breslov Research Institute, 1983.

———. *Tikkun.* Translated by Avraham Greenbaum. Jerusalem: Breslov Research Institute, 1984.

Neher, André. *The Exile of the Word: From the Silence of the Bible to the Silence of Auschwitz.* Translated by David Maisel. Philadelphia: Jewish Publication Society, 1981.

Nehunia ben Hakanah. *Sefer HaTemunah.* Jerusalem: Nezer Sharga, 1998.

Newman, Louis I., ed. *The Hasidic Anthology.* New York: Schocken Books, 1963.

Nomberg-Przytyk, Sara. *Auschwitz: True Tales from a Grotesque Land.* Translated by Roslyn Hirsch. Chapel Hill: University of North Carolina Press, 1985.

Nyiszli, Miklós. *Auschwitz: A Doctor's Eyewitness Account.* Translated by Tibere Kremer and Richard Seaver. New York: Fawcett Crest, 1960.

Opoczynski, Peretz. "Warsaw Ghetto Chronicle—September 1942." Translated by M. Z. Prives. In *To Live with Honor and Die with Honor: Selected Documents from the Warsaw Ghetto Underground Archives "O.S,"* edited by Joseph Kermish,Jerusalem, 101–11: Yad Vashem, 1986.

Ovid. *Metamorphoses: A New Translation.* Translated by Charles Martin. New York: W. W. Norton, 2005.

Ozerov, Lev. "Kiev: Babi Yar." In *The Complete Black Book of Russian Jewry,* edited by Ilya Ehrenburg and Vassily Grossman, translated and edited in English by David Patterson, 3–11. New Brunswick, NJ: Transaction, 2002.

Ozick, Cynthia. *The Shawl.* New York: Random House, 1990.

Ozsváth, Zsuzsanna. *In the Footsteps of Orpheus: The Life and Times of Miklós Radnóti.* Bloomington: Indiana University Press, 2000.

———. *When the Danube Ran Red.* Syracuse: Syracuse University Press, 2010.

Pagis, Dan. "Testimony." Translated by Stephen Mitchell. In *Holocaust Poetry,* edited by Hilda Schiff, 43. New York: St. Martin's Press, 1996.

———. "Written in Pencil in the Sealed Freightcar." Translated by Stephen Mitchell. In *Holocaust Poetry*, edited by Hilda Schiff, 180. New York: St. Martin's Press, 1996.

Pascal, Blaise. *Pensées*. Translated by A. J. Krailsheimer. New York: Penguin, 1995.

Patai, Raphael. *The Messiah Texts*. New York: Avon, 1979.

Patterson, David. *In Dialogue and Dilemma with Elie Wiesel.* Wakefield, NH: Longwood Academic, 1991.

Perl, Gisella. *I Was a Doctor in Auschwitz*. New York: International University Press, 1948.

Pesikta de-Rab Kahana. Translated by William G. Braude and Israel J. Kapstein. Philadelphia: Jewish Publication Society, 1975.

Pesikta Rabbati. Translated by W. G. Braude. 2 Vols. New Haven: Yale University Press, 1968.

Pirke de Rabbi Eliezer. Translated by Gerald Friedlander. New York: Hermon Press, 1970.

Pisar, Samuel. *Of Blood and Hope*. Boston: Little, Brown, 1979.

Plato. *Republic*. Translated by R. E. Allen. New Haven: Yale University Press, 2006.

Polen, Nehemia. *The Holy Fire: The Teachings of Rabbi Kalonymus Kalman Shapira.* Northvale, NJ: Jason Aronson, 1999.

Poliakov, Leon. *The Harvest of Hate*. Syracuse: Syracuse University Press, 1954.

Prager, Dennis and Joseph Telushkin. *Why the Jews? The Reason for Antisemitism*. New York: Simon and Schuster, 2003.

Radnóti, Miklós. *Foamy Sky: The Major Poems of Miklós Radnóti*. Translated by Zsuzsanna Ozaváth and Frederick Turner. Princeton: Princeton University Press, 1992.

Rashi, *Commentary on the Torah*. 5 Vols. Translated by M. Rosenbaum and N. M. Silbermann. Jerusalem: The Silbermann Family, 1972.

Rawicz, Piotr. *Blood from the Sky*. Translated by Peter Wiles. New York: Harcourt, 1964.

Remington, Blake William. 2015. *Read, Look, Go: Ethics and Dialogue in Holocaust Memorial Texts*. PhD dissertation. University of Texas at Dallas. Ann Arbor: ProQuest/UMI (Publication No. AAT 3719454).

Richardson, Ann. "The Ethical Limitations of Holocaust Literary Representation," *ESharp: Borders and Boundaries* 5 (Summer 2005): 1–19.

Ringelblum, Emmanuel. *Notes from the Warsaw Ghetto*. Translated and edited by Jacob Sloan. New York: Schocken Books, 1974.

Roberts, Geoffrey, ed. *The History and Narrative Reader*. East Sussex, UK: Psychology Press, 2001.

Rosenberg, Alfred. *Race and Race History and Other Essays*. Edited by Robert Pais. New York: Harper and Row, 1974.

Rosenfeld, Alvin. *A Double Dying: Reflections on Holocaust Literature*. Bloomington: Indiana University Press, 1980.

———. *The End of the Holocaust*. Bloomington: Indiana University Press, 2011.

Rosenzweig, Franz. *The Star of Redemption*. Translated by William W. Hallo. Boston: Beacon, 1972.

———. *Understanding the Sick and the Healthy*. Translated by Nahum Glatzer. Cambridge: Harvard University Press, 1999.

Rothberg, Michael. *Traumatic Realism: The Demands of Holocaust Representation*. Minneapolis: University of Minnesota Press, 2000.

Rousset, David. *L'Univers Concentrationnaire*. Paris: Éditions de Minuit, 1965.

Rubinstein, Donna. *I Am the Only Survivor of Krasnostav*. New York: Shengold, 1982.

Saadia Gaon. *The Book of Belief and Opinions*. Translated by Samuel Rosenblatt. New Haven: Yale University Press, 1976.

Sachs, Nelly. *Eli: A Mystery Play of the Sufferings of Israel*. Translated by Christopher Holme. In *Plays of the Holocaust: An International Anthology*, edited by Elinor Fuchs, 1–52. New York: Theatre Communications Group, 1987.

———. *O the Chimneys: Selected Poems*. Translated by Michael Hamberger et al. New York: Farrar, Straus, and Giroux, 1967.

Sacks, Jonathan. *Crisis and Covenant: Jewish Thought after the Holocaust*. Manchester, UK: Manchester University Press, 1992.

Salton, George Lucius. *The 23rd Psalm: A Holocaust Memoir*. Madison: University of Wisconsin Press, 2002.

Sandberg, Moshe. *My Longest Year*. Translated by S. C. Hyman. Jerusalem: Yad Vashem, 1968.

Scarry, Elaine. *The Body in Pain: The Making and Unmaking of the World*. Oxford: Oxford University Press, 1985.

Schiff, Hilda, ed. *Holocaust Poetry*. New York: St. Martin's Press, 1996.

Schneerson, Menachem M. *Torah Studies*. Adapted by Jonathan Sacks. 2nd Ed. London: Lubavitch Foundation, 1986.

Schoenberner, Gerhard. *The Yellow Star: The Persecution of the Jews in Europe, 1933–1945*. New York: Fordham University Press, 2004.

Schwarberg, Günther. *In the Ghetto of Warsaw: Photographs by Heinrich Jöst*. Göttingen: Steidl, 2001.

Schwarz, Daniel R. *Imagining the Holocaust*. New York: St. Martin's, 1999.

Schwarz-Bart, André. *The Last of the Just*. Translated by Stephen Becker. New York: Overlook, 2000.

Sefer Yetzirah: The Book of Creation. Translated with commentary by Aryeh Kaplan. York Beach, ME: Samuel Weiser, 1990.

Sforno, Ovadiah. *Commentary on* Pirke Avos. Translated with notes by Raphael Pelcovitz. Brooklyn: Mesorah, 1996.

Shapell, Nathan. *Witness to the Truth*. New York: David McKay, 1974.

Shapira, Kalonymos Kalmish. *Sacred Fire: Torah from the Years of Fury 1939–1942*. Translated by J. Hershy Worch, edited by Deborah Miller. Northvale, NJ: Jason Aronson, 2000.

Sifre on Deuteronomy. New York: Jewish Theological Seminary, 1993.

Singer, Isaac Bashevis. *Shosha*. New York: Farrar, Straus, and Giroux, 1996.

Sontag, Susan. *On Photography*. New York: Farrar, Straus, and Giroux, 1977.

———. *Regarding the Pain of Others*. New York: Farrar, Straus, and Giroux, 2003.

Spargo, R. Clifton, and Robert M. Ehrenreich, eds. *After Representation? The Holocaust, Literature, and Culture*. New Brunswick: Rutgers University Press, 2009.

Steiner, George. "The Long Life of Metaphor: An Approach to the 'Shoah.' " In *Writing and the Holocaust*, edited by Berel Lang, 154–74. New York: Holmes and Meier, 1988.

Stone, Dan. "Chaos and Continuity: Representations of Auschwitz." In *Representations of Auschwitz: Fifty Years of Photographs, Paintings, and Graphics*, edited by Yasmin Doorsy, 25–34. Oświęcim: Auschwitz-Birkenau State Museum, 1995.

———. "The Sonderkommando Photographs," *Jewish Social Studies* 7, no. 3 (2001): 112–48.

Strauss, Leo. *The Rebirth of Classical Political Rationalism: An Introduction to the Thought of Leo Strauss*. Selected by Thomas L. Pangle. Chicago: University of Chicago Press, 1989.

———. *Studies in Platonic Political Philosophy*. Chicago: University of Chicago Press, 1985.

Stroop, Jürgen. *The Stroop Report: The Jewish Quarter of Warsaw Is No More*! Translated by Sybil Milton. New York: Pantheon, 1980.

Struk, Janina. *Photographing the Holocaust: Interpretations of the Evidence*. London: I. B. Tauris, 2004.

Tal, Uriel. "On the *Study* of the Holocaust and Genocide," *Yad Vashem Studies* 13 (1979): 7–52.

Tillion, Germaine. *Ravensbrück*. Translated by Gerald Satterwhite. Garden City: Doubleday, 1975.

Tory, Avraham. *Surviving the Holocaust: The Kovno Ghetto Diary*. Translated by Jerzy Michalowicz. Edited by Martin Gilbert. Cambridge: Harvard University Press, 1990.

Tikkunei HaZohar. Jerusalem: Peihak Toveva, 1993.

Tosefta. Jerusalem: Wahrmann, 1970.

Touboul, Camille. *Un relais d'étoiles*. Montreal: Bibliothèque Nationale du Québec/ Les Éditions Julad, 1982.

Trepman, Paul. *Among Men and Beasts*. Translated by Shoshana Perla and Gertrude Hirschler. New York: Bergen Belsen Memorial Press, 1978.

"The Trial of Adolf Eichmann, Session 68," 7 June 1961. State of Israel Ministry of Justice. *The Nizkor Project*. Available at http://www.nizkor.org/hweb/people/e/eichmann-adolf/transcripts/Sessions/Session-068-01.html.

de Unamuno, Miguel. *The Tragic Sense of Life*. Translated by Anthony Kerrigan. Princeton: Princeton University Press, 1972.

Venezia, Shlomo. *Inside the Gas Chambers: Eight Months inside the Sonderkommando of Auschwitz.* Malden, MA: Polity Press, 2009.

Vital, Chayyim. *Kabbalah of Creation: Isaac Luria's Earlier Mysticism.* Translated by Eliahu Klein. Northvale, NJ: Jason Aronson, 2000.

———. *Shaarei Kedushah.* Jerusalem: Eshkol, 2000.

———. *The Tree of Life (Ets Chayyim).* Translated by D. W. Menzi and Z. Padeh. Northvale, NJ: Jason Aronson, 1999.

Vrba, Rudolf, and Alan Bestic. *I Cannot Forgive.* Vancouver: Regent College, 1997.

Waxman, Zoë Vania. *Writing the Holocaust: Identity, Testimony, Representation.* New York: Oxford University Press, 2008.

Weinreich, Max. *Hitler's Professors: The Part of Scholarship in Germany's Crimes against the Jewish People.* New Haven: Yale University Press, 1999.

Wells, Leon. *The Death Brigade.* New York: Holocaust Library, 1978.

Wiesel, Elie. *Against Silence: The Voice and Vision of Elie Wiesel.* 3 Vols. Edited by Irving Abrahamson. New York: Holocaust Library, 1985.

———. *Ani Maamin: A Song Lost and Found Again.* Translated by Marion Wiesel. New York: Random House, 1973.

———. *Evil and Exile.* Translated by Jon Rothschild. Notre Dame: University of Notre Dame Press, 1990.

———. *The Forgotten.* Translated by Marion Wiesel. New York: Summit Books, 1992.

———. *From the Kingdom of Memory: Reminiscences.* New York: Summit Books, 1990.

———. *The Gates of the Forest.* Translated by Frances Frenaye. New York: Holt, 1966.

———. "The Holocaust as Literary Inspiration." In Elie Wiesel et al. *Dimensions of the Holocaust,* 5–19. Evanston: Northwestern University Press, 1977.

———. *A Jew Today.* Translated by Marion Wiesel. New York: Random House, 1978.

———. *The Jews of Silence.* Translated by Neal Kozodoy. New York: Holt, Rinehart, and Winston, 1966.

———. *Legends of Our Time.* New York: Schocken Books, 1982.

———. *A Mad Desire to Dance.* Translated by Catherine Temerson. New York: Alfred A. Knopf, 2009.

———. *Night.* Translated by Marion Wiesel. New York: Hill and Wang, 2006.

———. *The Oath.* New York: Avon, 1973.

———. *One Generation After.* Translated by Lily Edelman and Elie Wiesel. New York: Pocket Books, 1970.

———. *Paroles d'étranger.* Paris: Éditions du Seuil, 1982.

———. *Somewhere a Master: Further Hasidic Portraits and Legends.* Translated by Marion Wiesel. New York: Summit Books, 1982.

———. *The Testament.* Translated by Marion Wiesel. New York: Summit Books, 1981.

———. *Le testament d'un poète juif assassin.* Paris: Editions du Seuil, 1980.

———. *The Time of the Uprooted.* Translated by David Hapgood. New York: Schocken Books, 2005.

———. *The Town beyond the Wall.* Translated by Stephen Becker. New York: Avon, 1964.
———. *Twilight.* Translated by Marion Wiesel. New York: Summit Books, 1998.
———. *Zalman or The Madness of God.* Adapted for the stage by Marion Wiesel. New York: Random House, 1974.
Wiesel, Elie, et al. *Dimensions of the Holocaust.* Evanston: Northwestern University Press, 1977.
Wiesenthal, Simon. *Die Sonnenblume: Von Schuld und Vergebung.* Hamburg: Hoffman and Campe, 1970.
———. *The Sunflower.* Translated by H. A. Piehler. New York: Schocken Books, 1976.
Wistrich, Robert. *Hitler and the Holocaust.* New York: Modern Library, 2001.
———. *A Lethal Obsession: Anti-Semitism from Antiquity to the Global Jihad.* New York: Random House, 2010.
Wittgenstein, Ludwig. *Tractatus Logico Philosophicus.* Translated by C. K. Ogden. London: Kegan Paul, Trench, Trubner, 1922.
Wollaston, Isabel. "The Absent, the Partial, and the Iconic in Archival Photographs of the Holocaust," *Jewish Culture and History* 12, no. 3 (2010): 439–62.
Wrzos-Glinka, Stanisław, Tadeusz Mazur, and Jerzy Tomaszewski, eds. *1939–1945: We Have Not Forgotten.* Warsaw: Polania Publishing, 1960.
Yaakov Yosef. *Toledot Yaakov Yosef al HaTorah.* 2 Vols. Jerusalem: Agudat Beit Vialipoli, 1944.
Young, James E. "Interpreting Literary Testimony: A Preface to Rereading Holocaust Diaries and Memoirs," *New Literary History* 18 (1987): 403–23.
———. *Writing and Rewriting the Holocaust: Narrative and the Consequences of Interpretation.* Bloomington: Indiana University Press, 1988.
Zalman, Schneur. *Likutei Amarim Tanya.* Translated by Nissan Mindel et al. Brooklyn: Kehot, 1981.
Zelizer, Barbie. *Remembering to Forget: Holocaust Memory through the Camera's Eye.* Chicago: The University of Chicago Press, 1998.
———, ed. *Visual Culture and the Holocaust.* New Brunswick: Rutgers University Press, 2001.
The Zohar. 5 Vols. Trans. Harry Sperling and Maurice Simon. London: Soncino, 1984.
Zusak, Markus. *The Book Thief.* New York: Alfred A. Knopf, 2007.
Zylberberg, Michael. *A Warsaw Diary.* London: Vallentine, Mitchell, 1969.
Zyskind, Sara. *Stolen Years.* Translated by Margarit Inbar. Minneapolis: Lerner, 1981.

Index

www.ingramcontent.com/pod-product-compliance
Lightning Source LLC
LaVergne TN
LVHW040757070826
844660LV00025B/1171

* 9 7 8 1 4 3 8 4 7 0 0 4 7 *